Managing Change

A Human Resource Strategy Approach

ADRIAN THORNHILL

PHIL LEWIS

MIKE MILLMORE

MARK SAUNDERS

FINANCIAL TIMES

PRENTICE HALL

An imprint of **PEARSON EDUCATION**

Harlow, England · London · New York · Reading, Massachusetts · San Francisco · Toronto · Don Mills, Ontario · Sydney
Tokyo · Singapore · Hong Kong · Seoul · Taipei · Cape Town · Madrid · Mexico City · Amsterdam · Munich · Paris · Milan

PEARSON EDUCATION LIMITED

Edinburgh Gate
Harlow
Essex CM20 2JE
England

and Associated Companies around the world

Visit us on the World Wide Web at
www.pearsoned-ema.com

_____

First published 2000

ISBN 0 273 63065 2

British Library Cataloguing in Publication Data
A CIP catalogue record for this book can be obtained from the British Library

10 9 8 7 6 5 4 3 2 1
04 03 02 01 00 99

Typeset by 32
Printed and bound in Great Britain by Henry Ling Ltd., at the Dorest Press,
Dorchester, Dorset

Contents

Preface

This book was conceived as something of a departure from many others. As a team, we have been involved in teaching the management of change and human resource management for several years. There is a range of books devoted to each of these disciplines. These reflect the different approaches to these subject areas. We set out to write a book which would produce a degree of synthesis between particular aspects of these subject areas.

Our course was set in 1993 when we devised a keystone module for an MA in the Management of Human Resources. This was entitled 'Managing change through people' and it sought to encompass a joint focus related to change and the use of a range of human resource strategies. We have refined this module twice since its initial conception, although it maintains this joint focus. Of course, the use of human resource strategies is integrally linked to the management of change. However, we felt that this relationship was not as developed as we would have wished in the books that we used. We therefore decided to design a book ourselves that focused specifically on the relationship between strategy and change, and in particular the relationship between the use of human resource strategies and the management of change. This book is the result.

There are two principal elements to the relationship between the use of human resource strategies and the management of change. One of these focuses on the role that human resource strategies may play in helping to generate organisational change. We consider this aspect of the relationship between these strategies and intentions to realise change. However, we recognise that this aspect of the relationship is likely to be problematic in terms of implementation. Like many others, we do not believe that the implementation of change is a simple process, based on rationality, which may be carried through without major or even minor consequences. We do not subscribe to a unitarist view of social and work-based relations. Much of the content of the book therefore explores the second aspect of this relationship, related to the implementation of change and the role that human resource strategies may play in this process. Thus, while human resource strategies may help to generate change, there is a need to consider how they are being used in relation to its implementation and resulting outcomes.

In recognising the potential for unintended outcomes from the implementation of strategic change, especially where this centres on people at work, we realise that the contents of this book will only consider part of the complexity that results in practice. This is not to apologise for its contents but to recognise the breadth of this subject area. We therefore hope that the use of this book will provide you with at least a starting point through which to explore these various facets of the relationship between the use of human resource strategies and the management of change. We hope that you will find it stimulating and as a means to raise questions as well as to supply answers.

Acknowledgements

We would like to thank those who helped to make the production of this book possible. In particular, we would like to thank all of those who granted access and provided co-operation to allow us to generate the case studies that are a key feature of this book. These case studies are divided into two categories, which appear as the first and second case studies in each chapter (other than the introductory Chapter 1).

The majority of the first case studies in the chapters are based on organisations that we have been able to name. Some of these are based on published information. However, in most cases they are based on data we collected from participants in these organisations. In one case, a change of ownership meant that we are unable to name the organisation. We would like to thank those who facilitated access to this organisation and permission to use it as the context for a case study, although we have not named them in order to maintain anonymity. In the other cases, permission has been kindly granted to name the organisations, for which we are most grateful. We would therefore like to thank the following people who granted access, provided data and/or granted permission: Paul Bissell, Rewards Consultant, and Deborah Rees, Job Families Implementation Manager, for permission to use the Nationwide Building Society case study in Chapter 2; also Nationwide's Corporate Communications and Group Legal departments for granting permission to use this case study; John Dowds, Human Resource Development Manager, for permission to use the DuPont case study in Chapter 3; Alex Lewis, Personnel Executive, for permission to use the Siemens Standard Drives case study in Chapter 5; Colin Court, Manager Human Resources Development, Melanie Morris, HR Officer, James Newman, Business Centre HR Manager and Lucy Adkinson, X Teams Co-ordinator, for permission to use the Xerox case study in Chapter 6; Barry Brown, Customer Services Director, for permission to use the Midland Mainline case study in Chapter 7; Bill Connor, General Secretary of USDAW, for information supplied and permission granted in relation to the Tesco case study in Chapter 8; P. Asselin, Sales Development Director, for permission to use the Barclays Edotech case study in Chapter 10, and Kevin Gowing for facilitating access.

Although the second case study in each chapter is based on a real organisation, or in some cases a combination of experiences drawn from the organisations to which we have been granted access, these are not named where they are based on primary data. In order to maintain the anonymity of these organisations, we have not named the many individuals who granted access and provided co-operation. Naturally, without their help we would not have been able to construct these case studies. We would therefore like to thank each person, although we cannot do so in name.

We would also like to thank Christopher Mabey, Graeme Salaman and John Storey, and Blackwell Publishers, for permission to use their Open Approach to HRS diagram from page 69 of *Human Resource Management: A Strategic Introduction*.

Our thanks also go to Sadie McClelland, our Commissioning Editor at Pearson Education, who has provided excellent and continued support during the writing of this book. We would also like to thank all of the staff at Pearson Education who have supported us through this project. It is always pleasant to be treated in a genuinely friendly way. Thanks are also due to Denise Skinner, from University College Northampton, for her helpful comments.

Finally, our thanks go, once again, to Jan, Jenny, Alice, Jane, Andrew, Katie, Stephen, Jennifer, Jemma and Benjamin for putting up with the long hours when we absented ourselves to think and write. We hope you will find that it was worth the effort.

Adrian Thornhill, Phil Lewis, Mike Millmore and Mark Saunders
March 1999

About the authors

Adrian Thornhill, BA, PhD, PGCE, FIPD, is Head of the School of Human Resource Management at Gloucestershire Business School, Cheltenham & Gloucester College of Higher Education. He teaches HRM and employee relations to postgraduate, undergraduate and professional courses and is involved in research degree supervision. Adrian's main research interest is related to managing organisational downsizing and redundancy, on which he has co-written a book which is also published by Financial Times Management. He has also published several articles on this aspect of managing change. He is co-author with Mark and Phil of *Research Methods for Business Students*, published by Pearson Education. He has undertaken consultancy in both public and private sectors.

Phil Lewis, BA, PhD, MSc, MIPD, PGDipM, CertEd, is a Principal Lecturer in Human Resource Management and MA HRM course leader at Gloucestershire Business School, Cheltenham & Gloucester College of Higher Education. He teaches employee relations and HRM to postgraduate, undergraduate and professional courses. Phil's research interests are reward management and performance management, on both of which he has published several articles. He is co-author with Mark and Adrian of *Research Methods for Business Students*, published by Pearson Education. He has undertaken consultancy in both public and private sectors. Prior to his career in higher education Phil was a training adviser with the Distributive Industry Training Board.

Mike Millmore, BA, MA, MSc, PGCE, FIPD, is a Principal Lecturer in Human Resource Management and HRM undergraduate co-ordinator at Gloucestershire Business School, Cheltenham & Gloucester College of Higher Education. He teaches HRM to postgraduate, undergraduate and professional courses. Mike's main research interests are related to recruitment and selection, training and development and HRM rhetoric versus reality. He has undertaken consultancy in both public and private sectors. Prior to his career in higher education he was a Training Manager in a large international electrical/ electronic engineering company. He has also worked for nine years as a senior general manager.

Mark Saunders, BA, MSc, PGCE, PhD, is Head of the Human Resource Management Research Centre at Gloucestershire Business School, Cheltenham & Gloucester College of Higher Education. He teaches HRM and research methods to postgraduate, undergraduate and professional courses and is involved in research degree supervision. Mark's main research interests are related to employee mobility, managing organisational downsizing and redundancy, and research methods. He has published several articles on these aspects of managing change. He is co-author with Phil and Adrian of *Research Methods for Business Students*, published by Pearson Education, and has also co-authored a book on business statistics. He has undertaken consultancy in both public and private sectors, prior to which he was Principal Research Officer for Hereford and Worcester Social Services.

An introduction to managing change: a human resource strategy approach

Learning objectives

Having completed this chapter, you will be able to:

■ Define the term strategy.

■ Evaluate alternative approaches to the development of strategy and appreciate their implications for managing change and the use of human resource (HR) strategies.

■ Recognise organisational and environmental factors that affect the nature of strategy and their implications for managing change and HR strategies.

■ Analyse levels of strategy and their implications for change and HR strategies.

■ Discuss the implementation of change and its impact.

■ Evaluate the role of HR strategies in implementing change.

■ Understand the approach of this book to managing change.

INTRODUCTION

The focus of this book is about managing change and the role of HR strategies in this process (or processes). We believe that the answer to the question, 'is there a role for HR strategies in managing change?', is a clear 'yes'. Many books discuss how change may be managed. However, there are few that focus on this particular question. This is not to query the value of other books on managing change. These reflect the diversity of approaches that exist in relation to this subject. However, we took a deliberate decision to focus on HR approaches rather than attempt to describe and discuss approaches related to, for example, systems theory or organisation development. Undoubtedly we draw on concepts developed and used by academics and practitioners working with these approaches to managing change. Where this is the case, we are naturally grateful to the bodies of work developed around such approaches to the management of change.

Instead, our focus leads us to seek answers to two further questions related to the initial, general one posed above. These are 'how may HR strategies help to generate organisational change?' and 'what is the role for HR strategies in helping to implement change?' Both questions have a strategic focus and we recognise that, in practice, they are clearly interrelated. The inclusion of 'help' or 'helping' in each question also recognises that the role of HR strategies in managing change will not be an exclusive one. However, we believe that the potential of HR strategies in the management of change has not been properly addressed in other approaches to this subject. Undoubtedly this is related to the relatively short period in which academics have been expressly thinking and writing about the strategic role of human resource management (HRM). We will return to the distinctiveness of the approach adopted in this book in the last section of this introductory chapter.

This chapter provides you with an understanding of the context in which HR strategies may be used to generate or implement change. However, it is important to remember that the reality of developing organisational strategy is unlikely to follow a highly rational and normative model. This reality will affect the nature of the change process that will follow and have implications for the use of HR strategies, in terms of both generating and implementing change. The next section therefore seeks to explore briefly approaches to developing organisational strategies and the organisational as well as the environmental factors that influence their development. It also describes different levels of strategy within organisations. This allows the implications that follow from these approaches and levels for managing change and the use of HR strategies in particular to be discussed. The third section explores issues related to the implementation of change, focusing principally on different practices in attempting to introduce change. In the fourth section we provide an overview of the implications for the use of HR strategies which may follow from these different practices in attempting to implement change. This will provide you with a framework within which to place the remaining chapters, each of which focuses on a specific HR strategy.

Strategy, change and human resource strategies

The need for strategic change arises from the formulation and implementation of the strategy that underpins the direction and activity of an organisation. Alterations to the strategic direction and activity of an organisation may therefore necessitate changes to its structures, systems, culture, managerial approach and technology. However, strategy is a difficult concept to characterise and understand in an organisational context. This is due to a number of reasons. First, the practice of formulating and implementing strategy varies between organisations, e.g. deliberate versus emergent (discussed later). Second, our understanding of how strategy is determined depends not only on the environmental circumstances faced by organisations but also on the cultural and political issues that operate within them. Third, strategy operates at a number of organisational levels, and strategic decisions taken at a higher level clearly affect strategy and change at a lower level including that related to human resources. We discuss the implications of each of these three aspects of strategy in relation to our focus on managing change and their links to HR strategies in this section.

Defining, formulating and implementing strategy and its implications for change

Johnson and Scholes (1993) identify a number of characteristics that help to define strategy. These lead them to offer the following definition of strategy:

> Strategy is the direction and scope of an organisation over the long term: ideally which matches its resources to its changing environment, and in particular its markets, customers or clients so as to meet stakeholder expectations. (Johnson and Scholes, 1993: 10)

This definition recognises internal (resource) as well as external (environmental) factors affecting organisations and the need for change as part of the process of strategic adaptation. The process of matching resources so that an organisation may be able to operate effectively in its 'marketplace' clearly suggests identifying and developing its resource capability or organisational competence. In addition, it points to the need to recognise other resource implications that stem from this matching process and to respond to these through appropriate change (Johnson and Scholes, 1993; Burnes, 1996). This may result in the restructuring of existing resources and other attempts to use these more efficiently, or acquiring new resources, perhaps by replacing some existing ones.

This approach to strategy, focusing on the internal, resource capability of an organisation as well as the challenges which it faces in its external operating environment, has the potential to enhance the role that HR strategies may contribute to the change process as an organisation attempts to adapt itself strategically (Purcell, 1995). Although an organisation's human resources are only one aspect of its resource base, this approach suggests that recognising and developing these resources will not only help an organisation to match them to changes in the environment but also create 'distinctive capabilities' to seek (further)

3

competitive advantage (Kay, 1993; Purcell, 1995). Burnes (1996: 142) recognises that 'the capabilities of an organisation, in terms of its structure, systems, technology and management style, restrict the range of strategic options the organisation can pursue'. If an inadequate resource base has the ability to restrict the capability of an organisation in relation to competitors, the development of its resource capability may, conversely, help it to develop the scope of its strategic options. We now explore this argument in relation to the formulation and implementation of strategy in practice.

Strategy as a deliberate process

There are essentially two views of the process of formulating and implementing strategy. The classical, or textbook, view advocates a linear, rationalistic and deliberate process, driven from the top of an organisation. This process involves a number of strategic planning steps including analysing the organisation's environment and its resources, establishing organisational mission and objectives, identifying and evaluating strategic options, and then implementing and evaluating chosen strategies (*see*, for example, Certo and Peter, 1988; Johnson and Scholes, 1993). Underpinning this approach to strategic management is a range of techniques and tools, ranging from a SWOT analysis to a variety of diagrammatic and quantitative methods.

This approach to the formulation and, in particular, the implementation of strategy would provide a 'neat' model to which to attach the HR strategies discussed in this book. To use Purcell's (1989) terminology in relation to strategy, the need for and direction of such HR strategies would flow logically from the 'first-order' strategic decisions taken 'upstream' in relation to the formulation of an organisation's future direction. Thus, the design of HR strategies to help to implement the overall strategy of an organisation would be part of the same linear, rationalistic and deliberate process described in the previous paragraph. However, while this approach may occur in broad terms in particular cases, the development of strategy is unlikely to happen in reality in such an apparently planned and orderly manner in many others.

Strategy as an emergent process

In contrast to the formalised strategic planning process outlined above, Mintzberg (1987) refers to the approach of 'crafting strategy'. He sees the development of strategy as analogous to the approach of the craftswoman or craftsman, whose knowledge and skills means that they conceive of (formulate) as well as execute (implement) their work in an integral manner. This provides a powerful contrast to the formal planning approach. Mintzberg's work suggests that organisational strategies often emerge from the work of those in an organisation and the opportunities that become apparent rather than being deliberately planned. Thus, the formulation and implementation of strategy is, in practice, a more integrated or fluid process, rather than being different stages in a deliberately planned and formal process.

This emergent strategy approach has implications for HR. The existence of an emergent strategy will need to be recognised (Mintzberg, 1987), so that appropriate HR strategies may be formulated and implemented to encourage behaviour to promote and support this change. In this way, change is more likely to be characterised by incremental rather than major shifts in strategy. However, in spite of the greater level of unpredictability and uncertainty that may be associated with this approach to the development of strategy for the formulation of HR strategies, we do not believe that this reduces their need or potential value. Indeed, we would argue that the HR strategies that are developed to support such emergent strategies have a greater propensity to become effective in particular circumstances, as we now discuss.

Organisational strategies which are emergent are likely to be understood by those who work in an organisation where they have been involved in the development of these strategies in some way. This contrasts with a situation where a strategic plan results in a low level of 'ownership' or even a lack of knowledge about it (Johnson and Scholes, 1993). This greater level of understanding and involvement may also, perhaps, be associated with the generation of increased levels of commitment to the goals of the organisation. Indeed, Quinn (1993) argues that one of the reasons for developing organisational strategy in an incremental manner is to generate employee effort and commitment in relation to the emerging strategy. Johnson (1993: 60) supports this view:

> strategies must be developed in stages, carrying the members of the organisation with them, and by trying out new ideas and experiments to see which are effective and to induce commitment within the organisational through continual, but low scale change. This is what has become known as 'logical incrementalism'.

We believe that this emergent approach to the development of organisational strategy has clear implications about the need for appropriately designed HR strategies. These implications have a clear relationship to the range of HR strategies we discuss in this book. These strategies may be divided into two categories. First, where appropriate HR, cultural and structural strategies are in place this should help to foster the development of emergent strategies. Second, specific strategies will also need to be designed to respond to the development of emergent strategies, in order to support them. As an example of the first category, Quinn's (1993) discussion about how to promote an incremental approach to develop organisational strategy emphasises, in particular, the use of employee involvement as a key HR strategy in this process (*see* Chapter 8). Related to both categories, Mintzberg (1987) believes that the development of emergent strategies in organisations promotes learning. This will need to be recognised and supported through HR strategies related to, in particular, recruitment and selection, training and development, and reward, as well as through cultural and structural strategies. The value of integration between emergent organisational strategies and HR ones returns us to the earlier argument about the development of 'distinctive capabilities', including human competences. The acquisition of distinctive capabilities through supportive HR strategies may help to broaden the range of an organisation's strategic options and thus further promote the potential for the development of such emergent strategies.

Mintzberg (1987, 1994) also recognises the existence of an approach to the development of strategy that leads to what he terms 'umbrella strategies'. In this approach, senior managers produce guidelines which others use to develop the details of an operable strategy. The first part of this approach to strategy development is deliberately set out while the second part is allowed to emerge. This umbrella strategy approach lends itself to the two types of integration outlined in the previous paragraph. In other words, HR strategies may be implemented initially to help to realise the strategic guidelines that have been established by senior managers by promoting the development of strategies at business unit level. Secondly, other HR strategies may then be devised to meet the resource implications raised by the development and implementation of these emergent strategies at business-unit level.

Environmental, cultural and political influences and their implications for change

We now discuss the second difficulty of characterising and understanding strategy and how this affects organisational change. This relates to another aspect of the rationalistic approach to formulating strategy, which promotes the notion that strategy is determined objectively with due regard to the environmental factors confronting an organisation. The nature of environmental pressures on a specific organisation may be very varied. In general terms these may include: government policies and the impact created when these are changed; demographic, social and educational changes; the effect of legal regulation or deregulation; technological changes; the availability and cost of finance; the influence of market structures; and the dynamics of labour markets. These may be compounded by, for example, effects of the globalisation of business, the location and impact of multinational companies, the European Union and changes in political stability in different parts of the world (*see* Rothwell, 1995, for a fuller discussion of such factors).

While environmental pressures will undoubtedly affect the formulation of strategy, the way in which these external factors are understood, and any responsive strategies formulated, will involve a process of social construction related to the cultural and political dimensions that operate within organisations. Thus, environmental factors will be interpreted and resulting strategies constructed through the cultural filters and political interests that operate in differing ways in different organisations (*see*, for example, Johnson, 1993; Nicholson, 1993; Burnes, 1996). This highlights choice or at least variation about the manner in which organisations respond to the need for change in relation to the same stimuli. Our definition of organisational culture, discussed in Chapter 3, follows Brown (1998: 9) who refers to 'the pattern of beliefs, values and learned ways of coping with experience that have developed during the course of an organisation's history'. It will be these 'beliefs, values and learned ways of coping' which will shape, at least partially, managers' assumptions about environmental pressures, and ways of responding to these. In particular, it affects their diagnosis of what needs to be changed and how this should be implemented (Johnson, 1993).

One outcome of this culturally filtered process of perceiving the changing environment may be the inadequacy of the way an organisation responds to external pressures, because its learned ways of coping from past experience prove to be insufficient in the current climate. This is likely to result in the need for further, more fundamental strategic change in the future and the need to change the underlying assumptions on which culture is based. However, the very nature and purpose of these underlying assumptions means that culture will not be easy to change, not least because those such as senior managers who exercise the greatest organisational power will do so in part because of the culture which operates in their organisation (Pfeffer, 1993; Johnson, 1993).

In this context, there is a potential role for HR-centred strategies to be used to attempt to change or realign the culture of an organisation. This may be linked to either a 'top-down' or a 'bottom-up' process of organisational change. We introduce these concepts in the next section of this chapter and discuss them in detail in the context of facilitating cultural change in Chapter 3. In general terms, in order to facilitate the change of an organisation's culture, an organisation may use one or a combination of the following HR strategies to alter its dominant system of practices, values and underlying assumptions:

- a recruitment strategy of replacing managers with those from outside;
- restructuring the organisation;
- downsizing the workforce;
- training programmes to re-educate employees or support their development;
- a new reward strategy and performance management to alter employee behaviours or reinforce emergent ones; and
- an employee involvement strategy (*see* Chapter 3 and other strategy-specific chapters).

However, the extent to which organisations adopt a rational approach and use such HR strategies to bring about change, arising from the inadequacy of their strategic responses to past environmental pressures, is open to question. A strong or established culture may be difficult to alter, even where it fails to recognise how the environment is affecting the organisation and thus to allow it to respond appropriately (Pfeffer, 1993). Change may eventually occur, but this may be forced by the adverse affect on an organisation's performance and take place some time, even years, after environmental pressures have started to exert an impact (Johnson and Scholes, 1993). The appointment of outsiders may thus be particularly important in this context to promote change since these organisational newcomers will not, at least initially, be subject to the cultural filters operating within the organisation (Johnson, 1993). The use of such a strategy to replace managers through external recruitment may in turn lead to the use of other HR strategies to promote further change.

An organisation's political system and the exercise of power within it also need to be taken into account in order to understand decisions about strategy, the allocation of resources and organisational change (*see*, for example, Morgan, 1986; Burnes, 1996). Organisations may be seen as being composed of different groups of stakeholders, each with a particular set of interests. Conflict may result where these interests differ. Dominant managers or groups of managers in an organisation may therefore seek to exercise discretionary power, as well as any formal authority vested in them, to influence the outcome of decisions that will affect their interests. The manager or group of managers attempting to exercise such influence may draw on the prevailing organisational culture to provide some legitimacy for her, his or their action. However, this political perspective may also operate independently by being used to challenge this culture in situations where change is already occurring and there is a new, emergent coalition of powerful interests (Johnson, 1993; Carnall, 1995; Burnes, 1996). Other, less powerful individuals who nevertheless exercise some degree of influence over the implementation of strategy and the management of change may also act in such a way that they have some effect on the way in which this is implemented in practice and perceived by others in the organisation.

The need to consider this political perspective therefore adds a further important dimension to our understanding of the development of strategy and its relationship to the management of change. It has a particular implication for our understanding of the formulation and implementation of HR strategies. As Burnes (1996: 127–8) points out in relation to the design of the structure of an organisation,

> The dominant coalition is the one which has the power to affect structure. The reason why this is so important is that the choice of structure will automatically favour some groups and disadvantage others ... Consequentially, structural decisions are not rational. Such decisions arise from a power struggle between special-interest groups or coalitions, each arguing for a structural arrangement that best suits them.

This exercise of choice about structure may also be extended to the way in which other strategies, including HR ones, are designed or used in practice. It is therefore inappropriate to view HR strategies as rational and objective entities as they exist within a value-laden system. HR strategies will also be subject to the political interests of the dominant groups in organisations who design and use them (Pettigrew, 1987). This recognition is important for what follows in this book, rather than being a potential weakness. Theory may be flawed because it reflects noble aspirations as well as being logical and rational. Practice, by contrast, reflects the varying interests of people. A sound theory needs to recognise the limitations that are built into strategies and systems devised by people, especially where one interest has dominated their design.

Levels of strategy and their implications for change

We now consider the third aspect of characterising and understanding strategy referred to at the start of this section and its implications for managing change through HR strategies. This relates to the organisational levels at which strategy occurs and the way in which decisions taken at a higher level affect those taken at a lower level. Three levels of strategy have been recognised (*see*, for example, Purcell, 1989).

'First-order' or corporate strategies

The highest level is concerned with the overall or corporate strategy of an organisation. This relates to the definition of strategy that we used above, concerned with the 'direction and scope of an organisation over the long term' (Johnson and Scholes, 1993: 10). Purcell (1989: 70) refers to the nature of these strategies as '"Upstream", first-order decisions' to indicate their status in relation to lower-order ones and the likely way in which other levels of strategy will flow from these higher-order strategies. A further distinction may be made at this level between corporate and business strategies, related to the nature of multi-product and multi-divisional organisations. Purcell (1995: 66) succinctly summarises this distinction as follows:

> Multi-product and multi-divisional firms have to make a distinction between corporate and business strategies; between those taken at the centre covering the whole enterprise, and those taken lower down at division or business-unit level and related to the products made and the markets served.

Various writers (e.g. Certo and Peter, 1988; Johnson and Scholes, 1993; Burnes, 1996), identify a range of corporate strategies which may be grouped within four broad categories. These categories are shown in Table 1.1.

Table 1.1 Four categories of corporate strategy

Stability	e.g. continuing with an existing strategy, consolidation
Growth	e.g. product development, market penetration, market development, or diversification involving internal investments, joint ventures, acquisition or merger
Retrenchment/Withdrawal	e.g. harvesting a business by using its existing competencies and resources but reducing costs, investments and running it down; closing down some existing locations; divesting existing businesses
Combination	using a mixture of the strategies referred to above

These corporate strategies may be seen to have implications for the nature of HR strategies, allowing for the differing approaches to the development of strategy discussed earlier. We return to these possible implications later in this section.

Second- and third-order strategies

The second and third levels of strategy are seen by Purcell (1989) as being 'downstream' of corporate strategy. The second level of strategy concerns the organisational structures and operating procedures that are put into place to support first-order decisions. The third level concerns functional strategies, including those related to HR, which are developed in the context of the first two levels. All three levels have strategic significance since they each affect the long-term direction of an organisation and the attainment of its goals.

However, the nature of the linkages between these three levels in organisations in practice is open to question and debate. Any implication that there is a process of deliberately fitting one to another in organisations is likely to be met by the response that such a highly rational and normative suggestion ignores the reality of developing strategy and the way in which managers operate. In any case, the extent of integration between these levels of strategy may also be questioned where third-order strategies are only developed in a reactive manner in relation to the other two levels (*see*, for example, Beaumont, 1993; Mabey and Iles, 1993). Nevertheless, we now focus on some of the linkages that have been advanced in the HR literature, which develop the notion of HR strategies being developed in response to corporate strategy or organisational circumstances.

Suggested linkages between corporate and HR strategies

A number of linkages between corporate and HR strategies have been suggested in the literature. These may be placed into three categories (*see*, for example, Storey and Sisson, 1993; Mabey and Salaman, 1995). One of these suggests that the nature of HR strategies should be determined by the life-cycle stage of an organisation. Four life-cycle stages have been identified by Kochan and Barocci (1985): organisational start-up; growth; maturity and decline. These life-cycle stages may be related, in part, to the strategic categories described in Table 1.1. The implication is that the nature of HR strategies will be contingent on the life-cycle stage of a particular organisation. This has implications for a number of the HR strategies discussed in this book. For example, the HR emphasis in the start-up cycle of an organisation will be related to attracting high quality staff, partly by paying market rates or better, and establishing skill requirements for future development and a suitable organisational culture. However, organisations confronted by conditions of decline will be more likely to focus on restructuring, cost controls, redundancies and outplacement activities (*see*, for example, Kochan and Barocci, 1985; Storey and Sisson, 1993; Mabey and Salaman, 1995).

Another category suggests that the focus of HR strategies should be contingent on the nature of the corporate or business strategy being pursued. Claims about the nature of this type of relationship have been advanced in particular by Schuler and Jackson (1987), based on a typology of three generic business strategies. These business strategies relate to either the pursuit of innovation, quality enhancement or cost reduction. Each strategy is designed to secure a different route towards competitive advantage. They may be related to some of the strategic facets referred to in Table 1.1. Schuler and Jackson (1987) identified the nature of HR policies and employee behaviours that they believe are implied by each of these business strategies. For example, an innovation strategy, related say to product development, is likely to be characterised by structures that encourage co-operation and creativity (e.g. through an emphasis on project-based teams); performance appraisal that recognises developmental and team-based activities; and investment in training and career development. Conversely, a cost reduction strategy is likely to be characterised by, for example, structures that emphasise control and low investment in training.

Table 1.2 Miles and Snow's three broad types of strategic behaviour

Strategic type	Description and implications for HR strategies
Defenders	Organisations focused on a narrow and relatively stable product-market niche. Results in the use of relatively stable technology, organisational structures and methods of working. Competitive advantage maintained through embedded expertise, production skills and the pursuit of cost efficiencies and control. Doing it better rather than seeking change.
Prospectors	Organisations that actively search for new product and market opportunities. High level of innovation resulting in different types of products and use of multiple technologies. Thus likely to be characterised by a divisionalised structure and to need high-level skills in product R and D, market research and technologies. Also likely to generate frequent change and to invest in new skills and 'divest' old ones.
Analysers	Organisations operating in a position that combines elements of the previous two categories. They maintain a range of high quality products produced through embedded efficiencies as well as seeking to develop into new areas. Thus, they may be characterised by bureaucratic methods and control in part of the organisation and by higher levels of discretion, innovation and involvement in another part.

A different approach to business strategies by Miles and Snow (1984) may also be seen to have contingent implications for the nature and focus of HR strategies. Miles and Snow identify three strategic types of organisational behaviour. They refer to these as Defenders, Prospectors and Analysers. These are briefly described in Table 1.2, along with some of their suggested implications for the nature of HR strategies. There are clearly similarities between the categories of Miles and Snow and the other strategic categorisations referred to in this chapter.

A further category suggests that the focus of HR strategies should be contingent not only on the nature of the corporate or business strategy being pursued but also on the type of organisational structure associated with this. The relationship between organisational strategies and appropriate structures is explored further in Chapter 2. We may refer briefly here to a number of forms of organisational structure identified in the literature. These relate to:

■ a simple organisational form;
■ a functional, bureaucratic form;
■ a multi-divisional form to cope with diversification into a number of related products;
■ a holding company composed of broadly self-managing businesses as a means to cope with unrelated diversification; and
■ a global structure that needs to cope with a range of products in a number of countries (*see*, for example, Fombrun *et al.* 1984).

The suggestion follows that the nature and focus of HR strategies should be related to the particular form of organisational structure as well as the strategic direction of an organisation (*see*, for example, Fombrun *et al.* 1984; Storey and Sisson, 1993).

However, the reality of these suggested or implicit linkages between corporate strategies, structures or life cycles, on the one hand, and HR strategies, on the other, is much more problematic than these reported formulations may suggest. While these linkages may appear to be reasonably logical and even useful, they may be based more on deduction than empirical data (*see*, for example, Hendry and Pettigrew, 1990). We saw earlier that the process of strategy development is affected by cultural and political factors, which will also affect perceptions about the need for change, its management and the way in which HR strategies may be used. We also recognised above that the development of strategy is unlikely to be an entirely rational and deliberate process, with business strategies emerging in parts of the organisation. We recognised in this context that there might be a strong local link between an emergent business strategy and HR strategies if the situation is also characterised by an appropriate managerial approach and employee involvement.

These factors suggest that the situation may be too complex for any simple linkage to be made between business and HR strategies. Storey and Sisson (1993) point out that for a linkage even to be considered, a business strategy will need to be clearly apparent to the managers of an organisation. They suggest that 'where such strategies are available they are often extremely vague' (Storey and Sisson, 1993: 69). The reality of devising and implementing business strategy also points to a significant measure of complexity. Mabey and Salaman (1995: 40) point out that 'experience suggests that strategic decision-making, either corporate or HR, is incremental, piecemeal, *ad hoc*, incomplete, and negotiated and only partly rational'. The complexity suggested by these aspects also needs to be placed alongside other factors that may impinge on any straightforward linkage suggested between business and HR strategies. These may include the presence or absence of trade unions, legal regulation and other impinging factors that also affect decision making about HR strategies. A greater range of factors is thus likely to affect the reality of choosing HR strategies than has been suggested by the literature outlined above (e.g. Boxall, 1991; Storey and Sisson, 1993; Mabey and Salaman, 1995).

However, this conclusion does not discount the potential impact that particular strategies, structures and organisational circumstances may have on the use of HR strategies. Rather, the conclusion reached above discounts any straightforward and uniform linkage between these factors. We may explore the way in which particular strategies and structures may affect the use of HR strategies through the work of Purcell (1989, 1995). He focuses specifically on potential linkages related to multi-divisional organisations. We acknowledge the work of Purcell in allowing us to construct the remainder of this sub-section.

Organisations that follow a strategy based on diversification will develop complex and more vertically decentralised organisational structures, characterised by a multi-divisional structure. This raises a question about decentralisation and accountability; in other words, how the corporate centre manages the different parts of an organisation. Diversified organisations, especially 'unrelated diversifiers' (e.g. holding companies), may use a form of portfolio planning as the means to allocate resources and performance targets, based on expectations about the growth rate and market share of each business in their portfolio. Purcell (1989) concludes that this approach to strategic management reduces the scope for the development of HR strategies across the organisation since business unit managers will be concerned to meet the financial targets established for them rather than focus on corporate HR issues, even where these have been identified. As each business unit pursues the targets set for it, it will be likely to develop separate HR strategies that focus on its own unit-level needs.

Based on work by Goold and Campbell (1987), Purcell (1989) differentiates between three approaches to managing diversified organisations, which allows the implications of the linkage between diversification, divisionalised structures and HR strategies to be explored further. The first approach, referred to as strategic planning, involves organisations that seek to develop competitive advantage from the businesses in their portfolio, based on a longer-term orientation. The second, termed financial control, involves 'companies [that] focus more on financial performance than competitive position. They expand their portfolios more through acquisitions than through growing market share' (Goold and Campbell, 1987: 10, cited in Purcell, 1989). The third category, referred to as strategic control, is something of a hybrid between the other two categories. Purcell (1989) develops the significance of these approaches for the scope and nature of HR strategies. Diversified organisations that use the strategic planning approach are more likely to develop, for example, strategies for training and development and performance management, related to their more longer-term, organic orientation. By comparison, the use of the financial control strategy is characterised by short-termism and the need to achieve demanding targets. This encourages further decentralisation in order to increase control and accountability. As a consequence HR policies which reflect this approach are likely to be characterised by 'hard', structural strategies related to restructuring, leanness, downsizing and redundancy.

More recently, Purcell (1995) has discussed the value of developing a greater role for organisation-wide, or horizontal, HR strategies in such organisations. This is based on the approach of recognising and optimising the resource capability of the organisation as a whole in order to seek competitive advantage. Purcell (1995: 83–4) argues that

> the identification of key resources and the means needed to convert them into sources of sustained competitive advantage ... no longer [suggests] that the operating subsidiary is the most appropriate unit of the organisation. ... rather than an exclusive concern with market growth and attractiveness, niches and segmentation, the language becomes one of maximising strengths of resources and capabilities to achieve synergy – the development of a core competence.

This is more likely to occur in an organisation of related business activities, where an internal labour market exists, or where one can be created through this type of approach. We return to this relationship between structural and HR strategies in particular when we discuss the introduction of job families in Chapter 2.

Summary

We have seen that strategy is far from being a completely rational and planned process. The emergence of organisational strategies, and the way in which these are affected by the nature of an organisation's cultural paradigm and the interplay of dynamic political issues within it, have important implications for the nature of HR strategies and the management of change. The nature of first-order and second-order strategies will also affect the scope for and focus of HR strategies, although not in a rational and uniform manner.

We have also seen that HR strategies have the potential to generate strategic change. This may be realised through their potential to affect an organisation's cultural paradigm, to develop its resource capability, and to foster and support newly emerging business strategies. This is, of course, not to deny that HR strategies emerge and exist within the context of the factors that affect their choice, design and implementation. The potential for strategic change involving the use of HR strategies therefore needs to be evaluated within the context of all the factors that have been considered in this section. In addition, we also need to consider the manner in which any such change is implemented and the way in which those it affects receive it. We therefore proceed to consider these aspects of the management of change.

The implementation and impact of change

The implementation of strategic change is likely to be problematic. This is especially likely to be the case in situations where this type of change involves people, and 'in which personal relationships and emotional responses are predominant' (McCalman and Paton, 1992: 18). Mabey and Salaman (1995) consider a number of perceptions about the management of change that will affect reactions to it. Amongst these factors are whether change is perceived as 'deviant or normal' and 'threatening or desirable' (Mabey and Salaman, 1995: 73). Change judged as deviant will be perceived as imposed and outside prevailing cultural norms. This is likely to generate resistance at various levels. Change seen as threatening is also likely to meet resistance and this will require careful implementation to overcome the fear associated with this perception. Perceptions about the nature of change and the need for it will therefore affect reactions to it.

The methods used to implement change will have an important role in affecting the nature and strength of these reactions. By methods, we refer to whether change is implemented as a 'top-down' or 'bottom-up' approach, whether its intention is transformational or incremental and whether it is a rapid or gradual process. There are clearly links between these facets of the implementation of change. Choice between these approaches will affect perceptions about the degree to which change is accepted or resisted and whether it is seen as imposed and controlled or, to some extent, participative. In addition, the exercise of choice between these approaches may affect the extent to which any resultant change is intended (that is, planned) or unintended (unplanned). We consider these aspects of implementation and their possible implications.

Top-down change is associated with the strategic planning approach discussed in the previous section and is designed and driven by an organisation's senior management. Nicholson (1993) believes that it will be necessary to use this approach to bring about radical change in an organisation. Another advantage of this approach is suggested by Mabey and Salaman (1995: 105) linked to the provision of 'a clear, sustained direction that is well resourced and co-ordinated'. However, where this approach is associated with a 'transformational' approach to change (e.g. Beckhard, 1992) its impact and effectiveness are frequently criticised. Change that is intended to be transformational will affect many aspects of an organisation and levels within it. It will require the creation of a new mission and future direction, alterations to the dominant values, beliefs and perceptions in the organisation with fundamental implications for the organisational paradigm and distribution of power, new structures and methods of working. In this sense, such change is seen as radical and discontinuous (*see*, for example, Levy and Merry, 1986; Beckhard, 1992).

Beer *et al.* (1990) are amongst those who criticise this type of approach to change because they believe that its use is not effective. They do not believe that intended change will be generated simply by changing organisational structures and imposing new systems. The change that is realised will not be that which was intended. This has clear implications for the use and nature of HR strategies, as we discuss in the next section. Pettigrew and Whipp (1991: 176) are amongst those who also criticise this approach and it is worth considering the following quotation from them to understand why.

> [T]he evidence from our research suggests that rigid or programmatic conceptions of the translation (change) process are of little use in understanding how that process works in practice. ... The subsequent interpretation by those affected and the myriad local adjustments are of equal importance. The translation process is the outcome of multiple actions. Sequential, linear programmes of implementation fall down because organisations fail to fit such straitjackets. In practice, attempting to carry out a given strategy or seeking to act out a plan invariably leads to its re-formulation. ... Putting a concept into practice leads to valuable clarification of the original.

Mabey and Salaman (1995: 74) refer to this process as one of 'co-construction'. In this process any attempt to implement change will be interpreted and acted upon by the individuals and groups who are affected by it. This may result in these individuals or groups adopting behaviours that effectively minimise or even negate the purpose of the intended change. The top-down approach to change may also be criticised where it is used in environmental conditions associated with a high level of unpredictability. This may result in the design and attempted implementation of changes that have a low level of credibility with those affected by them.

Perceptions about change will affect its acceptance and may lead to forms of resistance. We have seen that such reactions will be shaped by perceptions about the need for and nature of change, and the way in which it is implemented. In this context, we also need to add perceptions about the expected outcomes or impact of change, which we discuss latter in this section. In practice, there will be relationships between these facets. They are singularly and jointly capable of generating forms of resistance (or acceptance). We now focus on issues of implementation in particular.

Resistance to change may occur at a number of levels in an organisation, from senior managers down. We saw in the previous section that the dominant culture in an organisation is capable of masking the need to introduce change. Even when the need for change is recognised this will be interpreted through the prevailing organisational culture. Transformational change is of course likely to be aimed at changing this prevailing culture, resulting in conflict and clear implications for the use of HR strategies, as we discuss below. We also saw that the organisational culture and structures of an organisation confer power on individuals and groups. Managers and others may attempt to influence the implementation of change in order to maintain their power, with the outcome that some of its intentions are subverted.

More generally, resistance may arise from past personal investments, uncertainty, identification with previous organisational routines and ideological objections. Organisational participants may resist attempts to change the tasks that they undertake, their methods of working, those with whom they work and the way in which they are rewarded because of their sense of familiarity with these aspects and investments in forms of job control. In contrast, a situation of change may be associated with uncertainty and threat, and organisational participants may attempt to import as many of the practices with which they are familiar to their new work situation. Some participants, especially managers, may have been responsible for or involved in the introduction of previous organisational routines and may experience a 'loss of face' and sense of resistance to changes to these practices (Mabey and Salaman, 1995: 112). More generally, transformational change will alter the ethos of an organisation and lead many who have long service to regret the passing of the previous set of values. This undoubtedly helped some of the privatised public corporations in Britain in the 1990s to achieve high downsizing targets. Resistance to change may be seen as a form of withdrawal, and complete withdrawal with compensation may be seen as a preferable alternative by some organisational participants who will be most resistant to the need to adapt to a new situation and values.

Resistance to transformational change is likely to be higher in comparison to the 'task alignment' or bottom-up approach described by Beer *et al.* (1990) (discussed later). Beckhard (1992: 96) suggests ten organisational prerequisites which 'must exist before transformational change can be achieved in an organisation'. These are summarised in Table 1.3. The nature of these points is supported or complemented by other authors (for example, Huse, 1980).

A major distinction may be drawn between a top-down led attempt to generate transformational change and a bottom-up approach to bring about incremental change. The bottom-up perspective is associated with the emergent approach to the development of organisational strategy, discussed in the previous section. It is

Table 1.3 Beckhard's ten organisational prerequisites for transformational change

Priority	Prerequisite
1	Ensuring senior management commitment to the proposed changes which needs to be visible to all participants throughout the organisation.
2	Producing a written statement about the future direction of the organisation that makes clear its new objectives, values and policies.
3	Creating a shared awareness of conditions to produce a common perception that change must be implemented.
4	Assembling a body of key managers and other important opinion-formers to gain their commitment to the change process so that this may be disseminated more widely.
5	Generating an acceptance that this type of change will require a long time to implement fully even though there may be short-term, dramatic changes as part of the overall process of transformation.
6	Recognising that resistance to change is part of the normal process of adaptation, so that managers can be educated to be aware of this and equipped to manage this reaction.
7	Educating participants about the need for change and training them with the necessary competence to be effective, to overcome resistance and gain commitment.
8	Persevering with the change process and avoiding blame where an attempt to implement a facet of this process fails. Such negative action will generate resistance and reduce necessary risk-taking behaviour.
9	Facilitating the change process with necessary resources.
10	Maintaining open communication about progress, mistakes and subsequent learning

Source: Developed from Beckhard (1992).

'bottom-up' in the sense that, according to Beer *et al.* (1990), the change process commences in an operational part of an organisation away from its corporate centre, and is led by the operating unit's general manager rather than its corporate management. The change process will focus on a specific business problem and the strategy to overcome this will emerge through the efforts of those engaged in this situation. Beer *et al.* outline a number of stages in order to realise effective change, summarised in Chapter 3, in Fig. 3.6. These are underpinned by the use of, for example, team working, joint problem solving, producing a shared vision through involvement, and equipping those involved with competencies which are specific to the requirements of the change situation. Beer *et al.* support the redeployment or release of those who do not fit into the changing situation and replacement of these employees by others to facilitate change. They believe that the implications of this emerging strategy and incremental change process for other functions in the organisation need to be worked out through experience rather than being imposed. When each part of the organisation has recognised the need to change and how best to implement this within the overall requirements of the 'new' organisation, Beer *et al.* believe that this is the appropriate time at which to formalise the structures and systems that have emerged.

This type of approach may be less likely to create the forms of resistance that we discussed earlier. Principally, it is designed to generate commitment to the process of change through involvement and 'ownership' in its implementation. It is also designed to alleviate the creation of resistance to change through developing competence and teamworking. Huse (1980) advocates a number of ways to reduce resistance that fit with this approach to managing change. These include identifying the personal benefits that can accrue to those involved in the change process in order to gain their participation. For some, these may include the opportunity to develop and advance through the evolving change process. These ways of reducing resistance also include recognising the role that cohesive work groups may play in terms of facilitating participation in change, supporting the members of a group through the change process and reducing resistance to it (McCalman and Paton, 1992; Mabey and Salaman, 1995). The use of teamworking in this type of change may therefore be important to the achievement of success.

However, whether this form of change is more acceptable as well as more effective is open to question. Organisational factors such as culture, ownership and structure, and the nature of environmental pressures, will undoubtedly influence the choice of change process, perceptions about this choice and the nature of any outcome. There is perhaps a wider consensus about the period required for any type of change. Incremental change by definition suggests a series of steps or movement by small amounts. Quinn (1993) refers to incremental change as a continuous process, without any discernible beginning or end. The achievement of transformational change also needs to be seen as a long-term phenomenon. Although this type of change may be associated with the announcement of some dramatic changes to the organisation, the completion of any transformation is likely to take place over a lengthy period of time (Beckhard, 1992; Mabey and Salaman, 1995).

Indeed, the division between these types of change may become blurred. Beer *et al.* (1990) believe that once incremental change reaches a critical mass within an organisation this will promote its effective transformation as the organisation's senior management introduce new structures and systems to match the changes emanating from below. The use of an umbrella strategy (Mintzberg, 1987, 1994) will produce a hybrid approach to change combining elements of top-down and bottom-up approaches to its design and implementation. In this scenario, the corporate centre will establish directions and targets leaving the design of the changes necessary to achieve these to the operating divisions or business units (Beer *et al.*, 1990; Mabey and Salaman, 1995). Quinn (1993) also states that there is likely to be influence from the top in what is apparently a bottom-up and incremental approach to strategic change in order to affect its direction.

We also referred to the impact of change earlier in this section. The impact of change needs to be seen not only in terms of its level of acceptance or resistance but also in relation to the displacement of personnel from an organisation. Both transformational and incremental forms of change may lead to the need for redeployment within or severance from an organisation. For example, Beer *et al.* (1990) recognise the role that redeployment and severance may play in facilitating change where forms of resistance occur as a result of the process unfolding in a situation of incremental change. The impact of change may be seen as an independent factor where people are adversely affected, but even in this type of situation the careful implementation of change may help to alleviate its impact on those directly and indirectly affected. Examples of this are discussed in Chapter 9.

This discussion about the implementation and impact of change clearly has a number of implications for the use of HR strategies in these processes. We therefore move to discuss the role of HR strategies in these various approaches to implementing change.

The role of human resource strategies in implementing change

In this section, we address three issues. First, we consider notions of strategic human resource management and an organisation's overall HR strategy, as the means to embrace its philosophy and approach to the management of employees. These concepts are introduced to relate them to the debate in previous sections about different approaches to the formulation and implementation of change; and to pose the question 'how does an organisation set about discovering which approach to HR strategy design may be the most effective?' Second, we categorise a range of alternative change processes and identify the HR initiatives that may be embodied in these processes. Third, we examine a key question about the change process, 'who will be responsible for leading its implementation?'

Strategic human resource management and discovering which approach to HR strategy design may be most effective

Strategic human resource management came to the fore as a way of thinking about the role of people in organisations in the mid 1980s as a result, principally, of the writing of the schools at Harvard (Beer *et al.*, 1984) and Michigan (Fombrun *et al.*, 1984). Since then, it has become an element of organisational conventional wisdom that the organisation's HR activities should chime with its overall strategy. Hendry and Pettigrew (1990: 21) present the central components of strategic human resource management. These are:

1 the use of planning;
2 a coherent approach to the design and management of personnel systems based on an employment policy and (HR) strategy, and often underpinned by a 'philosophy';
3 matching HRM activities and policies to some explicit business strategy;
4 seeing the people of the organisation as a 'strategic resource' for achieving 'competitive advantage'.

Hendry and Pettigrew's four components are reflected in most writers' definitions of strategic HRM. Like Hendry and Pettigrew, Beer *et al.* (1984) leave an element of discretion in the choice of the activities to be embodied in the HR strategy. However, they emphasise that the strategy is designed to achieve certain HR outcomes. They are specific about these outcomes, which they see as employee commitment, competence, congruence (reconciling individual with organisational goals) and cost-effectiveness. Guest (1987) too identifies four outputs of HRM: flexibility, quality, employee commitment and integration (of HR with the business strategy; between HR initiatives; and line managers with HR philosophy). The assumption here is that whatever the HR activities pursued, there will be fixed goals that will be the outcomes of these activities. However, in practice, this may not necessarily be the case. For example, the company facing extreme product market pressure to produce as cheaply as possible a product which requires very little employee skill may be very conscious of the HRM goals of integration and cost-effectiveness but much less enthusiastic about pursuing employee competence and commitment. It may be an intrinsic part of the HR strategy to treat employees as highly dispensable. In this case, expenditure on training and policies to secure high employee commitment would be seen as wasteful. Mabey and Salaman (1995: 44) call this approach to HR strategy design 'closed', where 'the essence of HR strategy lies in the application of a specific and limited range of policies in every situation'. This may be rather harsh on Beer *et al.* and Guest because they only specify fixed goals. However, it does serve to highlight the comparison Mabey and Salaman make between this and their so-called 'open' approach to formulating HR strategy. Here, there is no attempt to prescribe a particular HR strategy, or indeed the outcomes. What is important is that the HR strategy should be appropriate to the 'particular circumstances and particular strategies' (Mabey and Salaman, 1995: 44) of the organisation. Mabey and Salaman's 'open' approach to formulating HR strategies is illustrated in Fig. 1.1.

To summarise the Mabey and Salaman model, the operating environment in which the organisation finds itself gives rise to the development of a corporate strategy. This requires HR outcomes (or desired employee behaviours) that are specific to the particular organisational context to be adopted if the corporate strategy is to be achieved. These HR outcomes, or desired behaviours, are pursued through the HR strategy which consists of three 'key levers' (structural, cultural and personnel strategies). These are 'intended to subsume all aspects of organisation which have an impact on employees' behaviour' (Mabey and Salaman, 1995: 46). Moreover, there is an important conceptual assumption, related to the achievement of integration. This takes two forms: external integration (where HR strategy is consistent with corporate or business strategy) and internal integration (where the structural, cultural and personnel strategies being used are integrated with one another). Where integration is achieved in this situation, Mabey and Salaman believe that the desired employee behaviours will be developed, except where the intended HR strategy is beyond an organisation's existing resource capabilities. They concede that this is a 'fantastically idealised picture: in reality achieving it is extremely rare, and the risk in these rarefied discussions of abstract principles of HRS

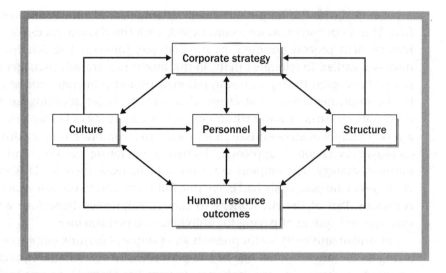

Fig. 1.1 The 'open' approach to HR strategies

Source: Mabey and Salaman (1995: 46). Reproduced with permission.

is that people begin to believe that the world is really like this' (Mabey and Salaman, 1995: 46–7). Nonetheless, we argue that this 'open' view has much to commend it as a means of analysing HR strategy. This is because it allows us to consider and represent the design of organisationally specific HR strategies from not only a top-down, strategic planning perspective but also a bottom-up, emergent one. This point is developed in the following paragraphs. What is also clear is that change is at the very heart of the 'open' model, and it may be seen as implicitly pointing to the complexity of the processes involved. We think that the key to this is in the phrase 'desired employee behaviours'. In this respect, we follow the thinking of Beer *et al.* (1990) and argue that lasting change is most likely to be a consequence of what employees do in their everyday jobs rather than the trumpeting of change programmes driven from the top by management rhetoric.

The 'open' model suggests that discovering which approach to HR strategy design may be the most effective is simple – at least in conceptual terms. Given that the 'open' model is based on a contingency approach, this therefore involves discovering what is appropriate to particular organisational circumstances, including the nature of corporate strategy formulation, and constructing appropriate personnel, structural and cultural strategies. In the context of our earlier discussion, this reinforces the two principal alternative approaches to HR strategy design that we discussed. The first of these suggests that the arrows in Fig. 1.1 are moving principally in a downward direction from corporate strategy through to desired employee behaviours. The second of these, related to the bottom-up, emergent approach discussed earlier, suggests that the arrows in Fig. 1.1 are moving upwards. In the context of the 'open' model, this proposes that what may be termed existing employee behaviours may be the driver for change in the personnel, structural and cultural strategies leading to a change in organisational strategy.

Let us deal with the 'corporate strategy driving desired employee behaviours' view first. This is consistent, as we would expect, with the classical model of the strategic management process outlined by, for example, Johnson and Scholes (1993) and discussed earlier. To reiterate briefly, in this model the strategic management process is seen to progress through a linear, rationalistic and deliberate process culminating in the implementation of strategy. This stage includes adopting an appropriate organisational structure and HR strategies. The case study of Finbank in Chapter 7 is a good example of an organisation following the 'corporate strategy driving desired employee behaviours' approach. Finbank's operating environment dictated a business strategy that emphasised a drive to increase income. This implied that employees who previously had been 'rule followers' had to become much more sales conscious. Part of the HR strategy to change employees' behaviour was a reward management system of paying for individual job performance.

The British university sector presents an example of existing employee behaviours acting as the driver for change in the personnel, structural and cultural strategies leading to a change in organisational strategy. For example, in one institution the existing research expertise of staff acted as the catalyst for the creation of research centres. The identity of these centres reflected this expertise. An important part of the personnel strategy was to develop this employee expertise and to supplement it with appointments of new staff possessing similar expertise. This led to the creation of a corporate strategy that embodied the desire to gain more external funding as a result of a growing research reputation. Of course, it is a moot point as to whether the institution had already decided upon this strategic objective and was simply maximising its existing resources or whether the resources were driving the strategy.

The range of alternative change strategies and the HR initiatives embodied in these processes

There is a further perspective to consider in terms of designing appropriate HR strategies. This concerns the design of individual HR strategies in relation to the focus of the change process. Especially where an organisation is attempting to pursue a planned, as opposed to a more emergent, approach to change, it will intentionally choose one or more change strategies related to those that we now discuss. Several writers (e.g. Chin and Benne, 1976; Kotter and Schlesinger, 1989; Jones and Bearley, 1986) have categorised the types of change strategies that may be adopted. These seem to fall into three main types: first, strategies that imply education and employee involvement activities; second, those that lead to a change in personnel; and third, strategies which necessitate changes to structures and systems. The HR strategies that are likely to be associated with each of these change strategies are shown in Table 1.4. Clearly achieving major change through sweeping away numerous previously influential managers is quite different to a gradual process of change through training and developing employees lower down the organisation who perform daily the necessary routine jobs of the organisation.

Training and development is a time-honoured method of seeking to change the attitudes and behaviours of employees. These may not all be quite as ambitious as

Table 1.4 A typology of change strategies and associated HR initiatives

Type of change strategy	HR activities	Advantages	Disadvantages
Education and employee involvement	▪ Management development ▪ Employee training e.g. change workshops ▪ Quality group programmes ▪ Joint consultation ▪ Team briefings and other forms of employee communications ▪ Performance management ▪ Employee counselling	▪ Greater sense of employee ownership ▪ Fresh ideas introduced ▪ Longer-lasting change	▪ Time consuming ▪ Slow ▪ Expensive ▪ May meet resistance through negative attitudes to change
Changes in personnel	▪ Severance ▪ Redundancy programmes ▪ Recruitment and selection	▪ Impact ▪ Speed	▪ Dealing with the negative consequences for employees ▪ Possibly expensive
Changes to structures and systems	▪ Changes to organisational structures including employee accountabilities ▪ Changes to reward systems ▪ Changes to performance management ▪ Changes to career management ▪ Changes to employee relations structures (e.g. consultation and bargaining)	▪ Longer-lasting change ▪ Re-generation of employee knowledge and skill ▪ Re-generation of tired systems	▪ Slower to have impact ▪ May be difficult to establish causal link changes to structures and systems and organisational change

the famous 'Putting People First' programme run by British Airways in the 1980s (Höpfl, 1993). However, this is one of the first initiatives that managers consider when introducing major change. Clearly, there is a limit to the potential of this approach. There are numerous reasons why training may be ineffective as a way of introducing change. Not the least of these is the 'big new management idea' syndrome. There is also often the feeling that employees are being brainwashed into change acceptance.

The same may be true of employee communication programmes. The chances of HR initiatives based on employee education are often thought to be greater when there is genuine employee involvement. Rather than being told how to think and behave, employees are given the opportunity to devise ways in which changes may be implemented to solve problems that face everyone in the organisation. These examples indicate differences between top-down and bottom-up approaches within this change strategy focus of re-educating and seeking to involve employees.

The biggest disadvantage of a change strategy based principally on education and employee involvement is the likelihood that change will be manifested slowly. Changes in behaviour may be apparent quickly. Getting the checkout assistant to smile at customers may be easy to accomplish (Ogbonna, 1992). However, embedding positive attitudes to the customer through the transmission of a message that the checkout assistant really means the smile is quite another matter. This is likely to be related again to the level of involvement felt by this person. Indeed, the nature of the treatment of many through processes of organisational change is likely to reduce whatever sense of involvement they may feel, with negative rather than positive consequences for the organisation. In this sense, engendering genuine involvement at the cost of speed is more likely to lead to a positive outcome in relation to desired employee behaviours.

If major strategic change is a priority then changes in personnel are almost inevitable. Changes in personnel at the top of the organisation may not be entirely rational judged by the criterion of competence. However, such changes symbolise the necessity to change. In this case change is highly visible and may be accomplished very quickly. However, it may not only be at the top of the organisation where personnel changes may be made. Significant change may be achieved by moving key people from one job function to another to inject fresh skills, experience, ideas and enthusiasm. More topically, jobs have moved to other organisational locations, often in another country. There can also be few organisations that have not lost staff in recent years because of changes in strategic direction. Chapter 9 goes into detail on the ways in which downsizing programmes are operated and their organisational implications.

This last aspect points to the third type of change strategy, that of restructuring. Again, it is unnecessary to go into detail here because this is dealt with in detail in particular in Chapter 2. It is sufficient to say here that alterations to the way that work is organised are of great importance in managing change. Of equal importance is the way that the people who do the work are organised. This is likely to affect patterns of employee accountability and of communication. Accountability for job performance raises the issue of performance management. Chapter 5 notes the potential of this HR initiative to complement HR change, perhaps in concert with a change in the reward system where pay is linked more closely to individual job performance (*see* Chapter 7).

You will notice that we have now moved toward the central subject of this book – the capacity of particular human resource initiatives to assist in the process of organisational change. But before we leave the general debate in this chapter to move to the more detailed accounts in the relevant chapters it is worth making the point that assigning the type of change strategy to one of the three above is far too simplistic. In reality, these strategies are not mutually exclusive. For example, structural change may lead to changes in personnel as the organisation loses employees. This may have been the subject of extensive joint consultation. In addition, a communication programme to explain to employees the need for the change, and to allay the fears of these who may not be directly affected, may have preceded this.

Who will be responsible for leading the implementation of the change process?

In Table 1.3 we noted how Beckhard (1992) stressed the importance of assembling a body of key managers and other important opinion-formers to gain their commitment to the change process so that this may be disseminated more widely. We also noted the importance of equipping those responsible for implementing change with the necessary competence to be effective through overcoming resistance and gaining commitment.

This raises the question of the best choice of principal person(s) to implement the change process. Mabey and Salaman (1995) suggest that there are three sources for the choice of candidate(s): line managers, HR specialists and external consultants.

Line managers

It is a recurrent theme throughout this book that the responsibility for conducting HRM in recent years has moved from the HR specialist to the line manager. Indeed, it was noted earlier in this section that Guest (1987) specifies one of the goals of strategic HRM as integration of line managers with HR philosophy. It is often they who communicate plans to their workforce, explain the relevance of those plans to the pursuit of the overall business strategy, operate the personnel procedures and monitor the performance of those procedures. In addition, they perform the critical function of managing the resources necessary for effective implementation of the strategy.

As Chapter 2 explains, one of the reasons for this assumption of greater responsibility by line managers for managing employees is organisational structures which hold line managers more accountable for the economic performance of their unit of the organisation. It follows from this that they have a close interest in the contribution that their workforce is making to the unit's goals. Arguably, this will increase the likelihood that managers will take personnel issues 'seriously'.

Mabey and Salaman (1995) note that HR changes will stand a greater chance of being implemented effectively if they are conducted by line managers because of their greater 'local' knowledge. They have a better idea of what will work and what will not. However, there is a fear that line managers may be so close to the situation that they do not see the need for change as sharply as the 'outsider'. Additionally, they may be so concerned with the pressing, everyday minutiae of managing the work of their unit that change issues may be constantly put in the 'pending tray'.

Human resource specialists

It would be wrong to conclude that the increasing importance of the line manager signals the demise of HR specialists. They have a key role to play in implementing change. The strategic HRM approach, depicted in Fig. 1.1, points to the HR specialist in a 'changemaker' role (Storey, 1992). In this the HR specialist has a close awareness of the organisation's operating environment and business plans, devises the personnel strategies to generate the HR outcomes in Fig. 1.1 and is in a position to ensure congruence between personnel, structural and cultural strategies. Mabey and

Salaman (1995) note also that HR specialists have an important role in securing the resources necessary for the change programme and selling the ideas of HRM changes to other managers.

This somewhat optimistic portrait of the role of the HR specialist in implementing change seems not to be borne out by the evidence. Storey (1992), in a study of fifteen UK organisations, reports that there was little evidence of the HR specialists adopting the changemaker role. The lack of status of the personnel function in the UK has long been noted (*see,* for example, Sisson, 1994) as an impediment to HR specialists playing a strategic role through influencing business strategy. The point remains, however, that strategic HRM does afford HR specialists the opportunity to make a major contribution to organisational change.

External consultants

In addition to line managers and HR specialists working in concert in the implementation of organisational change, the services of an external consultant may be called upon. The external consultant may adopt a variety of roles from providing change recipes 'off the shelf' for the client, through recommending courses of action based on problem diagnosis to helping managers to implement measures which those managers have designed.

Mabey and Salaman (1995) suggest that the engagement of external consultants affords managers two main advantages. First, they bring a fresh, 'objective' perspective to organisational problems, which may be helpful as a catalyst in developing novel solutions. In addition, they often bring to the organisation experience of problems and solutions in other organisations. However, there can be a major disadvantage in the engagement of an external consultant. This is where the consultant works on the early phases of the change project and is not in place to follow through or evaluate its success. This disadvantage may be overcome by the adoption of what Schein (1988) called the 'process consultation' model of consultancy. This is where the process consultant helps the client to perceive, understand and act upon process events in the client's environment (discussed in more depth in Chapter 10). An important part of process consultancy is the consultant passing on his/her skills to client managers in order that they may become a process consultant in their own organisation (Coghlan, 1993).

The approach of this book

We saw earlier how the nature and emergence of organisational strategies affects the scope for and nature of human resource strategies. From different perspectives and sources of literature, we highlighted a number of conceptual and observable differences to the nature of strategy formulation and change management. We recognised that these different approaches to strategic management, combined with their political nature, and the implications of particular organisational configurations, have clear implications for the design and use of HR strategies.

However, the key conclusion is that their value and importance remain unchallenged. Indeed, the absence of any considered and promoted HR strategy is likely, for example, to have significant adverse implications for a planned change strategy, or in relation to the resource capability required to realise a recognised emergent strategy. The complexity and political nature of change involving people is likely to lead to issues in the design and implementation of HR strategies even in cases where some attempt has been made to involve those affected in an objective way.

Our approach in the remainder of this book is therefore to seek to analyse and evaluate the way in which a range of HR strategies may either help to generate organisational change and/or implement it. In focusing exclusively on these HR strategies, we do not suggest that others, including HR strategies not included because of the need to restrict the number of pages this book contains, are not also of great significance. Neither has it been our intention to produce any material that might be accused of being prescriptive. Rather, it has been our goal to explore and critically evaluate the role of a number of important HR strategies in the processes of managing organisational change. This focus is intended to produce a book that plugs a gap between others that discuss broader approaches to change management and those that explore and evaluate HR strategies and HRM but which do not explicitly major on their change role.

In seeking to fulfil this focus, the chapters following this one adopt a similar pattern in the way that they are composed. Like this chapter, the others commence by expressing a number of learning objectives. You may care to preview these to gain some overall feel for the material in the book.

Each of the chapters following this one includes an initial case study. This introduces change management events related to the HR strategy being discussed in the chapter in the context of a real, and in all but one case a named, organisation. The purpose of this initial case study is to raise and illustrate important issues that relate to the subject of the chapter and as a means to introduce theoretical material and related discussion in the substantive text that follows. In this way, the issues raised in particular case studies are directly referred to in the discussion in the main body of the associated chapter, to explore links between theory and practice.

Each chapter following this one also contains a number of 'self-check questions'. These will allow you to reflect on material contained in the chapter, and in several cases, these questions also allow you to explore this material in relation to the associated case study. Answers are provided to the self-check questions at the end of the relevant chapter.

Each chapter following this one also contains a second case study. These case studies are accompanied by a number of focus questions to allow you to explore and discuss important issues. These case studies should therefore allow you to reflect further on the theoretical material introduced in the main body of the chapter with the intention of reinforcing your learning.

We therefore hope that you will find the material in this book helpful in a number of ways that will help you to reflect and learn about the role of these HR strategies in managing change.

REFERENCES

Beaumont, P.B. (1993) *Human Resource Management: Key Concepts and Skills*, London: Sage.

Beckhard, R. (1992) 'A model for the executive management of transformational change', in Salaman, G., Cameron, S., Hamblin, H., Iles, P., Mabey, C. and Thompson, K. (eds), *Human Resource Strategies*, London: Sage/Open University.

Beer, M., Spector, B., Lawrence, P.R., Quinn Mills, D. and Walton, R.E. (1984) *Managing Human Assets*, New York: Free Press.

Beer, M., Eisenstat, R.A. and Spector, B. (1990) 'Why change programs don't produce change', *Harvard Business Review*, November/December, 158–66.

Boxall, P.F. (1991) 'Strategic human resource management: beginnings of a new theoretical sophistication', *Human Resource Management Journal*, 12(3), 60–79.

Brown, A. (1998) *Organisational Culture*, 2nd edn, London: Financial Times Pitman Publishing.

Burnes, B. (1996) *Managing Change: A Strategic Approach to Organisational Dynamics*, London: Pitman.

Carnall, C.A. (1995) *Managing Change in Organizations*, London: Prentice Hall.

Certo, S.C. and Peter, J.P. (1988) *Strategic Management: Concepts and Applications*, New York: Random House.

Chin, R. and Benne, K. (1976) 'General strategies for effecting changes in human systems', in Bennis, W., Benne, K., Chin, R. and Corey, K. (eds), *The Planning of Change*, New York: Holt, Rinehart and Winston.

Coghlan, D. (1993) 'In defence of process consultation', in Mabey, C. and Mayon-White, B. (eds), *Managing Change*, London: Paul Chapman/Open University.

Fombrun, C.J., Tichy, N.M. and Devanna, M.A. (1984) *Strategic Human Resource Management*, New York: John Wiley.

Guest, D. (1987) 'Human resource management and industrial relations', *Journal of Management Studies*, 24(5), 503–21.

Goold, M. and Campbell, A. (1987) *Strategies and Styles: The Role of the Centre in Managing Diversified Corporations*, Oxford: Blackwell.

Hendry, C. and Pettigrew, A. (1986) 'The practice of strategic human resource management', *Personnel Review*, 15(5), 3–8.

Hendry, C. and Pettigrew, A. (1990) 'Human resource management: an agenda for the 1990s', *International Journal of Human Resource Management*, 1(1), 17–43.

Höpfl, H. (1993) 'Culture and commitment: British Airways', in Gowler, D., Legge, K. and Clegg, C. (eds), *Case Studies in Organisational Behaviour and Human Resource Management*, London: Paul Chapman.

Huse, E. (1980) *Organization Development and Change*, St. Paul, Minn.: West Publishing.

Johnson, G. (1993) 'Processes of managing strategic change', in Mabey, C. and Mayon-White, B. (eds), *Managing Change*, London: Paul Chapman/Open University.

Johnson, G. and Scholes, K. (1993) *Exploring Corporate Strategy*, 3rd edn, Hemel Hempstead: Prentice Hall.

Jones, J. and Bearley, W. (1986) *The Organisational Change-Readiness Survey (OCRS)*, Carmarthen: Organisation Design and Development Inc./MLR Ltd.

Kay, J. (1993) *Foundations of Corporate Success*, Oxford: OUP.

Kochan, T. and Barocci, T. (eds) (1985) *Human Resource Management and Industrial Relations*, Boston: Little Brown.

Kotter, R. and Schlesinger, H. (1989) 'Choosing strategies for change', in Asch, D. and Bowman, C. (eds), *Readings in Strategic Management*, Basingstoke: Macmillan.

Levy, A. and Merry, U. (1986) *Organisational Transformation*, New York: Praeger.

Mabey, C. and Iles, P. (1993) The strategic integration of assessment and development practices: succession planning and new manager development', *Human Resource Management Journal*, 3(4), 16–34.

Mabey, C. and Salaman, G. (1995) *Strategic Human Resource Management*, Oxford: Blackwell.

McCalman, J. and Paton, R.A. (1992) *Change Management: A Guide to Effective Implementation*, London: Paul Chapman.

Miles, R.E. and Snow, C.C. (1984) 'Designing strategic human resource systems', *Organisational Dynamics*, 13(8), 36–52.

Mintzberg, H. (1987) 'Crafting strategy', *Harvard Business Review,* July/August, 66–75.

Mintzberg, H. (1994) *The Rise and Fall of Strategic Planning,* Hemel Hempstead: Prentice Hall.

Morgan, G. (1986) *Images of Organization*, London: Sage.

Nicholson, N. (1993) 'Organizational Change', in Mabey, C. and Mayon-White, B. (eds), *Managing Change,* London: Paul Chapman/Open University.

Ogbonna, E. (1992) 'Organisational culture and human resource management: dilemmas and contradictions', in Blyton, P. and Turnbull, P. (eds), *Reassessing Human Resource Management*, London: Sage.

Pettigrew, A. (1987) 'Context and action in the transformation of the firm', *Journal of Management Sciences,* 24(6), 649–670.

Pettigrew, A. and Whipp, R. (1991) *Managing Change for Competitive Success,* Oxford: Blackwell.

Pfeffer, J. (1993) 'Understanding power in organizations', in Mabey, C. and Mayon-White, B. (eds), *Managing Change,* London: Paul Chapman/Open University.

Purcell, J. (1989) 'The impact of corporate strategy on human resource management', in Storey, J. (ed.), *New Perspectives on Human Resource Management*, London: Routledge.

Purcell, J. (1995) 'Corporate strategy and its link with human resource management strategy', in Storey, J. (ed.), *Human Resource Management: A Critical Text*, London: Routledge.

Quinn, J.B. (1993) 'Managing strategic change', in Mabey, C. and Mayon-White, B. (eds), *Managing Change,* London: Paul Chapman/Open University.

Rothwell, S. (1995) 'Human resource planning', in Storey, J. (ed.), *Human Resource Management: A Critical Text*, London: Routledge.

Schein, E.H. (1988) *Process Consultation: Its Role in Organization Development*, 2nd edn, Reading, Mass.: Addison-Wesley.

Schuler, R. and Jackson, S. (1987) 'Linking competitive strategies with human resource management practices', *Academy of Management Executive*, 1(3), 207–19.

Sisson, K. (ed.) (1994) *Personnel Management: A Comprehensive Guide to Theory and Practice in Britain*, Oxford: Blackwell.

Storey, J. (1992) *Developments in the Management of Human Resources*, Oxford: Blackwell.

Storey, J. and Sisson, K. (1993) *Managing Human Resources and Industrial Relations*, Buckingham: Open University Press.

Organisational structure and the management of change

Having completed this chapter, you will be able to:

■ Explain what is meant by organisational structure and its significance for change.

■ Outline approaches to the design of organisational structures, their implications for change and the people who work within them.

■ Identify the principal forms of organisational structure, their main effects on those who work within them and their relationship to change.

■ Appreciate the relationship between organisational structure and HR strategies.

INTRODUCTION

It is our aim in this chapter to demonstrate the significance of organisational structure in relation to the management of change. The variety of organisational forms and the range of reasons advanced for their existence means that this is an area of considerable complexity. The existence of such structural choice may mean that organisations seek to change their structure(s) in order to pursue notions related to greater organisational effectiveness, efficiency and performance. This may in part be driven by a strategy of cost reduction and, perhaps, also one of improving quality. It may also be driven by a desire to become more responsive to changing circumstances. For organisations operating in a market environment, this change along with others will be aimed at improving competitiveness and ultimately the gaining of competitive advantage. However, these strategic aims for changing organisational structures may overlook the human resource implications of the changes that take place.

Organisational structure is clearly also a human resource domain. It affects the way in which people at work are organised and their work co-ordinated, the nature of the relationships they develop, their feelings about these aspects and the way in which they carry out their work. It also affects the attributes required of those who work in particular types of structure and it has implications for the management of their performance. It is therefore also the aim of this chapter to outline the relationship between organisational structure and these various human resource related aspects. This chapter seeks to consider this by focusing on both the different approaches to the design of organisational structures that have been conceptualised in the literature and the principal forms of structure that have been recognised.

Two case studies are used in this chapter to explore key issues. The first of these examines structural change at Nationwide Building Society. This case study illustrates an attempt to integrate human resource considerations in the structural approach that was adopted. The second case study, which we refer to as Flexco, illustrates an example where the human resource implications of restructuring were not appropriately considered and discusses some of the consequences that followed from this situation.

CASE STUDY 2.1

Structural change at Nationwide – the introduction of job families

Nationwide describes itself as 'The World's No. 1 Building Society'. In 1998 it had total assets of £47 billion and employed approximately twelve thousand people. In the same year, the Society's Directors faced a significant challenge to its status as an organisation that is mutually owned by its members. Three resolutions were advanced in relation to changing the Society's mutual status. The majority of the members who voted on these resolutions declined to change the Society's mutual status. However, this challenge, and other changes occurring in the operating environment of financial services organisations, have led Nationwide to respond to the environment in a variety of ways. One of the key challenges in relation to these developments has been the need to control costs, with a view to demonstrating to members the continuing benefits of the Society's mutual status.

The following extracts from the Directors' 1998 Report illustrate these pressures and their response to them:

> The past year has been one of the most challenging and most successful in the Society's history. In a turbulent and increasingly competitive financial services world, the Society has honoured its commitment to deliver real value to its members and has experienced unprecedented growth. ... By operating on narrower margins than our main bank competitors, we have achieved product pricing which has rewarded the loyalty of existing members and has attracted new customers. ... At the same time, our administrative expenses as a percentage of mean gross total assets have fallen from 1.25% to 1.21%. The net result is an increase in our operating profit before provisions from £308.1 million to £413.7 million. (Nationwide, 1998)

The need to compete in the changing financial services industry and to demonstrate to members tangible benefits of its mutual status lies behind, at least in part, the introduction of an HR initiative that is growing in popularity more generally. This is the restructuring of jobs into what have become known as 'job families'.

Nationwide defines a job family as 'a number of jobs from different parts of the business, which can be grouped by a common set of skills and accountabilities'. This definition is similar to that of others. For example, Kearns and Huo (1992: 10) define a job family as 'a group or cluster of jobs that are in some manner related'. The introduction of job families into Nationwide was accompanied by related structural changes such as restructuring, de-layering and some downsizing in parts of the organisation. These changes were deliberately planned to coincide to prevent employees having to experience different facets of structural change in consecutive periods. However, it is also important to recognise the introduction of job families in Nationwide as an integrating form of structural change. In many organisations, structural alterations may occur as a series of 'piecemeal' changes. In Nationwide, the development of job families may be seen as driving and integrating these other forms of structural change in order to create a consistent and coherent outcome. We develop this integrating theme for changing structure during this case study.

The development of job families in Nationwide and their subsequent introduction has therefore resulted in a significantly reshaped organisational structure. The previous structure consisted of eleven numerical grades, rising from 11 to 1, plus a number of further levels related to senior managerial executives, divisional directors and main board executive directors. This old structure, although offering employees clarity of position and direction for progression, was seen as being excessively hierarchical and somewhat bureaucratic. It was characterised by nearly 1600 job descriptions so that those who achieved small changes in the nature of their jobs may have been able to apply for a re-grading.

In addition, the structure was also seen to lack flexibility. This was particularly significant in relation to the Society's wish to take rapid decisions. Competitors were being seen to reduce their response times in relation to providing decisions to customers, typically about mortgage applications. This was a particularly important part of Nationwide's business objectives. The Society needed to match if not exceed target response times. Thus a flatter, more responsive, flexible and customer focused structure was seen to be required.

Because of these needs, eleven job families arranged in five levels have been introduced into Nationwide. These job families and organisational levels are shown in Fig. 2.1.

Level 1 families focus on service and support roles within the organisation. There are four such families related respectively to transacting business with external customers; providing secretarial or administrative support within the organisation; providing specialist support such as information services; and manual support. Level 2 has three families consisting of those who generate customer business, those who offer internal specialist advice, and those who are first-line managers in the organisation. Level 3 is composed of senior managers who, in turn, are divided into two job families. These are heads of department who are respectively concerned with managing a major 'business-facing' resource area or leading the development of a professional support function.

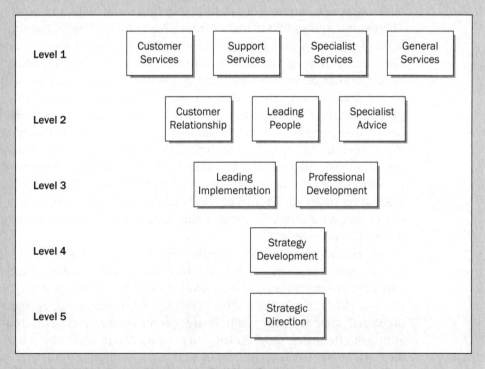

Fig. 2.1 Job families in Nationwide Building Society
Source: Nationwide Building Society. Reproduced with permission.

Level 4 is a single job family of the organisation's general managers who are responsible for developing and implementing the strategy of the Society in respect of a particular group function or functions. Level 5 is a single family of the executive directors of the Society, responsible for its strategic direction and overall performance.

The introduction of job families in Nationwide has effectively involved a 're-layering' of its organisation, rather than simply a programme of de-layering. Rather than simply removing particular layers and leaving others in place, the introduction of job families brought about a much more fundamental review that was designed to produce a consistent structure appropriate to the various needs that had been identified. The previous structure of grades has been subsumed within the appropriate levels of the new form and the roles associated with these old grades retained, modified or replaced accordingly. This has produced a more appropriate structure in terms of organisational flexibility and customer responsiveness, as we now discuss.

In replacing the previously much taller organisational hierarchy with five levels, it was also agreed as a fundamental principle of the new structure that all employees within a particular level would have to report to a manager at a higher level. These changes have effectively helped to flatten the structure of the organisation and reduce the bureaucratic nature of decision making. Previously some queries may have had to be passed up several layers before a decision could be taken and then passed down again for implementation. Some organisations that have simply de-layered may have created information gaps that are filled by those who remain assuming a larger area of responsibility in order to cope with this change. However, within each of the first two levels of the organisation of Nationwide in particular, there is sufficient differentiation of roles through the range of job families, as well as within them, to allow different tasks to be covered effectively. Consequently, many managers have both a wider span of control and a greater range of roles to manage. Potentially this will transform the role of managing more into one of leadership and allow managers to develop a fuller understanding of the links within the broader area for which they are now responsible.

As part of its 'holistic' approach to creating a new organisational form, Nationwide replaced the multitude of job descriptions that described its old structure. In their place, it developed fewer, broader job descriptions. For example, there are now ten job descriptions at Level 1 and five at Level 2. These provide each employee with a statement of the generic competences and attributes required at each job level. These broad job descriptions therefore not only provide a simpler and more transparent approach but also suggest a number of potential advantages for Nationwide and its employees. For Nationwide, these include an ability to improve its:

■ understanding of the nature and distribution of the skills and competence in the organisation;
■ response times to potential human resource planning issues;

▶

- identification of the potential progression of individuals and their training and development needs; and
- outcomes related to better utilisation and efficiency.

Individual employees will be able to understand more fully how their job relates to a similar role in another part of the organisation and other jobs into which they would like to be promoted. Thus, employees will be able to understand how their job relates to others in the same job family and to posts in other job families. Employees themselves should therefore be able to adopt a more proactive approach in pursuing their own required training and development needs where this is appropriate. This development may be focused within their existing job family or another family, or perhaps be intended to lead to a job outside of the organisation.

This approach to structuring the organisation is therefore potentially much more integrative than many traditional approaches. We have already described it as a holistic approach to the design of organisational structure. This is because it has the capacity to lead to the potential integration of HR strategies related to training and development, career management, reward, performance management, involvement, communication and organisational culture. Of course, the extent to which these HR strategies are integrated and effective in practice in relation to the use of job families will depend on their implementation and evaluation in Nationwide. Nevertheless, the potential for this integration clearly exists and demonstrates how organisations may follow the lead of Nationwide in developing this type of approach in designing their organisational structures.

Structure and strategic change

The significance of structure for change

Organisational structure may either act to facilitate or inhibit the fulfilment of the goals of an organisation. This is illustrated by Fritz (1994: 9), who believes that the structure of an organisation has a strong influence on its ability to realise change successfully:

> Structure is the most important and powerful influence there is within the organization. If we don't deal with structure, we won't be able to change the organization fundamentally. With an understanding of structural principles we can redesign our organization so that change will finally succeed ...

The example of the Nationwide case study illustrates the potential linkages between the nature of structural change and a range of HR strategies that may lead to significant organisational change. Where an organisation's structure proves to be deficient, this may therefore act to impair the intended outcomes of change as well as the overall goals of the organisation. Child (1984) has outlined a number of potential organisational consequences that may arise from structural deficiencies.

These include: poor quality and delayed decision making; ineffective co-ordination within groups or between functions, with the potential for conflict; and lack of adaptability to changing circumstances. Deficiencies such as these will clearly affect the scope for and the nature of change in an organisation.

Structural deficiencies may also adversely affect the realisation of third-order or functional strategies (*see* Chapter 1), such as the human resource ones discussed in this book. We may see potential conflict between, for example, the intended aims of a performance management system or a strategy for involving employees and the way in which an organisation is structured. An effective structure will establish clear lines of accountability and will devolve this appropriately through decentralisation and 'empowerment' (*see* Chapter 8). This type of structure should allow performance to be monitored and involvement to be realised. However, a deficient structure may effectively impede the development of the attributes and behaviours desired from a performance management system, and render false an organisation's espoused claims about empowerment in relation to a strategy of employee involvement.

The reason for the lack of congruence between the aims of these strategies and the structure of an organisation may be deeper than simply the existence of an inappropriate reporting relationship. It is also likely to be related to, and underpinned by, other factors such as an inappropriate style of management and the existence of a power culture. Indeed, in Chapter 1 we recognised that the formation of structure is influenced significantly by those who exercise the greatest power within an organisation. This therefore returns us to the proposition that structure may be largely the result of considerations based on the exercise of power, rather than the outcome of some rational process related to an objective assessment of an organisation's operating environment. Where this is the case, the structure of an organisation and style of management may be opposed in practice to the introduction of human resource strategies that are intended to lead to involvement in and commitment to the organisation.

These factors indicate that organisational structure implies more than simply a means to subdivide the work of an organisation and to co-ordinate the various tasks that result. Looked at from a 'bottom-up' perspective, organisational structure will have an important influence on those who work within it. Organisational structure may thus significantly affect levels of employee morale, the nature of communication between those in the structure, the development of informal, as well as formal, relationships, and resulting motivation (Child, 1984; Mintzberg, 1993; Francis, 1994; Fritz, 1994). These factors will also be related to the nature of employees' commitment and conflict in an organisation. Clearly, this may have either negative or positive repercussions and will affect the scope for and the nature of change in an organisation.

Structural choice and change

In the previous sub-section, we referred, somewhat generally, to structures being either deficient or effective. We now look at these terms in the context of managing change and discuss structures that are more likely to be effective, where these support the aims or direction of change. This is not a straightforward, or even necessarily a wise, process. Theories which suggest how organisations *should be* structured are open to the charge of being overly rationalistic or unitaristic, or both. These theories may be differentiated from the political perspective that seeks to recognise how organisations *are* structured in practice, at least to some degree. We have already referred back to Chapter 1, where we recognised that the design of structure may not be related to rational factors. Instead, structure may at least partially reflect the parochial interests of a particularly influential managerial coalition. This suggests an approach to decision making about structures that may be more rational for the influential individuals concerned than for the fulfilment of the espoused aims of the organisation. It also indicates that such decision making is underpinned by a pluralist perspective rather than an unitarist one. We return to this influence on the design and change of structure later in this section.

There are three perspectives on the design of organisations that relate to our present purpose. The first of these examines the claim that there is a universal set of principles which can be used in the design of the structure of any organisation. This classical universal approach to organisational structure was promulgated in the first sixty to seventy years of the twentieth century, as noted by Child (1984) and Francis (1994). However, the notion of a set of universal principles was also re-advanced in the 1980s through the publication of the 'excellence' literature (Peters and Waterman, 1982). Some formulations of universal principles may suggest an ideal form of organisational structure which if attained would restrict, if not eliminate, the need to alter this in response to changing environmental circumstances. The second perspective relates to contingency theory. This suggests that organisational strategy and structure are contingent on the circumstances confronting an organisation. Thus, as these circumstances change there will be a need to alter both strategy and structure (*see*, for example, Child, 1984; Mintzberg, 1993; Francis, 1994). A third perspective relates to the need to achieve consistency between the various facets of organisational design within a particular organisation (*see*, for example, Child, 1984; Mintzberg, 1991, 1993). This appears to place greater emphasis on the fit between the various elements of an organisation's structure in order to achieve operational effectiveness than on its fit to the external environment. We will consider each of these in turn in relation to the need to manage change, before returning later in this section to the perspective related to political influence and the exercise of power.

Classical universal approach to organisational structure

The development of the so-called 'scientific management' approach in organisations in the early twentieth century, along with technological changes, led to increasing standardisation of work and the notion that there was 'one best way' to organise it. This approach was designed to increase managerial control over organisational work (*see*, for example, Braverman, 1974). A similar idea, focusing on universally applicable principles, was applied to the design of organisational structure. A number of structural principles were advanced which were believed to be applicable in all organisations (*see*, for example, Francis, 1994). Contingency theory, defined below, originally developed from attempts to test the validity of classical universal theory. The work of early contingency theorists (Burns and Stalker, 1961; Woodward, 1965) as well as that of subsequent ones demonstrated that the notion of universally applicable principles for the design of organisational structures was incorrect. The notion of 'one best way' was in effect substituted by a recognition that the design of an appropriate structure for an organisation will depend on a number of characteristics of that organisation and the environmental factors that confront it. In other words, an appropriate structure will be contingent on the nature of these characteristics and factors.

However, the publication of the 'excellence' literature in the 1980s led to the advancement of yet more universal principles. These were based on a number of attributes of chosen organisations that had performed successfully, in terms of growth and financial returns, over a number of years. The inference was that if other organisations applied the principles derived from this excellence group, they would also benefit. While a number of the eight attributes derived by Peters and Waterman (1982) have structural, as well as cultural, characteristics, three of these in particular relate to structure. One attribute suggests adopting 'leanness' in relation to the design of the organisation and its staffing. A second suggests a model of accountability based on devolving responsibility through decentralisation while ensuring centralised control over core values and through financial targets. A third advocates the creation of small, empowered teams on a flexible basis, whose sole task would be to find a relatively rapid solution to a significant business problem, rather than working through a bureaucratic or formal route to solve the issue.

We will never know the extent to which the publication of this work and the dissemination of its ideas actually affected the thinking of those who were responsible for making decisions about corporate strategy. It is the case that strategies related to these principles have been particularly influential in organisations in many countries over the recent past. These strategies include structural changes related to leanness, de-layering, downsizing, decentralisation, autonomy, teamworking and flexibility. The widespread adoption of these strategies may therefore be taken as evidence of a tendency towards the adoption of a universal approach to structuring organisations. However, the adoption of these structural strategies may also be explained by other causes. These include changes in organisations' operating environments, such as those related to globalisation and the subsequent need to increase competitiveness. In addition, some of these structural strategies may be claimed to exhibit a much longer history than some current writing suggests, e.g. aspects of flexibility. Finally, any widespread adoption of these structural strategies may be explained by a 'universal' inclination to adopt cost reduction strategies, rather than dissemination of a management theory related to the advocacy of a generally applicable set of principles.

In any case, the universal applicability of these principles or attributes has been questioned. Simple, lean structures may be applicable in some situations but not in others. The resulting use of de-layering and downsizing aimed at producing lean and efficient organisations, which are responsive to their environment, may instead produce anorexic ones which are associated with meanness rather than leanness (Kinnie *et al.*, 1998). Devolving responsibility through decentralisation may also be inappropriate in particular situations (Child, 1984). This is discussed later in this sub-section. In addition, the validity of the attributes themselves has been questioned because of both the methodology used to derive them (e.g. Raimond, 1993) and the subsequent performance of the 'excellence' group of companies. The nature of these organisations' subsequent performance in changing environmental circumstances has raised questions about any approach to their structure which does not take into account contingent variables evident in their operating environments.

Self-check question	**2.1**	*What other criticisms may be made against the classical universal approach to the design of organisational structure?*

Contingency approach to organisational structure

A number of contingency variables have been recognised in the literature (e.g. Child, 1984; Mintzberg, 1993). These include the growth, size and diversity of an organisation, the nature and impact of the environmental factors that act upon it, and the level of complexity of the technologies that it uses. We focus on the organisational and environmental contingencies in this discussion in order to explore and evaluate this approach to designing organisational structure. Contingency theorists believe that where an organisation's structure has not been designed to take account of the demands created by the environment and the characteristics of the organisation this will adversely affect its effectiveness and performance. Where this approach is applied in practice, it may lead to a wide range of structural solutions. In reality, other factors are likely to make the use of this approach difficult or unrealistic, as we discuss later in this section. Nevertheless, the logic of this approach has led to a number of relationships being suggested in the literature between types of contingent factors and appropriate organisational structures, as we now outline.

A number of structural changes are likely to become necessary as organisations grow and employ greater numbers of staff. Small organisations are likely to be characterised by a simple structure within which there is functional flexibility and a high level of direction and control from the manager or chief executive, who may also be at least a part owner. In contrast, large organisations have traditionally developed their structures to incorporate functional specialisation, delegation of authority and procedural standardisation and formalisation, creating a situation of greater internal complexity. This latter type of structure, associated with large organisations, is mechanistic and bureaucratic, as defined by the presence of specialised tasks and jobs, clearly identified procedures and responsibilities, and hierarchical structures. In large organisations, co-ordination therefore becomes a significant issue, as does the design of jobs, the motivation of those who work in such a system and the identification and management of effective performance.

However, as Child (1984: 223) points out, organisational structure will be affected by 'multiple contingencies, such as environment plus size'. Because of the resulting interaction between these contingencies, size will not act as the sole determinant in choosing an appropriate structure, even though it is seen as a very significant factor according to contingency theory. We therefore turn to consider the impact of environmental factors on the design of organisational structure.

Mintzberg (1993) identifies four environmental dimensions. These relate to stability, complexity, diversity and hostility in the environment. Stability refers to the level of certainty or predictability that is evident, with a dynamic or variable environment being characterised by uncertainty or low predictability. Complexity concerns the number of environmental elements that confront an organisation, with a complex environment being characterised by the presence of numerous external factors. Diversity relates to the range of activities of an organisation, so that a business would be likely to face greater uncertainty where it had diversified into a number of different markets. Finally, hostility refers to the level of competition faced by an organisation, as well as the presence of other threats to its competitive position.

These environmental dimensions will interact between themselves, affecting the type of organisational structure that will be appropriate in a particular combination of circumstances, according to contingency theory. Figure 2.2 shows the interaction between only two of these environmental dimensions, namely complexity and stability, and the structural implications of these interactions that are believed to result according to this contingency approach.

Environmental complexity

	Simple ←————————————————————→ Complex
Stable	The stable environment promotes a bureaucratically based structure and the limited environmental interaction encourages centralised decision making.	While the stable environment promotes a bureaucratically based structure, the environmental complexity requires decentralised decision making linked to a divisional structure.
Variable	Environmental variability requires a structure that encourages flexibility, adaptability and responsiveness. Limited environmental interaction makes centralised decision making possible whilst the variable or dynamic nature of this environmental niche means that this is also desirable.	Environmental variability requires a structure that encourages flexibility, adaptability and responsiveness. However, environmental complexity also requires decentralised decision making. This will result in an organisational structure with a high level of internal complexity.

(Left axis: Environmental stability, Stable → Variable)

Fig. 2.2 Structural types related to the interaction between environmental complexity and stability

Figure 2.2 shows that it will not be appropriate for all large organisations to adopt a mechanistic and bureaucratic approach to the design of their organisational structure because of the interaction between these variables. This type of bureaucratic structure is likely to be more appropriate in large organisations that operate in relatively stable and simple environments (*see*, for example, Mintzberg, 1993). Similarly, this type of structure will also be more appropriate for organisations that supply one market, especially where they enjoy a position of market leadership or domination. In each of these cases, the level of environmental uncertainty is (fairly) low.

However, in environments characterised by variable conditions an alternative structural model will be more appropriate. Similarly, where an organisation faces environmental complexity, or where it has diversified into different markets and created a situation of complexity of its own making, an alternative set of structural arrangements will be necessary. Intense competition is also likely to demand a higher level of responsiveness than that offered by the adoption of a mechanistic and bureaucratic structure. The alternatives to such a mechanistic and bureaucratic structure are characterised by greater flexibility and different levels of decentralisation or centralisation.

We therefore digress at this point to consider a range of alternative structures by briefly examining the principal forms of organisational structure identified in the literature. After this examination, we will return to evaluate the contingency approach and then outline the third approach to organisational structure, which is the consistency perspective.

Principal forms of organisational structure and their effects on those who work within them

Organisational structures have changed in relation to the development of increasingly complex and variable or dynamic environments as well as changes in the purpose of organisations such as diversification (*see*, for example, Chandler, 1962; Miles and Snow, 1984b). Chandler's (1962) work on the rise of industrial enterprise in the USA charted the development of organisational structures that were used to adapt to the changing nature and strategies of American capitalism. Miles and Snow (1984a, 1984b) have summarised these developments and produced a typology of five organisational forms. We have referred to two of these forms already. These are the simple organisational structure and the functional structure.

Simple organisational structures

The simple organisational structure is suitable for small organisations supplying a single product, or set of related products, within a defined market. An example may be a professional practice serving a particular location. This type of structure is inherently centralised, with one person or perhaps a small number of people exercising control over the direction and operation of the organisation. The nature of both the managerial style adopted and the work undertaken will significantly affect the character of working relations that result in this type of structure. In this sense, its impact on those who work within it will depend also on these other factors. However, a simple structure should be responsive to the need for change where this type of organisation is 'customer focused' and based on an 'entrepreneurial approach'.

Functional and divisionalised forms of organisational structure

Introducing a functional organisational structure is designed to overcome the inability of a simple structure to respond to an organisation's increasing internal complexity arising from its growth. The adoption of a functional structure therefore leads to the creation of a number of specialised managerial roles and departments that typically include areas such as production or service provision, product development, sales and marketing, finance and human resources. The second case study in this chapter incorporates an example of this type of structure. Indeed, many organisations use this type of structure. Although this type of structure involves some delegation of authority (vertical decentralisation), power and control continue to be vested in line managers and focused on those in the most senior positions (Mintzberg, 1993). This type of structure is associated with the bureaucratic model we briefly outlined earlier. Mintzberg (1979, 1993) called the developed form of this type of structure the 'machine bureaucracy' because of its mechanistic and standardised approach to organising work.

However, functionally arranged organisations, characterised by bureaucratic principles of standardisation and formalisation, have been criticised for not being sufficiently responsive to complex environmental circumstances (e.g. Chandler, 1962; Miles and Snow, 1984b). Organisations require a different form of structure to be able to respond to a complex or diverse operating environment. For these organisations, the third type of structure in Miles and Snow's (1984a) typology is more appropriate. This is the divisionalised form of organisational structure. In this structure, different products, or groups of products, or service areas are organised into separate operating divisions. Different regions supplied by an organisation may also be organised into corresponding operating divisions (see, for example, Child, 1984). Many well-known organisations structure themselves using one or more of these divisional forms. The managers of a semi-autonomous division will thus be able to focus on the particular issues faced by their operating unit and take more rapid action.

While Mintzberg (1993) recognises that the use of a divisionalised structure will involve some decentralisation of decision making, he points out that this will be restricted. This will only occur vertically down to the senior managers of each division so that these middle-ranking managers in the organisation are permitted to exercise power along with its corporate managers. From a human resource perspective, this may help to motivate these divisional managers, provide them with developmental experience and a clear route for upward progression (Child, 1984). However, there may be little effective difference for others who work in each product division, other than the fact that a centralised bureaucratic structure has been replaced by a similar functional structure for that particular division. In other words, a divisionalised structure may continue to be characterised by a mechanistic and bureaucratic design affecting most of the people who work within it, although this does not have to be the case (Mintzberg, 1993).

The human costs of working in such mechanistic and bureaucratic structures under Tayloristic principles of managing people have been recognised for a long time (*see*, for example, Braverman, 1974; Mintzberg, 1993; Francis, 1994). Structures that emphasise managerial control over work are likely to be met by forms of resistance and attempts at counter-control. Employees may develop forms of job control that restrict their work effort and output. Indeed, Crozier (1964) found that the employees he studied used the bureaucratic procedures imposed by their organisations to their own ends in order to prevent their managers from treating them in an arbitrary way. These types of structure are therefore associated with a range of potential outcomes that will impact adversely on human resource strategies aimed at engendering employee involvement and performance as well as broader strategies related to innovation and change.

As we recognised in the previous sub-section, a bureaucratic structure may also prove to be inappropriate when an organisation is confronted by variable/dynamic or hostile environmental conditions. Contingency theory suggests that in these situations the appropriate form of organisational structure is likely to be a centralised one that permits an 'entrepreneurial' approach rather than one characterised by pre-established bureaucratic routines and behaviour. For example, Child (1984: 223) found that 'high performing companies in a variable environment tended to be particularly free of a bureaucratic style of structure: they were highly centralised and without much formalisation'. Mintzberg (1993) suggests that a centralised organisational structure will need to be introduced, at least on a temporary basis, where an organisation is confronted by a situation of particular hostility from its environment (*see also* Morgan, 1989). Where an organisation has already been adversely affected by such environmental conditions and needs where possible to be 'turned around', usually under a new management regime, an entrepreneurial and centralised organisational structure will also be appropriate (*see*, for example, Mintzberg, 1991).

The discussion in this section so far has highlighted some of the tensions around the dimensions of organisational structure. These include:

- determining the appropriate level of behavioural or procedural standardisation;
- the extent to which decision making should be centralised or decentralised;
- the extent of specialisation that is appropriate (*see*, for example, Pugh *et al.*, 1968).

A problematic relationship is particularly evident between the respective desires for managerial control, organisational efficiency and responsiveness to external conditions and intended markets. The simple organisational structure allows for the achievement of these three goals in variable or dynamic environmental conditions where the leading manager(s) adopt an appropriate approach – perhaps encapsulated by the term 'entrepreneurial'. Because of the lack of standardisation and formalisation, this type of organisation remains organic and adaptable.

We have seen how standardisation and specialisation are likely to develop in an organisation that develops a functional structure where it operates in a fairly stable and simple environment. This may help to preserve managerial control and organisational efficiency but may also impair the organisation's ability to be responsive where the operating environment becomes more variable or dynamic, or where the organisation itself diversifies and encounters greater environmental complexity. Responsiveness may be regained in the event of diversification by introducing some vertical decentralisation through a divisionalised structure, while seeking to maintain managerial control and efficiency by retaining other elements of a bureaucratic structure. However, a more problematic position will confront an organisation that faces both a more complex and variable or dynamic environment. The desire to achieve managerial control, organisational efficiency and responsiveness in this situation is likely to lead to a more complex organisational structure. Such a structure will be designed to promote managerial control and optimise efficiency while allowing a greater measure of decentralisation and a more flexible and organic form, in order to be responsive to the uncertain conditions confronting the organisation. One manifestation of this type of organisation is the matrix form of organisational structure, the fourth type in Miles and Snow's (1984a) typology (*see* Fig. 2.3). We consider this form now before discussing other possible forms below.

Matrix forms of organisational structure

The matrix structure combines a functional, hierarchical form with a product-, market- or project-centred arrangement. As an illustrative example of this type of organisational design, Fig. 2.3 shows the functional form on the vertical axis and the product or market basis on the horizontal axis of this structure. In other words, one of these

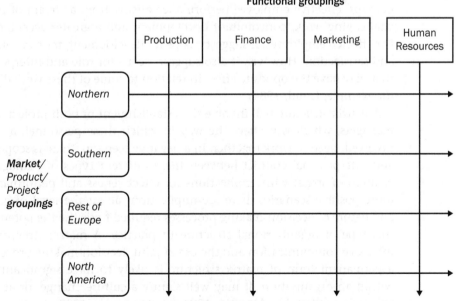

Fig. 2.3 Representation of a matrix organisation

approaches to managing is overlaid on the other, to create an integrated or multidimensional structure (Child, 1984). This type of structure is designed to combine the efficiency suggested by a functional approach to organisational design with the responsiveness implied by a product- or market-centred approach (*see*, for example, Miles and Snow, 1984b). In this way, a matrix form is seen to be more likely to be suited to an operating environment characterised by both variability and complexity (Mintzberg, 1993). However, because it operates on the basis of a shared, dual approach to decision making and control it may well be problematic to operate in practice because of differences between the people who exercise, and share, authority within this type of structure. We will consider some of these HR focused issues of this type of organisational structure in the discussion that follows in this sub-section.

As we may expect, in practice this organisational structure has a number of variations. It may be introduced on a temporary or permanent basis, and as a structure for the whole or a part or parts of an organisation. The 'temporary' use of this type of structure emphasises the importance of project- and team-based structures in this approach to organisational design. The level of uncertainty confronting an organisation may lead it to establish special project teams to deal with the problems that face it and in order to utilise effectively the specialised, and perhaps limited range of, skills that it possesses. Such project teams may be formed or re-formed according to the needs of the organisation and the environmental or market problems confronting it. A recent example of this has been the use of cross-functional teams by many organisations to ensure Year 2000 compliance, thereby stopping the millennium bug from affecting the organisation's computers.

The use of this project-based approach suggests a number of potential advantages, related to the organisation and its employees. For the organisation, it suggests responsiveness to circumstances, the attainment of employee flexibility, as well as, perhaps, effective employee performance arising from a stream of interesting and challenging work, concomitant development and a greater acceptance of change. For affected employees, it suggests scope for development, motivation, involvement and satisfaction. However, it also suggests scope for role and interpersonal conflict that may have the opposite effect in relation to some of these work dimensions (*see*, for example, Child, 1984).

A matrix structure will involve the establishment of both project and functional managers, which will affect the way in which these personnel, as well as others involved, need to work together. In a negative scenario, there is scope for confusion and interpersonal conflict between these different types of manager and for the creation of stress, with implications for effectiveness and performance. Even in a more positive scenario, there are implications about the level of communication and nature of decision-making processes required to realise the potential benefits of this type of organisational structure in practice. A matrix structure will require intensive communication and the use of joint decision-making processes. Adopting a permanent form of matrix structure is likely to have significant repercussions within an organisation. It may well signify a culture change, or at least the final stage of one (Bartol and Martin, 1994, cited in Senior, 1997), for the organisation. It will also require great care in relation to the selection and training, as well as the role definitions, of those who are placed into the management and other key jobs in this type of structure (*see* Chapters 4 and 6). The significance of the need to define these roles and select and train for them carefully is illustrated by the potential for shifts in power and struggles for control where this has not been considered or achieved effectively.

There are essentially three variations in relation to control in a matrix structure (Knight, 1977). In an 'absolute' or 'pure' matrix structure, which Knight called the 'overlay form', functional managers and project or product managers jointly share power and exercise authority. These managers will still commence their roles within this structure from different perspectives: in other words, from their functional or project/product perspective; but will need to work closely together to achieve an outcome. Francis (1994: 68–9) has summarised this position of interdependency from within differing perspectives:

> Every individual in the organisation is responsible to a functional manager for the technical aspects of the work and to a product or project manager for the way in which the task in hand is co-ordinated with other tasks relating to the same product or project.

The requirements of this type of arrangement clearly indicate potential scope for conflict and attempts to achieve ascendancy. Other employees may also be affected adversely, where they are exposed to role conflict in situations where they are expected to undertake different roles and answer to various managers, and may suffer from stress.

An alternative to the pure or absolute form of matrix structure is for either the functional manager or the project/product manager to hold overall authority. The first scenario has been called the 'co-ordination' matrix and the second situation the 'secondment' matrix (Knight, 1977). Our experience suggests a further variation, whereby overall authority switches between the functional manager and project/product manager, depending on the particular context or project. We refer to this as the 'variable control' matrix (*see* Fig. 2.4). Each of these variations suggests

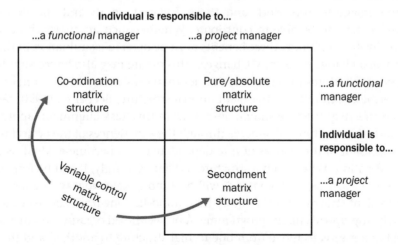

Fig. 2.4 Individual responsibility under different types of matrix structure

that there is still scope for conflict, even where overall, formal power and control has been established. This potential for conflict has led Mintzberg (1993) to suggest that this type of structure is only really suitable for organisations that have achieved operational and interpersonal 'maturity'. This may be characterised by an organisational culture that emphasises openness, co-operation and learning (*see* Chapters 3 and 6 in particular). This will be in addition to other requirements before this type of structure is adopted (*see*, for example, Davis and Lawrence, 1977; Child, 1984).

Project-based organisational structures

Another variation of this type of organisational design is a project-based structure. This may have features that overlap with those of a matrix structure, although it is not necessarily an alternative label for this organisational form. For example, Morgan (1989) suggests that a project-based approach may be used in an organisation that is still formally based on a functional structure. In this situation, the organisation's capacity to respond to its environment and to innovate is likely to be generated by the use of project teams rather than through its functional arrangements.

This is similar to the 'task alignment' approach advocated by Beer *et al.* (1990) (*see* Chapters 1 and 3 for a fuller discussion of this approach). They advocate the introduction of *ad hoc* organisational structures, centring on various types of project teams, to help to bring about organisational change. This approach is intended to engage employees in the generation of solutions to the problems faced by an organisation – to some extent, as a 'bottom-up' approach to strategy formation and implementation (*see* Chapter 1). Beer *et al.* (1990) believe that the use of project teams in this type of situation will lead to a number of specific benefits, culminating in the generation of more effective change in comparison to a top-down, 'programmatic' approach. These benefits include: the opportunity for participants to develop an understanding of the problems facing that part of the organisation for which they work and to devise solutions that are 'owned' jointly; as a result, the development of commitment to this work and those engaged on it; and the development of competencies to be able to contribute. Whether such an approach generates, or is more likely to generate, these benefits must be open to examination in the context of particular change situations. Change of this nature may also be seen as blending top-down and bottom-up approaches, rather than only being driven from one direction. Nevertheless, in relation to organisational structure, Beer *et al.* (1990) believe that a more effective structure should emerge from this 'task alignment' approach. This is because the structure will emerge through the experiences of the project teams. It will be cognisant of those areas of interdependence that become evident, which require co-ordination. When such a structure has emerged fully, it can be formalised in the organisation. This, they contend, will be a more effective way in which to generate an efficient structure for the future than imposing one from above at the outset of a purely 'top-down' change programme. A project-based organisation may therefore be used as a means to move from one formal structure to another, and thus it may be seen as a transitional structural state and a facilitator of other types of change.

Our discussion in Chapter 1 about the nature of HR strategies is clearly relevant to this project-based, emergent approach to strategic and structural change. In Chapter 1, we differentiated between HR strategies that are introduced to generate organisational change and those that are used to foster or support it (recognising the scope for overlap in practice). This project-based, emergent approach to change will benefit from the introduction of a range of HR strategies that are designed to foster and support it. These include the introduction of appropriate recruitment and selection, training and development, performance management and employee involvement strategies and practices (discussed in various later chapters). Where strategies already exist for these HR areas, they will need to be evaluated and modified to ensure that they are congruent with this type of change.

We now illustrate the significance of these different approaches to HR that may be adopted in this type of change scenario by using the example of employee involvement. Employee involvement may be seen to be implicit, and necessary, in a 'bottom-up', emergent change scenario. This type of change requires the expertise of those engaged in project-based teams and their commitment to develop solutions and a new direction. Ideally, any new formal structure will be intended to capitalise on these aspects. However, Beer *et al.* (1990) recognise that this bottom-up approach to employee involvement may be clearly differentiated from an imposed employee involvement strategy, which is 'rolled out' across the organisation from the top down. The former type of employee involvement will need to be developed in the specific setting of the emergent change scenario. The latter, imposed type of strategy is less likely to be effective because it has not been designed for such a specific setting. Beer *et al.* (1990) also distinguish between these different approaches to HR strategy by seeing the imposed, comprehensive approach as aimed at changing attitudes and the emergent, context-specific and supportive approach being aimed at altering behaviours. The behavioural approach is seen as being much more effective, the attitudinal one being likely to become 'crowded out' by other organisational events (*see*, for example, Guest *et al.*, 1993).

A similar distinction may be made between other HR strategies in the context of this type of change scenario. For example, a general programme of attitudinal training aimed at changing the culture of an organisation is less likely to be successful than specifically designed training aimed at developing behavioural competencies identified as necessary in the newly emerging organisation. Indeed, this latter approach to training may contribute more effectively to a shift in attitudes, and hence the changing of some facets of organisational culture, although this effect is also likely to depend on other aspects of organisational climate. In the context of an emergent change scenario, the use of structural forms such as project-based teams may therefore be seen as the primary driver of change, with a supporting role being conducted by appropriately formulated HR strategies.

However, even where this relationship is recognised and applied, the process of change may still be problematic and affected by conflict. Mintzberg (1993) refers to the types of organisations covered by our discussion of matrix and project-based structures as 'adhocracies'. Adhocracies are, according to Mintzberg, prone to political power struggles and characterised by conflictual relations, not least because of their organic and potentially changing structures. He equates the nature of these types of relationships to a form of social Darwinism, through which the fit survive.

Some discussion of the use of project-based teams ignores this aspect of this type of structure. Project-based teams may in reality be collections of representatives from different interest groups, each one of which may be promoting a conflicting solution to a particular problem or project focus in order to further the interests of their group. This possibility points to a more pluralist dynamic in the use of such an approach to facilitating change, in comparison to the implicit sense of unitarism that may be read into some discussions that promote this approach. This possibility indicates the need to consider the dynamics and training needs of, as well as the cultural background to, such a team-based strategy, if it is to be effective in practice. There is a sizeable body of literature that considers the creation and use of effective teams (e.g. Johnson and Johnson, 1997).

Network forms of organisation

We have considered how matrix and project-based structures are more suited to environmental conditions characterised by both complex and variable or dynamic conditions. Another form of organisation suited to this type of environment is the so-called network organisation. There are different categories or types of networks. These have been termed internal networks, vertical or stable networks and dynamic or loosely coupled networks (*see*, for example, Miles and Snow, 1984a; Morgan, 1989; Snow *et al.*, 1992; Senior, 1997).

Internal networks are essentially strategic business units or profit centres that use market pricing as the basis for supplying components or services from one part of an organisation to another. This arrangement is used to promote organisational efficiency and innovation. The second case study in this chapter incorporates an example of this type of arrangement. Many large organisations have moved to establish this type of internal structural arrangement.

Vertical or stable networks involve different organisations, centred on a core organisation, working together to produce and supply a good or service. The example often cited is that of the motor industry. Vertical integration is limited in this industry, so that at least some of the parts of the car that you drive may have been made by a range of firms that supply the company whose name your car displays. The distribution network for a particular make of car will also be owned by a range of other organisations, approved by and contracted to the particular manufacturer. These types of network generally remain stable over long periods. For the core organisation in such a network, this has the benefit of spreading the costs of investment and their exposure to risk and controlling their supply costs. For the organisations that supply parts or distribute the final product, this should generally ensure a steady flow of work and income. For the core organisation, this type of organisational arrangement is also known as outsourcing. Other examples of vertical networks may be found in a range of other industries such as manufacturing, clothing and retail (e.g. Benetton; Marks & Spencer).

Dynamic or loosely coupled networks differ from the previous form in that they are less likely to be dependent on a particular organisation and, by definition, are also likely to be less stable. This type of arrangement is essentially a co-operative one between a number of organisations to develop and exploit a perceived commercial opportunity, perhaps where none is large enough or has sufficient resources to achieve this in isolation. Examples may be found in construction, in order to undertake large projects that bring together a range of capabilities. Such a network arrangement therefore has the benefit of allowing a number of specialised organisations to pool their resources to mutual advantage. Larger organisations that co-operate to pool their resources in some way, in relation to a particular opportunity, may prefer to develop a more permanent organisational arrangement. This may point to the creation of a strategic alliance or joint venture.

In general terms, there appear to be a number of HR implications arising from these types of network arrangements and structural relationships. These include issues related to co-ordination, co-operation, communication, product quality, training and development, performance management, involvement and commitment. The use of an internal network will affect the nature of co-ordination and communication within the organisation, suggesting the need for the development of co-operative relations based on internal customer relationships. In turn, this is likely to have implications for the nature of HR strategies relating to, amongst others, recruitment and selection, training and development and the design and management of appropriate performance standards.

A vertical network adds a further layer of complexity to the effective management of people engaged in this type of arrangement. Co-ordination, co-operation and communication will not only need to be achieved within each constituent organisation in this type of network but also between them. The core organisation may seek to ensure the adoption of particular standards in supplying organisations within the network by requiring them to adopt an approved and verifiable system of quality management. This in turn will raise HR implications related to, most obviously, employee training and selection. The core organisation may also use its supplier network, or part of it, to hold down costs in this area, with particular implications for the nature of the treatment of those who work in one of these supplier organisations. Where a core organisation decides to develop its strategy of outsourcing this may lead it to restructure and reduce its workforce as it downsizes. In effect, this vertical network strategy may allow the core organisation to become smaller with an altered internal organisational structure. This outcome may therefore lead to a lower level of internal complexity, but a need to engage 'key' personnel to co-ordinate effectively its vital external relationships.

The issue of external complexity and co-ordination is most evident in relation to the use of a loosely coupled network. This type of network arrangement suggests the need to generate a high level of shared understanding, communication, trust and co-operation. It seems likely that each core employee of a constituent organisation in such a network will need to become a 'key' member in ensuring the success of this type of arrangement. This has clear implications about the selection and performance management, as well as the commitment attributes, of those who work in this type of network.

Self-check question	2.2	*Why do you think that we considered the principal forms of organisational structure within the context of the discussion related to the contingency approach to the design of structures?*

Evaluating the contingency approach to organisational structure

We have considered the principal forms of organisational structure within our discussion of the contingency approach to the design of organisations because, in theory, it is possible to see how environmental and organisational factors influence or shape each form. However, in reality, choice of organisational structure will be subject to aspects other than those contingencies suggested above, and these aspects may supersede such contingent variables. Child (1984) provides a very useful evaluation of contingency theory when applied to organisational design. His evaluation includes consideration of other aspects related to organisational performance, environmental dependency, the impact of multiple contingencies, structural variations and choice (that may be based on non-technical factors) and an absence of rationalistic assumptions.

Some examples from the work of Child (1984) will illustrate the essence of these aspects. Structure is only one of several variables that will affect organisational performance. It is therefore possible for a relatively successful organisation to be operating with a structure that is apparently a poor fit in relation to its operating environment (and vice versa). Organisations in a position of market dominance will be less affected by competition and less dependent on recognising the consequences for them that flow from their operating environment. They will therefore be able to exercise greater freedom in relation to choice about organisational structures without having to suffer the consequences of resultant inefficiencies, at least for some time. The existence of several contingency factors affecting an organisation simultaneously was recognised earlier. While, as Child (1984) discusses, contingency theory may be seen to cope with this by pointing to the adoption of an internally differentiated structure, or structures, in an organisation, this reality also leads to structural variations and the exercise of choice. Such choice may be based on sub-optimal or social considerations. It may also be based on lack of knowledge about structural alternatives, constrained by current ('fashionable') thinking and affected by past developments. This is likely to lead to significant variations between apparently similar organisations operating in the same environment (Stacey, 1993). It is also the case that organisations will seek to affect their operating environments and intended markets in a way that is beneficial to their economic interest. This will undoubtedly lead to the exercise of choice and structural variations as organisations adopt different strategies to attempt to achieve this beneficial environmental interaction and some notion of competitive advantage.

This evaluation of the contingency approach to the determination of organisational structure returns us to the consideration of political influence and the exercise of power that we referred to earlier and discussed in Chapter 1. In Chapter 1 we recognised that structure confers power and that, of course, it is determined by those in positions of power. While a range of factors, including the contingencies considered above, will undoubtedly affect the design of organisational structure, it would nevertheless be naïve to think that political influence and the exercise of power do not play a significant role in determining choice about structures. Structural choice based on political influence and the exercise of power therefore limits considerations about rationality and underlines the importance of subjective factors (*see*, for example, Pfeffer, 1981, 1992; Child, 1984; Robbins, 1987).

Consistency approach to organisational structure

The issue of structural variations between similar organisations operating in the same environment leads towards a consideration of why each of these may still be effective. This points to the extent to which the various elements of organisational design within such organisations are internally consistent (*see*, for example, Child, 1984; Mintzberg, 1991). The essence of this approach to choosing or changing structure is that whichever form is chosen there will need to be a high degree of internal consistency between the elements of the structure in order to promote organisational effectiveness.

Child (1984) provides different examples of this which relate to the potential conflict between the respective organisational desires to exercise managerial control, be responsive and be effective that we outlined earlier. As one example, an ostensibly decentralised structure that maintained mechanisms to ensure high levels of centralised control would be likely to lead to conflict, dissatisfaction and lowered morale in comparison to an organisation that operated on a more consistent basis. In this scenario, organisational effectiveness would be impaired by the conflict between the quest for control and the search for responsiveness. Conversely, a decentralised organisational structure that did not include sufficient integrating mechanisms would be likely to be ineffective (*see*, for example, Lawrence and Lorsch, 1967).

This clearly points to the need to examine the effectiveness of an organisation's structure from the perspective of its internal fit, or consistency, as well as its fit to the external environment (*see*, for example, Mintzberg, 1991). From an HR perspective, the inference to be drawn from this approach is that an organisational structure that is internally inconsistent is more likely to lead to adverse HR implications than one that is consistent.

Self-check question	2.3 *How would you summarise the key differences between the classical universal, contingency and consistency approaches to the design of organisational structure?*

Summarising the HR implications of structural choice and change

Our discussion about the relationship between organisational structure and change, and structural choice has indicated a number of important HR implications. These fall into two categories. First, implications arising from the effects on people who work within a particular form of organisational structure and their reactions to these. This will clearly have consequences for the management of those who work within these organisational structures. Second, implications arising from these forms of organisational structure in relation to the scope for and nature of HR strategies. These categories of implications would appear to go some way towards substantiating Fritz's assertion that 'structure is the most important and powerful influence there is within the organization' (1994: 9). While there will be other key influences that operate jointly with structure to affect the management of change, such as organisational climate and culture, there can be little doubt about the central role of structure in any change process.

We may summarise the HR related implications arising from organisational structures in two ways: first, by listing the ways in which various structural forms may affect organisations and those that work in them (these are summarised below); second, by discussing the way in which different structures may affect the scope for and nature of human resource strategies in organisations.

Organisational structure can be seen to influence:

- the nature and fulfilment of organisational strategy
- organisational responsiveness to external change and competitiveness
- scope for innovation
- organisational capability to cope with uncertainty
- organisational performance and effectiveness
- product and service quality
- the nature and effectiveness of co-ordination
- the organisation of work and job design
- the nature of decision making (accountability and responsibility)
- the location and exercise of power and control
- the generation and level of organisational conflict (and co-operation)
- organisational culture
- motivation and commitment/alienation
- the scope for and nature of employee involvement and performance
- the nature of and channels for communication
- formal and informal relationships
- group processes, teamworking and network relationships
- career paths and scope for development
- the nature of employees' psychological contracts (discussed in Chapter 8)
- work-related stress.

Which items can you add to this list of implications? You may also care to re-read pp. 36–53 to consider further the linkages between the specific implications listed above and particular organisational forms.

We now turn our focus towards the way in which different structures may affect the scope for and nature of HR strategies in organisations. In Chapter 1, we discussed the implications of strategy and structure for the development of human resource strategies, with reference to divisionalised structures. In that discussion we recognised that the use of complex and more vertically decentralised organisational structures, characterised by a multi-divisional structure, could lead to a reduction in the scope to develop HR strategies across the organisation. Business unit managers in such a structure may become more concerned to meet the financial targets established for them rather than focus on corporate HR issues, even where these have been identified (Purcell, 1989).

We also recognised in Chapter 1 that this effect would depend not only on organisational structure but also on the strategic focus of different organisations. Thus, some divisionalised organisations may have a short-term focus on financial control and returns that reduces their scope to develop organisation-wide HR strategies. Other divisionalised organisations may adopt a longer-term strategic focus that encourages developmental HR strategies to be introduced and used across the organisation (Goold and Campbell, 1987). The nature of HR strategies may also be affected by a combination of a divisionalised organisational structure and the particular strategic focus of the organisation (*see* Chapter 1).

In a similar way, other more recent forms of organisational structure, such as network structures, will affect the scope for organisation-wide HR strategies. Again, this effect is likely to be in combination with the strategic focus of an organisation. The use of these structures may thus lead some organisations to recognise the importance of the contribution of their core groups of staff, in particular, and to adopt a developmental and strategic approach to the management of these people. Conversely, other organisations may adopt a more short-term focus based on financial controls and returns. These organisations may believe that they can 'poach' key members of staff from an external pool of labour, by rewarding them well, at least for a limited period. This second approach would be based on pragmatism and opportunism. It would not encourage the development of a range of integrated and longer-term HR strategies.

Self-check question	**2.4** *The discussion in this section has considered the impact of decentralised organisational structures on the development of HR strategies. How do you think a more centralised and bureaucratic form of organisational structure will affect the development of HR strategies?*

In Chapter 1, we also referred to Purcell's (1995) discussion about the value of developing a greater role for organisation-wide, or horizontal, HR strategies in decentralised organisations. This is based on the value of recognising and optimising the resource capability of an organisation as a whole in order to seek competitive advantage. Our first case study related to the structural approach of introducing job families in the Nationwide Building Society may be seen as a good example of this in action. Complex and decentralised organisational structures may lead to the breakdown of internal labour markets, and therefore adversely affect an organisation's ability to utilise its resource capability to optimal effect. The use of an integrative organisational structure across the Nationwide Building Society shows how this type of structural form may help to create a more transparent internal labour market in such an organisation.

The development of job families in Nationwide has led to the clear identification of the skills required at each level in the structure and the creation of developmental records that allow career development and succession to be recognised. It also facilitates lateral movements of staff across the Society, including between its divisions, as the need arises. This type of structure also encourages the development of other organisation-wide HR strategies, such as those referred to in Case Study 2.1. We therefore conclude that organisational complexity and the requirements for decentralisation do not lead inevitably to a reduced scope for organisation-wide HR strategies. In practice, this will be a function of both the nature of the structural form that is chosen and the strategy of the organisation.

SUMMARY

■ Organisational structure is a powerful influence on an organisation's ability to realise intended change. The choice of an organisation's structure will be likely to lead to a range of significant effects on those who work within it.

■ Organisations will need to promote HR strategies that are congruent with the nature of the organisational structure that they choose (or recognise the impact of their structure on their espoused HR policies and the practice and outcomes of the HR strategies that they promote).

■ Three generally exclusive perspectives have been conceptualised in the literature in relation to the design of effective organisational structures. These relate to the classical universal, contingency and consistency approaches to the design of organisational structure. It is also important to recognise other perspectives that affect the design of organisational structure, most notably the influence of a political one.

■ Several principal forms of organisational structure have been described and discussed. These relate to the following structural forms: simple; functional; divisionalised; matrix; project-based; and network. Theoretical linkages between these organisational forms and contingency variables have been recognised.

■ Choice of organisational structure has been recognised as leading to a problematic relationship between the respective desires for managerial control, organisational efficiency and responsiveness to external conditions and intended markets. Attempts to maximise centralised managerial control in situations requiring greater organisational responsiveness are likely to affect adversely the pursuit of effectiveness and working relationships.

■ These forms of organisational structure have been associated with multiple HR related implications. These implications need to be considered in relation to the design of any structure and managed during its use.

■ Decentralised forms of organisational structure may adversely affect the scope for and nature of organisation-wide HR strategies. In practice, this is likely to be a function of both the nature of the structural form that is chosen and the strategy of the organisation.

Restructuring at Flexco

Flexco commenced existence as a business unit of a large private sector organisation. This organisation had operations in a number of information technology applications. Flexco was originally set up as a service function to some of these operations. The parent organisation had experienced very rapid growth over a number of years. In the mid 1990s, its senior management decided to undertake a programme of internal rationalisation because it was felt that management control systems were inadequate and that it had exposure in a very wide range of operations. This review of operations led to a policy to outsource some non-strategic operations and to 'spin off' or divest the internal operating units associated with these operations. Flexco was one of these operations. Its senior managers decided to 'engineer' a buyout, and having raised the finance largely through an investment company it commenced operations as an independent company in its own right.

As a business unit of the original parent organisation Flexco had operated with a fairly simple but functionally arranged organisational structure. The general manager of the unit, who became the managing director of Flexco, had undertaken an overall co-ordinating role but with specific responsibility for the financial management of the business unit. Two other central business unit managers each had specific functional responsibilities. One was responsible for arranging contracts and co-ordinating service provision across the parts of the parent organisation that composed its business at that time. The other manager was responsible for service development and training. Other functional requirements were contracted from the corporate service provision of the parent organisation. In this way, personnel services were bought in from the parent organisation. The HR department was aware of its image as being a cost. Over the lifetime of the organisation, it had followed a strategy to counter this by developing a professional image and as a provider of value in the work that it did for the respective parts of the business. Flexco had therefore been able to draw on this central HR function whenever it required support in this area. A somewhat paternalist ethos had developed across the business, despite its outward appearance as having an entrepreneurial approach, with one outcome of this being that the organisation 'looked after' its employees and provided them with employment security.

The transformation of Flexco to an independent organisation therefore heralded further change for this business and those who worked for it. It would no longer have what had been in practice a guaranteed supply of contracts, nor the old parent organisation's financial backing and the support of its corporate service provision. It expected to continue to work for parts of the old parent organisation but had been told that it would not be given preferred status in relation to other providers. The strategy of outsourcing was seen as an opportunity to 'test the marketplace' to a greater extent than had been the case previously.

This exposure to market forces led to a number of structural changes. These were driven by a desire to cut costs, maximise the utilisation of those that worked for Flexco and increase the level of managerial control. The strategy of the new organisation was now focused outward towards their marketplace and competitors rather than just inward toward those parts of the old parent organisation for which they had traditionally worked. Thus, the new situation that they found themselves in was seen to offer a series of threats as well as opportunities. Although the old business unit had had a simple functional structure, supported by the parent organisation's corporate service provision, the organisation of work under the three central managers had developed around the use of bureaucratic procedures. This had been encouraged by the stable and generally repetitive nature of the work carried out within the old parent organisation. Because the old parent organisation had operations in a range of locations around the country, there were also a number of regionally based service centres, staffed by a regional manager and service support staff.

The structural changes that occurred were focused on these aspects of Flexco. The senior managers wished to see the development of a much higher level of functional flexibility. This was accompanied by a review of staffing levels in different functional and sub-functional areas and a consequential downsizing of the workforce. This particular process utilised voluntary severance and some compulsory redundancies. Indeed, in some areas more than the numbers of staff that needed to leave wished to do so and a decision was taken to 'let them go'. However, this also occurred amongst the service support staff and it was agreed that these staff would be 'paid off' but re-engaged on a flexible contract basis. Several of these staff were happy to proceed on this basis. This proved to be a more costly exercise than was first anticipated but was seen to offer significant cost savings after initial severance costs were absorbed. The result of this was a reduction in the total staffing to about 70 per cent of the buyout number and the creation of a core group of staff supported by other groups of flexible workers. Some of these, including several in the service support area, were now contracted as part of an 'on-call' network. Those who remained in the core were expected to absorb much of the work of those who left and there was a desire to introduce some sort of performance management system, although ideas about this were rather hazy.

The managers in the regional service centres were also affected by these strategic and structural changes. While in most cases they retained their jobs, the nature of their work changed significantly. Previously these managers had had a fairly comfortable existence co-ordinating the delivery of the contracts agreed with the old parent organisation for locations within their region. Now they were expected to maintain these contracts against commercial competition in the new 'open marketplace' and to win new work from other businesses. In addition, they were expected to assume responsibility for the management of the people that Flexco either employed or contracted to work in the region for which they were responsible. In the past, HR issues of almost any nature had been referred up to the personnel function of the old parent organisation's corporate service provision. Now, of course, this option did not exist.

Case study questions

1 How would you label the various organisational structures that have been referred to in the case study?

2 How do you think Flexco's workers will react to its changing organisational structures and the strategies used to implement these changes?

3 How do you think these reactions will affect Flexco's ability to realise its intended strategy?

4 What recommendations would you make to the senior management of Flexco in relation to the scope for and nature of HR strategies in this organisation?

REFERENCES

Bartol, K.M. and Martin, D.C. (1994) *Management*, 2nd edn, Maidenhead: McGraw-Hill International.

Baverman, H. (1974) *Labor and Monopoly Capital: The Degradation of Work in the Twentieth Century*, New York and London: Monthly Review Press.

Beer, M., Eisenstat, R.A. and Spector, B. (1990) 'Why change programs don't produce change', *Harvard Business Review*, November/December, 158–66.

Burns, T. and Stalker, G.M. (1961) *The Management of Innovation*, London: Tavistock.

Chandler, A.D. Jr (1962) *Strategy and Structure: Chapters in the History of the Industrial Enterprise*, Cambridge, Mass.: MIT Press.

Child, J. (1984) *Organization: A Guide to Problems and Practice*, London: Paul Chapman.

Crozier, M. (1964) *The Bureaucratic Phenomenon*, Chicago: University of Chicago Press.

Davis, S.M. and Lawrence, P.R. (1977) *Matrix*, Reading, Mass.: Addison-Wesley.

Francis, A. (1994) 'The structure of organizations', in Sisson, K. (ed.), *Personnel Management: A Comprehensive Guide to Theory and Practice in Britain*, 2nd edn, Oxford: Blackwell.

Fritz, R. (1994) *Corporate Tides: Redesigning the Organization*, Oxford: Butterworth-Heinemann.

Goold, M. and Campbell, A. (1987) *Strategies and Styles: The Role of the Centre in Managing Diversified Corporations*, Oxford: Blackwell.

Guest, D., Peccei, R. and Thomas, A. (1993) 'The impact of employee involvement on organisational commitment and "them and us" attitudes', *Industrial Relations Journal*, 24(3), 191–200.

Johnson, D.W. and Johnson, F.P. (1997) *Joining Together: Group Theory and Group Skills*, 6th edn, London: Allyn & Bacon.

Kearns, J. and Huo, Y.P. (1992) 'An empirical approach to job families in large, complex organizations', *International Journal of Manpower*, 13(3), 10–18.

Kinnie, N., Hutchinson, S. and Purcell, J. (1998) 'Downsizing: is it always lean and mean?', *Personnel Review*, 27(4), 296–311.

Knight, K. (ed.) (1977) *Matrix Management: A Cross-functional Approach to Organisation*, Farnborough: Gower Press.

Lawrence, P.R. and Lorsch, J.W. (1967) *Organization and Environment: Managing Differentiation and Integration*, Boston, Mass.: Harvard Business School Press.

Miles, R.E. and Snow, C.C. (1984a) 'Designing strategic human resource systems', *Organizational Dynamics*, 13(8), 36–52.

Miles, R.E. and Snow, C.C. (1984b) 'Fit, failure and the hall of fame', *California Management Review*, 26(3), Spring, 10–28.

Mintzberg, H. (1979) *The Structure of Organizations*, Englewood Cliffs, N.J.: Prentice Hall.

Mintzberg, H. (1991) 'The effective organization: forces and forms', *Sloan Management Review*, Winter, 54–67.

Mintzberg, H. (1993) *Structure in Fives: Designing Effective Organizations*, Hemel Hempstead: Prentice Hall International.

Morgan, G. (1989) *Creative Organization Theory: A Resource Book*, London: Sage.

Nationwide (1998) *Voting Matters 98*, Swindon: Nationwide Building Society.

Peters, T. and Waterman, R. (1982) *In Search of Excellence*, London and New York: Harper and Row.

Pfeffer, J. (1981) *Power in Organizations*, Cambridge, Mass.: Pitman.

Pfeffer, J. (1992) *Managing with Power: Politics and Influence in Organizations*, Boston, Mass.: Harvard Business School Press.

Pugh, D.S., Hickson, D.J., Hinings, C.R. and Turner, C. (1968) 'Dimensions of organization structure', *Administrative Science Quarterly*, June, 65–104.

Purcell, J. (1989) 'The impact of corporate strategy on human resource management', in Storey, J. (ed.), *New Perspectives on Human Resource Management*, London: Routledge.

Purcell, J. (1995) 'Corporate strategy and its link with human resource management strategy', in Storey, J. (ed.), *Human Resource Management: A Critical Text*, London: Routledge.

Raimond, P. (1993) *Management Projects: Design, Research and Presentation*, London: Chapman and Hall.

Robbins, S.P. (1987) *Organization Theory: Structure, Design and Applications*, Englewood Cliffs, N.J.: Prentice Hall.

Senior, B. (1997) *Organisational Change*, London: Financial Times Pitman Publishing.

Snow, C.C., Miles, R.E. and Coleman, H.J. Jr (1992) 'Managing 21st century organizations', *Organizational Dynamics*, Winter, 5–19.

Stacey, R.D. (1993) *Strategic Management and Organisational Dynamics*, London: Financial Times Pitman Publishing.

Woodward, J. (1965) *Industrial Organization: Theory and Practice*, London: Oxford University Press.

ANSWERS TO SELF-CHECK QUESTIONS

2.1 *What other criticisms may be made against the classical universal approach to the design of organisational structure?*

The classical universal approach is strongly associated with a philosophy of managerialism. Universal principles are advanced in the name of organisational responsiveness and efficiency. However, while they may be seen as furthering short-term managerial interests they do little to consider the consequences of those affected, nor, indeed, the longer-term implications of some of the practices that may flow from these universal principals. The available literature related to the use of forms of flexibility, leanness and downsizing would support this view about an absence of thinking about these people-centred and longer-term business consequences. While some of the practices associated with this approach may be seen as encouraging employee involvement, this is based on unitarist principles and does not consider more conflictual frames of reference.

2.2 *Why do you think that we considered the principal forms of organisational structure within the context of the discussion related to the contingency approach to the design of structures?*

A great deal of work has been undertaken through the second half of the twentieth century in order to recognise the way in which organisations have attempted to adapt themselves to the environments in which they operate. This has been related to the application of an open systems approach to organisational analysis. Our references to the work of British contingency theorists and to American writers such as Chandler (1962) illustrate how the design of and changes to organisational structures were related to this approach. We therefore considered these forms of organisational structure within our discussion of the contingency approach to the design of organisations because, in theory, it is possible to see how environmental and organisational factors influence or shape each form. However, we also recognise that choice of organisational structure will be subject to other aspects as we discuss in this chapter.

2.3 *How would you summarise the key differences between the classical universal, contingency and consistency approaches to the design of organisation structure?*

The classical universal approach is associated with the identification of so-called best practice principles that may be used in a variety of organisational settings. It is therefore associated with the notion of 'one best way'. The contingency approach requires a more situational analysis and believes that effective organisations will result from a structural design that takes account of the demands created by the environment and the characteristics of the organisation. The consistency approach allows for structural variation based on a broader range of aspects. It highlights the need to analyse the internal fit between the various elements of an organisation's structure in order to produce a higher level of effectiveness and performance.

2.4 *How do you think a more centralised and bureaucratic form of organisational structure will affect the development of HR strategies?*

Large organisations based on these principles were associated traditionally with the existence of an internal labour market. For certain groups of employees, this offered a pathway for progression linked to the provision of training and development, incrementally progressive rewards and security of employment. These characteristics are associated with a psychological contract that exchanges security and gradual progression in the organisation for loyalty and commitment. The bureaucratic approach also points to the creation of centralised rules that are likely to include those related to HR. Organisations based on centralised and bureaucratic principles are therefore likely to develop corporate HR strategies that are applied across the organisation.

However, the effects of such corporate HR strategies may be questioned in practice. Those outside particular groups may be excluded from the intentions of these HR strategies, especially in the context of recent developments to differentiate more strongly between core and peripheral groups of workers. Second, a centralised and bureaucratic organisational structure is likely to have an adverse impact on the intended outcomes of certain HR strategies in an organisation. We refer you back to the discussion on pp. 36–7 as an example of this type of effect. The impact of structures based around centralised controls and bureaucratic procedures may thus act to impair HR strategies aimed at promoting or improving employees' performance, involvement and commitment. This is likely to indicate a failure by those responsible to appreciate the lack of congruence between the impact of this type of structure and the aims of such HR strategies, if this is indeed their real aim.

Organisational culture and the management of change

Having completed this chapter, you will be able to:

■ Explain what is meant by organisational culture, levels of culture and the interactions between these levels.

■ Outline the three main perspectives through which organisational culture has been explored within organisations: integration, differentiation and fragmentation.

■ Discuss the importance of organisational culture in understanding and managing change through human resource (HR) interventions within organisations.

■ Identify the complexity of issues associated with aligning culture to the direction that an organisation wishes to take.

■ Link organisational culture change with other HR change interventions (e.g. organisational structure, performance management, recruitment and selection, employee commitment) and understand the role of HRM in managing culture change.

INTRODUCTION

Culture change is one of the most widely written about concepts in the populist change management literature typified by writers such as Peters and Waterman (1982) and Deal and Kennedy (1982). Messages from these and subsequent publications have been summarised by Hendry (1995) as twofold. First, organisational culture matters and, more importantly, the right culture can lead to improved performance. Following on from this the second message implicit in these publications is that an organisation's culture is a tangible phenomenon and can be changed. The importance of organisational culture might therefore be considered a result of the search by organisations for competitive advantage linked to 'buzz phrases' of the 1980s such as 'competitive advantage' and 'models of excellence' (Legge, 1994: 397). The implication is that, through a strong culture, an organisation can gain competitive advantage and corporate success.

Despite this, research evidence (also reviewed by Hendry, 1995) suggests that the link between an organisation's culture and its performance is weak. He argues that an organisation's culture is unlikely to accentuate positive attributes already possessed such as competitive advantage, overall performance or success. Rather the way in which an organisation's employees behave, and the assumptions upon which they base their behaviours, are likely to reduce the impact of negative attributes such as resistance to necessary change. As part of this we would agree with the contention of Whipp *et al.* (1989) that culture is one factor influencing an organisation's competitiveness over time. This implies that a culture change can assist in making a less effective organisation more effective.

Culture change within an organisation is clearly to do with employees. It places considerable emphasis upon the way an organisation manages people, for example through their recruitment and selection, their performance, the training and development programmes they follow and the hierarchies in which they are placed. As such it is formed by the things that human resource management (HRM) can influence (Hendry, 1995).

In this chapter we tend towards the perspective that organisational culture is an objective entity, and in particular that it is 'something an organisation has' (Legge, 1994: 405). This implies that organisational culture is something which can, at least theoretically, be manipulated and managed (*see* pp. 69–73 below). To this end we offer an analysis of a variety of ways in which this might be achieved and the contribution HRM might make. Within our analysis we recognise that, whilst a large number of views and prescriptions for changing culture abound, in reality the process is long term and complex needing careful study prior to attempting any strategy of change (Thompson, 1992; Bate, 1995). As in subsequent chapters we adopt Beer *et al.*'s (1990) model of change. This emphasises that change needs to occur at the level of employees' jobs rather than as a consequence of senior management's edicts. Thus although a culture change process might be initiated by senior management, for it to work it needs to be internalised by individual employees.

The main points in this chapter are illustrated by two case studies. The first,

DuPont Nylon, is set in manufacturing industry. It illustrates how a culture change programme was introduced and focuses upon employee responsibility and safety. The second case study examines British Airways, a service sector organisation in which culture change was part of a transformation from an operationally driven to a market led organisation.

CASE STUDY 3.1

Culture change at DuPont Nylon

DuPont Nylon's UK Gloucester site is one of a number of worldwide manufacturing facilities involved in DuPont's Global Nylon Business and specialises in the provision of products and services primarily to the European clothing industry. A well known brand manufactured at the site is the Tactel® nylon yarn for fabrics. The site was transferred to DuPont from ICI in 1993 as part of a takeover and employed 1100 people at that time.

Despite ICI being seen as a good employer, employee morale was low when DuPont purchased the Gloucester site. They had been told that 'nylon' was not part of the core ICI business and, whilst it was core to DuPont, employees were unsure of the reasons behind the takeover. Within three months of the takeover it was discovered that the nylon business was losing money and needed to be 'stabilised' prior to any development of the site. The message of a 30 per cent staff reduction across all departments was delivered to all employees by senior works managers. Compulsory redundancies followed for which the responsibility was devolved to the Gloucester site. The resulting workforce numbered approximately 700.

During 1994 DuPont Nylon re-outlined its fundamental business purpose as 'to be the world's most innovative and influential supplier of offerings related to nylon technology'. This was to be based around a number of key strategies including culture change: 'We will develop people's skills and the organization's capability to grow by creating a new culture that fosters continuous learning, flexibility and networking.' The new culture represented significant change for the Gloucester site which can be explored by examining the focus upon workplace safety.

Safety has always been important to DuPont. Company legend tells of an accidental explosion at the original manufacturing site in which workers were killed. Subsequent to this the owner rebuilt the site, including his own house within the factory area. The owner justified this by arguing that if the factory was safe for his employees it would be safe for him and his family. Today within DuPont it is commonly said that if you make an error regarding safety it is 'a good career opportunity', in other words acting safely is a condition of continued employment. The focus upon safety has wider significance, namely that every employee is responsible for her or his own actions. Within DuPont each employee is responsible for creating a safe environment. This contrasts with the old Gloucester site belief that managers were mainly responsible for ensuring a safe working environment for employees. DuPont emphasise that although it is managers' responsibility to create a safe environment, it is also each individual's responsibility to act safely within it. At the Gloucester site it was felt that if a culture of employees being responsible for their own safety could be established then it would be easier to introduce them to being responsible for other aspects of their jobs.

Safety at the Gloucester site can therefore be considered as part of a culture change to involve all employees fully in the business and, in particular, ensure that they take responsibility. The culture change was labelled the introduction of a 'High Performance Work Culture'. A core team of people was created to challenge the current view of the site's purpose: manufacturing (*see* Fig. 3.1).

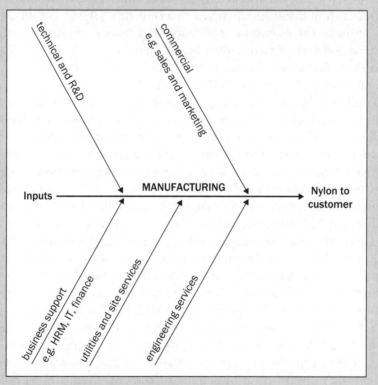

Fig. 3.1 The manufacturing focus at DuPont
Source: Developed from a diagram by John Dowds, DuPont, Gloucester.

The team argued that this was incorrect as it emphasised a core manufacturing role, other functions adding costs to this process. In contrast they developed the view that all site functions were equally important in adding value to the 'offerings' made to four groups of stakeholders: customer, community, employee and shareholder. This provided what they termed a 'unified focus' (*see* Fig. 3.2).

A training programme was instigated. This emphasised that it was not the product (nylon) but the process of satisfying the four groups of stakeholders' requirements that was important. The programme was designed to

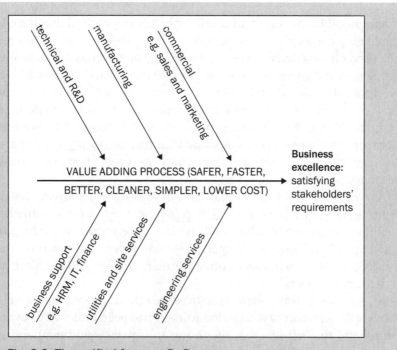

Fig. 3.2 The unified focus at DuPont

Source: Developed from a diagram by John Dowds, DuPont, Gloucester.

■ enable employees to understand what was going on;
■ improve employees' stakeholder orientation.

To enable the programme to be delivered to all employees the production shift system was altered, releasing eight days per employee per annum for communication, training and self-development. This meant that for the first time shift workers had the same access to training as day staff. Initially these were called 'communication days' to help emphasise the fact that communication at the site was a problem that needed addressing. A 'Development Centre' was physically identified as a visible symbol of DuPont's commitment to training for everyone. Topics covered included:

■ What do we do?
■ What do our competitors do?
■ What will the competition be doing in five years time?
■ What will we have to be doing in five years time?

As part of the programme employees were shown what happened in different areas of the site. This emphasised that all employees' actions had an impact. However, some employees still consider this to be general training rather than making any explicit links with their own work.

A visioning process had been undertaken jointly by site departments with DuPont's senior management. The outcome, 'Vision 2000', was shared on ▶

communication days with all employees. This emphasised that the Gloucester site could only compete through developing new products and led to a recognition of the need for new skills. However, the change process was not as simple as training employees and giving them power to make their own decisions. Many production workers still believed making decisions was the supervisor's job, not their own. Previously when they had been empowered to make their own decisions there had been problems. As a consequence they had subsequently been told to refer decisions to their supervisor. Because trust had been withdrawn there was a need to re-create a mindset in which they believed they were trusted to take responsibility.

A 'critical mass' of 84 natural leaders who were managers, design engineers, team leaders, members of the HR department etc. were identified to help the culture change. Others who could also influence people were added to the group, making 112 'influencers' in total. These employees had taken on the new 'trust culture' and were to influence others through their everyday actions and informal and formal contacts.

At the same time, new employee selection procedures were introduced. Previously, selection of production workers had been undertaken by the personnel officer and the first-line manager using an interview and mathematical aptitude test. As part of 'Vision 2000' it was recognised that employees needed to be teamworkers who used their initiative, rather than just machine operators. In addition it was important that existing production workers were not threatened through the introduction of additional educational requirements for such posts. A new selection process was therefore devised using teamwork exercises, aptitude testing and standard and behavioural interviewing. The teamwork exercise was used along with aptitude tests assessed by existing production workers to select applicants against predetermined criteria. The assessment team consisted of managers and people from the production teams. All those involved in the process subsequently scored each applicant, having equal influence regarding who received job offers. This process has been used subsequently by other DuPont UK sites.

It was also recognised that pay and appraisal systems did not reflect the culture the Gloucester site is trying to achieve. At the time of writing these systems are being revised. However, a return to the current safety record suggests some measure of the impact of the changes to date upon the site's culture. Prior to the DuPont takeover a staff raffle with the prize of a car was held if a target of one million employee hours without injury was reached. Under DuPont the average number of employee hours without injury is 7.5 million and there is no longer a raffle. HR managers argue this is because safety is now something which is automatic. All visitors and external contractors working at the Gloucester site are introduced to and expected to observe the same safety code as employees.

Organisational culture

One culture or many cultures?

As we already hinted in the introduction there are different perspectives upon organisational culture (Frost *et al.*, 1991). Most writers take one of two alternatives. Either they view culture as one of a series of metaphors, such as the organisation as a machine, used to help understand the complexity of organisations (for example Morgan, 1986); or (the majority) see it as an objective entity. Those writers who view culture as an objective entity use two distinct approaches. The first of these approach the subject in a way aligned to how anthropologists treat culture; that is as something an organisation *is* rather than a variable that can be manipulated by managers. The *is* approach argues that all an organisation's features and behaviours, including its systems, procedures, policies and processes, are part of its culture. As a consequence the culture can not be manipulated as a whole, or turned on or off, although it may be intentionally influenced (Pacanowsky and O'Donnell-Trujillo, 1982; Meek, 1988). Legge (1994) argues that this approach is self defeating. By defining culture as all an organisation's features and behaviours, its management becomes equivalent to managing behaviour in organisations. The alternative approach is to think of culture as a variable which an organisation *has* such as the set psychological predispositions that members of an organisation possess which lead them to act in certain ways (Schein, 1992a). This implies that culture is something which might feasibly be managed.

Given the arguments outlined above and the case study you will not be surprised that we have chosen to examine culture as something an organisation *has*. Despite this we recognise that implications for cultural change associated with the *is* approach are still likely to be of relevance, in particular the complexity and time consuming nature of the change process. As the basis for our examination we have used Brown's (1998: 9) definition:

> Organisational culture refers to the patterns of beliefs, values and learned ways of coping with experience that have developed during the course of an organisation's history, and which tend to be manifested in its material arrangements and in the behaviours of its members.

This definition uses the term 'culture' collectively to refer to more than a single set of attitudes or beliefs within any one organisation. A particular pattern of beliefs, values and behaviours will have proven valid and useful for the organisational group(s) that use it, and will therefore have been shared with new group members (Schein, 1992b). It therefore follows that the culture will need to change when the beliefs, values and learned ways no longer work or when the external environment necessitates different responses such as when the Gloucester site was taken over by DuPont.

The DuPont case study indicates that more than one culture can exist within an organisation. This was particularly evident in the desire of some employees to embrace the new 'trust culture' and take responsibility for their own actions while

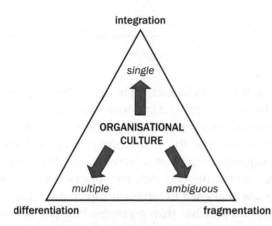

Fig. 3.3 Martin's perspectives on the study of culture

others, in particular production workers, still believed that making decisions was not their job. Martin (1992) terms this perspective on the study of culture 'cultural differentiation'. Within this she argues that manifestations of culture will be inconsistent; subcultures such as that of the production workers will exist and consensus will only be found within as opposed to between these groups. In addition she notes that managers may say one thing and do something else.

The differentiation perspective contrasts with the other two identified by Martin (1992): integration and fragmentation (*see* Fig. 3.3). The integration perspective implies that all members of an organisation share a common culture and there is consensus regarding the beliefs held and the behaviours expected. This concept of one culture in an organisation is easy to comprehend and would make the management of organisational culture more straightforward than the multiple cultures suggested by the differentiation perspective. Unfortunately, although assumed to be the only perspective by many managers of cultural change programmes, the integration perspective is only likely to be visible at an aggregate level and subcultures are also likely to exist. As we saw in Fig. 3.1, DuPont's Gloucester employees considered the site's core purpose was manufacturing. However, unlike others, manufacturing employees were paid on a weekly basis, and they regarded other departments and managers as less important, implying that subcultures also existed.

Martin's fragmentation perspective offers us an extreme alternative to the other perspectives. Within this researchers argue that they can detect very little consensus in the cultures they are studying. Rather than actually identify subcultures within organisations they suggest that consensus only occurs around specific issues which will rise and fall in their importance. As a consequence cultures are ambiguous, uncertain and difficult to comprehend.

Within this chapter we use a combination of Martin's integration and differentiation perspectives. The ideal of an integrated whole organisation culture in which the same beliefs are held by all members is unlikely to occur in reality. Rather an organisation such as a UK National Health Service (NHS) hospital will exhibit only some organisation-wide cultural consensus and consistency. In addition there will be differentiation such as between professional subgroups within the hospital. Research by Preston *et al.* (1996) emphasises this, arguing that historically each caring profession, such as doctors, nurses, or radiographers, has striven hard to maintain a separate professional (subcultural) identity. Within the hierarchy (whole culture) of the hospital profession, subcultures have developed with independent roles despite being dependent on others for the successful recovery of patients.

Preston *et al.* also argue that the existing culture and subcultures present an obstacle to the new framework of the NHS, represented by NHS Trust Boards and hospital managers. The framework represents a culture change to more patient-focused holistic care requiring greater interaction between professions. The example also serves to emphasise our second point, namely that culture must not be seen as a static entity, rather as an organic process which is created, sustained and changed by people (Bate, 1995). In other words, culture may be seen as an evolutionary process. The implications of this for HRM are twofold. The first relates to the need to discern and start to comprehend an organisation's culture prior to initiating change; the second to the need to keep in mind that the approach or approaches adopted to change or realign that organisation's culture to support its objectives are unlikely to remain the same over time.

Self-check questions	*Re-read the DuPont Nylon case study.*
	3.1 *What do you think are the main features of the corporate DuPont Nylon culture?*
	3.2 *What subcultures exist at the Gloucester site?*

How visible are organisational cultures?

Among the best known representations of organisational culture are Hofstede's (1994: 9) 'onion diagram' subtitled 'manifestations of culture at different levels of depth' and Schein's (1992a) 'levels' of culture. Each emphasises that organisational cultures manifest themselves in many ways. Some of these are visible and therefore relatively easy to discern when studying an organisation but, because of their shallow or superficial nature, the true meaning is difficult to decipher. These manifestations are Hofstede's 'symbols', 'heroes' and 'rituals' and Schein's 'artefacts' (*see* Fig. 3.4). Managers often think that just through changing these visible practices or artefacts they are able to effect a culture change. Unfortunately, for real change the process also needs to occur far more deeply, in the less visible levels.

The deepest levels of culture (Hofstede's 'values' and Schein's 'basic underlying assumptions') are invisible and, as a consequence, extremely difficult to discover. They provide what Argyris (1995: 21) terms the 'theories in use' upon which the more visible 'practices' or 'artefacts' of organisational culture are built. Hofstede (1994: 9) refers to these 'values' as the 'core of culture'. Such values are likely to have become so taken for granted that there will be little variation in them within a culture or subculture (Schein, 1992a). They will be communicated to new

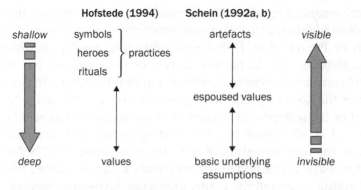

Fig. 3.4 A comparison of Hofstede's and Schein's representations of organisational cultures

employees, thereby transferring the culture. If these basic underlying assumptions are strongly held then group members will find behaviour on any other premiss inconceivable. For this reason changing these is likely to result in a true culture change which will also be reflected in 'practices' and 'artefacts'. However, because they are deeply and strongly held in individuals' subconscious, they are extremely difficult to change.

Between the deepest and shallowest levels Schein (1992a) introduces 'espoused values'. These are values connected with moral and ethical codes and determine what people think ought to be done, rather than what they necessarily will do. Often organisations present a particular view of their culture through formal documents, such as annual reports, mission statements and speeches by senior managers. While these predict much of the behaviour that is observed at the 'practice' or 'artefact' level, especially with regard to what people *say*, they may conflict with what people *do* (Schein, 1992a). For example, you will often have heard organisations say their human resources are their most important asset, yet sometimes their employment practices contradict this espoused value.

Changes at DuPont's Gloucester site are evident in a range of artefacts or practices, all of which are manifestations of the new culture. As we read, altering the shift work system to release eight days per employee per annum for training and the physical establishment of the Development Centre are both symbols of a culture change. Similarly, the story of the reconstruction of the DuPont factory surrounding the founder's home gives the founder almost hero-like status, emphasising commitment to safety and to employees and providing a role model (Deal and Kennedy, 1982). However, these provide us with no indication as to whether change is superficial or deep.

DuPont's espoused values are evident in the strategy 'to develop people's skills and the organization's capability to grow by creating a new culture that fosters continuous learning, flexibility and networking'. These appear to match the more visible practices and artefacts outlined in the case. However, whether the espoused values are congruent with employees' values or underlying basic assumptions or simply aspirations for the future is difficult to ascertain. Values and basic underlying assumptions cannot be discussed or directly observed by outsiders such as ourselves; they can only be inferred from the practices and artefacts which act as indicators (Brown, 1998). At the Gloucester site the increase in employee hours without injury provides us with an indication that safety is part of the underlying basic assumptions of the organisation's culture.

So we have a problem. The outward manifestations of culture are clearly visible and relatively easy to discern. Unfortunately, if only these are considered we cannot be certain that the less visible underlying values or basic assumptions have really changed. Yet for real cultural change to occur we need to ensure that not only are the practices or artefacts, such as messages provided through training sessions (such as those held in the Gloucester site's Development Centre), changed, but that they are also internalised as values or basic underlying assumptions by individual employees (Mabey and Mallory, 1994/5).

Self-check question	3.3	*Why do you think it is difficult for managers to measure their organisation's culture? Use examples from the DuPont Nylon case to illustrate your answer.*

How can organisations realign their culture?

As we outlined above, there has been considerable debate as to whether culture can be managed, much of it focusing on whether or not it can be modified. Given that it can be altered it therefore follows it can be managed and realigned to the strategic direction an organisation wishes to take. Bate (1995) argues that, within organisations, culture is a dynamic, continuously developing phenomenon. It therefore follows that if managers can manage organisations' cultures they can not only change culture but also prevent its change as well as abandon or destroy it (Ogbonna, 1993). In this section we explore possible frameworks for managing both gradual or developmental change and more radical or transformational change to a new culture. In particular we explore the use of top-down and bottom-up approaches and the roles that HRM can play within these.

Frameworks for managing the change

Lewis (1996) reviews a range of frameworks for managing cultural change. These, he argues, consist 'overwhelmingly of a number of steps' or questions (Lewis, 1996: 9) which outline an overall process. One of the most widely quoted of these is Lewin's (1952) three steps of unfreezing, moving and refreezing. Lewin's framework emphasises that before an organisation can be transformed to a completely new culture, the embedded culture must be unfrozen and made more susceptible to change. Subsequent to the change his framework highlights the importance of stabilising and institutionalising the new culture, in Lewin's words refreezing. As we can see in Fig. 3.5, these features are common in frameworks involving both questions and steps which offer a process.

Kilmann (1984, 1989)	Wilkins and Patterson (1985)
Five steps:	*Four questions:*
■ surfacing actual norms (more or less equivalent to surfacing the culture)	■ where are we now as a culture?
■ articulating new directions	■ where do we need to be going strategically as an organisation?
■ establishing new norms	■ what are the gaps between where we are as a culture and where we should be?
■ identifying culture gaps	
■ closing culture gaps	■ what is our plan of action to close the gaps?

Fig. 3.5 Typical frameworks for managing culture change

Like other frameworks (for example: Beer *et al.*, 1990; Beckhard, 1992) those in Fig. 3.5 emphasise the importance of knowing and understanding the current culture and strategic direction of the organisation prior to instigating any culture change. They then build upon this using what is presented as a relatively straightforward process. In essence this consists of: working out the desired strategy and the desired culture, presumably ensuring that the desired strategy and culture match, identifying gaps between actual and desired culture and taking steps to move the actual culture to the desired culture. However, the reality of achieving this is more complex. Organisations are dynamic phenomena and even those within similar backgrounds in similar environments are likely to develop different cultures (Hassard and Sharifi, 1989). Power relationships within the organisation and the transformation process will need to be managed and resources available will need to be sufficient to ensure that the changes are permanent (Beckhard, 1992). These, and other principles, have been illustrated by numerous case studies which 'purport to demonstrate successful cultural change' (Lewis, 1996: 10) and are summarised in Table 3.1.

From our earlier discussion it is therefore clear that prior to changing an organisation's culture a variety of elements need to be taken into account. Bate (1995) groups these into five foci. The first is a need to have a clear appreciation of the culture to be changed. To enhance appreciation the current culture needs to be placed within a historical context so that the ways in which it has developed are clearly understood. This second focus allows learning from past experience as well as avoiding 'corporate amnesia ... and the associated problems of repeating the same mistakes or endlessly re-inventing the wheel' (Bate, 1995: 141). Understanding of the current organisational culture needs to be integrated with the nature of the required change, in particular whether the existing culture can be further developed or a transformational change to a new culture is necessary. Bate (1995) refers to this third focus as the life cycle stage of the culture in the organisation. Through examining this the most appropriate HR interventions can start to be identified as well as potential problems.

Typologies of organisational culture change (for example Deal and Kennedy, 1982) suggest a wider environmental context which will also impact upon

Table 3.1 General principles for successful cultural change

■ Accepted and appropriate patterns of behaviours within organisations are defined by values and basic underlying assumptions.

■ Successful organisations tend to be those where the values and basic underlying assumptions encourage practices and behaviours which match the organisations' strategies.

■ Where values and basic underlying assumptions are incompatible with an organisation's strategy successful cultural change may be difficult to achieve.

■ If an organisation is contemplating change it first needs to establish whether the strategy necessitates a shift in values and basic underlying assumptions or if change can be achieved some other way.

■ Prior to any culture change, senior management must understand the implications of the new culture for their own practices, artefacts and espoused values and be involved in all the main change phases.

■ Adequate resources need to be allocated to support culture change and maintain it once it has been achieved.

■ Culture change programmes must pay careful attention to the organisations' power bases and opinion-leaders such as trade unions and employees' associations.

■ Culture change programmes must take into account an organisation's existing practices or artefacts such as approaches to recruitment, selection and retention, training, performance management and employee relations.

■ In order to create a change in culture, organisations need to decide how practices or artefacts will be amended to support the new espoused values and contradictory practices removed.

■ Every opportunity should be taken to reinforce the practices or artefacts and restate the espoused values of the new culture's values and basic underlying assumptions.

Source: Developed from Beckhard (1992) and Hassard and Sharifi (1989).

individuals' behaviours and an organisation's culture. This is Bate's fourth focus. Taking a broad interpretation of this we might even question whether it is ethical behaviour for organisations to try to alter their employees' values or basic underlying assumptions (Woodall, 1996). Bate's last focus returns to the organisation and contrasts what people in an organisation want with that organisation's needs. This emphasises the importance of understanding organisational politics, power bases and opinion-leaders (highlighted in Table 3.1) prior to attempting to change culture (Harrison, 1972; Handy, 1978). Cultural change will therefore occur from and within an existing organisational culture and be influenced by wider societal and national cultures.

Strategies for cultural change: top-down or bottom-up?

Strategies for creating change are often divided into two alternative approaches: top-down and bottom-up. The former, often termed 'programmatic change', are typically initiated and led from the top (Beer *et al.*, 1990) and have often been inspired by writers on corporate excellence (Hendry, 1995). The latter focus on incremental approaches in which change is developed from the bottom up, tied to an organisation's 'critical path' (Beer *et al.*, 1990) and spread through that organisation. For either approach to succeed it is crucial that employees have the capabilities to deliver the behaviours necessary to realise change (Mabey and Mallory, 1994/5). It therefore follows that an organisation can make a number of HR responses to support either approach ranging from piecemeal to coherent, tactical to strategic or, maybe, just afterthought!

Top-down approaches

Change initiated by senior managers typically looks towards organisation-wide consensus, focusing on the artefacts of culture (including employees' overt behaviour) and to a lesser extent their espoused values (Legge, 1994). As a consequence senior managers often rely on the HR function to manage the symbols of cultural change such as the organisational structure, the management of office space, and car parking allocations as well as provide educational and training interventions to change them directly. HR initiatives such as organisation-wide human resource development programmes (*see* Chapter 6) to enhance quality, excellence or empowerment might be introduced as part of top-down approaches although the outcome is likely to be representational learning (i.e. in the way participants talk) rather than behavioural learning (the way they do things).

Often managers will try a succession of HR interventions using only anecdotal evidence to evaluate the impact each is having. For example the introduction of performance-related pay (*see* Chapter 7) may force managers to differentiate between better and poorer performers. However on its own it will not help them to internalise the cultural context of the new standards by which performance is to be judged or the way in which poor performers will be dealt with. Ultimately it may therefore fail to create the desired organisational change resulting in perhaps another HR intervention such as training to manage poor performance. As a consequence the focus is on the process rather than understanding the organisation's problems and the consequent need for change (Beer *et al.*, 1990). In addition the succession of interventions tends to promote cynicism and scepticism thereby inhibiting change. Hendry (1995: 135) summarises these arguments:

> Programmatic change does not work because it typically fails to tackle three interrelated structural-cum-attitudinal factors – the requirement for co-ordination through teamwork, the need for commitment, and the need to develop new competencies. Company-wide change programmes address one only or, at best, two of these. Culture change programmes in particular dwell on the creation of commitment, but only at a very superficial level.

Top-down culture change programmes also suffer from three interrelated paradoxes (Legge, 1994). First, messages of initiative, autonomy and innovation are usually conveyed through highly bureaucratic methods such as team briefings or company-wide training initiatives. Second, transformation to the new culture is often seen as the task of a new leader. This can be problematic if, as in our earlier

NHS example, employees believe the new culture conflicts with their existing occupational culture. Finally, and building upon Legge's second point, if the values espoused by senior management are discordant with employees' sense of reality the new culture may be acted out cynically and without being internalised into employees' basic underlying assumptions.

This is not to say that HR interventions such as those we have mentioned are inappropriate to managing cultural change. They can play a valuable role when used in an integrative manner, ensuring that the implicit and explicit message provide 'consistent cues' to the desired culture (Brown, 1998: 166). Indeed research into significant factors behind successful cultural change interventions at organisations such as BT (British Telecom), Royal Dutch Shell, BA (British Airways) and Manchester Airport emphasise the importance of deliberately modifying organisation-wide HR practices such as reward systems (*see* Chapter 7) to reinforce desired cultural changes (Mabey and Mallory, 1994/5).

Bottom-up approaches

In contrast to a programmatic or top-down approach Beer *et al.* (1990) found that successful change usually started in one part of an organisation away from corporate headquarters. As you would expect, change in these organisations was led by general rather than senior managers. Rather than creating formal structures and systems these managers focused upon solving concrete business problems, a process Beer *et al.* (1990) termed 'task alignment'. The role of senior management was to specify the general direction and provide a climate for change as well as to spread lessons from both successes and failures. Task alignment, Beer *et al.* argued, could be achieved through a series of overlapping steps (their critical path) taken at the business unit or site level (*see* Fig. 3.6).

As you can see, there are some similarities between the bottom-up approach and the culture change frameworks outlined earlier (Fig. 3.5). Despite these we would

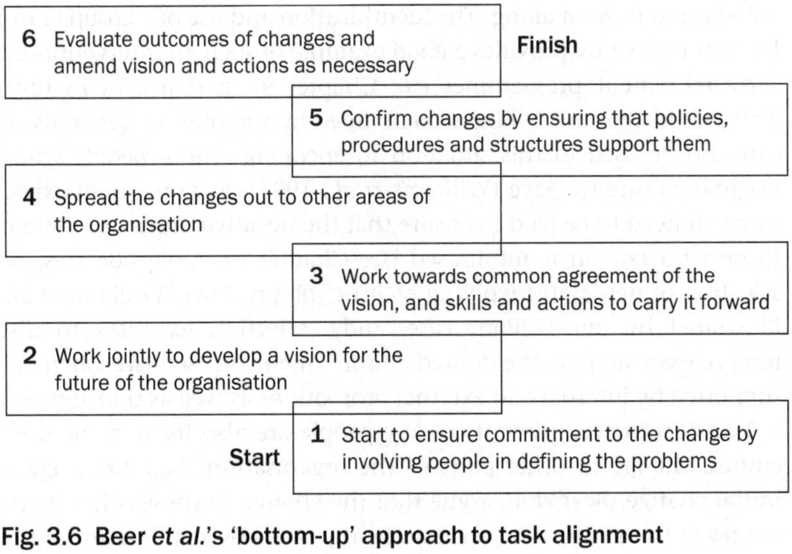

Fig. 3.6 Beer *et al.*'s 'bottom-up' approach to task alignment

argue that bottom-up task alignment offers a different approach for managing change. In particular it focuses on part of the organisation away from corporate headquarters and emphasises individuals' shared commitment and vision as a prerequisite to change. As in the other frameworks (Fig. 3.5) change is enabled by developing people's abilities, although now the desire to learn is enhanced by improved co-ordination and the need to work differently to solve concrete problems. Subsequent results generate stronger commitment to change resulting in a mutually reinforcing cycle of increasing commitment, co-ordination and abilities. This provides a role model for other parts of the organisation. Organisation-wide HR policies, procedures and structures such as recruitment and selection, reward systems, or roles and responsibilities within the hierarchies are only revised subsequently to reinforce and support the change.

HR related actions can, as you have probably already foreseen, be used to support such a process of culture change. In the early stages of Beer *et al.*'s (1990) bottom-up task alignment this is likely to involve managing or enabling employees from different levels and functions within that part of the organisation to meet, mobilise commitment and develop their shared vision (Fig. 3.6, stages 1 and 2). Once the vision has been defined employees will need to develop the skills required by the new culture. As part of this stage (3), HR initiatives such as training and management development programmes might be used (*see* Chapter 6). Such programmes can play a very important role in indoctrinating the desired culture as illustrated by use of employee training at Disneyland (Van Maanen, 1991). However, unlike the Disneyland experience, training in a bottom-up approach will usually aim to address needs directly identified by employees. As a consequence it is more likely to influence their basic underlying assumptions.

By stage 3 in the change process employees who have not accepted the new culture are likely to be highly visible. It will be apparent if the total number of employees is too large or too small for the new vision of the organisation. For both scenarios HR interventions can help to foster consensus of the new vision and generate the cohesion to move it along. The identification and use of a group of influencers in our DuPont case study provides a good example of such an intervention. Redundancy or early retirement programmes (*see* Chapter 9), perhaps, as in the case of Abbey National in the mid 1980s, accompanied by the offer of generous severance terms, can also be used in this situation to encourage those people who hold onto the original culture to leave (Williams *et al.*, 1993). As you would expect, considerable care will need to be paid to ensure that the negative impact of these programmes on those who remain is minimised (*see* Chapter 9). Alongside this, recruitment and selection of new staff involving realistic job previews (Williams *et al.*, 1993) and, as illustrated by our DuPont case study, selection exercises to discover whether interviewees support the desired culture might be used (*see* Chapter 4). This can be supported by internal and external promotions as well as transfers and secondments.

Transfers or secondments of key people are also likely to be used to spread the culture change to other parts of the organisation (Fig. 3.6, stage 4). As with the initial change, Beer *et al.* argue that the change in these other parts must again be managed from within rather than being forced by senior managers.

Beer *et al.* argue that alterations to policies, procedures and structures to support the change (new culture) should only be made once it is entrenched within part of the organisation, the right people are in place and it is working (Fig. 3.6, stage 5). Through working together employees have already learned what interdependencies are necessary and so the organisational structures to support this can be developed. Performance appraisal systems (*see* Chapter 5) need to be tailored to emphasise the basic underlying assumptions of the new culture. Answers to questions such as 'are past achievements or future potential more important?', 'should objective or subjective techniques be used?' and 'who undertakes the appraisal?' need to be aligned to the culture. Reward systems (*see* Chapter 7) need to reflect the espoused values of the culture in what is rewarded, the relative importance of individuals or teams and the way bonuses are given. Similarly defining job roles, writing new policies and applying human resource development systems (*see* Chapter 6) will, whether intended or not, send out messages to employees about accepted and desirable behaviour and the new culture. Many of the problems with implementing culture change strategies occur either because such systems are projecting inappropriate values or because they are giving out mixed messages (Hendry, 1995). The HR function can help co-ordinate and provide direction and control to overcome this.

The final stage in the process of bottom-up task alignment relates to evaluating and adjusting strategies in response to problems. This emphasises the evolving nature of culture as it interacts with both the internal and external environments. However, as in earlier stages it also emphasises the importance of evaluating the changes and sharing the outcomes of evaluations undertaken as part of the process (*see* Chapter 10).

So, should we always take a bottom-up approach? Reading the arguments above you might feel that the answer should be an unqualified 'yes'. However, this is not always the case. Whilst Beer *et al.*'s (1990) research has shown that a bottom-up approach is more likely to achieve effective change this does not mean that top-down approaches will not work. Every organisation's culture is unique and a product of that organisation's past as well as the wider environment within which it exists. As we can see it therefore follows that the appropriateness of the chosen strategy will depend upon what an organisation wishes to achieve through culture change.

Bate (1995) identifies a series of parameters through which an organisation can explore what it wishes to achieve through cultural change and the appropriateness of different cultural change strategies. He terms these the 'design parameters for cultural change' (1995: 203) and argues that their relative importance, weight and value will differ both between organisations and over time within an organisation. We outline these in Table 3.2.

What might be effective or appropriate in one situation may not be in another. For example 'expressiveness' is unlikely to be important where culture change is concerned with further developing an existing culture, in effect more of the same. Conversely where transformational culture change is desired, as at DuPont's Gloucester site, expressiveness is an essential component. Requirements of an

Table 3.2 Design parameters for cultural change

Parameter	Aspect of the organisation	Description
Expressiveness	Affective component (feelings)	The ability of the cultural change approach adopted to express a new symbol which captures employees' attention and excites or converts them
Commonality	Social component (relationships)	The ability of the culture change approach adopted to create a shared common understanding and sense of common purpose amongst a group of employees or the whole organisation.
Penetration	Demographic component (number/depth)	The ability of the culture change approach adopted to spread throughout all levels of an organisation and to affect employees' basic underlying assumptions
Adaptability	Development component (process)	The ability of the culture change approach adopted to adjust to changing organisational and wider environmental circumstances
Durability	Institutional component (structure)	The ability of the culture change approach adopted to create a lasting culture

Source: Developed from Bate (1995).

organisation are also likely to change over time. At the start of a culture change process, expressiveness may be considered more important whilst commonality and penetration are considered less important. However, as the process continues and the new culture is spread throughout all levels of the organisation, commonality and penetration may become more important.

Relationships between these parameters and the top-down and bottom-up approaches are summarised in Table 3.3. As we can see, the two approaches' effectiveness differs across the parameters. This suggests that it is not just a case of choosing which approach will best fit with an organisation, as no one approach will provide everything required. Rather the strategy for culture change needs to be tailored to the precise requirements of the organisation at a particular time. A top-down approach can enable relatively rapid change in an organisation's practices. HR interventions such as organisation-wide training and communication can be used to help inspire employees to adopt the new culture at the practice or artefact level, offering the impression of a culture change. However, if the culture change is also required to be durable it will need to be combined with a bottom-up approach over a longer time period. This can help ensure that the new culture becomes part of the employees' basic underlying assumptions.

Managing organisational cultural change is therefore extremely complex. It needs to take account of the existing culture, whether developmental or transformational change is required, as well as a range of internal and external factors. As part of this process employees need to be managed. The reality of this challenge is clearly

Table 3.3 Relative effectiveness of top-down and bottom-up approaches to cultural change across different parameters

Parameter	Level of effectiveness of	
	Top-down approaches	Bottom-up approaches
Expressiveness	*High* – deal in simple messages and specialise in communicating these effectively and reasonably quickly at the practice/artefact level	*Low* in short term – focus on concrete problem generates lots of detail rather than a new symbol
Commonality	*Low* – promoted unifying feeling often ceases after formal programme ends; methods often lead to resistance and lack of common ownership	*High* – operates through shared understanding and creates a culture of trust and understanding
Penetration	*Variable* – depends on ability of interventions to affect more than just practices or artefacts; highly structured programmes likely to reach all employees	*Low* in short term – involves only part of the organisation; *High* in long term – involves discussing proposals and implications with employees
Adaptability	*Low* – tend to be inflexible and imply instant fix; programmed nature implies conformity and devalues deviance	*High* – concrete problem led, willing to accommodate new views and find best fit with organisational requirements
Durability	*Low* – based on senior management's desires; lack of ownership by employees likely to be highest with transformational change	*High* – employees are keen to preserve what they have created; especially high when a development of existing practices which employees own rather than transformational change

summarised by Whipp *et al.* (1989: 583) who state: 'culture is a Pandora's box: both academics and practitioners should not make any easy assumptions about their control of the contents'.

<table>
<tr><td>Self-check questions</td><td>3.4 How might an organisation use HR interventions as part of a culture change process?</td></tr>
<tr><td></td><td>3.5 Why might organisations choose a top-down approach to culture change?</td></tr>
</table>

SUMMARY

■ Organisational culture can be viewed in a variety of ways. In this chapter we have explored culture principally from the perspective of something an organisation *has* rather than something an organisation *is*. Culture is one of a range of factors which influence an organisation's competitiveness over time. A culture change can therefore help make a less effective organisation more effective.

- Organisational culture refers to the patterns of beliefs, values and learned ways of coping within an organisation. These are visible in the structures and processes of the organisation and the ways its employees behave. Within an organisation there may be elements of organisation-wide cultural integration alongside differentiation between subgroups.

- An organisation's culture is most visible in its practices or artefacts and to a lesser extent its espoused values. HR interventions are largely concerned with structural means of influencing and supporting these visible manifestations.

- For permanent cultural change to occur the basic underlying assumptions upon which these practices or artefacts are based need to be changed. As these are deeply and strongly held within each employee's subconscious they are difficult to change, especially over the short term.

- Strategies for changing culture can adopt a range of approaches. These are often divided into top-down (programmatic) and bottom-up (critical path) approaches. Bottom-up approaches have more chance of achieving cultural change because they start from concrete problems related to the organisation whereas top-down approaches start with people's values. The choice of approach is, however, dependent upon what an organisation wishes to achieve and the time frame available. It is also likely to be revised during the change process.

- Top-down and bottom-up approaches can be supported by a range of HR interventions. These include defining job roles, developing and implementing procedures for recruitment and selection, pay and reward, redundancy, and providing appropriate training and employee development. Interventions need to project the same values as the desired culture.

- Managing culture change is a complex process and neither academics nor HR practitioners should make assumptions about the ease of control of its contents.

CASE STUDY 3.2

Culture change at British Airways

At the start of the 1980s British Airways (BA) faced severe financial difficulties. A survival plan, guided by the then chairman Sir John King, had reduced staff from 60 000 to around 38 000 using a combination of voluntary redundancies and natural wastage. Unprofitable routes were abandoned and surplus assets sold off. By 1983 the airline had been returned to profitability.

To ensure longer-term success a transformational change in the way the business was run was required. The newly appointed chairman, Colin Marshall, embarked on a culture change to turn the airline from one which was operationally driven to one which was market-led (Höpfl et al., 1992). Blyton and

Turnbull (1998: 71) state that 'for many commentators [this] ... provides the best instance of intensive and ambitious commitment to culture change in the last ten years'. Over this period the company's culture was to be changed from what many perceived to be authoritarian (Colling, 1995) to one which was service driven and market-led (Goodstein, 1990).

BA undertook extensive market research and listened to the ideas and concerns of people both inside and outside the company (Heifetz and Laurie, 1997). This revealed gaps between customer and employee expectations regarding service delivery. Staff focused on routine and functional aspects of their jobs and while customers expected this as a minimum level of service, they also expected warmth, friendliness and attention to their personal needs. This emphasised the need for a sharpened focus on customer service.

The strategy adopted by Colin Marshall and corporate managers was to change the values, practices and relationships throughout the company by creating trust throughout the organisation (Heifetz and Laurie, 1997). This was to be achieved by developing the workforce (Colling, 1995). In November 1983 BA launched its 'Putting the Customer First' campaign supported by a massive commitment to corporate training and communications (Blyton and Turnbull, 1998). As part of this the 12 000 BA staff in direct contact with customers, such as those employed on check-in desks and as cabin crew, went through a two-day training programme (Höpfl et al., 1992). Entitled 'Putting People First', the programme focused upon the individual and actively involved employees in developing ideas for improving customer service. The programme gave substance to senior management's notion of service through a considerable investment in time and money (Höpfl, 1993). In addition, the chairman tried to attend every event, thereby emphasising his visible commitment. Subsequently the programme was extended to staff not involved in direct contact with customers such as pilots and baggage handlers, using the premiss that their customers were other BA employees. This provided all employees with an emotional context through which they could respond and change (Höpfl, 1993).

In 1984 a new corporate identity for Personnel was introduced and a new Human Resources Director appointed. As part of this, administrative procedures formerly attached to the personnel role were devolved to line managers. In addition all HR employees were offered a week-long residential programme which focused on developing their consultancy skills to manage change (Höpfl, 1993). Other HR interventions such as profit sharing were used to reinforce employees' feelings of belonging and involvement.

The high level of commitment by senior management gave a clear message to all employees, but particularly managers, that they had to support the initiative (Storey, 1992). This was the most critical dimension of the change programme and necessitated changes in the style of the managers and management (Blyton and Turnbull, 1998). Managers were expected to adopt the new shared vision and

▶

adapt their style of management from a prevailing domination of roles and procedures to one which was more open, visible and dynamic (Höpfl et al., 1992). Training called 'Managing People First' was introduced in 1985 (Höpfl, 1993). This consisted of a one-week programme for all 1400 management personnel 'aimed at removing internal blockages and converting participants to Marshall's organisational values – caring, achievement, creativity, innovation and profit' (Bate, 1995: 195).

Managers' adoption of the vision was evaluated through a new performance appraisal system for all managers and rewarded through a new performance-related pay system. These emphasised both 'the "how" and the "what"' of managers' achievements (Höpfl et al., 1992: 27). Thus the changes were not only about 'caring'. As one manager put it, 'Don't be deluded into thinking the change was about being nice to each other, it was about effectiveness, performance and survival' (Höpfl et al., 1992: 34). Managers were also expected to be more visible, a requirement which many managers equated with working longer hours (Blyton and Turnbull, 1998).

The culture change programme was ongoing and supported by further interventions throughout the decade. In November 1985 the 'A Day in the Life' programme was launched emphasising the benefits of collaborative working. As before, the appearance of the chief executive or a director was used to show top-level commitment (Höpfl et al., 1992). A range of other programmes followed such as 'To Be the Best', launched in 1987, which focused upon growing market competition and the importance of delivering excellence in service.

Changes in managerial attitudes were undoubtedly achieved. However, alongside this there was also undoubtedly resistance by some employees who treated programmes they attended and messages heard with considerable cynicism (Blyton and Turnbull, 1998). In addition a relatively high incidence of industrial conflict throughout the 1980s introduces some doubts regarding the depth of the culture change (Colling, 1995).

The 1990s recession, combined with deregulation and the resultant competition in the airline industry, has forced BA to re-examine its mission. BA's mission to be 'Fit for Business' and to 'Close the Gap' (Blyton and Turnbull, 1998) represents the response to this. This has necessitated buying into other airlines to become a global carrier and, at the same time, continuing to reduce salary costs through a variety of measures. Thus employees appear to be receiving mixed messages. On the one hand they are being asked to improve the quality of service offered. At the same time resources available are being reduced to lower costs. In 1991 BA again announced redundancy measures to deal with over-staffing. Research undertaken at the time suggests that employees did not see these redundancies as a betrayal of caring company values promoted during the 1980s (Höpfl et al., 1992).

Case study questions

1 What do you think senior management wished to achieve through the BA culture change programme?

2 To what extent do you believe the culture change programme at BA addressed employees' basic underlying beliefs as well as their practices?
Give reasons for your answers.

3 Did the culture change programme at BA involve a top-down or bottom-up approach, or a combination of approaches?
Give reasons for your answers.

4 How would you introduce a culture change programme to an organisation in a similar situation to that of BA?

REFERENCES

Argyris, C. (1995) 'Action science and organizational learning', *Journal of Managerial Psychology*, 10(6), 20–6.

Bate, P. (1995) *Strategies for Cultural Change,* Oxford: Butterworth-Heinemann.

Beckhard, R. (1992) 'A model for the executive management of transformational change', in Salaman, G., Cameron, S., Hamblin, H., Iles, P., Mabey, C. and Thompson, K. (eds), *Human Resource Strategies,* London: Sage, pp. 95–106.

Beer, M., Eisenstat, R.A. and Spector, B. (1990) 'Why change programs don't produce change', *Harvard Business Review,* November/December, 158–66.

Blyton, P. and Turnbull, P. (1998) *The Dynamics of Employee Relations,* 2nd edn, Basingstoke: Macmillan.

Brown, A. (1998) *Organisational Culture,* 2nd edn, London: Financial Times Pitman Publishing.

Colling, T. (1995) 'Experiencing turbulence: competition, strategic choice and the management of Human Resources in British Airways', *Human Resource Management Journal,* 5(5), 18–32.

Deal, T.E. and Kennedy, A.A. (1982) *Corporate Culture: The Rites and Rituals of Corporate Life,* Reading, Mass.: Addison-Wesley.

Frost, P.J., Moore, L.F., Louis, M.R., Lundberg, C. and Martin, J. (1991) *Reframing Organizational Culture,* Newbury Park, Calif.: Sage.

Goodstein, L.D. (1990) 'A case study in effective organizational change toward high involvement management', in Fishman, D.B. and Cherniss, C. (eds), *The Human Side of Corporate Competitiveness,* Newbury Park, Calif.: Sage.

Handy, C.B. (1978) *The Gods of Management,* London: Penguin.

Harrison, R. (1972) 'Understanding your organization's character', *Harvard Business Review,* 50 (May/June), 19–128.

Hassard, J. and Sharifi, S. (1989) 'Corporate culture and strategic change', *Journal of General Management,* 15(2), 4–19.

Heifetz, R.A. and Laurie, D.L. (1997) 'The work of leadership', *Harvard Business Review,* 75 (Jan/Feb), 124–34.

Hendry, C. (1995) *Human Resource Management: A Strategic Approach to Employment,* Oxford: Butterworth-Heinemann.

Hofstede, G. (1994) *Cultures and Organisations: Software of the Mind; Intercultural Co-operation and its Importance for Survival,* London: HarperCollins.

Höpfl, H. (1993) 'Culture and commitment: British Airways', in Gowler, D., Legge, K. and Clegg, C. (eds), 2nd edn, *Case Studies in Organizational Behaviour and Human Resource Management,* 2nd edn, London: Paul Chapman, pp. 117–25.

Höpfl, H., Smith, S. and Spencer, S. (1992) 'Values and valuations: the conflicts between culture change and job cuts', *Personnel Review*, 21(1), 24–38.

Kilmann, R.H. (1984) *Beyond the Quick Fix: Managing Five Tracks to Organizational Success*, San Francisco: Jossey-Bass.

Kilmann, R.H. (1989) 'A completely integrated program for creating and maintaining success', *Organizational Dynamics*, 18(1), 5–19.

Legge, K. (1994) 'Managing culture: fact or fiction', in Sisson, K. (ed.), *Personnel Management: A Comprehensive Guide to Theory and Practice in Britain*, 2nd edn, Oxford: Blackwell, pp. 397–433.

Lewin, K. (1952) *Field Theory in Social Science*, London: Tavistock.

Lewis, D. (1996) 'The organizational culture saga – from OD to TQM: a critical review of the literature. Part 2 – applications', *Leadership and Organization Development Journal*, 17(2), 9–16.

Mabey, C. and Mallory, G. (1994/5) 'Structure and culture change in two UK organisations: a comparison of assumptions, approaches and outcomes', *Human Resource Management Journal*, 5(2), 28–45.

Martin, J. (1992) *Cultures in Organizations: Three Perspectives*, New York: Oxford University Press.

Meek, V.L. (1988) 'Organizational culture: origins and weaknesses', *Organizational Studies*, 9(4), 453–73; reprinted in Salaman, G., Cameron, S., Hamblin, H., Iles, P., Mabey, C. and Thompson, K. (eds) (1992), *Human Resource Strategies*, London: Sage, pp. 192–212.

Morgan, G. (1986) *Images of Organization*, Beverley Hills, Calif.: Sage.

Ogbonna, E. (1993) 'Managing organizational culture: fantasy or reality?', *Human Resource Management Journal*, 3(2), 42–54.

Paconowsky, M.E. and O'Donnell-Trujillo, N. (1982) 'Communication and organizational culture', *The Western Journal of Speech and Communication*, 46(1), 115–30.

Peters, T. and Waterman, R.H. (1982) *In Search of Excellence*, London and New York: Harper and Row.

Preston, D., Smith, A., Buchanan, D. and Jordan, S. (1996) 'Symbols of the NHS: understanding the culture and communication process of a general hospital', *Management Learning*, 27(3), 343–57.

Schein, E.H. (1992a) *Organizational Culture and Leadership*, 2nd edn, San Francisco: Jossey-Bass.

Schein, E.H. (1992b) 'Coming to a new awareness of organisational culture', in Salaman, G., Cameron, S., Hamblin, H., Iles, P., Mabey, C. and Thompson, K. (eds), *Human Resource Strategies*, London: Sage, pp. 237–53.

Storey, J. (1992) *Developments in the Management of Human Resources*, Oxford: Blackwell.

Thompson, K. (1992) 'Cultural strategies: introduction', in Salaman, G., Cameron, S., Hamblin, H., Iles, P., Mabey, C. and Thompson, K. (eds), *Human Resource Strategies*, London: Sage, pp. 189–91.

Van Maanen, J. (1991) 'The smile factory: work at Disneyland, in Frost, P.J., Moore, L.F., Louis, M.R., Lundberg, C. and Martin, J. (eds), *Reframing Organisational Culture*, London: Sage, pp. 58–76.

Whipp, R., Rosenfeld, R. and Pettigrew, A. (1989) 'Culture and competitiveness: evidence from two mature UK industries', *Journal of Management Studies*, 26(6), 561–85.

Wilkins, A.L. and Patterson, K.J. (1985) 'You can't get there from here: what will make culture change projects fail', in Kilmann, R.H., Saxton, M.J., Serpa, R. and associates (eds), *Gaining Control of Corporate Culture*, San Francisco: Jossey-Bass, pp. 262–91.

Williams, A., Dobson, P. and Walters, M. (1993) *Changing Culture: New Organizational Approaches*, 2nd edn, London: Institute of Personnel Management.

Woodall, J. (1996) 'Managing culture change: can it ever be ethical?', *Personnel Review*, 25(6), 26–40.

ANSWERS TO SELF-CHECK QUESTIONS

3.1 *What do you think are the main features of the corporate DuPont Nylon culture?*

DuPont Nylon's espoused corporate culture is one of continuous learning, flexibility and networking focusing on their employees' skills. This is stated as part of the organisation's strategy. DuPont believes that all employees are important and valued and should be fully involved in the business. The case illustrates this in a variety of ways. These include:

- a fundamental business purpose of producing 'offerings related to nylon technology' rather than a manufacturing site;
- involving senior managers in the communication of bad news about redundancy;
- a focus on safety and, in particular, employee safety.

3.2 *What subcultures exist at the Gloucester site?*

This question is difficult to answer as the new culture is still evolving. At the time we wrote the case at least two distinct cultures were evident. These were typified by those employees who had bought into the new culture of taking responsibility for their own actions and those who still believed that 'management' were responsible for making decisions. Employees who had embraced the new culture, typified by the 'High Performance Work Culture' and 'Vision 2000', probably included the 112 'influencers' identified to help the cultural change. Other employees, including many production workers, still believed that taking decisions was the supervisors' job, not their own. These formed a second distinct cultural subgroup. It is also likely that there were distinct subcultures for each of the functions identified in Figs 3.1 and 3.2, although these are not discussed in the case!

3.3 *Why do you think it is difficult for managers to measure their organisation's culture? Use examples from the DuPont Nylon case to illustrate your answer.*

The short answer to this question is reasonably straightforward. Whilst the outward manifestations of culture are easy to discern (relatively visible) the deeper underlying meanings upon which these are based are far more difficult to decipher. In particular, the values upon which the culture is based are held within individuals' subconscious and are only articulated in their practices and perhaps the organisation's espoused values.

Outward manifestations of a culture change at the Gloucester site include changes to a range of practices or artefacts such as

- introducing a High Performance Work Culture;
- altering the shift system to release eight days per employee per annum for communication, training and self-development;
- physically identifying a development centre;
- introducing a new selection procedure which involves the production teams;
- focusing on safety and the removal of the staff raffle and targets for hours without employee injury.

While these suggest cultural change it is impossible to be clear whether or not such changes are real or just cultural compliance. For example some employees still see training to emphasise the impact of their actions as generalist rather than making specific links with their own work. Despite this the increase in employee hours without injury described in the case suggests that cultural change has begun to reach the underlying basic assumptions and could be taken to imply that employees find unsafe behaviour inconceivable.

3.4 *How might an organisation use HR interventions as part of a culture change process?*

HR interventions are likely to be used to support and facilitate cultural change rather than initiate it. It is important that such interventions are aligned to the desired culture, and therefore the overall strategy of the organisation, and that they project values appropriate to both the strategy and the culture.

Symbols of organisational change such as the management structure, office space and car parking allocations can be used to reinforce the new culture. Training interventions can also be used to help to educate employees about the reasons for the change and the new desired behaviours.

HR systems can be designed and implemented to support the desired culture. For example performance measurement and reward schemes can be used to monitor and reinforce desirable behaviours in employees. Similarly recruitment, retention and redundancy can be used to help ensure that employees' skills and preferred approaches to working match an organisation's requirements.

Whether top-down or bottom-up strategies are adopted it is important that the HR interventions used provide consistent clues to the desired culture.

3.5 *Why might organisations choose a top-down approach to culture change?*

Top-down approaches may be appropriate in particular circumstances or at particular times during a culture change process. Re-examining Table 3.3 highlights those of Bate's (1995) design parameters of culture change for which a top-down approach is more effective. In particular the table emphasises the ability of top-down approaches to communicate simple messages quickly. Thus, where expressiveness is essential to culture change or to a particular stage of the culture change process, a top-down approach may be most appropriate. This is especially true when all that is required is changes at the practice/artefact level or when rapid change is required.

Top-down approaches may also be effective where it is essential that the new culture's message is spread throughout all levels of an organisation. The ability of the message to penetrate in such cases depends on the communication process being highly structured, as illustrated by the BA case. However, it must be remembered that in the short term, such an approach is likely to generate some resistance to the new culture's values and basic underlying assumptions. In contrast bottom-up approaches are more likely to generate a shared understanding and ownership of the new culture, although initially only amongst a subgroup of employees rather than the whole organisation.

Recruitment and selection and the management of change

Having completed this chapter, you will be able to:

■ Discuss traditional approaches to the recruitment and selection process and explore their limitations when applied to a changing environment.

■ Identify how recruitment and selection can contribute directly to a variety of organisational change scenarios.

■ Outline how recruitment and selection processes can be developed to accommodate planned and unplanned change.

■ Link recruitment and selection processes to other human resource (HR) change interventions e.g. organisational structure and culture, human resource development, and employee relations.

INTRODUCTION

Recruitment and selection has recently been held largely responsible for spicing up the life of youngsters across the world, causing abject misery to children in Wales and beyond, and scuppering the world's biggest merger plans. You have probably participated directly in the recruitment and selection process, not least because of your experiences as applicants and interviewees for job vacancies, yet despite this familiarity the linkages claimed in this opening paragraph may not be readily apparent.

The Spice Girls pop phenomenon resulted from a careful and deliberate recruitment and selection strategy designed to create a group capable of redefining the pop market (Moloney, 1998). Within the first year of its launch this 'product' grossed in excess of £40 million and the promoter's investment was recouped from their first album – girl power indeed! In stark contrast to this success story is the incalculable misery visited on children in care by the recruitment of paedophiles into children's homes. Welch (1998: 30) cites that in Wales alone '33 of the 40 homes are implicated in [child abuse] activities going back more than two decades' and poor recruitment and selection processes were identified as contributing significantly to this appalling situation. 'The breakdown of the world's biggest merger, which would have created a £100bn drugs behemoth' (Pain, 1998) was attributed to factional infighting and personality clashes between Glaxo Wellcome and Smith Kline Beecham's senior management and the inability to recruit a chief executive from their number.

These examples illustrate not only the importance of recruitment and selection to organisational success or failure but also its relationship with change management. The Spice Girls were the outcome of a deliberate change in market strategy whereas mergers represent corporate-level strategic change. The children's homes scenario, arguably, reflects an unplanned crisis demanding changes in future practice. However, as suggested by two of these examples, evidence suggests that careful recruitment and selection practice is not the norm (Lundy and Cowling, 1996), with most organisations adopting what is termed the 'traditional' approach (Scholarios and Lockyer, 1996). What forms the main body of this chapter is an exploration of the inappropriateness of this traditional model to change management and how it can be adapted to take account of both planned change and an imperfect, unpredictable future. Here we draw heavily on the strategic management literature to demonstrate how recruitment and selection can play a significant role in facilitating, sustaining and initiating organisational change. This leads us on to consider an alternative strategically driven recruitment and selection model.

The main points in this chapter are illustrated by two case studies. The first, Protection *Royale*, is set within the financial services sector and illustrates how a staffing crisis precipitated a move from a largely traditional to a more strategic recruitment and selection process. The second concerns Unicol, an education establishment, and examines how a merger and resultant changes in strategic priorities impacted on the whole recruitment and selection process of one of its departments.

Recruitment and selection at Protection *Royale*

Protection *Royale*, a leading player in the composite insurance business, has consolidated over time to become one of the largest direct insurers in the UK. Its headquarters, based in Dorking, reported a turnover in 1998 of over £2780 million and its future strategy is directed towards becoming the undisputed market leader in the UK insurance market. The company is organised divisionally around its four core business areas.

This case traces developments in recruitment and selection within one of these divisions – Financial Consultancy Services – which is acknowledged as having an increasingly important role to play in pursuit of corporate objectives. This division employs Sales Consultants whose primary role is to market Protection *Royale*'s insurance products to insurance brokers. These brokers then consider Protection *Royale*'s products along with those of other insurance companies when making recommendations to individual customers purchasing insurance through this medium. The basic job description and person specification (detailing those attributes associated with effective role performance) had remained much the same since the early 1990s. Labour turnover amongst these staff was very low at approximately 4 per cent and when vacancies arose little difficulty was experienced recruiting replacements as a relatively undemanding person specification meant that many people in the labour market matched its requirements. Replacements were found using a well established recruitment and selection process which, in brief, comprised

- advertising in financial services media
- use of specialist recruitment agencies
- recommendations from existing staff
- shortlisting from application forms/CVs
- interviews
- role plays
- psychometric testing
- references.

Despite its growing strategic importance, concerns over the division's business performance began to surface in 1997 eventually leading to a review of its operations. During the early and mid 1990s the division's product lines marketed by Sales Consultants had proliferated, partly in response to the growing technical complexity of the financial services industry. The resultant lack of product specialisation was undermining customer confidence and contributing towards a deterioration of Protection *Royale*'s overall standing in the marketplace.

These developments prompted a reappraisal of the division's work and resulted in a major shake-up of staff and the precipitation of a staffing crisis. This necessitated the development of improved recruitment, selection and retention strategies designed to address the immediate crisis and at the same time support

▶

longer-term strategic priorities. What began to emerge was a need for a smaller and more focused product range and high-performing staff who were able to project their products on to the 'best advice lists' of brokers (i.e. where Protection *Royale*'s products are strongly endorsed by brokers to their customers). Of these the latter was seen as crucial and prompted a detailed assessment of existing staff against a much more demanding personnel profile. An emerging person specification for Sales Consultants began to coalesce around: excellence of product knowledge; interpersonal skills associated with influence and persuasiveness, and the negotiation skills involved in anticipating and countering broker reservations.

An added complication had been introduced in 1994 by the PIA (Personal Investment Authority), established following the Financial Services Act 1988, which required financial sales practitioners to hold Financial Planning Certificate qualifications. This represented a potential threat to the staffing base as current employees might be either unwilling or unable to obtain these qualifications. In addition these qualifications needed to be built into the emerging person specification for new recruits resulting, almost overnight, in a substantial reduction in the number of people within the external labour market who could meet the requirements of the revised specification.

The reappraisal of the division involved an assessment of current staff against the anticipated transformation in the role and profile of Sales Consultants. Assessments resulted in staff being rated as 'suitable', 'unsuitable' or 'possibles', i.e. those who, following training and development, might meet the grade. What resulted was a significant and rapid reduction in the workforce through resignations, redundancies and transfers that seriously undermined the ability of the division to meet its performance targets. At first this was not perceived as a crisis because line managers believed they could personally head-hunt replacements despite a radically altered labour market and their lack of experience. However, failure to make a single appointment using this method meant the situation rapidly assumed crisis proportions. Not only was immediate business performance being undermined but threats to longer-term objectives quickly became apparent. The reputation of Protection *Royale* amongst brokers was steadily deteriorating and this was also making the company less attractive to potential applicants.

At the initiation of the Personnel Department alternative recruitment and selection strategies were devised and implemented in 1998 with line managers and personnel specialists working in concert. These comprised the following:

- Identification of recruitment champions charged with developing and driving through the strategy and reporting back regularly on outcomes.
- Adoption of recruitment objectives as key performance indicators for line managers and personnel staff. As one ex-employee put it, 'any failure to deliver would result in those responsible losing their heads'.
- Introduction of a dual recruitment and selection strategy. The first continued the practice of direct recruitment from the external market but this now

involved the use of a professional search agency. The role of the agency was to identify suitable candidates who were positively oriented towards joining Protection *Royale*. At this stage Protection *Royale* took over the process and put candidates through a selection process designed to assess fit with the organisational culture and job competence. The second, responding to the contraction in the labour market, involved the recruitment of a cadre of trainees who would follow a 15-to 18-month training and induction programme leading, if successful, to their appointment as Sales Consultants.

▪ For both strategies recruitment and selection was geared to a revised job description and person specification of the 'ideal candidate'. The latter was extrapolated into a series of competencies and became the main driver of the recruitment and selection process for both direct entrants and trainees following its adaptation to provide greater emphasis on potential and trainability.

▪ For direct entrants multiple selection methods were adopted for assessing referrals from the search agency. Methods were chosen for their relevance to the competencies being assessed. A matrix was produced identifying which methods would be used to assess each competence. Selection methods included completion of a competency-based application form, situational testing (i.e. based on samples of required job knowledge, skills and attitudes), psychometric testing to assess aptitudes, competency-based interviews, role-play simulation exercises, presentations and references.

▪ Recruitment of trainees driven through national advertising. Advertising invited respondents to telephone in for a brief interview and lines were staffed all week including Sunday. Selection began at this stage through assessment of responses to standardised questions and, for successful and interested parties, led to the arrangement of a screening interview. Recruitment was supported by a detailed information pack for candidates.

▪ Selection of trainees via assessment centres. These employed similar selection methods to those described earlier for direct entrants.

▪ Thorough induction of trainees following appointment. A dedicated manager was appointed to support trainees who were also able to maintain regular contact with their designate managers to discuss their progress or any other concerns.

▪ Extensive training for all line managers involved in any aspect of recruitment and selection. Training was supported by a very detailed (54-page) pack providing step-by-step guidance on all aspects of the process. There was an emphasis throughout on standardisation including interview questions.

Following the introduction of these procedures an initial cohort of eight trainees was recruited and they all successfully completed their training programme during 1999. On 'graduation' from the training programme each trainee was placed in their designated regional sales office.

Recruitment and selection: definitions and models

What do we mean by recruitment and selection?

For our purposes we have adopted what is arguably the most common approach to defining recruitment and selection. This simply views recruitment and selection as a systematic process applied to meeting an organisation's staffing requirements through filling identified vacancies. This process can be broken down into a series of stages which Wright and Storey (1997: 212) summarise as 'defining the vacancy, attracting applicants, assessing candidates and making the final decision'.

This perspective of recruitment and selection, which we interpret here as including internal promotions, concerns a process that is meant to be reciprocal (*see* for example Watson, 1994). This acknowledges that candidates as well as employers are involved in a decision-making process and that the way the process is conducted may have a significant impact on employer attractiveness and employee retention.

It is possible to disaggregate this perspective into its two distinct but integrated and overlapping components (*see* Fig. 4.1). Recruitment is described as a positive attraction process designed to assemble a suitable pool of applicants against a given job vacancy. It commonly involves defining the job or role to be filled (job description), identifying personal attributes that are positively correlated with effective job performance (person specification), searching for people with those attributes, and persuading such people to apply for the vacancy. In contrast selection can be seen as a negative process of rejection that involves narrowing down the field of candidates until a suitable match against a given vacancy is found (Whitehill, 1991, cited in Wright and Storey, 1997: 212).

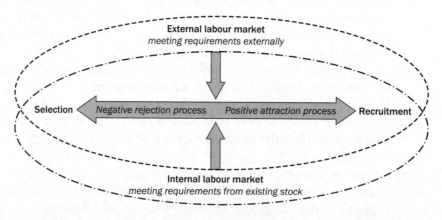

Fig. 4.1 Internal and external models of recruitment and selection

Internal versus external models of recruitment and selection

A commonly adopted framework of recruitment and selection sees the process as being essentially geared to either the internal or the external labour market. The internal model places emphasis on meeting the organisation's manpower requirements from its existing stock of employees. Here the use of the external labour market will be restricted mainly to low-level positions with the expectation that once recruited, investment in career development will promote upward mobility. In contrast the external model aims to meet its manpower requirements from outside the organisation. Both models are likely to be evident in any organisation at the same time but within an overall resourcing strategy where either the internal or the external model (*see* Fig. 4.1) is likely to predominate.

Both models have their advantages and disadvantages and their appropriateness will be contingent on organisational circumstances which will themselves change over time. Moscow McDonald's (*see* Vikhanski and Puffer, 1993) and Midland Bank's establishment of First Direct (*see* Martin, 1990) were both based predominantly on an internal resourcing model where external recruitment into low-level positions would be followed by career development and enhancement within the organisation. A major concern in both cases was to use recruitment as a vehicle for establishing cultural fit and reinforcing this through subsequent socialisation. However, external recruitment may also be used as an instrument of culture change 'as a symbol that "things are changing"', as was the case with the global telecommunications company AT&T (Miller, 1984). Schuler and Jackson (1987) identified that recruiting managers externally was positively correlated to business success in industries characterised by both growth and decline. The contingent nature of resourcing, however, is well illustrated by staffing strategies adopted by Chase Manhattan Bank. These moved from an internally to an externally driven model at a point of business turnaround and moved back to the internally driven model in the following period of stability as a way of promoting morale and commitment amongst employees (Borucki and Lafley, 1984).

Self-check question	**4.1**	*How would you classify Protection Royale's approach to recruitment and selection – internal or external? Give reasons for your answer.*

The 'traditional' model of recruitment and selection

To make real the rhetoric 'people are our most important asset' it might be expected that organisations would develop carefully considered recruitment and selection processes designed to meet their strategic imperatives and changing organisational circumstances. However, evidence suggests that recruitment and selection practice is conducted either in an *ad hoc*, haphazard fashion (Scholarios and Lockyer, 1996) or reflects the 'traditional model' (Wright and Storey, 1997).

Mike's research not only clarifies what we mean by the 'traditional model' but also provides evidence of its pervasiveness in companies operating in the West Midlands. Over the three years to May 1998 students studying for postgraduate management and professional personnel management awards have been asked to provide a flow chart depicting the totality of their organisation's recruitment and selection practice. The essence of approaching 250 responses has been distilled into one chart (Fig. 4.2).

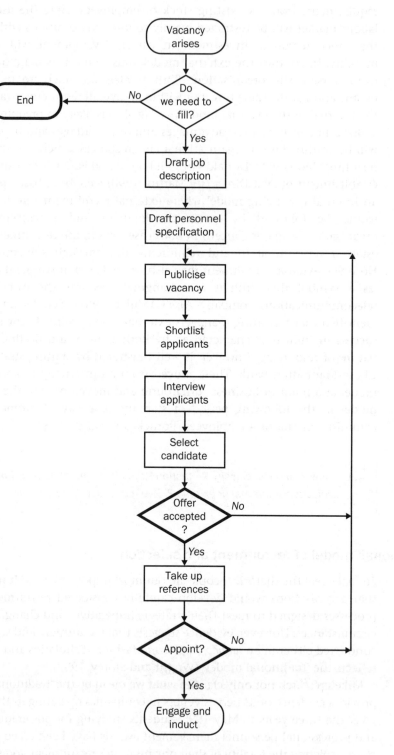

Fig. 4.2 The traditional approach to recruitment and selection

From this a number of central features of the traditional recruitment and selection model can be discerned:

■ It is geared to filling specific job vacancies. Invariably this was the starting point; it also frequently involved an exhaustive process for authorising the vacancy.

■ The process continues with the production of a job description, either using or up-dating a previous one, which is usually translated into a person specification.

■ Recruitment is predominantly through advertising but with significant usage of agencies and word of mouth.

■ A limited number of selection methods are used and invariably include shortlisting using application forms/CVs, interviews and references. Around 50 per cent of organisations additionally use testing for some vacancies.

■ It involves a decision-making process where candidates are meant to be assessed against the requirements of the job description and personnel specification.

■ It concludes with offer/reject letters and candidate acceptance/rejection with, increasingly, some negotiation of terms.

This model is basically directed towards fitting people to available jobs (Lawler, 1994) but for our purposes has limited utility as a lever for initiating, facilitating or sustaining organisation change. Although constructed around a series of systematic steps it may be apparent that it presents an incomplete picture. The flow chart makes no reference to any relationship with human resource planning let alone corporate strategy or any post-event evaluation.

It could be argued that the model is essentially static and reflects the status quo. Mike found little evidence that job analysis was being used to inform recruitment and selection processes. Where it was it was limited by a preoccupation with current (and in some cases previous!) job requirements therefore doing little to anticipate and account for future change scenarios or broader organisational needs. The traditional approach itself may be undermined by reducing a job-focused system to little more than a people-matching process. Here an emphasis on the interview as the key selection method provides ample opportunity for line managers to manipulate the process in order to select in their own image (Cockerill, 1989). This arguably reduces the process to little more than matching candidates to selectors (Gerstein and Reisman, 1983).

The apparent over-reliance on interviews and references may also impact adversely on the reliability and validity of selection decisions as these methods are widely acknowledged to be relatively poor predictors of job performance (Lundy and Cowling, 1996). Despite this, Mike found little evidence that organisations were evaluating the effectiveness of their selection methods. We would suggest that if employees are really considered to be such a valuable asset then the general absence of an evaluation stage in the recruitment and selection process may be construed as perverse.

Lastly we argue that the traditional model has a narrow focus in terms of stakeholder involvement. At best it can be described as a two-way process conducted between candidates and management representatives. At worst the overriding concern for fitting the person to the job subordinates candidates' needs to those of the institution, making the process ostensibly one-way. However, in both these scenarios the interests of internal and external customers, peers and service providers do not appear to be accommodated.

In summary the traditional model may be seen largely as a replenishment model more relevant to steady-state, bureaucratic organisations. This is not to say that any single appointment cannot potentially be a catalyst for change but where this occurs it is likely to be accidental as the model is not explicitly geared to managing change. The constituent parts of the traditional model, however, cannot be discarded as they remain, when utilised effectively, central to alternative approaches to recruitment and selection. It is important, therefore, to consider how the traditional model can be adapted to contribute more explicitly to organisational change. We return to this theme later in the chapter.

Self-check question	**4.2** *To what extent did Protection Royale's initial recruitment and selection processes reflect the traditional model depicted in Fig. 4.2?*

How recruitment and selection may contribute to organisational change

In response to change of almost endemic proportions a number of organisations have made significant shifts in the way that they manage their employees. Human resource management, the development of a flexible workforce and attempts to change organisational culture (*see* Chapter 3) may be identified as just three examples of such shifts. Here we argue that organisational responses to change and specific human resource interventions place new demands on recruitment and selection. The reactive nature of the 'traditional' model of recruitment and selection, which concentrates on matching individuals to well defined jobs, makes it an inappropriate vehicle for facilitating change management. This suggests the need to re-conceptualise recruitment and selection as a proactive, more broadly-based activity capable of supporting and, at times, driving organisation strategy (Scholarios and Lockyer, 1996). This conceptual shift can be identified in approaches to recruitment and selection that focus variously on fitting the job to the person rather than the person to the job, fitting the person to the organisation rather than the job, and selecting against core competencies or skills rather than the broad demands of a specific job. These perspectives are in no way mutually exclusive and are likely to share the common denominator that they are strategically driven.

In this section we particularly draw on strategically driven change which was identified in Chapter 1 as an important aspect of change management. Our approach to discussing the relevance of recruitment and selection to strategically driven change revolves around three concepts which are introduced briefly here and developed further immediately below (*see* Fig. 4.3). First, we have adopted Purcell's (1989) construction that strategy can be viewed as operating at three different levels starting with corporate strategy and moving through the strategic issues relating to organisation structures to end with functional strategies (in this case human

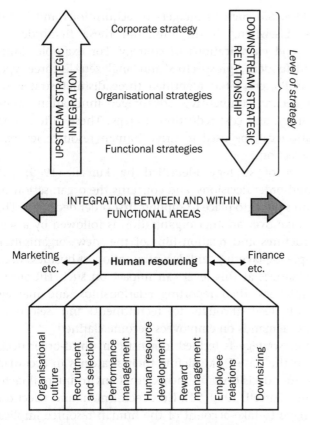

Fig. 4.3 **The strategic context of recruitment and selection**

resourcing). Second, the essential relationship between functional and corporate strategy, referred to by Mabey and Iles (1993: 16) as 'external integration', can be regarded as two-way. This acknowledges that much of what happens at the functional level flows directly from the demands of corporate strategy (i.e. functional strategy lies 'downstream' from corporate strategy). At the same time it is also recognised that the functional level can operate to influence the shape of corporate strategy (i.e. the functional level has an 'upstream' relationship with corporate strategy). Third, the various dimensions (or levers) of human resourcing should not only be integrated with corporate strategy but should also be 'internally integrated' (Mabey and Iles, 1993: 16–17) with each other. This would mean, for example, that within an organisation competing on the basis of quality all the HR levers should be mutually supporting the acquisition, development and retention of a workforce that can deliver this strategic imperative. This means recruiting quality staff, investing significantly in the development of the organisation's skills base, defining and rewarding quality performance, involving employees in continuous improvement, etc.

We start by examining how recruitment and selection can contribute to strategic change at the three levels identified by Purcell (1989) and discussed in Chapter 1. '"Upstream", first-order decisions are concerned with the long-term direction of the enterprise' (Purcell, 1989: 70) and embrace 'the big decisions taken in the corporate office' (Purcell, 1995: 63) such as mergers or acquisitions and divestment of an existing business. Elsewhere in the literature these first-order decisions are aggregated into broad classifications of strategy. For example, Miles and Snow (1984) identified 'defenders', 'prospectors' and 'analyzers' as three types of strategic behaviour whereas Porter (1985) identified three distinct strategies adopted by organisations to secure competitive advantage: innovation strategy; quality enhancement strategy; and cost reduction strategy. These different approaches to strategy classification can be used to drive human resource levers, in this case recruitment and selection.

The second level of strategy identified by Purcell (1989: 71) is termed 'downstream second-order decisions' and concerns the organisation structures and operating procedures put into place to support first-order decisions. Thus a decision to merge with or take over another organisation is followed by a set of decisions governing the structures and relationships of the 'new' organisation and could include, for example, de-layering and decentralisation of business decision-making (*see* Chapter 2). Changes at this level can impact on such HR areas as the roles performed by employees, their reporting relationships, and management style. These changes will feed through to recruitment and selection as revised expectations of and demands on employees become clarified.

The third level of strategy is termed 'downstream third-order decisions' where functional areas, in this case HRM, define their strategies in accordance with the first- and second-order decisions and the external environmental factors operating on the organisation (Purcell, 1989: 91). Here recruitment and selection, along with other HR levers, have to take account of the human resource implications of the first- and second-level strategic decisions taken by the organisation. It is this direct linkage of third-level functional areas to corporate strategy that is referred to by Mabey and Iles (1993: 16) as 'external integration'.

This linkage, however, is essentially one-way (or 'downstream') and as such does not meet the fuller definition of external integration that we favour, which incorporates a two-way relationship (i.e. 'upstream' as well as 'downstream'). From this perspective, external integration may only be achieved fully when HR issues, in this case recruitment and selection, not only serve first- and second-order strategies in a downstream relationship but also operate upwards to influence both strategic formulation and implementation (Lundy and Cowling, 1996). Hendry (1995) suggests that at one level this upstream relationship could result in corporate strategy being informed by changes in the labour market and at another being formulated around the people and skills the organisation has at its disposal. Mabey and Iles (1993: 16) suggest that this two-way relationship requires what they term 'institutional integration'. This is where the personnel/HR function is strategically integrated into the organisation and is more likely to occur where the head of function is a board-level appointment. We therefore follow our examination against Purcell's three levels of strategy by considering how recruitment and selection can operate in an upstream way to influence strategy formulation. This upstream relationship is consistent with the 'bottom-up' as opposed to the 'top-down' approach to change discussed in Chapter 1.

We next turn our attention to how recruitment and selection can facilitate and sustain strategic change through supporting other HR initiatives. This draws on the concept of 'internal integration' (Mabey and Iles, 1993: 16–17) where full strategic integration requires that the various elements of human resourcing cohere in a way that provides a consistent whole (Guest, 1987). This applies not only to recruitment and selection, human resource development, corporate culture, performance management etc. pulling in the same direction to achieve a corporate objective, for example quality enhancement, but also to the elements of the recruitment and selection process itself (Wright and Storey, 1997).

Given that we tend to favour the merits of bottom-up change (as explained in Chapter 1), you might think that we have adopted an overtly rational, deterministic approach to strategic change in this chapter. To an extent we make no apologies for this. We believe it is essential for recruitment and selection to reflect strategic priorities where they have been clearly espoused and are capable of translation into HR terms. However, to stop here would in our view provide an incomplete picture. It is equally important to consider how recruitment and selection can respond to less clear cut change scenarios. These would include, for example, those situations where strategy only emerges over time or in an unplanned way; where there is simply no strategic plan; unforeseen crises; and the challenges produced by an unpredictable future. The last element of this section therefore explores how recruitment and selection practice can be applied to reflect these uncertainties which we refer to as 'future imperfect'. Interestingly at Protection *Royale* changes in recruitment and selection practice were driven partly by deliberate changes in marketing strategy but also by unforeseen legislative changes that led to the redefinition of the potential labour market for Sales Consultants.

This unpredictable nature of change anticipates a significant shift in the recruitment and selection process from one that traditionally focuses on matching people to specific, well defined jobs to one where emphasis is placed on finding and selecting people who have the necessary attributes to be able to adjust to changing roles. This changes the focus from selecting people on the basis of their current skills repertoire to selecting people on their capacity to learn and adapt through training (Offerman and Gowing, 1993). These dilemmas are captured well by an IBM executive: 'I know we cannot plan our requirements for skills well enough over a two-year period. The chances of planning them over an employment lifetime are nil. Therefore the one thing we must plan for is flexibility of skill ... you have to employ people who are sufficiently intelligent, flexible in attitudes, determined, and prepared to take on any new job' (cited in Sparrow and Pettigrew, 1988: 41). However, in a way consistent with two-way external strategic integration, Offerman and Gowing (1993) go further than this. They suggest that organisations will only realise the full potential of strategies directed towards establishing a diverse workforce if they adapt their culture and working practices to make effective use of the range of talent recruited.

From what has been discussed so far in this chapter it is possible to delineate three approaches to human resource planning (HRP) that focus recruitment and selection

Table 4.1 Human resource planning choices

Change scenario	HRP approaches	Strategic selection choices	Selection criteria
Status quo	Provision of human resources for existing jobs	Select for short-term proficiency and accept the possibility of high levels of turnover if employees cannot cope with change	Operational criteria: attributes required for successful current job performance such as the abilities, knowledge, interpersonal skills and the beliefs and values that are required to meet current job demands
Planned/predictable change	Provision of human resources for envisaged future jobs	Select for longer-term adaptability to change, but accept that there will be limited knowledge of future changes and therefore some difficulties in assessing adaptability	Visionary criteria: attributes that are hypothesised as necessary for successful future job performance
Future imperfect: unplanned unpredictable change	Provision of human resources for jobs which cannot be prescribed	Follow a path of continuous modifications as the future unfolds, with numerous changes to selection systems (where reliance is on the external labour market) or vocational training systems (where the reliance is on an internal labour market)	Transformational criteria: attributes that are required to enable change to happen: the competencies for change rather than the changing competencies

Sources: Snow and Snell (1993), Sparrow (1994: 15) and Williams and Dobson (1995: 17).

activities on maintaining the status quo, responding to planned/predictable change or coping with an imperfect future characterised by unplanned/unpredictable change. Table 4.1 illustrates the selection foci under these three different change perspectives.

Our primary concern is with two of these three scenarios – planned/predictable change and unplanned/unpredictable change – and we now go on to examine in turn how recruitment and selection can contribute to these using the six points of reference identified earlier, i.e.

- recruitment and selection and strategic change at the first level (downstream, external integration);
- recruitment and selection and strategic change at the second level (downstream, external integration);
- recruitment and selection and strategic change at the third level (downstream, external integration);
- recruitment and selection and strategic formulation (upstream, external integration);
- recruitment and selection as a facilitator of other HR change initiatives (internal integration);
- 'future imperfect' – recruitment and selection beyond the horizon.

Having explored the potential relationships between recruitment and selection and these six points of reference we go on in the next section to consider how the traditional model might be reconstructed to more adequately address the demands presented by these different change scenarios.

Recruitment and selection and strategic change at the first level (downstream, external integration)

Under this scenario the objective of recruitment and selection is to resource the organisation with employees who will enhance its capacity to deliver its chosen corporate strategy. Arguably the key concern here is to identify those employees whose role behaviours will achieve this objective.

Schuler and Jackson (1987), for example, have attempted to do this by mapping out role behaviours that support either Porter's innovation, quality enhancement or cost reduction strategies. They have identified 12 behavioural continua (shown in Fig. 4.4) that can be used to generate a personal profile of those enabling behaviours that support the pursuit of these different strategies. They have identified, for example, that for an organisation pursuing an innovation strategy the following role behaviours would be appropriate: highly innovative behaviour; relatively high preference and ability for co-operative, interdependent behaviour; relatively high degree of risk-taking behaviour; highly tolerant of uncertainty; moderate concern for quality of output; moderate concern for quantity; balanced orientation towards process and results; and tendency towards longer-term focus (Schuler and Jackson, 1987). These behaviours form a template that can be used to drive an integrated set of HR levers designed to recruit, develop and retain appropriate employees against changing (as well as current) strategic objectives.

Self-check question	4.3	*Using Schuler and Jackson's continua what role behaviours do you think are appropriate to quality enhancement and cost reduction strategies?*

Taken at face value it seems highly plausible that different employee role behaviours will underpin different competitive strategies. However, although based on research, such frameworks may be overly prescriptive and should therefore be used cautiously. While such frameworks provide useful guidance, organisations will still need to identify and validate those role behaviours that support its own particular context in order to fully exploit the potential contribution that recruitment and selection can make to first-level strategic change. For Protection *Royale* this involved those attributes linked to the rapid assimilation of technical knowledge, persuasiveness, commercial awareness, negotiation and customer relations skills etc., although these had not been validated at the time of writing and would probably need to be refined in the light of any subsequent validation.

Highly repetitive, prescribed	**Degree of innovation**	Highly creative, unpredictable

Operates interdependently	**Exercise of self-autonomy**	Operates independently

Low	**Degree of risk-taking**	High

Highly inflexible and conservative	**Adaptability to change**	Highly flexible and adaptable

Avoids responsibility	**Responsibility preference**	Seeks and assumes responsibility

Comfortable with stability	**Comfort with uncertainty**	Tolerant of ambiguity

Low	**Concern for quality**	High

Low	**Concern for quantity**	High

Strong orientation towards process	**Concern for outcomes**	Strong orientation towards results

Limited/narrow	**Skills base and application**	Multi/broad

Low	**Degree of job and organisation involvement**	High

Short-term	**Time focus of behaviour**	Long-term

Fig. 4.4 Continua of employee role behaviours

Source: Developed from Schuler and Jackson, 1987.

Recruitment and selection and strategic change at the second level (downstream, external integration)

As with first-order strategic decisions there are likely to be contingent relationships between structures and processes on the one hand and staffing strategies and desired role behaviours on the other. For example, as you may have experienced, organisations regularly make major structural changes as they adapt to changing organisational circumstances. This has frequently involved a move away from bureaucratic, mechanistic structures towards organic organisations (Cockerill, 1989) and, more specifically, the imposition of de-layering to reduce hierarchy and produce flatter organisational structures (Sparrow, 1994).

The impact that this shift from bureaucratic to organic structures has had on managerial roles has been researched by Cockerill (1989). In the relative stability of bureaucracies planning, organising, monitoring and the use of rules, regulations and precedents to solve problems represent appropriate role behaviours. However, these lose their value in organic organisations where the more turbulent nature of the business environment undermines their validity. Here management behaviours that include networking, team building, information retrieval and innovative problem solving and decision making are likely to be more appropriate. Managers are expected to 'make things happen', that is to institute change that will improve organisational performance. Cockerill (1989: 54–5) identified a number of competencies associated with high performance management in rapidly changing environments ('information search; concept formation; conceptual flexibility; interpersonal search; managing interaction; developmental orientation; impact; self-confidence; presentation; proactive orientation; and achievement orientation') which he argues can be assessed reliably through selection methods involving direct observation and assessment centres.

This focus on management, however, is only half the equation. To more fully support changes to organisation structures similar thought needs to be given to the recruitment and/or development of line staff. Employees are likely to be expected to exercise higher degrees of discretion and autonomy in their work (empowerment), take more control of their personal development, be flexible and adaptable in their responses to changing patterns of work and work collaboratively within and across teams. This is likely to give rise to demands for similar sets of competencies to those identified earlier for managers and will almost certainly place greater emphasis during recruitment and selection on the assessment of social skills, interaction ability and group fit and may even lead to teams being given devolved responsibility for recruitment.

Recruitment and selection and strategic change at the third level (downstream, external integration)

Third-order strategy, as described in Chapter 1, concerns the strategic choices made at the functional level of organisations, in this case human resourcing, to deliver the strategic ends of the organisation (Evenden, 1993). For example, human resource management and culture change could represent two, sometimes interrelated, strategic responses within the HR function to the changing business climate of the 1980s and 1990s. Here we have chosen, by way of illustration, to show how recruitment and selection can be directed to support the introduction of HRM.

HRM has emerged as an approach to managing the human resources of an organisation partly in response to the increasing recognition given to employees as valuable assets but particularly because of its strategic alignment (Guest, 1987). To consider the impact recruitment and selection can have on its introduction we feel it will be helpful to identify a number of key dimensions associated with HRM which have been developed into a series of theoretical propositions by Guest (1987). He identified four key human resource goals: integration; employee commitment; flexibility/adaptability; and quality. Integration occurs when human resource policies are consistent with the strategic objectives of the organisation, cohere with each other as well as with those in other functional areas, are internalised by line managers and support the full integration of employees into the business. Where this is achieved it is predicted that change will be more readily accepted and conflict reduced, leading to an increased chance that strategic plans will be successfully delivered. Where employees exhibit commitment to their job and their organisation and its central objectives it is predicted that it will support high retention, superior performance and acceptance of change. Flexibility relates to organisation structures, job content and employee skills and behaviour and it is predicted that where present these attributes will enhance the organisation's responsiveness to change. The goal of quality is based on the prediction that where demanding jobs are performed by highly skilled employees reporting to competent managers high levels of performance will result. Within this construction recruitment and selection have a key role to play for organisations choosing to adopt or move towards an HRM approach. The key issues here are, first, to identify the attributes that are positively correlated with committed, flexible and high-quality employees and, second, to determine how to attract and select them. You are invited to explore these issues in more depth through the second case study in this chapter.

Another key dimension of HRM is the devolvement of much of the work of specialist personnel departments to line managers. Where fully effected this has the potential to radically alter their respective role responsibilities. For personnel specialists this may precipitate the development of an alternative model for delivering the department's work, create the need for the acquisition and development of a different skills base and involve redundancy. For line managers, given the low levels of concern for the staffing dimension of their role frequently observed, this redefinition of their role will place particular demands on their selection and development. If this is not addressed it is highly likely that any top-down intent to introduce HRM will be frustrated by a skills gap and inappropriate attitudes lower down the organisation.

Self-check question	4.4	*How can recruitment and selection contribute to culture change programmes?*

Recruitment and selection and strategic formulation (upstream, external integration)

We begin this subsection by illustrating the nature and importance of upstream, or two-way, external integration through reference to a short case. A large manufacturing company Mike worked for formulated an aggressive strategy to defend its dominant market position involving the expansion of its product markets and the company's share of those markets. This required significant increases in production levels. Personnel was expected to contribute by recruiting staff to meet the increased production targets. The personnel department highlighted that prevailing labour market conditions (at that time, full employment and labour shortages) precluded any large-scale recruitment making the production and marketing plans untenable thereby threatening the viability of the corporate strategy itself. The personnel department proposed an alternative strategy that involved the capital intensification of production work, restructuring and adoption of cost reduction rather than market assertiveness as the mainstay of the organisation's defender strategy. The department was instructed to stop interfering and get on with the recruitment campaign. Despite exhaustive efforts the demand for labour could not be met. This led in time to a staffing crisis and a collapse of the business strategy. Coupled with the inflow of cheaper foreign imports, this contributed significantly to the eventual demise of the organisation.

This scenario illustrates the potential dangers of operating the external integration relationship between human resourcing and corporate strategy through a one-way (downstream) interpretation. It may also show something about the credibility and/or status of the personnel function (institutional integration) in the case organisation. It also provides an example of how, through environmental scanning, human resource concerns can potentially influence higher levels of strategic planning. Evenden (1993: 223) argues that this represents a 'business case' for upstream strategic integration. He contrasts this with a 'social responsibility' case for upstream integration where strategy formulation is influenced by human resource initiatives concerning moral and ethical issues. This could arise, for example, through proactive approaches to equal opportunities that target recruitment strategies at the long-term unemployed, a group in which ethnic minorities are also significantly over-represented.

Another example where upstream integration may be evident is the promotion by the HR function of a 'managing diversity' strategy. 'Managing diversity' has been developed as a strategic response to the changing demographic complexion of the workforce and social values that emphasise the need for the full participation of all people in and at work. As such, using Evenden's analysis, it could be construed as representing both a 'business' and 'social responsibility' case for upstream strategic integration. However, we would argue that in practice its adoption is more likely to be driven by business arguments, as the following examples of managing diversity illustrate.

A number of companies, for example Burger King and Sainsbury, have developed recruitment and selection strategies to increase the number of employees from certain ethnic groups in order to exploit these groups' significant and growing importance as consumers (Evenden, 1993). L'Oréal in France found that recruiting a diverse workforce enhanced the creative capacity of the workforce on which it depended (Sadler and Milmer, 1993). Iles and Hayers (1997) point to how a number of organisations are selecting diverse, multi-national project teams to increase their flexibility and responsiveness in globally competitive markets. It can also be argued that the recruitment of a diverse workforce adds generally to an organisation's ability to meet the challenges presented by an imperfect future through the creation of a more flexible and adaptable workforce (Sparrow, 1994). Recruitment and selection processes have a key role to play in securing a diverse workforce and may require innovative practices to identify and attract suitable candidates from target groups (Paddison, 1990).

Recruitment and selection as a facilitator of other HR change initiatives (internal integration)

As discussed earlier, an important part of internal integration is the coherence between different elements of human resourcing (Guest, 1987; Mabey and Iles, 1993). Here we explore how recruitment and selection can support other human resource change initiatives using work restructuring to illustrate this. You might also like to work through how recruitment and selection can similarly be integrated with all the other HR areas covered by this book. For example in the next chapter we go on to consider performance management and the management of change and we could ask a number of questions with respect to recruitment and selection:

- Do different types of people respond better than others to a performance culture?
- If so how can we identify what characterises such people?
- Where will we find such people?
- How might we attract them to the organisation?
- What selection methods would provide the most reliable and valid measures of these attributes among prospective candidates?

A consistent feature emerging from our chapters on managing change through organisational structure (Chapter 2) and downsizing (Chapter 9) is that jobs will require restructuring in order to cope with the consequences of de-layering and the need 'to do more with less (staff)'. This has frequently led to redesigning work around self-managed teams which are assigned delegated responsibility for task completion. Such teams exercise high degrees of autonomy over interrelated activities such as production control, quality control, work allocation and problem solving. This demands a high level of involvement from and interaction between team members. Evidence suggests, however, that in practice work redesign along these lines has not always been successful because such changes have not been introduced within the context of a supportive infrastructure (Staniforth, 1996). Staniforth argues that in order to ensure internal integration, teamworking ability needs to be assessed during recruitment and selection, developed through training and reinforced through appraisal and reward systems. The composition of the team, however, has been identified as a critical success factor (McCombs et al., 1994). This places particular emphasis on the staffing function and stresses the importance of identifying, attracting and selecting those employees who are most likely to succeed under teamworking conditions (Flynn *et al.*, 1990).

Two sets of employee characteristics have been identified as predictors of effective team performance. The first concerns individual characteristics such as dependability, interpersonal skills, self-motivation and integrity and the second group membership characteristics such as leadership potential, assertiveness, participation, tolerance of ambiguity and capacity to cope with stress (Flynn *et al.*, 1990). In reporting on case studies where autonomous work groups (Flynn *et al.*, 1990) and high involvement work systems (Bowen *et al.*, 1991) have been successfully introduced such characteristics have been assessed through the use of multiple selection devices. These included:

■ application forms designed around the specified characteristics;
■ surveying previous employers using structured questions to secure reference checks against dependability and integrity;
■ work sampling;
■ attendance at a pre-employment training programme;
■ group interviews including current team members;
■ aptitude and personality testing; and
■ a series of group exercises to assess decision-making skills, problem solving and values orientation.

There was a heavy emphasis throughout on providing candidates with a realistic job preview, making selection genuinely a two-way process, and involving team members in the final selection decisions. A number of these features can be observed in Protection *Royale*'s development of their recruitment and selection process to cope with the changing nature of the work of Sales Consultants including a detailed information pack, and selection involving competency-based application forms, situational testing, competency-based interviews and group selection exercises as integral elements of their assessment centre. Both the Bowen *et al.* (1991) and Flynn *et al.* (McCombs *et al.*, 1994) studies also reported on methods used to evaluate the recruitment and selection process which were found to have promoted the formation of teams characterised by high productivity, high job satisfaction scores and low levels of absenteeism and labour turnover.

'Future imperfect' – recruitment and selection beyond the horizon

Although we have distinguished between predictable and unpredictable change we have so far been concentrating on how recruitment and selection can contribute to planned change. As discussed in Chapter 1, this suggests a degree of rationality to change management that will not always accord with reality. A major difficulty is that we cannot always predict accurately what lies ahead even within the adopted planning horizon, let alone what lies beyond it, with any degree of certainty. This is well illustrated by the financial services industry, within which the company in Case

Study 4.1 operates. The last few years have been characterised by significant rationalisation of the industry through mergers. A graphic example of this is that the relatively recent merger between Royal Insurance and Sun Alliance may shortly be followed by the takeover of Guardian Royal Exchange by the product of the former merger, Royal and Sun Alliance (Clark, 1999). Within this context it is easy to see how the strategic relevance of human resource plans and contingent recruitment and selection strategies can quickly be overtaken by events in the wake of a merger. A change in business strategy and/or radical adjustments to future staffing requirements (downsizing) may turn previous human resource and recruitment and selection strategies on their head almost overnight. Such uncertainties place an onus on recruitment and selection to generate a workforce that will be able to cope with the unexpected as well as the expected or planned. Two possible strategies may be appropriate in such situations: first, to recruit people who can adapt readily to change, and second, to recruit people who will become agents of change and/or shapers of the organisation's future destiny. This also gives rise to the prospect that recruitment and selection processes will be directed, in part, at jobs that do not yet exist.

One approach consistent with the recruitment of employees who can adapt to change is managing diversity. As identified earlier, this can build a rich mix of employees whose varied skills, experiences, values and culture increase the organisation's potential capacity to cope with change. Another approach is to recruit and select against the construct of 'the learning organisation' which Evenden (1993: 238) identifies as 'a strategy to develop an organisation that is sensitive to environmental change so that it creates opportunities and deals with threats by a process of continuous learning and adaptation that ensures its survival and growth effectiveness'. The implication for the staffing process is to incorporate characteristics appropriate to the learning organisation – such as 'experiments, admits mistakes, open, encourages ideas and makes joint decisions', as opposed to 'cautious, rationalises mistakes, defensive, discourages ideas and dominates' – into the personnel specification, and to develop recruitment and selection strategies to secure these attributes (Evenden, 1993: 238–9). The concept of the learning organisation is also relevant to managing change through human resource development and we will return to it in Chapter 6.

Another approach is to consider the extent to which management will hold the key to future organisational effectiveness and this has led to attempts to identify and select against appropriate competency criteria. Cockerill (1989) maintains that it is possible to identify high performance competencies that lead to effective managerial performance in changing environments. Eleven such competencies, identified earlier (p. 105), were used as the basis for managerial selection at National Westminster Bank using direct observation at work and 'simulated assessment centre conditions' (Cockerill, 1989: 54). BP and NatWest are cited by Williams and Dobson (1995: 21) as good examples of companies trying 'to ensure that they have the basic raw material in senior management to cope with a scenario where the only certain fact is that the future will be impregnated by change'. They see the use of what they termed 'transformational criteria' in recruitment and selection and training and development making a significant contribution to 'an organisation's renewal processes and the development of the learning organisation' (*ibid.*).

The change agent role of managers is well documented. Beer *et al.* (1990) suggest that line managers might be expected to play a pivotal role in initiating and managing change whereas Williams and Dobson (1995) point to the key role newly appointed chief executives may play in the process of strategic change. However, it is important to stress that change agents are not necessarily managers and may operate at various levels within the organisation and therefore it is arguably the characteristics of transformational leaders that are needed for organisations to manage change effectively (Tichy and Devanna, 1990). Bass (1990) stresses the increasing relevance of transformational leadership to future uncertainties in the business environment and suggests that research evidence identifies four key characteristics of such leaders:

■ *charisma* – where the leader provides vision and is able to generate respect, trust and pride;
■ *inspiration* – where high expectations are set and communicated;
■ *intellectual stimulation* – where rational, intelligent approaches to problem solving are promoted; and
■ *individualised consideration* – where the needs of individual employees are identified and supported through personalised approaches to their development needs.

Alternatively Legge's (1978) construction of the 'deviant innovator' could be applied, i.e. those personnel specialists who challenge the criteria by which organisational success is evaluated. This perhaps represents a different perspective on diversity and will be particularly valuable as an antidote to organisations that, for whatever reason, find they have assembled a management team that is too homogeneous (Sparrow, 1994). The potential for creating novel solutions to the problems that change can visit on organisations can also be enhanced by taking a team approach to recruitment and selection. The demanding lists of competencies sought in change environments (*see*, for example, Cockerill, 1989) may only be found in individuals who can walk on water! It may, therefore, be more appropriate to apply the competency template to teams so that members collectively have the capacity to initiate and manage change and cope with an imperfect future. This, however, implies that personnel specifications and appropriate recruitment and selection strategies need to be constantly recast as each team member is appointed in order to focus on the competency gaps that remain following each appointment. This would be important, for example, where new teams are being formed, perhaps along the lines of autonomous work groups described earlier.

These different change scenarios clearly place many demands on the recruitment and selection process and, given that the traditional model has been discounted as inappropriate, leaves us in need of a viable alternative. We now go on to outline one such possibility – strategic recruitment and selection.

Strategic recruitment and selection – the emergence of an alternative process

Strategic recruitment and selection starts from the premiss that an organisation's workforce makes a significant contribution to the achievement of strategic goals both now and in the future. The quality of the workforce is, in part, a function of the recruitment and selection process (Evenden, 1993). The concern to meet current and future strategic requirements as well as enabling adaptation to an imperfect future represents the starting point for a model of strategic recruitment and selection (*ibid.*). The bridge between strategy and the staffing process is often filled by human resource planning which aims to interpret and convert strategy into human resource plans (Rothwell, 1995). However, under the strategic model the essential elements of the recruitment and selection process are broadly similar to those outlined earlier under the 'traditional' model. The key difference is that strategic concerns drive their operation. This will mean that job analysis moves away from a narrow concentration on the current demands of specific tasks to a future-oriented process that also takes into account the wider demands of units or teams as well as the whole organisation itself (Bowen *et al.*, 1991). This changing requirement is encapsulated in the strategic job analysis technique propounded by Schneider and Konz (1989). This sets out to specify the knowledge, skills and abilities that will be relevant to anticipated future job roles and tasks to ensure their effective performance as well as to provide a procedure that can be applied to job roles and tasks that have not yet been anticipated. There is a similar change in emphasis in the generation of a personnel specification. The focus is no longer on identifying attributes associated with effective performance among current job incumbents but on those that are seen to be relevant to changing strategies and future uncertainties (Gerstein and Reisman, 1983). The person specification should therefore reflect changing patterns of work, the consequences of organisational restructuring, and different strategic priorities as well as being responsive to specific change programmes (e.g. culture change) and future uncertainties. It is critical that the specification provides sufficient detail for recruitment and selection processes to be targeted specifically at locating, attracting and assessing the desired attributes whatever they are.

The strategic model does not therefore reject traditional recruitment and selection methods, but develops and deploys them in ways consistent with overriding strategic concerns. For recruitment more thought will be given to likely sources of potential recruits and how to reach them. For selection the common reliance on shortlisting, interviews and references is likely to be eschewed in favour of more reliable and valid selection arrangements. This may involve supplementing these selection tools with purpose-built selection methods as well as the use of a greater array of off-the-shelf assessment tools. There will be concern to increase the reliability and validity of interviews and a more realistic appreciation of what they can and cannot measure as well as frequent adaptations to application forms and reference requests to reflect the explicit demands of different roles or jobs, for example, based around core competencies. Overall there is an implicit assumption that it will be insufficient to simply update existing job descriptions, interpret the personnel specification narrowly in terms of immediate job requirements, use the same array of recruitment media, produce standardised application forms and select by interview in a relatively arbitrary and cavalier way. The focus spreads to role and organisational requirements and in essence recruitment and selection is interpreted as a tailor-made activity designed to relate specifically to many emerging demands. This construction makes redundant any pretence to a prescriptive model. Each recruitment and selection activity is therefore viewed through a contingency framework that recognises that it will need to be adapted to each changing scenario.

This strategic approach requires a front-loaded investment strategy where there is a concern to recruit the 'right' competencies first time rather than invest later in rectifying 'poor' selection decisions and is exemplified by practice documented in inward investment companies such as Nissan and Toyota (Storey and Sisson, 1993) and a number of UK companies (Cockerill, 1989). This signals two further dimensions of strategic recruitment and selection. First, the cost of failure spotlights the importance of the decision-making process that underpins selection. The strategic model places much more emphasis on securing the active participation of relevant stakeholders within a more open decision-making framework. The inherent two-way nature of selection is honoured by giving candidates or potential candidates equality in the process. There is a concern throughout to provide a realistic preview of the job, role and organisation context to enable candidates to match their aptitudes, interests, etc. against any vacancy and thereby enable self-selection (Lawler, 1994). In addition the selection process itself will also be constructed with due regard to the impact it, and the decisions emanating from it, can have on the future lives of candidates. At the organisational level there will be concern to involve those who have a direct investment in any appointment, for example, subordinates, peers and service providers. Second, the front-loaded investment strategy arguably places a greater emphasis on the need to evaluate the whole process including the assessment of the reliability and validity of the personnel specification and the assessment methods utilised.

A definition of strategic recruitment and selection serves to bring these distinct but integral elements of the model together. According to Lundy and Cowling (1996: 240), 'If organisation selection is informed by the organisation's environment, linked to strategy, socially responsible, valid, periodically evaluated and maintained by knowledge of leading theory and practice, then such selection is, indeed, strategic'.

These principles enable the traditional model to be reconstituted into a strategic model of recruitment and selection (Fig. 4.5). Within this model and from our earlier discussion it is possible to distil a number of core dimensions that underpin strategic recruitment and selection (*see* Fig. 4.6).

Self-check question	4.5	*To what extent can Protection Royale's current recruitment and selection process be described as strategic?*

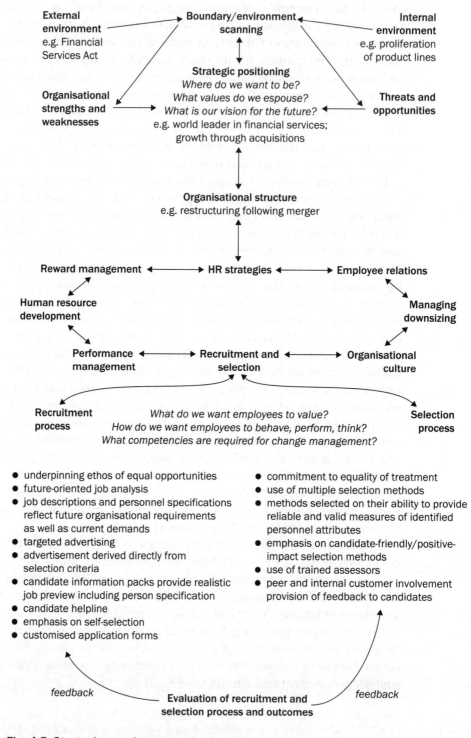

Fig. 4.5 Strategic recruitment and selection

Source: Developed from Millmore and Baker, 1996a.

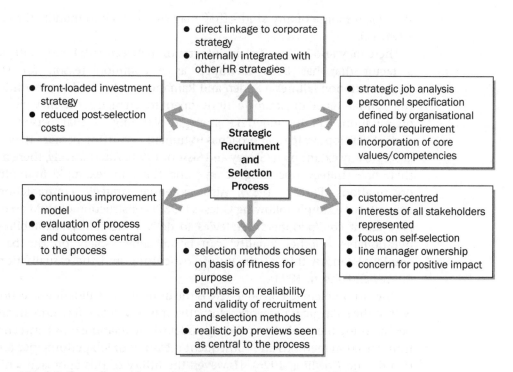

Fig. 4.6 Core dimensions of strategic recruitment and selection

Source: Developed from Millmore and Baker, 1996b.

There is, however, little evidence to suggest that practice is moving significantly in the direction of strategic recruitment and selection. Scholarios and Lockyer (1996) identify a gap between rhetoric and reality where evidence suggests little take-up of more sophisticated procedures and a continuing reliance on traditional approaches, while Lundy and Cowling (1996: 212) point to a 'paucity of cases which demonstrate strategic selection in action'. We now consider why this might be so.

The strategic model with its emphasis on tailor-made procedures is expensive in terms of both time and money. Because of this the potential for front-loaded investment in staffing processes may be restricted to large organisations and is, anyway, unlikely to be compatible with cost reduction strategies (Schuler and Jackson, 1987). The strategic model may also be perceived as demanding an unobtainable nirvana where selection is successfully made against a composite personnel specification embracing specific job requirements, group fit and organisation fit both now and in the future. Even if managers have time to work through these scenarios it may appear self-evident that compromises between these different demands may be necessary leading to sub-optimal decisions which could then threaten the integrity of the whole process. Another practical difficulty is that the short-term perspectives, rooted in accountancy traditions and traditional patterns of corporate ownership and said to characterise UK businesses, encourage managers to adopt quick-fix solutions (Storey and Sisson, 1993). A scenario familiar to many managers is 'that they may be under too much pressure to develop a strategic response of any kind – they may simply seek to muddle through' (Sisson, 1994: 12).

There may also be insufficient integration between HRM and strategic planning, a factor that has been identified as a common reason for HRM policy implementation failures (Golden and Ramanujam, 1985). Another difficulty is that the central tenet of strategic fit is open to challenge. It may be simply that organisations fail to undertake strategic planning or that personnel managers cannot develop strategic approaches to human resourcing because they cannot gain access to any extant plan (Storey and Sisson, 1993). Alternatively, there may be more than one strategy operating at any one time, for example in multi-divisional organisations (Purcell, 1989). Also, potential strategic contradictions may be evident. For example following Guest's (1987) construction of HRM an organisation may adopt core/peripheral strategies to deliver 'flexibility/adaptability', but it is questionable whether 'quality' can be sustained solely on the backs of core employees and within a climate of cost-cutting and the casualisation of labour (Storey and Sisson, 1993).

One last problem to consider here is the difficulty of validating selection decisions within the strategic framework. Most attempts to validate recruitment and selection decisions use the predictive validity model where relationships between predictions from selection methods and subsequent measures of job performance are correlated (Lundy and Cowling, 1996). However, the utility of this approach which is based essentially on current job performance is questionable where selection is being directed towards organisation fit and the future capacity of employees to manage change (Lawler, 1994). Organisations may therefore find it difficult to justify resource-intensive staffing processes without also investing in alternative concepts of validation (*ibid.*).

These potential obstacles could represent formidable impediments to the successful implementation of strategic recruitment and selection processes. However, as reported earlier, there are a number of organisations who are moving in this direction perhaps reflecting the adage 'to fail to plan is to plan to fail'. There are also inherent within the strategic model concepts whose careful application may serve to address and ameliorate these difficulties. We would particularly draw attention to recruitment and selection geared around managing diversity, the learning organisation, competencies associated with change management, managerial and key change agent appointments and using team selection as the basis for assembling the many disparate qualities likely to be demanded in the workforce of the future.

SUMMARY

- Recruitment and selection have the potential to make a significant contribution to the management of both planned and unplanned change. When integrated externally with corporate strategy and internally with other HR levers they represent powerful tools for facilitating, sustaining and initiating organisational change.

- The recruitment and selection process most commonly found in organisations – the 'traditional' approach – has limited application to change management despite its pervasiveness. Its narrow focus on immediate job demands and a tendency to preserve the status quo represent the antithesis of what is required from recruitment and selection when strategic priorities are changing and the future is uncertain.

- Increasingly recruitment and selection processes need to be responsive to a changing and uncertain business environment. Increased competition, the internationalisation of business and demographic shifts are examples of macro-level change leading to micro-level strategic responses such as restructuring, downsizing, de-layering, HRM, the flexible firm, mergers and culture change programmes. All of these place demands on the type of people required to staff an organisation with the presumption that their recruitment will facilitate the achievement of organisational objectives.

- Recruitment and selection can contribute to change management within a variety of change scenarios such as different competitive strategies, structural changes, the introduction of HRM and autonomous work groups. The dominant theme here was the potential to support planned change deriving from rational strategic planning processes. However, this represents an incomplete picture and it is possible for recruitment and selection to drive change, for example, through the targeted appointment of change agents or establishment of a diverse workforce, as well as equipping an organisation with those competencies relevant to managing unplanned change.

- An alternative, strategic, approach to recruitment and selection is more likely to be appropriate to changing business strategies and future uncertainties. This approach is not an easy option and requires significant front-loaded investment to fully exploit the contingent relationships between recruitment and selection and different change scenarios.

CASE STUDY 4.2

Recruitment and selection at Unicol

In 1984 Deepdale, a college maintained by its Local Education Authority, comprised seven academic and a number of non-academic departments and provided a range of both further education (FE – i.e. up to A-level) and higher education (HE – i.e. post-A-level) courses.

At this time three particular difficulties confronted the management team of its Business Studies Department. First, there was no evident departmental or corporate strategy. Second, its courses (or 'products') could largely be classified, using the BCG matrix (Purcell, 1989) as 'cash cows' or 'dogs'. Third, a human resourcing audit had revealed an impoverished staffing base characterised by a skewed (elderly) age profile, low turnover, lengthy service in post, limited recent

▶

practical experience to support the vocational nature of course programmes, lack of potential, inappropriate skills mix and an attitudinal set which was anti-management and resistant to change.

The department's courses were predominantly aimed at the part-time market and there were relatively few full-time courses or students. This created a further difficulty as the part-time market was far more volatile, being more susceptible to economic changes, and generated significantly less revenue than the full-time student market. A decision was therefore taken to develop a departmental strategy that reflected the perceived best interests of the department, college and students (customers). The strategy that emerged was designed to increase full-time student numbers significantly while maintaining part-time student numbers at their current level and rationalising part-time courses to meet local demands. These objectives were based on the delivery of high-quality programmes within areas of high demand which if achieved would lead to greater cost efficiency. The growth strategy coupled with more rigorous staff management, designed to 'ease' poor staff out, would provide the manoeuvrability necessary to address the problematic staffing profile.

A recruitment and selection strategy was developed around a staffing profile that stressed: high-quality lecturing skills (or the potential to develop them); recent, relevant work experience; professional qualifications; a positive orientation to change; flexibility and adaptability; commercial orientation (to help raise money to support such strategies); and a commitment to self-development. Higher-level academic and teacher training qualifications were regarded as desirable attributes as was previous lecturing experience. The college had in place a mandatory procedure that involved advertising internally and in the educational and local press, shortlisting from application forms and selecting via panel interviews and references. To overcome the perceived limitations of this process the department funded a number of supplementary activities. Recruitment was supported by: a professionally produced information pack that contained details of the vacancy, department, college and the local environment (housing, schools, etc.); open events and recruitment 'hot lines'; and advertising targeted at women returners and at employed and redundant professional practitioners. Advertising included the use of mailshots, professional magazines, public services (e.g. libraries) and newsagents. The prescribed selection methods were supplemented by work sampling tests (e.g. delivering a lecture) and panel interviews were structured (to ensure consistency) around behaviour-based questions where candidates were asked about how they behaved in certain situations. A line staff member was added to the interview panel and wherever possible students were included as active participants in work sampling tests along with line staff and managers.

By the end of the 1980s the department had radically changed its staffing base. It had developed its own human resource planning model and successive staffing audits confirmed an appropriate skill mix, balanced age profile, pockets of entrepreneurial ability, high-quality lecturing performance, a significant reduction in average length of service, excellent networking with local organisations and a number of recent recruits who had been fast-tracked into management positions. However, an anticipated increase in labour turnover among those predicted to be high-flyers had not materialised. Between 1984 and 1989 the department had expanded its full-time and overall student numbers by 100 per cent and 30 per cent respectively and by 1989 accounted for around 40 per cent of the college's income line and student numbers, employing 100 academic and 25 non-academic staff.

At the end of the 1980s higher education entered a period of turbulence. Government legislation removed maintained HE colleges and polytechnics from LEA control and established them as autonomous bodies. At the same time changes to the funding of HE meant that it was no longer financially viable to operate mixed-economy colleges like Deepdale which offered combinations of both FE and HE provision. In consequence it was decided to split Deepdale into separate FE and HE colleges and simultaneously merge the HE offshoot with another exclusively HE college to become Unicol in 1990. Staff from Deepdale were allocated to the split colleges on the basis of their teaching responsibilities and the HE element of the Business Studies Department became The Business School – one of five academic departments – in the newly created Unicol.

Anticipating the split and subsequent merger the management team of Deepdale's Business Studies Department conducted a strategic review and identified two particular difficulties for its HE component. First, its HE course portfolio was severely out of alignment with competing institutions as, consistent with its predominantly FE background, the department offered no undergraduate or postgraduate degree courses. The department had concentrated on delivering vocational Higher National Certificate and Diploma awards in Business Studies although its part-time provision included a limited range of postgraduate professional programmes. Additionally there was no formal departmental research activity. Second, the staffing profile had been deliberately structured around the course portfolio as described and was incompatible with the demands of HE. Among the 30 academic staff transferred to Unicol there was minimal experience of undergraduate and postgraduate teaching and virtually no experience of writing and publishing research papers. The prevailing departmental culture reflected Deepdale's FE bias and was regarded by the management team as being inconsistent with what they perceived an HE culture to be like (*see* Table 4.2).

The management team proposed a five-year strategy for HE based on 100 per cent expansion of student numbers to be met completely from and funded by the launch of a suite of undergraduate and postgraduate degree programmes. These would be designed to exploit existing established markets and market niches and would run parallel to the existing course portfolio. If successful this would lead to a significant expansion of staff numbers thereby providing opportunities to address problems presented by the FE profile of transferring staff.

▶

Table 4.2 The contrasting cultures of FE and HE as perceived by the Business Studies Department

FE culture	HE culture
Teaching environment	Learning environment
Vocational orientation	Academic orientation
Geared towards young, dependent students	Geared towards more mature, independent students
Premium on maintaining control and motivation	Premium on autonomy and self-motivation
Students as recipients of espoused wisdom	Students as critical and original thinkers
Research inactive	Research active
Responsive to local community	Responsive to national community
Promotion based on teaching and management performance	Promotion based on research and publications
Teaching as the focus for quality control and assurance	Research as the focus for quality control and assurance
Staff affiliated to professional bodies	Staff affiliated to academic communities
Emphasis on staff's practical experience	Emphasis on staff's postgraduate qualifications and research record

The strategy was approved by the designate chief executive of Unicol. Plans for the new degree programmes were developed and brought forward for approval. This was subsequently obtained but only on condition that new 'HE' staff were appointed to teach the second and third levels of the three-year degree programmes. This produced an interesting dilemma. Existing staff who had successfully developed these degree programmes would be precluded from teaching on all but the first level unless they could rapidly satisfy an HE staffing profile.

The new degrees were launched by The Business School in 1990 and for the 1990/91 academic year they were to be taught by existing staff with new appointments being made during that time to teach subsequent levels as they came on stream in successive years. As a result of environmental scanning the management team were aware that the recruitment and selection strategy that they were developing had to take into account a number of potential constraints:

- rapid expansion of the HE sector had generated intense competition for experienced staff;
- feelings of insecurity among HE staff meant they were staying put with their current employer;

- HE was facing significant year-on-year reductions in central (i.e. government) funding as a result of government policies;
- Unicol and its Business School had not yet had the opportunity to market itself and establish its credibility.

Case study questions

1 (a) Using the approaches outlined in Chapter 1, how would you classify the emerging strategies of the Business Studies Department in 1984 and the designate Business School in 1989?

  (b) What implications do you think these strategies would ordinarily have for recruitment and selection?

2 To what extent do you think the recruitment and selection process developed to meet the 1984 strategic plan could be described as strategic? Give reasons for your answer.

3 What competencies do you think are relevant for an HE lecturer and how can they be incorporated into and used to drive the recruitment and selection process?

4 Devise a detailed strategic recruitment and selection process to meet the changed circumstances of the Business School following the 1990 merger. How does this differ from the earlier process adopted for the Business Studies Department?

REFERENCES

Bass, B.M. (1990) 'From transactional to transformational leadership: learning to share the vision', *Organizational Dynamics*, Winter, 19–31.

Beer, M., Eisenstat, R.A. and Spector, B. (1990) 'Why change programs don't produce change', *Harvard Business Review*, November/December, 158–66.

Borucki, C.C. and Lafley, A.F. (1984) 'Strategic staffing at Chase Manhattan Bank', in Fombrum, C.J., Tichy, N.M. and Devanna, M. (eds), *Strategic Human Resource Management*, New York: John Wiley, pp. 69–86.

Bowen, D.E., Ledford, G.E. and Nathan, B.R. (1991) 'Hiring for the organisation not the job', *Academy of Management Executive*, 5(4), 35–51.

Clark, A. (1999) 'Royal plans takeover of GRE', *Daily Telegraph*, 23 January, p. 29.

Cockerill, A. (1989) 'The kind of competence for rapid change', *Personnel Management*, September, 52–6.

Evenden, R. (1993) 'The strategic management of recruitment and selection', in Harrison, R. (ed.), *Human Resource Management: Issues and Strategies*, Wokingham: Addison-Wesley, pp. 219–45.

Flynn, R., McCombs, T. and Elloy, D. (1990) 'Staffing the self-managing work team', *Leadership and Organization Development Journal*, 11(1), 26–31.

Gerstein, M. and Reisman, H. (1983) 'Strategic selection: matching executives to business conditions', *Sloan Management Review*, Winter, 33–49.

Golden, K.A. and Ramanujam, V. (1985) 'Between a dream and a nightmare: on the integration of the human resource management and strategic business planning process', *Human Resource Management*, 26(4) (Winter), 429–52.

Guest, D.E. (1987) 'Human Resource Management and industrial relations', *Journal of Management Studies*, 24(5) (September), 503–21.

Hendry, C. (1995) *Human Resource Management: A Strategic Approach to Employment*, Oxford: Butterworth-Heinemann.

Iles, P. and Hayers, P.K. (1997) 'Managing diversity in transnational project teams: a tentative model and case study', *Journal of Managerial Psychology*, 12(2), 95–117.

Lawler, E.E. (1994) 'From job-based to competency-based organisations', *Journal of Organizational Behaviour*, 15, 3–15.

Legge, K. (1978) *Power, Innovation and Problem-Solving in Personnel Management*, Maidenhead: McGraw-Hill.

Lundy, O. and Cowling, A. (1996) *Strategic Human Resource Management*: London, Routledge.

Mabey, C. and Iles, P. (1993) 'The strategic integration of assessment and development practices: succession planning and new manager development', *Human Resource Management Journal*, 3(4), 16–34.

McCombs, T., Elloy, D.F. and Flynn, W.R. (1994) 'A procedure for staffing the autonomous work team', *Recruitment, Selection and Retention*, 3(1), 17–23.

Martin, D. (1990) 'Recruitment: coin operators', *Personnel Today*, 6 March, 41–5.

Miles, R.E. and Snow, C.C. (1984) 'Designing strategic human resource systems', *Organizational Dynamics*, 13(8), 36–52.

Miller, E. (1984) 'Strategic Staffing', in Fombrun, D.J., Tichy, N.M. and Devanna, M. (eds), *Strategic Human Resource Management*, New York: John Wiley, pp. 57–86.

Millmore, M. and Baker, B. (1996a) 'Staff recruitment and selection: strategy for the future', *Managing HE*, 3 (Summer), 16–19.

Millmore, M. and Baker, B. (1996b) 'Staff recruitment: hitting the target', *Managing HE*, 4 (Autumn), 18–21.

Moloney, K. (1998) 'Seasoned professionals', *People Management*, 19 March, 34–40.

Offerman, L.R. and Gowing, M.K. (1993) 'Personnel selection in the future: the impact of changing demographics and the nature of work', in Schmitt, N. and Borman, W. (eds), *Personnel Selection in Organizations*, San Francisco, Calif.: Jossey-Bass.

Paddison, L. (1990) 'The targeted approach to recruitment', *Personnel Management*, November, 54–8.

Pain, D. (1998) 'Footsie recovers from merger breakdown shock', *The Independent*, 25 February, p. 23.

Porter, M.E. (1985) *Competitive Advantage: Creating and Sustaining Superior Performance*, New York: Free Press.

Purcell, J. (1989) 'The impact of corporate strategy on human resource management', in Storey, J. (ed.) *New Perspectives on Human Resource Management*, London: Routledge, pp. 67–91.

Purcell, J. (1995) 'Corporate strategy and its link with human resource management strategy', in Storey, J. (ed.), *Human Resource Management: A Critical Text*, London: Routledge, pp. 63–86.

Rothwell, S. (1995) 'Human resource planning', in Storey, J. (ed.), *Human Resource Management: A Critical Text*, London: Routledge, pp. 167–202.

Sadler, P. and Milmer, K. (1993) *The Talent-intensive Organisation: Optimising your Company's Human Resource Strategies*, Special Report No. P659, London: The Economist Intelligence Unit.

Schneider, B. and Konz, M.K. (1989) 'Strategic job analysis', *Human Resource Management*, 28(1) (Spring), 51–63.

Scholarios, D. and Lockyer, C. (1996) 'Human resource management and selection: better solutions or new dilemmas?', in Towers, B. (ed.), *The Handbook of Human Resource Management*, 2nd edn, Oxford: Blackwell, pp. 173–95.

Schuler, R.S. and Jackson, S.E. (1987) 'Linking competitive strategies with human resource management practices', *The Academy of Management Executive*, 1(3), 207–19.

Sisson, K. (ed.) (1994) *Personnel Management: A Comprehensive Guide to Theory and Practice in Britain*, 2nd edn, Oxford: Blackwell.

Snow, C. and Snell, S. (1992) 'Staffing as strategy', in Schmitt, N. and Barman, W. (eds), *Personnel Selection*, vol. 4, San Francisco: Jossey-Bass.

Sparrow, P.R. (1994) 'Organizational competencies: creating a strategic behavioural framework for selection and assessment', in Anderson, N. and Herriot, P. (eds), *Assessment and Selection in Organizations: Methods and Practice for Recruitment and Appraisal, First Update and Supplement*, Chichester: John Wiley, pp. 1–26.

Sparrow, P.R. and Pettigrew, A.M. (1988) 'Strategic human resource management in the UK computer supplier industry', *Journal of Occupational Psychology*, 61, 25–42.

Staniforth, D. (1996) 'Teamworking, or individual working in a team?', *Team Performance Management: An International Journal*, 2(3), 37–41.

Storey, J. and Sisson, K. (1993) *Managing Human Resources and Industrial Relations*, Buckingham: Open University Press.

Tichy, N. and Devanna, M.A. (1990) *The Transformational Leader*, Chichester: John Wiley.

Vikhanski, O. and Puffer, S. (1993) 'Management education and employee training at Moscow McDonald's', *European Management Journal*, 11(1), 102–7.

Watson, T. (1994) 'Recruitment and selection', in Sisson, K. (ed.), *Personnel Management: A Comprehensive Guide to Theory and Practice in Britain*, 2nd edn, Oxford: Blackwell, pp.185–220.

Welch, J. (1998) 'Process of denial', *People Management*, 19 February, 30–4.

Whitehill, A.M. (1991) *Japanese Management: Tradition and Transition*, London: Routledge.

Williams, A.P.O. and Dobson, P. (1995) 'Personnel selection and corporate strategy', in Anderson, N. and Herriot, P. (eds), *Assessment and Selection in Organizations: Methods and Practice for Recruitment and Appraisal, Second Update and Supplement*, Chichester: John Wiley, pp. 1–27.

Wright, M. and Storey, J. (1997) 'Recruitment and selection', in Beardwell, I. and Holden, L. (eds), *Human Resource Management: A Contemporary Perspective*, 2nd edn, London: Financial Times Pitman Publishing, pp. 210–76.

ANSWERS TO SELF-CHECK QUESTIONS

4.1 *How would you classify Protection Royale's approach to recruitment and selection – internal or external? Give reasons for your answer.*

Throughout there is evidence of the use of an external model. Sales Consultants were recruited directly from the labour market. This initially presented no difficulties as the personnel specification was relatively undemanding meaning that many individuals in the labour market could meet its requirements. Following the tightening of the specification reliance on the external market continued using, in addition, head-hunting as a recruitment vehicle.

When the difficulties in recruiting Sales Consultants became critical the direct use of the external labour market was continued as part of a two-pronged strategy. The second prong, the recruitment of trainees, is a little more difficult to classify and represents something of a hybrid. Recruiting trainees and developing them to become Sales Consultants bears the hallmarks of an internal model, albeit used in concert with the external model. However, trainees were predominantly recruited from the external labour market rather than existing employees and their point of entry into the organisation was above those entering at the base level.

4.2 *To what extent did Protection Royale's initial recruitment and selection processes reflect the traditional model depicted in Fig. 4.2?*

Initially at least, the recruitment and selection of Sales Consultants closely followed the traditional model. Recruitment appeared at this stage to be driven by the need to fill vacancies, with the process itself structured around the demands of the job as it was currently performed. There was no evident link with corporate strategy and it could be argued that a lack of human resource planning was demonstrated by a failure to plan in advance to forestall what became a recruitment crisis. The almost spontaneous recourse to head-hunting by inexperienced managers would also suggest that investment in recruitment and selection was end-loaded. In addition there did not appear to be any systematic evaluation of the process.

The traditional model, however, appears to have been applied very professionally. All stages were fully developed with recruitment and selection being driven by an agreed job description and personnel specification. Selection involved the use of multiple methods and it appears that the traditional approach satisfied well the organisation's recruitment needs for Sales Consultants.

4.3 *Using Schuler and Jackson's continua what role behaviours do you think are appropriate to quality enhancement and cost reduction strategies?*

Schuler and Jackson (1987) suggest that the following role behaviour profiles are appropriate for these strategies:

Quality enhancement strategy
Orientation towards repetitive, prescribed behaviour
Tendency to operate co-operatively and interdependently
Low level of risk-taking

High concern for quality of output

Moderate concern for quantity

High process rather than results orientation

High level of identification with and commitment to the organisation

Intermediate or longer-term focus.

Cost reduction strategy

Orientation towards repetitive, prescribed behaviour

Predominantly oriented to autonomous, independent behaviour

Low level of risk-taking

Preference for certainty and stability

Moderate concern for quality

High concern for quantity of output

High results rather than process orientation

Tendency towards short-term focus.

4.4 *How can recruitment and selection contribute to culture change programmes?*

We would identify at least three levels of contribution. First, it is necessary for employees to possess those capabilities, attitudes and values that support the new culture. In the example of DuPont (Case Study 3.1) these coalesced around a safety culture. Here, ongoing recruitment and selection should build such requirements into the personnel specification, and selection methods may need to be adjusted to meet its new demands. This was seen earlier in this chapter under our consideration of job design (pp. 108–9) where teamworking approaches resulted in selection methods to ensure compatibility among team members and their involvement in the selection of new team members.

Second, culture change will require the recruitment and selection of opinion-formers and natural leaders to support the change programme. These are likely to be recruited internally but where necessary will be recruited externally against an appropriate personnel specification. In the DuPont case, 112 'influencers' were 'recruited' to influence others through their everyday actions and formal and informal contacts.

Third, a new Chief Executive may be recruited specifically to drive through culture change, as seemed to be the case with the appointment of Colin Marshall at British Airways (Case Study 3.2). Even if not a specific objective the appointment of a new Chief Executive may often promote a reappraisal of corporate culture and the launch of a change programme.

4.5 *To what extent can Protection Royale's current recruitment and selection process be described as strategic?*

The dual recruitment and selection strategy has built on the professional application of the previous traditional model and a sophisticated approach displaying a number of strategic characteristics is now evident. The process reflects a front-loaded investment strategy, involves significant line management ownership and employs multiple selection methods. The trainee route appears to reflect a growing concern for human resource planning and a competency model is being used extensively to integrate the components of the process. Competencies are being used to structure the job description, the personnel specification, and the application form and to determine the choice of selection methods. Such measures should result in positive impact on applicants and candidates. The use of candidate information packs should reinforce this and contribute to a realistic job preview.

However, and importantly, there is little evidence of explicit strategic integration either 'externally' or 'internally'. It may simply be that we have insufficient information to assess strategic integration at this time and may need to reserve judgement. However, the reappraisal of the product portfolio and the reconstruction of the Sales Consultant role, and recruitment to this redefined role, around demanding performance criteria does appear to be consistent with Protection *Royale*'s market-leader strategy. There is also a clear internal integration link between recruitment and training with the introduction of the training scheme. On the other hand, given the lack of evident external strategic integration, it may well be that any strategic thrust associated with evolving recruitment and selection practices is likely to be more emergent than deliberate. We would also note that, against one of our features of strategic recruitment, there is no evidence that the process is being systematically evaluated, although in fairness it is arguably too early to do this.

CHAPTER 5

Performance management and the management of change

Having completed this chapter, you will be able to:

■ Define performance management by explaining the separate activities which constitute this approach to the management of people.

■ Explain the importance of processes in the effective conduct of performance management by recognising these as a process cycle.

■ Identify the role performance management plays in contributing to organisational change.

■ Link performance management with other important management themes, e.g. strategic human resource management, organisational culture and structure, and the search for employee commitment.

INTRODUCTION

Performance appraisal has traditionally been an important personnel management activity. It has often been seen by non-personnel staff as marginal to the mainstream of the organisation's activities and has therefore been perceived as bureaucratic and procedural – an unnecessary evil. But in recent years, in many organisations, the image of performance appraisal, however unfair it may have been, has changed. Performance appraisal is now seen in these organisations as part of a set of techniques for managing employee performance. Far from being marginal to the mainstream of the organisation's activities it is an intrinsic part of them. This has coincided with the school of thought that 'people are our greatest asset': a cliché maybe, but one which has had a profound effect on the rhetoric if not the practice of organisational life in recent years. If people are an organisation's greatest asset then it makes sense to treat people in the way that any other valued asset is treated: i.e. to set clear performance expectations for that asset, monitor progress against those expectations and take action to improve the performance where it may be less good than expected.

In this chapter we cast the net wider than performance appraisal by considering the broader approach of performance management, of which performance appraisal is a key component. We analyse performance management from a processual perspective. The touchstone of this approach is a performance cycle which details four key processes in performance management. Processes focus on what actually happens in systems and structures rather than dwelling on the systems and structures themselves. What forms the main body of this chapter is an analysis of the way in which these processes are implemented. This analysis underpins the way in which performance management may contribute to organisational change. The chapter assumes a model of change propounded by Beer *et al.* (1990): that change happens at the level of people's jobs, not as a consequence of senior executive edicts. The real contribution which performance management can make to organisational change is through the actions of line managers and individual employees in acting out these processes. The analysis places particular emphasis on the role of line managers in implementing the performance management processes. Their belief in the value of performance management and actions to support that belief are crucial.

The chapter's main points are illustrated by two case studies. One, Siemens Standard Drives, is set in manufacturing industry and illustrates how performance management may assist in transformational change. The second concerns Premierco, an organisation in the insurance industry where performance management is very much swimming with the 'cultural tide' and therefore assisting in incremental organisational change.

Performance management at Siemens Standard Drives

Based in Congleton, Cheshire, Siemens Standard Drives is the global headquarters for the Variable Speeds Drives business of the German electronics giant Siemens AG. It employs 430 in the design and manufacture of specialist electronic control equipment used in a wide range of industrial applications. In 1996 it had 5 per cent of a world market dominated by Japanese competitors Fuji, Mitsubishi and Yaskawa. Its target is an 8 per cent market share by 2001 and to be the market leader with over 10 per cent by 2005.

To achieve this ambitious objective Siemens embarked on a nine-month process re-engineering project (process engineering is defined by Wastell *et al.* (1994: 23, quoted in Burnes (1996: 172)) as 'initiatives, large and small, radical and conservative, whose common theme is the achievement of significant improvements in organisational performance by augmenting the efficiency and effectiveness of key business processes'). It was clear that significant process improvements would be required. The company adopted a programme called 'World Class for 2000', the aim of which was to benchmark with other manufacturers and adopt the best processes in all areas and thus engender a culture of world-class practices. These included:

- a zero defects culture;
- cellular and team-based manufacture;
- daily cell meetings to discuss and agree targets;
- minimum stock at all stages of the manufacturing process;
- just-in-time Kanban delivery from suppliers direct to cell;
- visible and agreed performance measures which form the basis for regular performance feedback;
- a multi-skilled and highly flexible workforce;
- total satisfaction of customer demand.

Much was made of the ability of process re-engineering to bring a new start for the company. The adoption of this new approach was made easier through the commencement of a new production management team and a new personnel manager. The first task of this team was to restructure the manufacturing operation to align personnel roles with the new structure.

The company had been structured on traditional functional lines. This meant that there were too many layers of responsibility, decision making was slow and personnel management responsibility was unclear and therefore ineffective. In order to meet the new operating strategy the structure was changed radically. The new structure is built around two main production segments. One of these manufactures printed circuit boards (PCBs) and the other assembles and tests final products. Each production segment adopts a cellular manufacturing approach with 20-strong production teams headed by a group leader who has total responsibility for all aspects of the team's operation. The production groups are ▶

product-based and have all the constituent parts of an autonomous cell (*see* Chapter 2), i.e. operators, a technician, a line feeder, and a test operator. For example, a product-based group in the PCB segment has total responsibility for the generation of an assembled, tested and packaged PCB.

The group is responsible and accountable for its output and operation. The issue of accountability is crucial to success. If a team member is not performing adequately the group leader is empowered to remedy this situation. Initially this would be by giving assistance to the individual to improve performance. In the event of such improvement not materialising the group leader has the power to terminate the individual's contract and recruit a replacement. This new approach was well received by the majority of production staff. However, in the early stages of this process approximately 10 per cent of employees decided they could not meet the new principles and left by mutual agreement.

The role of the group leader is vital. A few of the nine group leaders had been supervisors previously. However, they all accepted that with the new role carrying full operational responsibility and accountability the job could not have been more different. Most of the group leaders had previously been PCB or mechanical assembly operators. They were selected for the new group leader posts on the basis of their business awareness and people management potential. Their training for the new role emphasised team building abilities. The senior management hope that the enthusiastic example they set to their team members will be infectious. Group leaders hold their own quality meetings and daily 'early bird' meetings to discuss important issues for the day. They select, train and appraise team members. Siemens Standard Drives is also adopting an annualised hours system whereby team members work a differing amount of hours weekly, albeit that an annual target must be reached. The group leader plans staffing levels as part of this system. The key aspects of teamworking are shared ownership of objectives, skills training, performance feedback, communication meetings and, most importantly, 'no secrets'. Part of the culture change which the company has sought is the generation and publication of shared values. The values agreed by the teams which are prominent are openness, honesty, trust and respect.

Performance management is a vital aspect of the group leader's job. It has three elements. The first entails setting individual performance objectives. This is done six-monthly by group leaders. Siemens uses the management by objectives approach where objectives are cascaded from overall business objectives through the four-tier company hierarchy to operators. These objectives are displayed clearly at the entrance to the production area. The criteria emphasise quality, efficiency, attitudes (in particular, flexibility) and attendance. The link between these criteria and overall business performance is obvious and demonstrable.

Dialogue between the group leader and member is the second element. This has two components: an assessment of the member's performance against objectives set and a discussion of the member's training and development and career planning needs. Managers stress the need for a dialogue characterised by 50 per cent input from both group leader and member. A crucial part of this dialogue is the views of the team member on the ways in which he or she thinks the company may be managed more effectively. This dialogue is seen by managers to be a vital aspect of the 'open and honest' values they are seeking to create.

The third element of performance management is the outputs of the process. Siemens Standard Drives is currently in the process of designing a performance-related pay system which will be based on performance objectives. In the recently adopted appraisal system described above the group leader makes it clear to each team member how progress through the pay structure can be achieved. This conversation is documented, and 'owned' by the team member.

All employees are clear that in a performance management system driven by business objectives those employees who do not add value to their team through achievement of their individual objectives are held accountable for such failure. In such cases, improvement targets are agreed by the team member with the group leader and the implications of failure to meet these targets is made clear. In most cases the necessary improvement has been forthcoming. But in some cases team members have been the subject of the disciplinary measures which have been taken publicly and in accordance with the disciplinary procedure, with some dismissals.

The new approach has had considerable success in the twelve months since it was introduced. Labour efficiency has increased from 58 per cent to 78 per cent and delivery performance from 72 per cent to 94 per cent.

Performance management: old wine, new label, new flavour

What is performance management?

Clark (1995: 187) indicates that 'there is no single universally accepted model of performance management in use'. It is a term which originated in North America and is used to describe an integrated set of techniques which have had an independent existence under their own names (e.g. performance appraisal). Storey and Sisson (1993) note that at its broadest the term can mean any activity which is designed to improve the performance of employees. At its narrowest performance management is used to refer to individual performance-related pay. The definition we adopt in this chapter is that which emphasises the three basic activities recognised by Storey and Sisson (1993). These are:

1 setting clear objectives for individual employees which are derived from the organisation's strategy and departmental strategies (or, as they call this, 'departmental purpose analysis');
2 formal monitoring and review of progress towards these objectives;
3 using the outcomes of the review process to reinforce desired employee behaviour through differential rewards and identifying training and development needs.

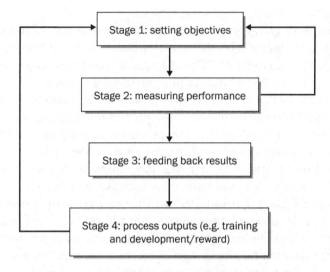

Fig. 5.1 The performance management cycle
Source: Adapted from Clark (1995).

Clark (1995) stresses one additional performance management activity which you will have noticed is emphasised at Siemens Standard Drives: that of feeding back to the employee the results of the formal monitoring.

Clark, like Storey and Sisson, emphasises that performance management's set of processes is operated in a cycle (*see* Fig. 5.1). In Clark's cycle there is a stage which is placed *after* the four stages of setting objectives, measuring performance, feeding back results and rewarding based on results. This stage entails the possible amendment of objectives and changing the activities which contributed to the performance measure. This creates a direct feedback loop to the setting of objectives.

Storey and Sisson (1993) also build in feedback loops. Employees have their objectives set in accordance with corporate or departmental strategy. A feedback loop is evident at this point to allow amendment to the objectives in the light of particular departmental strengths and weaknesses. At the next stage formal monitoring and review of progress towards those objectives takes place. This generates the outcomes of differential rewards and identification of training and development needs. Another feedback loop is inserted after this stage 'to allow renewed individual objectives so that the department may adjust its mission in the light of enhanced performance levels achieved' (Storey and Sisson, 1993: 134).

Self-check questions	5.1	*Why do you think stage 3 of the performance management cycle shown in Fig. 5.1, feeding back results, is so important?*
	5.2	*What skills do you think line managers must use in order for stage 3 to be performed effectively?*

Why is there such interest in performance management?

A major study of performance management (Institute of Personnel Management, 1992) claims it offers several advantages. Among these are:

- more effective employees able to meet increased product market competition;
- a greater opportunity for employees to share in the organisation's vision and the way to realise that vision;
- the pushing of key decisions down the organisational structure to line managers and supervisors (note the importance of this at Siemens Standard Drives);
- a greater acceptance of accountability by line managers of the necessity to make such decisions (note the importance of this at Siemens Standard Drives); and
- reward structures which forge a clear link between individual and/or group performance.

You will note that these claimed advantages for performance management have a missionary zeal about them suggesting that they have an important part to play in the generation of organisational change. They are a long way from the traditional 'just another piece of personnel bumph' view of performance appraisal so prevalent in many organisations.

We will now explore in more detail the ways in which performance management may contribute to organisational change. These are: communicating the organisation's mission; making employees more effective by linking their performance objectives to those of the organisation; involving employees in decision making; assisting restructuring through the devolvement of decision making; making managers manage; linking employee rewards to individual performance; reducing trade union influence; and developing employees in line with organisational goals.

How performance management may contribute to organisational change

Communicating the organisation's mission

Performance management is characterised by the major influence the organisation's strategic objectives have upon the definition of unit, department, team and individual performance objectives. Siemens Standard Drives is a good example of this. The mission is to be market leader by 2005. This provides a clear focus and rationale for all the change the company is promoting. The challenge for senior managers is to get all employees to be committed to the mission.

The pursuit of employee commitment to the organisation's mission is something which has dominated people management thinking in recent years. Beer *et al.* (1984) specified commitment as one of their 'HR outcomes'. Guest (1987) identified commitment as one of the four goals of HRM together with strategic integration, flexibility and quality.

Legge (1995: 180) suggests that the orthodox interpretation of commitment 'is operationalised in terms of three factors: a strong desire to remain a member of the organisation; a strong belief in, and acceptance of, the values and goals of the organisation; and a readiness to exert considerable effort on behalf of the organisation'. Guest (1987) argues that the theoretical proposition which follows from this orthodox interpretation of commitment is that organisational commitment will result in high employee satisfaction, high performance, longer tenure and a willingness to accept change.

The research evidence on the effects of employee commitment is inconclusive, not the least reason being the difficulty of separating cause and effect (Legge, 1995). For example, you may be asking: does the opportunity to negotiate individual performance objectives *cause* employee commitment or does a committed employee define the objective-setting process as negotiation where, in truth, it is little more than imposition with a cursory opportunity for the individual to disagree? What this suggests is that testing the theoretical proposition that employee commitment leads to specific outcomes is extremely difficult.

However, we need to make two points here. The first is that managers have taken this theoretical proposition as an act of faith on the assumption that employees who 'sign on' to the organisation's goals are more likely to be effective performers than those who are at best apathetic or at worst alienated. Notwithstanding the complexity of the topic masked by its seeming simplicity, it is a compelling argument. The second point is that without the communication of the organisation's mission, commitment to it is impossible. Performance management offers an excellent opportunity not only to introduce the mission but to reinforce it consistently through regular reviews of individual performance.

Making employees more effective by linking their performance objectives to those of the organisation

Much of the writing on HRM in recent years has stressed the importance of integrating human resource activities with the strategic objectives of the organisation (Beer *et al.*, 1984; Fombrun *et al.*, 1984). This may take the form of, for example, selecting the sort of people who have the potential to deliver a contribution specifically to organisational objectives and training them in such a way that such performance may be realised. But performance management offers the most obvious link. As you saw at Siemens Standard Drives, the performance objectives of individuals are derived from the organisation's objectives.

This raises the question of the extent to which designing a clear link between individual job and organisational objectives will actually create that connection in practice. For reassurance, doubting managers may turn to goal-setting theory (Locke *et al.*, 1981). Goal-setting theory has a long history which has been substantiated over 30 years of research. The components of the theory are that:

- clear and challenging goals lead to higher performance than easily attainable goals, those goals at which you try your best or no goals;
- goals affect performance by directing employees' attention and effort, increasing their determination to succeed and motivating them to develop strategies for achievement;

■ goal-setting is most likely to improve employees' task performance when goals are clear and challenging; employees have sufficient ability to achieve them; supportive managers give regular feedback on the level of progress being made; tangible rewards, such as money, are given for goal achievement; and employees accept their goals.

Many performance management schemes involve setting employees challenging goals. An oil company in which we did research call them 'stretch goals'. An insurance company whose performance management scheme Phil studied (Lewis, 1998) emphasised that rewards would only be given to those employees who demonstrated *improved* performance; performing at last year's level, however good, simply wasn't good enough. You may be thinking that this reveals a particularly 'hard' side to performance management. What it does imply is the necessity for managers to ensure that the *opportunity* is available for individuals to demonstrate improved performance.

You may have noticed the close relationship between the performance management cycle in Fig. 5.1 and the last set of components of goal-setting theory listed above (i.e. the necessity for goals to be specific and sufficiently challenging, the subjects to have sufficient ability, feedback to be provided to show progress in relation to the goal, rewards such as money being given for goal attainment, a supportive manager and assigned goals accepted by the individual). The first stage (setting objectives), the second stage (measuring performance) and the fourth stage (process outputs, in particular, reward) relate to goal-setting theory.

The acceptance by the individual of assigned goals suggests that mere imposition of goals by managers is unlikely to lead to goal acceptance, goal pursuit and, therefore, organisational change in line with strategic objectives. There may be two reasons why managers impose rather than negotiate objectives. The first relates to what Marsden and Richardson (1992) call 'information asymmetry'. This occurs when managers control all the information relevant to performance management. They set objectives, define performance measures, conduct appraisals and decide rewards. It is easy to see why some managers may prefer to do this: it enables them to retain the power which they derive from their managerial status and it makes them less accountable for their actions. We explain below how performance management has the capacity to change the organisation by making managers more accountable to their employees. This happens at Siemens Standard Drives where dialogue is encouraged to foster the 'open and honest' values the organisation is seeking to create. The second reason why managers may impose rather than negotiate objectives is structural. In many large organisations, such as the building society where Phil studied performance management, the objective-setting process is a mini-industry (Lewis, 1998). Goals are 'handed down' to over 700 branch managers through their area managers. In reality there is little scope to amend the content of these goals which relate to the *outputs* (e.g. mortgage sales) the manager is expected to achieve. However, there is scope for area managers to negotiate *process* goals, on the way in which the branch managers perform their duties (e.g. leadership style of branch staff).

The provision of feedback to show progress in relation to the goal is the third stage of the performance management cycle. This is a powerful indicator of performance management effectiveness. Some organisations have weekly, monthly or quarterly progress meetings and reviews. This is a very demanding and time consuming process for managers. This element of the performance management cycle needs managers who are not only prepared to spend the time, but who are committed to the style of management which is consistent with emphasis upon giving feedback. Their concern is for management *processes,* rather than outputs being their sole concern. This 'new style' managerialism is characterised less by concern for the technical side of individuals' jobs than by talking to them about what they do to ensure everything is right for them to do their jobs. The 'new style' manager is supportive, a team leader, a coach and facilitator. This is precisely the vision senior managers have for group leaders at Siemens Standard Drives, confirming the impressions of Storey (1992) in his research at fifteen mainstream UK organisations.

Giving rewards such as money for goal attainment raises the contentious question of individual performance-related pay which we cover in some detail below. Suffice it to say at this stage that for many employees the achievement of goals is a reward in itself, providing that other preconditions of goal-setting theory have been met.

Involving employees in decision making

This is a significant way in which performance management may potentially contribute to organisational change. You will remember that we indicated above that employee commitment is one of the *goals* of HRM. Employee involvement is one of the most significant *processes* whereby this goal may be realised. Among the strongest advocates of this philosophy is Walton (1985). Walton argued that employees are more likely to respond to and feel involved in situations where they are provided with an opportunity to undertake work that offers enrichment, broader responsibility in relation to typical approaches to job design, and satisfaction. From this, an increased contribution may result. While this apparently ideal scenario is questionable in relation to its suggested causal linkages and actual practice, performance management may be seen to offer the opportunity for involvement and an encouragement to contribute.

This opportunity for employee involvement in the performance management system comes before the cycle begins. ACAS (1996), although referring specifically to appraisal-related pay, stress the importance of involving employees in the design of schemes from the outset. ACAS recommend, in particular, that there should be employee involvement in decisions on such issues as the coverage of the scheme, how it will operate, and the resources and training to be provided. It seems reasonable to assume that if employees have had a say in the design of the scheme they are more likely to accept its legitimacy than if the scheme is imposed upon them. Involving employees at the scheme design stage is also a tangible recognition by managers that they do not possess the monopoly on good ideas. This may be a significant indication to employees of the willingness of managers to be open in their operation of performance management.

One of the most powerful ways in which individuals may become involved in the performance management process is through self-appraisal. This may play an influential role in the performance management cycle in that it involves employees in assessing their own performance against set goals and planning ways in which performance may be developed. This will often lead to a re-formulation of goals, thus linking back to the first stage of the performance management cycle. Not the least reason for the power of self-appraisal as an employee involvement technique is the tendency for individuals to be more critical of themselves than their managers would be, as McKenna and Beech (1995) note in an example of Michelin workers. This gives managers the opportunity to give positive feedback to the employees, thus building their confidence.

Self-check question	5.3	*Individual employees are likely to be more critical of themselves than their managers would be. Why do you think this is the case?*

Advocates of self-appraisal argue that its real value is the promise it holds for positive action to follow as a consequence of the performance appraisal process. Where appraisal is by the line manager only, there is a danger of mere lip-service being paid by the employee. The argument is that self-diagnosis will result in ownership of solutions which will lead to action, and genuine organisational change. This resonates with the bottom-up view of organisational change propounded by Beer *et al.* (1990). Their view is that real change comes about at the grass roots of the organisation, at the level of the work people do, not on major change programmes pushed down the organisation from the chief executive.

Increasingly, individual employees are becoming involved in the appraisal of their managers, so-called 'upward appraisal'. This is part of the opening out of the assessment process to what has become known as '360-degree appraisal'. In this approach, feedback of performance of the individual being appraised may be taken from a variety of sources, for example: other managers with whom the individual comes into contact; customers and colleagues. Offering employees the opportunity to comment on the way in which they are being managed is a powerful symbol of genuine employee involvement through performance management. Upward appraisal may, of course, be approached by employees as a chance to pay off old scores. Alternatively it may be a case of pseudo-involvement by managers who seemingly note employees' comments but take no action as a consequence of those comments. But if it is treated as a genuine development opportunity the initial discomfort felt by appraisers and those managers being appraised may well result in a significantly different way in which organisations manage their people.

Assisting restructuring through the devolvement of decision making

In their model of strategic HRM, Mabey and Salaman (1995) hypothesise that structural, cultural and personnel strategies, when aligned with each other and with the overall business strategy of the organisation, should result in employee behaviours consistent with the demands of the business strategy. Some writers are critical of this model. It is accused of being overly rational in its assumptions about the way in which strategy is determined (Legge, 1995). This rationality excludes the 'emergent' (Mintzberg and Waters, 1989) model of strategy determination. It assumes that strategy is 'top-down' without the possibility of human resource strengths shaping strategy. According to this rationalist view, 'HRM is cast purely in a reactive, implementationist role' (Boxall, 1992: 68).

An equally fundamental criticism is the highly deterministic role of strategic HRM which assumes that the integration of strategic HRM policies and practices will have a beneficial effect upon the performance of the organisation. This is a considerable assumption, not the least because of the difficulty of subjecting the assumption to empirical test due to its complex, all-embracing nature (Noon, 1992). These deterministic assumptions of SHRM mask the complexities of organisational life. To think that simply aligning policies and practices will yield 'success' ignores the host of variables which may conspire to render such an outcome unlikely, one of which may be the resistance of employees who have not 'signed on to' the organisation's mission. In short, SHRM's deterministic perspective is based on assumptions of rationality and unitarism which disregard the political realities of organisational life (Keenoy, 1990).

Strategic HRM has become an important way of thinking about the employment relationship. These criticisms of a strategic HRM, of which structure is a significant element, seem to us to be perfectly valid. But it cannot be denied that many organisations have seen restructuring as an important plank in their organisational change strategies (*see* Chapter 2). One of the key elements of this has been the decentralisation of their organisational structures in that responsibility for decision making has been pushed down the organisational hierarchy to the level where the job is undertaken. The creation of teamworking at Siemens Standard Drives is a typical example.

You may see such restructuring as sound common sense; after all, who better to make decisions about the way work is undertaken than those who do the work? On the other hand, you may see it as an inevitable outcome of the enormous amount of de-layering which has taken place in recent years with the resultant decline in the number of middle managers in organisations. This seems to be a good example of 'soft' versus 'hard' HRM (Legge, 1995). Is giving people development opportunities the main driver, or is it simply cost reduction? Maybe the answer in many organisations is an element of both, with the 'soft' explanation providing a convenient rationale for the 'hard'.

But what role does performance management play in assisting the devolvement of decision making through restructuring? To answer this it is necessary to focus our thoughts on the fundamental building-block of organisational structure which many organisations have introduced: the strategic business unit. The IPM report (Institute of Personnel Management, 1992) argues that performance management allows a better understanding of the contribution of the business unit to overall organisational performance.

This better understanding is achieved in two ways. First, it means that individuals and teams are likely to be much more responsible for their performance if they can see precisely what it is they are supposed to achieve, particularly if they have had a hand in setting the objectives. The second way is that performance management, through its close relationship between unit goals and organisational goals, is potentially a powerful way of ensuring the optimum use of resources. A good example of this is the Siemens Standard Drives annualised hours system which seeks to make optimum use of the most costly of their resources: labour. Teams are set targets for labour utilisation which implies the necessity for more hours to be worked when product demand is greater and less hours worked when demand is less intense. This has at least two outcomes which have important effects on organisational change. First, it means that employees, and in the case of Siemens Standard Drives, their trade unions, need to be more flexible in their thinking about the nature of their relationship with their employer. The needs of the customer dictate the demands for work, not the needs of the employee. This is a good example of the customer-driven thinking which managers would like to think is now prevalent in most organisations. The second outcome is, as far as senior managers are concerned, the most significant: costs are controlled, rendering the organisation more competitive in the product market.

Self-check question	5.4	*It has been argued that performance management may allow a better understanding of the contribution of the business unit to overall organisational performance. What assumptions underpin the two ways in which this may be achieved ?*

Making managers manage

Closely allied to the role of performance management in contributing to organisational change through assisting the devolvement of decision making through restructuring is the role of line managers in conducting the performance management process. There are two aspects of this which we discuss below: first, the importance of line managers in delivering what has become known as 'human resource management' of which performance management is a key part; second, the accountability for their actions which performance management imposes upon line managers.

In the UK there has been a tendency for managers to be technicians who do not always appreciate the importance of 'people policies'. This is because many of them see their own technical specialism as their priority. Consequently, managers often experience difficulty with many of the complex interpersonal skills which are necessary in performance management. Storey (1992: 35) talks of the line manager's role in human resource management becoming one of 'transformational leadership', seizing the initiative for managing people from the personnel specialist. The leadership style is one of facilitation rather than autocracy. The skills of facilitation are particularly necessary in the first and third stages of the performance management cycle: the setting of objectives and the provision of feedback to the individual.

Storey and Sisson (1993) suggest that short-term concerns govern the thinking and behaviour of many British managers. They argue that this gives rise to 'quick-fix agreements, firefighting solutions; and Tayloristic job design methods which are built on command and control rather than the more time-consuming consensus-seeking methods' (Storey and Sisson, 1993: 76). If the 'softer' elements of the performance management cycle are to be promoted then line managers need a longer-term investment perspective on their management of employees which will lead to the involvement of individuals in the cycle rather than exclusion from it.

It has been noted earlier in this chapter that performance management imposes upon line managers accountability for their actions. Storey and Sisson (1993) point out that the role of managers and supervisors is critical to the implementation of performance management. It is they who must define the required standards of performance and behaviour, explain these to their subordinates, take tough decisions about assessments, communicate these decisions to subordinates, and defend their judgements if asked.

The desire of organisations to thrust more accountability for performance on managers flows from the perception that this is something that managers tend not to do well. This is accounted for by Kanter (1987) in terms of the desire not to make, announce and defend difficult and uncomfortable decisions. The consequence of this is statistical distributions of individual performance-related pay which concentrate on the middle ranking, thus defeating the object of paying for differentiated performance, and managers who 'hide' behind their decisions, claiming that they fought on behalf of their employees and lost, or that their hands are tied by the budget or the policies of the personnel department (Lawler, 1990).

Kessler and Purcell (1992: 22) too found evidence of the desire to 'make managers manage'. As they note, individual performance-related pay 'is often seen as a means of forcing a manager into a direct one-to-one, usually face to face relationship with their employees'. They also noted in their research how the pressure on managers came additionally from employees who, as one of their interviewee managers noted, 'are interested in money, and they're going to be badgering you to do it'.

Linking employee rewards to individual performance

Performance-related pay is the aspect of performance management which has received most attention in recent years. Much of the literature on performance-related pay (e.g. Marsden and Richardson, 1992) has been critical. It has dwelt on its dysfunctional aspects, for example, its lack of success in motivating employees due in part to its perceived lack of fairness. However, it is our contention that in spite of performance-related pay's operational shortcomings it does have the facility to generate organisational change. This is principally due to its power to communicate the message to employees that the organisation's culture is changing from one which is 'business as usual' to one in which the need to perform at a higher level than hitherto is necessary. In other words, the message is generally that the organisation is getting 'tougher'.

Organisational culture is dealt with in detail in Chapter 3. Here we will remind you only of sufficient detail in order that you may understand the importance of culture to performance-related pay. The most useful working definition of organisational culture to adopt for the purpose of demonstrating the culture change potential of performance-related pay is that of Schein (1992). Schein talks of organisational culture as operating at three levels. Level one is symbols (although he refers to these, rather more narrowly, as visible artefacts or creations). These symbols may be the chief executive's reserved parking space, or, at the other extreme, the existence of a single-status canteen in which all grades of employee eat. Both communicate a message about the culture of the organisation, or what senior managers would like to think of as the culture of the organisation.

Schein argues that symbols enable little more than a superficial description of, say, behaviour. In order to understand why this behaviour occurs one must look for espoused values that govern behaviour. This is Schein's second level. To establish the espoused values it is necessary to note what people say is the reason for their behaviour. Values may typically be found in mission statements or the sort of 'good news stories' which managers would like to think underpin the actions of people in organisations. But Schein argues that a third level is really necessary to understand a culture and comprehend more completely values and behaviour. This involves uncovering the underlying assumptions of which group members are often unaware but which usually influence strongly how they perceive, think and feel about issues. We think that performance management and, in particular, performance-related pay, is a visible artefact – a symbol, which is being created by management in order to challenge the pattern of basic assumptions which may exist in the organisation, thus changing the organisation's culture. This will lead to employees perceiving, thinking and feeling about the employment relationship in a particular way – the way that management feel is consistent with the long-term goals of the organisation. Symbols proliferate in performance-related pay systems. They convey clear impressions about the changed role of the system itself, the employee, the manager and the organisation. Table 5.1. summarises the symbols enshrined in performance-related pay: the values to be created and underlying assumptions challenged by the use of these symbols.

The potential of performance-related pay to change organisational culture is, of course, linked to the way in which it is implemented. Two of the major implementation problems have been employees' inevitable perceptions of unfairness and the typically low amounts of money devoted to schemes in recent years. Your own experience of individual incentive payments may have convinced you that it is not possible to please 'all the people all of the time'. Certainly, the research evidence illustrates that many schemes have encountered significant problems in this respect. It may be, however, that this does little to dilute the cultural message that 'the world is changing'. For example, the employee may

Table 5.1 The symbols enshrined in performance-related pay; the values to be created and underlying assumptions challenged by the use of these symbols

Symbol	Value to be created	Underlying assumptions to be challenged
Changed basis of pay from 'rate for the job' or length of service to individual performance	Necessity for employees to be 'achievers' Greater sense of fairness by paying high performers at a higher rate than lower performers	The organisation values loyalty Experience deserves higher pay because it will lead to better job performance Organisation will pay the same to all, regardless of performance
Clear goals set for performance consistent with business goals	Employees to be goal-directed and key part of the organisation	Employees are isolated from the organisation – only managers are concerned with corporate goals
Managers who monitor employee performance	Managers must 'manage' Managers and subordinates must be more performance conscious	Managers are technical experts first and people managers second
Pay as an individual aspect of the employment relationship	Self-reliance in employees – not all employees are the same	Collective bodies are responsible for determining pay: it is the responsibility of someone else
Pay increases have to be justified by individual and organisational performance	Greater awareness of labour costs in employees and managers	The organisation can always afford increases in pay

perceive the organisation to be unduly harsh in imposing a performance-related pay scheme which threatens the long-cherished advantage of annual increments based on length of service. But the cultural message is unambiguous.

The case of low amounts of money in the 'pot' to distribute through the performance-related pay scheme is a different issue. Cascio (1989) and Lawler (1990) suggest that anything less than 10 per cent of salary is too little to be of consequence to employees. Low inflation has meant that the pot has often equated to approximately 3 per cent in the mid 1990s. This means that organisations have not been able to pay 10 per cent to even the outstanding performer. The majority of employees, in the middle of the normal distribution, will receive the going rate, approximately 3 per cent, causing them to say 'why bother?' In such circumstances performance-related pay is not perceived as performance-related, with the result that the cultural message becomes much less powerful.

There are other ways in which linking employee rewards to individual performance may contribute to organisational change. However, these are given detailed treatment in Chapter 7 on reward management. At this stage we will just mention the possible advantage of the creation of a more effective workforce. This is based on the assumption that higher payments accruing to more effective employees will have the effect of retaining these individuals. Conversely, the less effective employees will see their pay level falling in real terms and will decide to leave. There has been no research to test this proposition, perhaps because the introduction of performance-related pay on a wide scale coincided with a tight labour market for employees and consequent fears of job insecurity. In addition, the less effective employee is likely to be the least marketable and will decide to stay in spite of falling pay.

Before leaving the topic of pay linked to individual performance it is worth mentioning a situation where it threatens the prospect of organisational change. West *et al.* (1994) argue that individual performance-related pay may make employees more reluctant to innovate and take risks because they will be more concerned with narrow, short-run issues which are in their set of individual performance objectives. Nobody wants to threaten their pay award. This suggests the necessity to include innovation in the performance management measurement criteria.

Reducing trade union influence

Performance management, and performance-related pay in particular, strikes at the well-established union principle of 'the same rate for all': a move away from collectivist to individualist principles. Heery (1992: 3–4) argues, with support from local government case study examples, that some employers have clear anti-union motives for wishing to introduce performance-related pay. He cites examples of organisations which have used performance-related pay as the occasion to de-recognise trade unions, although he points out that this is by no means an inevitable consequence of its introduction. A more likely motive is the weakening of collective bargaining. This can affect bargaining structure in two ways: by reducing its *scope* and *depth*.

The typical situation in which bargaining scope is reduced is where the size of the performance-related pay 'pot' is negotiated collectively but the allocation to individual employees is at the discretion of line managers. This is favourable to the circumstances in which, Heery (1992: 4) argues, bargaining depth is reduced: i.e. where the union is involved in consultation over the type of performance-related pay scheme but has limited influence over the outcomes.

A second negative outcome of performance-related pay for trade unions is that it is likely to reduce the perceived need of members for collective representation (Heery, 1992). This is for four reasons. First, the instrumental value of union membership may decline as the role of collective bargaining diminishes. Second, the individual nature of performance-related pay may lead to a weakening of the collective ethos of trade unionism. Third, members may perceive performance-related pay as indicating reduced management support for unions and so may indirectly discourage membership. Fourth, if schemes meet employee aspirations for recognition and reward, the amount of grievances will reduce thus reducing the need for union representation.

Heery's (1992) conjecturing for trade unions is not all gloom. He envisages the possibility of performance-related pay actually *increasing* the perceived need by employees for unions. This may be a consequence of feelings of inequity and bias in the application of schemes and increased management control associated with closer monitoring of performance.

The empirical evidence of management attempting to lessen trade union influence is inconclusive. Kessler and Purcell (1992: 21–2; also Kessler, 1994) point out that in at least three organisations in which they did research, management was 'consciously attempting to weaken trade union power through performance-related pay'. This was vividly illustrated in a quotation from a personnel director who, in stressing the quest for individualising the employment relationship in the organisation, in which performance-related pay was to play its part, said this process 'began with cutting the power of trade unions, in the traditional collective bargaining sense, off at the knees' (Kessler and Purcell, 1992: 22). Storey, in his study of HRM in fifteen organisations, confirmed that personnel specialists were concerned 'to break at least partially away from collective pay arrangements and to introduce some variations based on individual performance' (1992: 108).

Not all the evidence points to employers wishing to reduce trade union influence through the introduction of performance management and performance-related pay. A local government quantitative survey (Local Authorities' Conditions of Service Advisory Board, 1990) found little evidence of the desire of employers to lessen trade union influence. Virtually no respondents indicated that they had introduced performance-related pay to 'individualise employment relations'. However, connecting personnel policies to the introduction of performance-related pay revealed some indication of a desire to reform employee relations. The report notes that 'in a number of cases [performance-related pay was] associated with a switch from national to local collective bargaining' (LACSAB, 1990: 26). In addition 55 per cent of respondents said that introducing PRP was related to the wish for better employee communications and 41 per cent indicated that it was linked to better employee involvement in management decision making through quality circles or similar initiatives.

Other studies by Cannell and Wood (1992) and Thompson (1992) record little support for performance-related pay as an anti-union measure. Although Cannell and Wood note that several of their respondents had introduced performance-related pay in order to emphasise greater individual responsibility only two had made it the central part of their employee relations policy.

Developing employees in line with organisational goals

Traditionally, one of the key purposes of performance appraisal has been the recognition of the individual's training needs and a recognition of the potential the individual possesses for career advancement. The very term 'performance management' suggests that such functions are downgraded in the current trend towards a rather 'harder' approach to managing performance. To some extent this is confirmed in the Institute of Personnel Management (1992) research, where it is noted that reward outcomes of performance management tended to dominate development outcomes. Even so, nearly three-quarters of responding organisations used performance management to identify the training needs of individuals in their current jobs and over half did so to recognise needs for future development. In addition, nearly four out of ten organisations used performance management to recognise individual potential, and 21 per cent used the scheme for recommending employees for promotion. This evidence suggests that training and development is still seen as a valuable element of performance management in spite of the conventional wisdom that including pay and training in the same appraisal process is not good practice. It is clear that training and development has enormous potential for contributing to organisational change, as explained in Chapter 6. An effective system for identifying training and development needs is clearly important. This is the role which performance management plays.

Self-check question	5.5	*Conventional wisdom suggests that including pay and training in the same appraisal process is not good practice. Why do you think this is?*

SUMMARY

■ Performance management may be represented by a cycle of activities which comprises four stages: setting objectives; measuring performance; feeding back performance results; and deciding appropriate outputs.

■ Performance management can assist in organisational change by communicating the organisation's mission.

■ Linking the organisation's objectives to individual performance objectives can also contribute to organisational change.

■ Involving employees in performance management is a powerful way of changing organisations, particularly through the medium of self-appraisal.

■ In decentralised organisational structures performance management can assist organisational change through making business units more responsible for their performance.

■ Performance management renders managers more accountable for their actions.

■ Performance management has significant capacity to change organisational culture.

■ The influence of trade unions may be lessened by performance management.

CASE STUDY 5.2

Performance management at Premierco

Premierco sells life insurance, unit trusts, pensions and mortgages. It was founded in the early 1970s and grew rapidly with high profits throughout the 1970s and 1980s. It has over 4000 employees. Premierco is part of a major industrial group and one of the largest retail financial services organisations in the UK.

The culture of Premierco is dominated by meritocracy. It is a fact of life at Premierco that people expect and receive recognition for success. As one employee put it, 'here at Premierco there is a constant atmosphere of how to win, how to be successful … you have to be quite tough to survive here – they put a lot of pressure on you'.

Premierco employees are young and 'positive'. One employee said of the atmosphere at Premierco that 'you sort of get dragged along by the infectious nature of it'. Other managers talked of the 'buzz of enthusiasm around the place' and the way in which new ideas are taken up by Premierco managers with great enthusiasm.

Premierco pays high salary levels relative to other employers in the locality in which it is situated. This aspect of employment is prized by employees, many of whom bought their houses at a time when prices were high. The housing price slump of the early 1990s, together with small pay increases, has meant that generally employees are money-conscious, irrespective of their psychological predispositions.

In view of the meritocratic nature of Premierco and the competitive values of its employees it is predictable that the company has a very clear view of the type of employee it wishes to recruit. Premierco values 'performance-conscious' employees. Managers use such adjectives as adaptable, young, meritocratic, motivated, ambitious, driving – people who will 'fit in' with Premierco's way of doing things.

The company issues to all employees a document called the *Premierco Approach*. The document emphasises the role of hard work in Premierco but gives equal significance to the intention to reward hard work in a generous manner. There is similar stress placed upon the importance of respect for the individual, who is to be treated in a manner 'exactly as we would like to be treated ourselves'. At Premierco there is no collective employee representation, either by trade union or staff association.

Consistent with the meritocratic nature of Premierco is a lack of tolerance for poor performance. Premierco managers are under no illusion about the necessity to ensure that performance is engendered by more than rhetoric. The key to this is a performance management system. The principal reasons performance management was introduced were: the desire to improve the performance of all employees; getting more 'behaviour for our bucks'; saving pay bill money; and distinguishing between the good and not so good performers.

The desire to improve the performance of all employees is consistent with the company's strategic objectives. While there was no strong impression that employees were underachieving in Premierco, the desire was for employees to achieve even more. This is best illustrated by the clear instruction in the guidelines for performance pay that payments should only be given to those who have demonstrated *improved* performance.

This case study concerns only the performance management system for junior and middle managers. The key determinant of improved management performance is the process of setting objectives and monitoring performance against those objectives. A typical contract will specify, on four pages, 24 objectives, in as measurable a form as possible, against which the manager will be reviewed. This gives the manager explicit standards which reflect the need for improved performance. In addition, Premierco managers have a high achievement orientation. Set them a target and they will strive to achieve it. This suggests that the role of pay in performance management is important in giving direction to managers.

Getting more 'behaviour for our bucks' is important at Premierco who have a policy of maintaining a minimum level of full-time staff: coping with the extra demand for staff through temporary appointments and imposing longer hours on extant full-time staff. This makes Premierco a very demanding employer. The company pays well but it expects a lot in return. Adding pay to the performance management process emphasises the relationship between employee effort and pay.

Saving pay bill money is achieved through breaking the expectation of an automatic annual increase. This means that pay increases are only given to those managers who have demonstrated improved performance in the past year and who are not at or near the top of the pay scale for their grade. That way, the pay bill is used to nurture only those employees who are deemed to be worthy of it.

There is a strong strand of fairness in the quest to distinguish between the good and not so good performer. The logic is 'why should the other guy who works less hard than me get the same increase?' This is always prevalent as a response to the question posed about the reasons for the introduction of performance pay. But in Premierco managers were sure that their colleague managers were giving 100 per cent.

There are often weekly, monthly or quarterly progress meetings and reviews. There is also the annual appraisal at which all employees complete a self-appraisal. This is shared with the reviewing manager who has done the same. The object is to reach a consensus. The output of the process is the setting of future objectives and planning training and development needs. The future objectives for managers are written into a performance contract which typically will have over 30 result areas grouped into six categories.

Performance measures for managers are precise and demanding. Managers may be measured on: keeping within budget; meeting service quality standards; meeting financial controls; relationships with other departments and relationships with staff. This latter criterion is measured by means of a questionnaire completed by staff on the performance of their manager as a people manager.

▶

Many managers think of the major benefit of the system as there being 'no surprises' at the end of the year when the final performance rating was announced. This is because of the considerable amount of time devoted to giving performance feedback to the recipient managers by the managers implementing the system. This is typical of the way Premierco managers manage. They are characterised by attention to management processes, not outputs. The management of people is seen by all Premierco managers as vitally important. Perhaps the best summary of this 'new style' managerialism at Premierco came from an operations manager who had obviously given the matter a great deal of thought. She confessed she knew little about the technical side of the jobs her people did. She thought her job was to talk to them about what they did and make sure everything was right for them to do their jobs. She summarised her management philosophy thus; 'if you treat them correctly you'll get that back twenty times over from them. They will want to do it for you.'

There are two features of performance management at Premierco which are typical of performance-related pay schemes. First, employees do not know what the reward for a particular rating will be prior to its award. This situation is brought about, partly, by the system which operates whereby awards are linked not only to performance but also to position on pay scale. Therefore a manager who is high on the scale receives less for the same level of pay. It is also due to the fact that the pay award is not declared until the latter part of the review year. The second feature is that in recent years the size of pay awards has been small. This has been particularly marked at Premierco because increases in the 1980s were generous: 10 to 12 per cent had not been unusual. But in recent years the average award has been approximately a quarter of that.

However, if the success of performance management can be estimated by the extent to which it is accepted by its recipients then it was certainly successful at Premierco. The reaction of recipient managers interviewed was overwhelmingly positive. They saw performance management as conducted fairly by managers who believed in the scheme. Moreover, they perceived its congruence with the meritocratic values which the company had traditionally preached and they had absorbed.

Case study questions

1 To what extent do you think that performance management may be equally appropriate for a less demanding employer than Premierco?

2 How relevant do you think the level of employee acceptance of performance management is an indicator of its success?

3 What other indicators of success could be used?

4 To what would you attribute the seeming success of performance management at Premierco?

5 What long-term problems do you think Premierco may face in maintaining the seeming success of performance management?

REFERENCES

ACAS (1996) *Appraisal Related Pay,* London: ACAS.

Beer, M., Spector, B., Lawrence, P.R., Quinn Mills, D. and Walton, R.E. (1984) *Managing Human Assets*, New York: Free Press.

Beer, M., Eisenstat, R. and Spector, B. (1990) 'Why change programs don't produce change', *Harvard Business Review*, November/December 158–66.

Boxall, P. (1992) 'Strategic human resource management: beginnings of a new theoretical sophistication?', *Human Resource Management Journal*, 2(3), 60–78.

Burnes, B. (1996) *Managing Change: A Strategic Approach to Organisational Dynamics*, 2nd edn, London: Pitman.

Cannell, M. and Wood, S. (1992) *Incentive Pay: Impact and Evolution,* London: Institute of Personnel Management and National Economic Development Office.

Cascio, W. (1989) *Managing Human Resources*, 2nd edn, New York: McGraw-Hill.

Clark, G. (1995) 'Performance management', in Mabey, C. and Salaman, G. (eds), *Strategic Human Resource Management*, Oxford: Blackwell.

Fombrun, C., Tichy, N. and Devanna, M. (1984) *Strategic Human Resource Management*, New York: John Wiley.

Guest, D. (1987) 'Human resource management and industrial relations', *Journal of Management Studies*, 24(5), 503–21.

Heery, E. (1992) 'Divided we fall? Trade unions and performance-related pay', paper for LSE/TUC Trade Union Seminar, 19 March.

Institute of Personnel Management (1992) *Performance Management in the UK*, London: Institute of Personnel Management.

Kanter, R.M. (1987) 'From status to contribution: some organisational implications of the changing basis for pay', *Personnel*, January, 12–37.

Keenoy, T. (1990) 'Human resource management: rhetoric, reality and contradiction', *International Journal of Human Resource Management,* 1(3), 363–84.

Kessler, I. (1994) 'Performance related pay: contrasting approaches', *Industrial Relations Journal*, 25(2), 122–35.

Kessler, I. and Purcell, J. (1992) 'Performance related pay: objectives and application', *Human Resource Management Journal,* 2(3), 16–33.

Lawler, E.E. (1990) *Strategic Pay: Aligning Organisational Strategies and Pay Systems*, San Francisco, Calif.: Jossey-Bass.

Legge, K. (1995). *Human Resource Management: Rhetorics and Realities*, Basingstoke: Macmillan.

Lewis, P. (1998) 'Managing performance-related pay based on evidence from the financial services sector', *Human Resource Management Journal*, 8(2), 66–77.

Local Authorities' Conditions of Service Advisory Board (LACSAB) (1990) *Performance Related Pay in Practice: A Survey of Local Government in 1990*, London: LACSAB.

Locke, E., Saari, L., Shaw, K. and Latham, G. (1981) 'Goal setting and task performance: 1969–1980', *Psychological Bulletin*, 90(1), 125–52.

Mabey, C. and Salaman, G. (1995) *Strategic Human Resource Management*, Oxford: Blackwell.

McKenna, E. and Beech, N. (1995) *The Essence of Human Resource Management*, Hemel Hempstead: Prentice Hall.

Marsden, D. and Richardson, R. (1992) *Motivation and Performance Related Pay in the Public Sector: A Case Study of the Inland Revenue*, Discussion Paper No. 75, Centre for Economic Performance, London School of Economics.

Meyer, H.H. (1975) 'The pay for performance dilemma', *Organisational Dynamics*, Winter, 39–50.

Mintzberg, H. and Waters, J. (1989) 'Of strategies deliberate and emergent', in Asch, D. and Bowman, C. (eds), *Readings in Strategic Management*, Basingstoke: Macmillan.

Noon, M. (1992) 'HRM: a map, model or theory?', in Blyton, P. and Turnbull, P. (eds), *Reassessing Human Resource Management*, London: Sage.

Schein, E. (1992) 'Coming to a new awareness of organisational culture', in Salaman, G. (ed.), *Human Resource Strategies*, London: Sage.

Storey, J. (1992) *Developments in the Management of Human Resources*, Oxford: Blackwell.

Storey, J. and Sisson, K. (1993) *Managing Human Resources and Industrial Relations*, Buckingham: Open University Press.

Thompson, M. (1992), *Pay and Performance: The Employer Experience*, Brighton: Institute of Manpower Studies.

Walton, R. (1985) 'From control to commitment in the workplace', *Harvard Business Review*, March–April, 77–84.

Wastell, D., White, P. and Kawalek, P. (1994) 'A methodology for business process redesign: experiance and issues', *Journal of Strategic Information Systems*, 3(1), 23–40.

West, M., Fletcher, C. and Toplis, J. (1994) *Fostering Innovation: A Psychological Perspective*, London: British Psychological Society.

ANSWERS TO SELF-CHECK QUESTIONS

5.1 *Why do you think stage 3 of the performance management cycle shown in Fig. 5.1, feeding back results, is so important?*

The most obvious response is that if employees don't know how their manager thinks they are performing, they cannot be expected to adjust performance. But, as with most obvious answers, this is often overlooked by busy line managers. They may not subscribe to the 'if nobody tells me to the contrary then I must be doing OK' school of thought but they reinforce it through their lack of feedback-giving.

This is the occasion when managers and individual employees can sit down and take stock in a cool, analytical way without immediate problems dominating the thought processes of both. Look again at the performance management cycle in Fig. 5.1. The forward arrow to stage 4 suggests that the feeding back of results conditions individual employees for the rewards they may receive, or prepares them for the development opportunities they are going to pursue. Similarly, the backward pointing arrow indicates the possibility of the feeding back of results stage leading to adjustment of performance objectives and measurement criteria.

5.2 *What skills do you think line managers must use in order for stage 3 to be performed effectively?*

Many line managers think that to perform the feedback stage effectively it is necessary to be 'good with people'. We accept that it is helpful if managers enjoy this part of the job and we realise that many managers don't. After all, the skills needed here are not easy. But we would argue that the key skills can be learned. Among these is giving honest, clearly understood feedback based on observable examples of behaviour. Many managers believe in the 'feedback sandwich' which involves some criticism sandwiched between two outer layers of positive comments. Another key skill is the drawing out of self-evaluation of the individual employee. Self-criticism is likely to be owned by the employee to a far greater extent than criticism from the line manager.

5.3 *Individual employees are likely to be more critical of themselves than their managers would be. Why do you think this is the case?*

This may be a function of people not wishing to 'blow their own trumpet', a traditional British cultural norm. On the other hand the reasons may be rather more subtle. It could be a device to extract praise from their manager ('oh! I really think you do yourself an injustice'). Alternatively, it could be purely instrumental: if the employee downgrades her own performance, the manager is less likely to respond with higher performance targets than had the self-rating of performance been exaggerated.

Interestingly, there is some evidence that a difference may be evident when employees are asked to compare their job performance with that of peers. A study by Meyer (1975) found that when employees were asked to self-rate their performance in comparison with that of their peers they consistently rated themselves above average. In fact only 2 per cent of Meyer's sample rated themselves below average while 5 per cent rated themselves as average. The remaining 93 per cent rated themselves as above average with the average percentile at 77. Since the majority of employees are likely to have their performance rated as 'average' in any distribution of employees, the implications for demotivation are obvious.

5.4 *It has been argued that performance management may allow a better understanding of the contribution of the business unit to overall organisational performance. What assumptions underpin the two ways in which this may be achieved?*

The assumptions are those which are questioned by the critics in the earlier part of the section headed 'Assisting restructuring through the devolvement of decision making' (pp. 137–8). It is assumed that organisations are rational, unitary bodies. What we mean by this is that goals are set in a rational top-down manner, communicated throughout the organisation and understood by all employees who are keen to see their achievement. Our own knowledge of organisational life tells us that this is often far from the truth. Goals are often not clearly communicated and understood, even if they have been set in a rational way. What this may lead to is employees constructing their own interpretation of the content of these goals: an interpretation which may be at odds with the 'official' version. Therefore, the definition of goals may be messy and complex rather than clear and straightforward.

The reference to organisations being unitary bodies notes the assumption so often made by managers in particular that all organisational members wish to pursue the 'official' goals. This may not be the case. An alternative assumption is that organisations are political bodies consisting of interest groups which define and pursue their own agenda which may, at best, be a reconstructed version of the 'official' agenda or, at worst, reflect an effort deliberately to subvert the 'official' version. An obvious example is the overtime issue which traditionally has been an employee relations battleground in many organisations. Managers have a clear interest in containing overtime in order to maintain labour costs whereas employees may wish to 'manufacture' overtime in order to supplement their earnings.

5.5 *Conventional wisdom suggests that including pay and training in the same appraisal process is not good practice. Why do you think this is?*

The reasoning is that employees are more likely to be interested in issues related to their pay than in training. This may lead to employees concealing the self-diagnosed need for training and development because they feel it will prejudice the performance rating they are given, leading to a lesser performance-related payment. What suffers here is the vitally important role performance appraisal plays in identifying training needs.

The way many organisations have resolved this potential conflict is to have more than one appraisal interview annually with each separate interview concentrating on a different purpose.

Human resource development and the management of change

Learning objectives

Having completed this chapter, you will be able to:

■ Discuss how human resource development can be regarded as a vital dimension of HRM on the one hand and yet may attract low levels of organisational commitment to its practice on the other.

■ Explain the concept of 'strategic human resource development'.

■ Identify the role human resource development plays in contributing to organisational change.

■ Outline the human resource development role played by managers and how manager and management development is central to the effective management of change.

INTRODUCTION

Human resource development (HRD) has been identified as the vital component of human resource management (Keep, 1989). It could also be argued that HRD lies at the very heart of managing change through people because the consequence of any change process is that people will need to think and/or behave differently. This will apply whether the change is operational, for example adjustments to working practices or the introduction of new policies and procedures such as performance appraisal, or strategic, where change will be more dramatic and pervasive, as with a culture change programme. From these examples we can see that different behaviours will be required either at the level of individual employees, work groups or units or even, potentially, the whole workforce. Irrespective of the degree or scope of change some type of HRD process will be inevitable to move staff from where they are now to where the organisation wants them to be.

The central status that this rationale suggests for HRD is, however, not always reflected in practice. At the macro or national level investment in education and training has been criticised for being inadequate and misdirected with no coherent strategy (Ashton and Felstead, 1995; Kelleher, 1996). At the micro or organisational level HRD is too often regarded as a luxury which cannot be afforded when times are hard. It may be one of the first budgets to be cut during recession. This was graphically illustrated by the large-scale dismantling of apprenticeship training schemes during the 1980s, a factor which has contributed significantly to the skills shortage now being widely experienced. Company-based HRD activity has also been criticised for its over-reliance on structured training events with a concern that it is too rarely internalised as a key management activity.

In this chapter we hope to challenge the attitudes that underwrite current HRD practice by systematically examining how it can contribute to all levels of strategic change while at the same time arguing that the processes of manager and management development can help achieve greater commitment to HRD. It will become apparent that we have not been able to find space for all areas of topical HRD interest such as career planning and Investors in People. We have chosen to focus on those aspects of HRD that we feel are particularly relevant to managing change. However, towards the end of the chapter we have chosen to specifically explore one such topical area – the learning organisation – and go on to show how this approach to HRD can be integrated with management development and strategic change. Although we express doubts about the efficacy of the learning organisation concept we are attracted to its conceptual plausibility which plays down an over-reliance on structured off-the-job training events while emphasising the development opportunities offered through everyday experiences.

The two case studies in this chapter have been deliberately selected for their similarities. They both concern the contribution HRD can make to work restructuring that is being driven by strategic change. However, in the first, Xerox, change is introduced within an organisational context that is very conducive to HRD interventions. In the second, Dales, the opposite is true and the case is, therefore, as much to do with the relationship between HRD, culture and attitudes as it is with the knowledge and skills development necessary to underpin the introduction of teamworking.

Human resource development at Xerox

The Document Company, Xerox, at Mitcheldean is part of the Xerox Corporation. The site manufactures digital document office products. Approximately 2300 staff are employed on site of which 1800 are directly engaged on production work.

For a number of years Xerox has sought to gain competitive advantage through the relentless pursuit of customer satisfaction. Exceeding customer requirements in every part of the business is seen as the route to increased productivity, growth, investment and business stability. This strategic commitment has prompted the development of a management model (XMM). There are currently a series of supporting company-wide programmes, notably the 'Customer First' and 'Employee Satisfaction' initiatives.

For manufacturing, 'Business Units' meeting the ever-changing demands of customers involved an early commitment to teamworking which is evolving over time into the development of 'X Teams' (Fig. 6.1). Under 'Team Xerox' traditional flow line systems were reconfigured into manufacturing teams in the early 1980s. Subsequently, higher productivity demands led to their development into 'Self-Managed Work Groups' (SMWG) at the beginning of the 1990s. However,

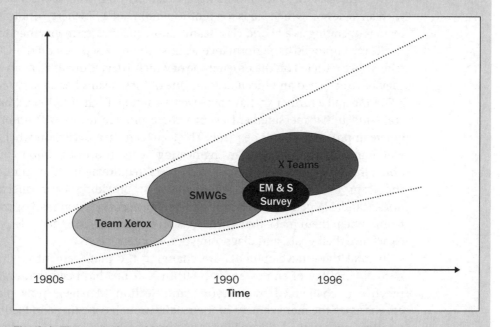

Fig. 6.1 The evolution of X Teams at Xerox

Source: Xerox Ltd (Manufacturing), Mitcheldean, Gloucestershire.

▶

employees signalled through the regular 'Employee Motivation and Satisfaction Survey' (EMSS) that greater emphasis on effective team performance as an important part of continuous improvement was desirable. This led in the mid 1990s to the 'X Team' initiative where the focus was on empowerment, leading to high performance.

While manufacturing continues to be organised around teams, grouped into Business Units, this evolutionary process has transformed roles and responsibilities. Previously Section Managers heading the teams were responsible for the traditional diet of managerial responsibilities – daily communication, disciplinary issues, identifying development needs, allocation of work etc. The underlying concept of teamworking was to move decision making progressively to the point at which decisions are likely to have the most impact, i.e. those who do the job. 'X Teams' are essentially a process that enables production teams to take far more responsibility for the day-to-day running of their work area; ownership of their performance and results; and setting targets, monitoring and formulating actions for improvement.

Progression to an X Team is voluntary. An existing team seeking this designation must first find a sponsor. This is usually their line manager or her/his manager. The team itself can be any identifiable group of employees with a common purpose/output and may include their direct line manager. The process starts with teams conducting a self-assessment exercise against four sets of criteria: customer assurance; process management; team motivation and satisfaction; and empowerment. Once the assessment has been agreed by the 'sponsor' it is validated with an 'assessor' which leads to an official rating of 1–7 where 7 indicates that the team is operating as a 'world class team'. Subsequent assessments then take place as the team improves its performance against the four sets of criteria. Currently 36 teams have enrolled on the programme of which 10 have qualified as an X Team (i.e. they have achieved an official rating). One of these teams has already progressed to a 5 rating and a further six have achieved a 4 rating. Each criterion set has a 7-point scale and initial measurement against these provide teams with information on where improvements can be made. The team can then decide on what and how it will improve, e.g. through re-engineering work processes, improving skills or obtaining better understanding of customers' requirements. The sponsor supports the team by helping with self-assessments; providing clear direction, goals, understandable performance measures and agreed work boundaries; coaching the team to help them make their own decisions, effectively use the tools available and to achieve their goals; and diagnosing development needs.

In total these developments are changing the management environment. A natural corollary of empowerment within X Teams has been that organisational practice is challenged by everyone and Section Managers now place greater emphasis on the management of their staff through coaching and facilitating with less time personally dedicated to managing operational issues. However, although more teams are seeking X Team status the concept, its development and indeed designated X Teams are still in their infancy. Nevertheless they represent a long-term commitment that is integral to planned changes to the management style and culture of the organisation which, of course, will not happen overnight.

The evolution of teamworking, therefore, should not be seen in isolation. It consistently stresses the same key values of XMM, Customer First and Employee Satisfaction. It is regarded as a significant conduit for translating these into reality for shop floor teams and helping them drive actions which also support the direction of the company. In summary X Teams have been initiated to support Xerox's vision for the millennium, drive performance to world class standards and impact positively on profitability and employee and customer satisfaction.

The progressive movement to X Teams has inevitably impacted on the skills, knowledge and attitudes required of the workforce. From what has been said so far this is clearly evident amongst three groupings of employees: production operatives, Section Managers, and 'sponsors'. Changes to the structure of jobs have simultaneously involved the vertical integration of tasks, the exercise of interpersonal skills and movement to an empowered culture. This has involved, for example, a move from centralised to team-based material acquisition; the successful integration of new team members; and the translation of strategy into operational activities.

Underpinning Xerox's approach to managing its human resources is a framework of 23 'Leadership Attributes' and 9 'Cultural Dimensions' (*see* Table 6.1 for examples). These drive the HR processes of development, recruitment and selection, and performance review.

Table 6.1 Examples of Xerox's Leadership Attributes/Cultural Dimensions

Leadership attributes	Cultural dimensions
No. 5 Decision making ■ Takes decisions in a timely manner ■ Wherever possible manages by facts ■ Uses best sources of information available as a basis for decisions in uncertain situations ■ Assumes responsibility for the results of decisions made ■ Takes calculated risks to seize opportunities	**No. 7 Open and honest communication** ■ Sensitive to concerns and feelings off others ■ Does not treat disagreement as disloyalty ■ Encourages feedback, dialogue and information sharing ■ Fosters openness and trust through personal behaviour ■ Confronts conflict openly
No. 6 Quick study ■ Understands processes, technologies and issues quickly ■ Identifies cause/effect relationships ■ Generates original ideas ■ Reduces complex situations to the essential elements ■ Fully understands problems and recognises their implications for the business	**No. 8 Organisation reflection and learning** ■ Sees problems as learning opportunities ■ Role model in self-development ■ Encourages others to learn from successes and failures ■ Treates new ideas with respect ■ Encourages sharing of knowledge

▶

	Site Induction	Leadership Through Quality	Intro to Dept	Foundation Programme	Customer 1st	Failsafing	Process Knowledge	NVQ Level 1	Matrix Labels	Coloured Labels	Engraver	Zebra Printers	Windows PC	Embosser	Dot Matrix	Press	Addressograph	Card Press
Operator 1	✓	✓	✓	✓	1/98	✓	✓	4/98	4/98	4/98	3/98	✓	✓	✓	✓	✓	✓	✓
Operator 2	✓	✓	✓	✓	1/98	5/98	✓	4/98	✓	✓	✓	12/97	✓	✓	✓	✓	✓	12/97
Operator 3	✓	✓	✓	✓	1/98	5/98	✓	4/98	4/98	4/98	3/98	✓	✓	✓	✓	✓	✓	✓
Operator 4	✓	✓	✓	✓	1/98	5/98	✓	4/98	4/98	4/98	3/98	✓	✓	✓	✓	12/97	✓	✓

Fig. 6.2 Learning matrix for an X Team

Source: Xerox Ltd (Manufacturing), Mitcheldean, Gloucestershire.

From its inception the move towards teamworking has been supported by a series of training/development initiatives. To support 'Team Xerox', team building days were held, and supported by a series of formal training courses. The productivity-focused SMWGs and X Teams were underpinned by NVQs and multi-skilling which were mapped on a learning matrix (Fig. 6.2) for each team. The HRD activity within the organisation, however, is also clearly moving with the evolving needs of its customers. The launch of 'The Skills Partnership' in January 1998 is a measure of how the integration of HR functions is needed to support the modern learning organisation. This team is an amalgamation of the traditional functions of resourcing, training and development. The boundaries between these are blurred in this new service organisation. Their mission is to provide the services that help their business centre customer teams and individuals acquire the skills they need to be successful in world markets. They therefore engage any activities that support people, development and learning and look to the introduction of new skills from outside the organisation to provide continuous freshness in that learning. Driven by the Manager of Human Resourcing and Development the physical infrastructure has been transformed from a traditional office environment into one that resembles a high street shop. This sends out powerful signals about the modus operandi of the HR function. It represents an accessible service committed to meeting the needs of its internal clients. While previously the approach was not entirely prescriptive, the ethos now is very much based on consultation leading to many of the training needs being identified from the bottom up.

The development needs of X Team members are likely to be met through three different routes. First, there are company-wide initiatives such as customer service training and TQM that all employees undertake normally through off-the-job formal courses. Second, product training operates to ensure that new developments and progress through the multi-skilling matrices can be accommodated. This is likely to involve off-the-job courses but dependent on identified needs could be met in part or in full through on-the-job training. However, whereas the first two routes are mandatory the third is optional and is driven more by individual employees themselves. Here there is an increasing reliance on self-development and the use of direct day-to-day experiences as learning vehicles.

The third route focuses on self-development as a means to address identified needs. These may well be identified through the annual Performance Feedback and Development Review Process which is underpinned by the 'Leadership Attributes' and 'Cultural Dimensions' and uses a combination of self-assessment and manager feedback. Alternatively, the team itself, individually or collectively, including its sponsor, may drive the process. Table 6.1 provides a number of explicit examples that relate to employee development. In addition the onus is on all team members to recognise the importance of development to organisational success; serve as a role model for personal and professional growth; coach teams to achieve high performance and self-managing capability; and devote time to development needs. The identification of individual and team development needs can therefore be driven by the team itself and often arises directly from operational issues or the continuous improvement process.

Teams can also draw on the support of the Team Facilitator – a post specifically created to service X Teams – to discuss both development needs and how to meet them. Throughout the emphasis is on team members, the sponsor and 'Skills Partnership' working in concert to analyse gaps and identify appropriate development strategies. A good example here is that of X Team sponsors. A detailed support pack provides guidance on role responsibilities and self-assessment, and consultation with the Team Facilitator and their X Team members can be used to identify development needs. These may be met through a variety of methods including formal education, training courses, shadowing, special projects, mentoring etc. In this way the whole principal of empowerment underpinning X Teams also becomes an important dimension of the HRD process which in itself is an important vehicle for progressing towards the designation of a 'world class' team.

Human resource development: the vital component or poor relation of HR change strategies?

What is human resource development?

As is the case elsewhere in the HR literature there is some debate within the area of training about definitions and terminology. Throughout this chapter we have used the umbrella term human resource development – or HRD – partly because of its increasing usage and acceptance (Harrison, 1993b) and partly because of its consonance with the strategic thrust of managing change through people (Garavan *et al.*, 1995) which is one of the central features of this book.

We use HRD to refer to those processes directed towards equipping employees with the skills, knowledge and attitudes necessary to achieve corporate objectives both now and in the future. These processes can be targeted at or initiated by the individual employee, groups/units or the organisation and, therefore, embrace self-development as well as top-down interventions. This construction echoes Harrison's definition of HRD (1993b: 300) as

> the skilful provision and organisation of learning experience in the workplace in order that business goals can be achieved. It must be aligned with the organisation's mission and strategic goals in order that, through enhancing the skills, knowledge, learning ability and enthusiasm of people at every level, there will be continuous organisational as well as individual growth.

These perspectives of HRD are interpreted here as including the terms education, learning, training and development which when referred to in this chapter are seen as an integral part of the wider HRD framework.

HRD is strongly associated with internal resourcing strategies as described in Chapter 4. As a means of enhancing workforce skills it can be viewed as a direct alternative to recruiting from the external labour market (Keep, 1992). In reality the choice is not so stark, as both processes can be regarded as complementary and, as illustrated in Chapter 4, internal and external models are frequently used in tandem. This complementary nature of recruitment and HRD is well illustrated by the use of the former to select employees with a demonstrable capacity to learn and develop in a way commensurate with managing an imperfect future. This juxtaposition is well illustrated by Upton (1987, cited by Keep, 1992: 324) who stated 'a company is only as good as its personnel – so it's vital to choose and train the best'.

HRD – the vital component?

The above definitions of HRD, taken together with its alignment to recruitment and selection, point to its external integration with corporate strategy and internal integration with other HR policy levers (Mabey and Iles, 1993). These relationships have been well illustrated by Harrison (1993a: 40) in her 'wheel of HRM functions'. We have developed this in Fig. 6.3 to reflect the HR levers covered in this book and to build in the two-way strategic linkage that we believe is an essential dimension of external integration. For a fuller explanation of these strategic linkages we would refer you to Case Study 2.1 and pp. 98–103.

In an examination of company practice Harrison (1993c: 379) identifies HRD as 'the critical function in the human resources wheel'. This status is primarily afforded to HRD because it can be internally integrated with all other HR levers and mirrors closely arguments advanced by Keep (1992) that corporate training strategies represent the vital component of HRM. Harrison (1993b: 324–5) reasons that the 'development of people virtually absorbs all HRM processes', such as 'recruitment and selection ..., strategies for motivating, retaining and rewarding people ..., appraisal and development of people ...'. For Keep (1992: 335) commitment to

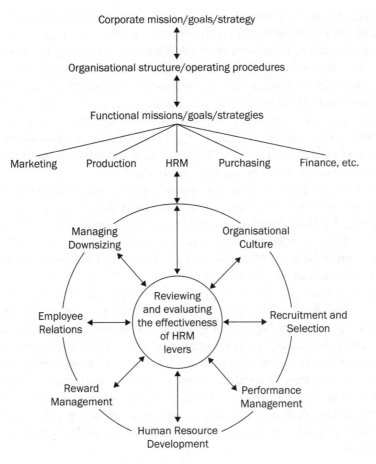

Fig. 6.3 **The wheel of HRM functions**

Source: Developed from Harrison, 1993a: 40.

training can be used as the acid test for determining whether an organisation has adopted HRM policies:

> If the training and development of its employees is not afforded high priority, if training is not seen as a vital component in the realization of business plans, then it is hard to accept that such a company has committed itself to HRM.

These arguments, however, may reflect rhetoric more than reality as evidence consistently points to low levels of HRD investment in the UK (Kelleher, 1996).

HRD – the poor relation?

In stark contrast to the argument that HRD is a vital component of HRM, evidence suggests that there is a chronic under-investment in HRD in the UK. This has been identified as a prime reason for the poor performance of the UK economy (Keep, 1992; Ashton and Felstead, 1995). The critique that can be constructed is disturbingly pervasive. At the macro level the national education and training infrastructure, particularly when subjected to international comparisons, has been criticised for consistently failing to address the needs of industry (Kelleher, 1996). Training initiatives have been criticised variously for failing to provide consistent direction (Ashton and Felstead, 1995), concentrating on the certainties of vocational relevance rather than the longer-term knowledge demands relevant to an imperfect future (Kelleher, 1996) and, simply, a lack of overall investment (Storey and Sisson, 1993). Education has been similarly criticised (Keep, 1992) with the relatively low participation rates of 16-year-olds in post-compulsory full-time education (Ashton and Felstead, 1995) and educational attainment of UK managers (Storey and Sisson, 1993) being particularly cited.

At the micro level, despite the reliance placed on a market-based system by successive governments, the practice of individual organisations is similarly disturbing. Under-investment in HRD, whether measured in terms of budgets or training days, is regularly reported, particularly among low-skill occupations (Ashton and Felstead, 1995). For example Storey and Sisson (1993) point out that the average investment in training among our European counterparts has been estimated at 3 to 5 per cent of employment costs compared with less than 2 per cent in Britain and that UK companies invest less heavily in training managers compared with France, Germany, Norway or Spain. All too frequently HRD fails to be regarded as a managerial priority or something that should be fully integrated through a learning culture into everyday practice (Storey and Sisson, 1993). The traditional patterns of corporate ownership, dominance of accountancy traditions and short-termism that characterise our business inheritance arguably provide infertile conditions for what is essentially a long-term commitment. Given this rather depressing resumé, the inclusion of a chapter on HRD in this book might be questioned.

Self-check question	**6.1** *To what extent might HRD be classified as either a vital human resource component or a poor relation in an organisation known to you?*

The relevance of HRD to the management of change

While acknowledging the above pessimistic construction we would argue, first, that investment in HRD can play a key role in initiating and facilitating change. This perspective is encapsulated in the HRD mission of Thorn Lighting Ltd, UK (Harrison, 1993c: 379) which is directed at 'positioning the organization to adapt to whatever comes along and to take advantage of it, turning threats into challenges, and rising to these challenges in ways that produce increased benefit to the company and workforce'. Indeed, an adverse impact on a company's innovative capacity and responsiveness to change has been identified as one of four critical consequences found to result from under-investment in training (Prais, 1990, cited by Harrison, 1993b). At Xerox it can be seen that HRD is an integral component in engineering changes to work practices designed to lead to 'world class' performance.

Second, while any claim that HRD is the vital component may be challenged, its symbiotic relationship with all other HR levers is in our view self-evident. We will seek to demonstrate this view later but meanwhile point out that HRD is commonly regarded as an integral component of wider HR strategies designed to create new working practices and a more highly motivated, flexible and autonomous workforce (Keep, 1989). At Xerox multi-skilling, a commitment to continual self-improvement using development opportunities and empowerment through teamworking are held to have a number of advantages for employees. These include personal growth, involvement, employability, recognition and extrinsic performance rewards.

Third, deficiencies in the national framework of education and training place the onus on individual companies to meet their own training needs. It is a sobering thought that as long ago as 1993 Storey and Sisson (1993: 161) suggested that 'organizations already have in place 7 of the 10 employees they will have in year 2000'. Such a statistic, coupled with the ever increasing dynamic of change, might suggest that any over-reliance on external resourcing strategies is becoming increasingly untenable.

How human resource development may contribute to organisational change

Strategic change and HRD (first-order strategic integration)

In much the same way as the emergence of HRM was followed shortly afterwards by its strategic derivative SHRM (Miller, 1989), so HRD has become increasingly linked with strategy formulation, implementation and change. As outlined in Chapters 1 and 4, this strategic integration operates externally (Mabey and Iles, 1993) at a number of different levels – first-order corporate decisions; second-order organisation structure and operating procedure decisions; and third-order functional decisions (Purcell, 1989) – and internally across the range of HR levers (Mabey and Iles, 1993).

For Harrison (1997) this strategic derivative (SHRD) involves the alignment of human resource development activities with the organisation's vision, mission and strategic goals whereby continuous organisational as well as individual growth is achieved through enhancing the knowledge, learning ability, motivation and skills of employees at all levels. From this perspective the whole essence of SHRD can be interpreted as a change process.

For our purposes this construction of strategic integration provides a useful starting point. Here SHRD is geared to facilitating the achievement of organisational goals and with its reference to continuous organisational and individual growth provides the potential for SHRD to influence strategy formulation. We would emphasise this position as for us full strategic integration is inherently a two-way relationship where functional decisions, in this case HRD, not only support changes to and implementation of strategy but also inform strategic formulation. What is missing, however, is any reference to 'internal integration', that is the extent to which HRD strategies and practice cohere with other elements of the human resourcing function (Guest, 1987; Mabey and Iles, 1993).

The internal integration dimension is picked up well in Mabey and Salaman's model of 'strategic training and development' (1995: 131). Within their model internal integration can be interpreted as one of two dimensions of strategic fit. Internal integration is evident because within their model training and development is set within an overall human resource strategy where the various HR policies and activities mutually reinforce each other. External integration is evident through the alignment of training and development activities to organisational objectives. This is achieved by directly linking training and development to the organisation's strategic priorities. In addition their model stresses the importance of 'senior management support', 'involvement of line managers' and 'motivation of trainees'. This anticipates the promotion of a culture of learning where line managers and staff are actively involved in diagnosing training needs and selecting training methods. Line managers are also expected to engage in hands-on training, assuming responsibility for much of its delivery (Mabey and Salaman, 1995: 131).

Their comprehensive interpretation of strategic fit reflects closely the criteria used by Guest (1987) to define integration – one of four human resource policy goals making up his conceptual framework of HRM. For Guest, integration occurs when human resource policies are consistent with the strategic objectives of the organisation (alignment with organisational objectives), cohere with each other (integration with HRM policy), are internalised by line managers (involvement of line managers) and support the full integration of employees into the business (motivation of trainees and senior management support).

Taking the first of these dimensions the logic for linking HRD with corporate strategy may appear self-evident. At one level it can be argued that, when strategically driven, HRD can contribute significantly to the implementation of strategic change by ensuring that employees possess the necessary capabilities to manage the new demands presented (Johnson and Scholes, 1993). The direct consequences for HRD will of course be contingent on the nature of strategic change which may be triggered in a number of ways. Based on life cycle models it may be that the organisation is simply proceeding over time from one phase to another, e.g. from growth to maturity (Garavan, 1991). Alternatively an organisation may be deliberately embarking on a different competitive strategy, for example moving from an innovation to a quality enhancement strategy (Schuler and Jackson, 1987). In contrast more rapid or even transformational change may be driven by first-order corporate decisions such as mergers and acquisitions.

In facilitating first-order strategic change it is possible to delineate a number of different HRD responses. First, whatever the drivers of strategic change a central HRD question will be 'What do our people need to be good at?' (Twigg and Albon, 1992: 87). This may manifest itself in a set of organisational competencies. Here Xerox's 'Leadership Attributes' and 'Cultural Dimensions' provide a comprehensive specification that drives all HR processes. A number of these were identified earlier in Table 6.1; other examples include strategic thinking and implementation, customer-driven approach, decision making, managing teamwork, leading innovation, personal drive, overall technical knowledge, results orientation, action orientation etc. Responses to competitive pressures that lead to technical change and new product development will almost certainly point to deficiencies in the skill base of existing employees. HRD represents an important lever for addressing any skill gap revealed.

Second, the change processes themselves are likely to place additional demands on employees. There may be a general requirement for employees to cope with uncertainty. More specifically, say, the move to a quality enhancement strategy may require employees to absorb a different cultural set and to think about their roles in new ways (Garavan, 1991). Rather than a simple focus on skills an appropriate strategic HRD response under these conditions might be to foster a climate of learning which also has a longer-term objective of helping the organisation and its employees cope with future unpredictable change.

Third, the strategic change process itself needs to be initiated and sustained and here the purpose of SHRD may at one level be to act as a catalyst for change and at another to develop change agents. An example of the former is the use of training by Sainsbury to drive through a change programme directed towards establishing a customer service culture (Williams and Dobson, 1996). An example of the latter is the development of transformational leaders or change agents around those competencies which when acquired 'enable change to happen' such as 'envisioning, teambuilding, conflict management, persuasiveness' (Williams and Dobson, 1995: 17).

Fourth, there is likely to be a requirement to develop functional HRD strategies to reflect the organisation's broad business requirements. Using the life cycle model, SHRD in the growth stage would coalesce around activities such as the initiation of career development programmes, management development, inducting new staff and developing high-performance teams. In contrast the HRD function threatened with or immersed in the decline stage is more likely to direct its strategic effort to managing change and turnaround, culture change, project and problem-centred teams and handling downsizing (Garavan *et al.*, 1995: 22).

Last, HRD may have an important role to play when problems arise over strategy implementation. Garavan *et al.* (1995) suggest that implementation failures frequently involve HRD as both a contributory cause and a possible solution. For example, if managers failed to provide adequate leadership and direction it might be because they lacked the necessary management skills of communication, team building, delegation and problem solving. Similarly if HRD was more involved during the process of strategy formulation it might help the organisation to identify and tackle people problems that might otherwise surface later to thwart strategy implementation. Interestingly, at Xerox general management skills, customer focus and a strategic orientation are promoted through the HR framework.

The above points are consistent with our earlier contention that full external integration envisages HRD contributing to strategic planning as well as responding to it. This may be particularly evident where the HRD function promotes a learning culture that builds in a potential capacity amongst employees and the organisation as a whole to change the status quo and develop innovatory responses to strategic challenges. Although it is too early to evaluate, an underpinning objective of Xerox's X Teams is that they will develop the capacity to drive organisational improvement from the bottom up.

Self-check question

> **6.2** *On the basis of available data to what extent would you describe Xerox's approaches to HRD as strategic? Give reasons for your answer.*

In summary, a strategically integrated HRD function has the potential to make a significant contribution to organisation success through its capacity to initiate, sustain and facilitate strategic change. We now consider how HRD can contribute to organisation change arising from second-order strategic change. Our particular focus is the impact that restructuring resulting from de-layering and downsizing can have on the very nature of work itself.

Work restructuring/job design and HRD (second-order strategic integration)

Job design and workforce skills have increasingly made their way on to the managerial agenda for change in the 1990s. This is largely for two reasons. First, recessionary pressures and cost reduction strategies have led to organisations trying to do more for less. Often this means substantial downsizing or de-layering with the two frequently being synonymous as layers of management are removed from the organisation. When they are applied in tandem the consequence for the remaining workforce is that levels of output may have to be maintained, or even increased, while at the same time the displaced managerial processes need to be absorbed into the job specifications for those that remain (*see* Chapter 9). Second, the emergence of more volatile markets has generated the need for product diversity and adaptive responses to an uncertain business climate. The watchword here is flexibility both in terms of work processes and workforce skills (*see* Chapter 2). This is certainly true in the Xerox case where X Teams are seen as a flexible production system designed to establish and respond to customer requirements. However, it is also true that their evolution has run alongside a number of redundancy programmes that have significantly reduced the size of the workforce.

This increasing interest in work processes and workforce skills is reflected well in the growing array of initiatives that have found their way into business vocabulary. These include multi-skilling; lean production systems; cellular manufacturing; autonomous work groups; self-managed teams; empowerment; and high involvement work organisations. Xerox's X Teams reflected several of these during their evolution. These approaches, however, share a number of underlying work design principles:

- organisational restructuring including de-layering, matrix structures/project teams, fewer and broader job grades and revisions to individual job descriptions (Heyes, 1998);
- horizontal restructuring or job enlargement where tasks, i.e. 'the actions and responsibilities undertaken in any function' (Kelleher, 1996: 140), of similar levels of skill and responsibility are combined;

- vertical restructuring or job enrichment where tasks involving higher levels of skill and responsibility are introduced (Kelleher, 1996);
- teamworking where the skills required to handle every task are assembled by combining the talents of individuals (Cappelli and Rogovsky, 1994).

It is frequently argued that work restructuring can contribute simultaneously to the pursuit of competitive advantage and employee job satisfaction through a focus on enhancing the autonomy, variety, identity, meaningfulness and feedback associated with work (Cappelli and Rogovsky, 1994). On this basis you may well question why it has taken management so long to rekindle their interest in work design and how this interest squares with their longstanding historical opposition to employee participation.

Whenever work is restructured it almost inevitably leads to changes in the required skill base, i.e. 'the combination of knowledge and ability possessed by individual workers' (Kelleher, 1996: 140). This skills base can usefully be constructed around three dimensions. First, there are applied or technical skills arising from technological change with multi-skilling predicated by the need to learn the jobs of colleagues and to cross hierarchic job boundaries (Heyes, 1998). Heyes interprets this as a move away from Tayloristic perspectives based around narrow, low-level skills towards a broad and high skill specification that includes, for example, skills associated with quality control, work scheduling, stock inventories and maintenance functions. Second, there are conceptual skills (Kelleher, 1996) which are frequently demanded by the vertical integration of work particularly where it embraces managerial responsibilities. Examples include quality assurance, problem solving, risk assessment, preventative maintenance and customer service. Third, there are behavioural skills which are strongly associated with management processes and effective team organisation (Cappelli and Rogovsky, 1994). Examples here could include giving and receiving feedback, negotiation, leadership, communication, group dynamics and personnel functions such as recruitment, training, performance appraisal and discipline.

Whatever management's motivation for work restructuring the implications it has for HRD should now be readily apparent. Almost every work redesign initiative will carry with it the need to develop additional and/or different skills in the workforce. This potentially represents a formidable training and development agenda, particularly given the multidimensional nature of the skills base.

The implications of work restructuring for HRD can be well illustrated by reference to research conducted in manufacturing companies by Parker *et al.* (1994). They identified dimensions of the skill base associated with effective performance in high-involvement work organisations. These, arranged in their broad categories together with a few construct examples, are presented in Table 6.2. You may also identify that there are clear similarities between these dimensions identified by Parker *et al.* and Xerox's integrating HR framework comprising their 'Leadership Attributes' and 'Cultural Dimensions'.

When the current employee skill base is assessed against such a template, specific training needs will emerge. Organisations will then need to develop specific HRD interventions to address these needs and are likely to do so against the conventional

Table 6.2 Dimensions of effectiveness in high-involvement work organisations

Process ownership	1 *Ownership of the production process.* 2 *Goal/task-oriented.* 3 *Multi-skilled/broad knowledge of the process,* e.g. characterised by individuals who: can competently execute many tasks of the production line; possess good cross-functional awareness of production processes; are familiar with the company product range; have a broad, technical skill base; are adaptable and cover for others.
Social skills	1 *Social confidence,* e.g. characterised by individuals who are forward in opening up constructive discussion; contribute positive ideas verbally; are not afraid to ask difficult questions; show a strong desire to learn through open enquiry; are willing to question rather than just accept. 2 *Effectiveness of communication within and across group boundaries.* 3 *Teamworking and co-operation.*
Personnel style	1 *Flexibility/adaptability.* 2 *System/planful,* e.g. characterised by anticipatory and evaluative behaviour; planned/systematic approach to achieving results; assessing information available before starting a task.
Loss prevention	Characterised by employees who exhibit good housekeeping skills, display good attention to detail and deliver both quality and output consistently.

Source: Developed from Parker *et al.*, 1994: 11.

decision options confronting HRD practitioners, e.g. on-the-job versus off-the-job training or internal versus external provision. Possibilities might include NVQs, which are designed to provide practical skill development (Kelleher, 1996), competency-based training programmes and the use of open learning as a vehicle for acquiring theoretical knowledge. The role of on-the-job HRD interventions is developed more fully later when we consider the learning organisation.

HRD interventions, however, while being a necessary lever for the successful implementation of work restructuring programmes are, on their own, unlikely to be sufficient. Integration with other HR levers, such as recruitment and selection, reward and performance management that may be constructed around a pay-for-skill basis, employee relations and the management of downsizing which may have precipitated job redesign initiatives, will be of paramount importance.

A second caveat is that the HRD portents for effective work restructuring are not particularly encouraging. Approaches to HRD frequently focus on knowledge and skill dimensions and neglect attitudes perhaps in the hope that appropriate attitude change will automatically flow from behavioural change! The national training framework with its rigid hierarchy of vocational qualifications is unlikely to 'provide the flexibility required to offer qualifications that recognise the innovative nature of the range of tasks and skills now demanded' (Kelleher, 1996: 150). The business conditions that frequently spawn work restructuring programmes may well lead to disinvestment in training rather than challenge the myopic managerial stance on training. Last, managers may not be of a sufficiently high calibre to handle the challenges to traditional command and control structures presented by restructuring. This clearly places a premium on manager and management development, issues that we return to later.

Self-check question

6.3 *How might work restructuring initiatives be undermined by a failure to invest in HRD directed at behavioural skills and/or attitude change?*

How HRD can facilitate change at the functional level (third-order strategic integration)

Having considered how HRD can contribute to both first- and second-order strategic change, our focus now shifts to consider how HRD can impact on third-order functional change (Purcell, 1989). Here we return to our earlier consideration of internal integration and argue that HRD can be shown to support all of the other HR change levers considered in this book. Mabey and Salaman (1995: 132) go so far as to envisage HRD as the 'pivotal link' that forges the relationship between 'business and human resource strategy'. Viewed from this perspective it lends credence to Keep's (1992) analysis that corporate training strategies are the vital component in the development of human resource management practice and Harrison's (1993c: 379) observation that HRD is 'the critical function in the human resources wheel'.

Our central argument here is that functional-level change within human resourcing almost invariably involves a training dimension. Viewed from this perspective HRD can be regarded as an integral element of change directed through a multiplicity of HR change levers. It is not surprising therefore that you will find explicit links to HRD throughout the book. It is not our intention here to repeat these. Instead we simply illustrate the potential contribution that HRD can make to facilitating change at the functional level through a few brief references to this material.

In the first case study in Chapter 2, for example, it can be seen that not only have structural changes at Nationwide impacted on training and development and career management but these have in turn facilitated the 're-layering' of the organisation. Following the creation of job families employees are able to see more clearly how their job relates not only to other similar roles in other parts of the organisation but also to jobs into which they may seek promotion. This enables employees to be more proactive in identifying and addressing their own required training and development needs. This in turn helps to internally resource jobs and roles within the new structure as employees acquire the necessary skills and competences required by the organisation.

In Chapter 3, training and development was identified as an important ingredient of programmes designed to change an organisation's culture. At DuPont (Case Study 3.1) training was used as a vehicle not only to help employees understand what was going on but also to improve their stakeholder orientation. The 'Development Centre' created to help deliver training also became identified as a visible symbol of DuPont's commitment to training for everyone reinforcing the message that all employees were involved in shaping the future of the organisation. This chapter also stressed that employees will frequently need to develop the different behaviours (skills, knowledge and attitudes) required by a new culture if culture change is to be effectively realised.

In Chapter 7, multi-skilling and teamwork will be identified as a necessary corollary of broad banding as an approach to pay determination. This has obvious HRD implications which are even more explicit under skill-based pay systems where pay progression is dependent on the acquisition of new skills by employees. This may represent a simple proxy measurement of employee performance. However, in Chapter 5 the intricacies of performance management are explored with managers' ability to provide feedback to their staff being seen as an important indicator of its effectiveness. This represents only one skills area where manager development can be viewed as an integral component of change management.

Development of managers

Given the many links that can be made between HRD and managing change it was difficult to decide what to include in this chapter. In addition to focusing on a variety of links to strategic change we felt it was essential to recognise and reflect the vital role played by managers in change management. We do this in two ways. First we present here an HRD overview of manager development that focuses on two key interrelated perspectives: the critical relationship between organisational performance and the quality of its managers; and managers' role responsibilities for developing their staff. Second, in a later section, we draw on the work of Beer and Eisenstat (1996) to illustrate how corporate strategy, management development and the principles of a learning culture can potentially be woven into an integrating framework. Before we move on, however, we need to distinguish between the use here of the terms 'management development' and 'manager development'. The former refers broadly to the management processes in organisations that operate to help or hinder the achievement of strategic goals. This will include 'specific management practices and organizational arrangements' (Beer and Eisenstat, 1996: 125) and will involve line staff as well as managers, for example, through upward communication mechanisms. The latter refers to the specific development of managers (i.e. those who are responsible for the work of others) against organisational requirements based on an analysis of their training needs.

The strategic complexion of manager development is readily discernible if we accept that an organisation's ability to secure current and future competitive advantage is dependent, in part, on the quality of its managers. Arguably the importance attached to developing managers should increase the more dynamic an organisation's business environment becomes. It is not surprising therefore that, in a survey of European companies commissioned by the Ashridge Management Research Group, 'managing on-going organisational change' was the most commonly cited priority when developing managers (Lundy and Cowling, 1996: 274). However, success in this arena is inextricably bound up with the ability of managers to secure effective performance from their staff. This obviously incorporates a number of human resource dimensions including HRD.

Development of their staff is seen here as one of the critical HR role responsibilities of managers. As they make operational the organisation's business plans it is arguably line managers who are best placed to assess the current and future training and development needs of their staff (Garavan, 1991; Mabey and Salaman, 1995). In addition, they can play an important role in constructing and implementing HRD strategies designed to develop the requisite skills, knowledge and attitudes amongst the workforce. Particularly for job-related training it will be necessary for managers to exhibit coaching and mentoring skills and to facilitate learning through shared experiences (Garavan, 1991). One of the clear structural changes associated with the evolution of X Teams at Xerox has been the redefinition of managers' roles. As reported in the Xerox case, section managers now place greater emphasis on staff management through coaching and facilitating, with less time dedicated to managing operational issues.

Unfortunately this upbeat message sits rather uneasily in the context of the UK economy. As discussed earlier, the prevailing climate at both the national and individual organisation level is not particularly favourable to HRD. A number of factors impact adversely on the quality of our managers and operate to marginalise their staff development responsibilities. An initial difficulty arises over role definition and the ownership of HRD. Managers may not necessarily regard training as part of their role, either because they have not connected generally with their HR responsibilities or because they believe that its ownership resides elsewhere with training specialists. This position is likely to be reinforced where the customary response to identified training needs is to send the employee on a course rather than to undertake job-related training. Alternatively even if dual responsibility for HRD is accepted there is a danger that the two protagonists will conflict. Twigg and Albon (1992) report that managers and training specialists are frequently critical of each other over respectively their lack of business focus and short-term profit mentality that precludes investment in the development of people. These relationships can become so polarised that the two parties can seem to be operating in two different worlds – hardly a recipe for success. The reconfiguration of the HR function at Xerox into the 'Skills Partnership' represents an interesting development and, with its emphasis on collaboration between HR specialists and line managers, not only should avoid such polarisation but could generate very constructive working relationships.

A further difficulty is that even managers who understand that HRD is an integral aspect of their staffing responsibility may fail to deliver against this role. At one level they may simply lack the motivation. This is not so irrational as it may sound, for the longer-term payback strongly associated with HRD is not consistent with the predominantly short-term focus adopted by many organisations. Also if the cynical view that you only get the behaviour that you either measure or pay for is accepted then any failure to incorporate HRD into a manager's performance criteria will result in the expenditure of minimum effort in this area. As Storey and Sisson (1993: 171) have lamented, 'Rarely is it the case in British companies that the extent to which a manager develops his or her own immediate staff is regarded as the critical measurement of how well that manager is doing the job.'

At another level managers may simply lack the necessary competence to execute their HRD role effectively. Garavan (1991) cites the inability to appraise performance, identify training needs and empathise with subordinates together with a lack of listening and counselling skills as the most commonly identified shortcomings. These competence deficiencies may reflect the relatively low education and training base of some British managers referred to earlier and HRD approaches that rely more on throwing managers in at the deep end than on their methodical, continuous development (Storey and Sisson, 1993). A particular difficulty is that what training there is tends to be concentrated towards the lower end of the management hierarchy (Garavan, 1991). Particular concern has been expressed that insufficient attention is paid to the development of senior managers, given their critical contribution to organisational performance (Mumford, 1998). Where senior managers neglect their own personal development it can also establish poor role models, potentially reinforcing the negative attitudes line managers have towards HRD.

Unfortunately we are faced with the dilemma that managers may sustain an anti-training attitude out of rational self-interest, despite its potential for facilitating organisational change. Keep (1992) outlines a rather depressing scenario where poorly educated and trained managers brought up within traditional authoritarian control and command structures conspire to deny subordinates training opportunities because their effective development may subsequently threaten the manager's own managerial prerogative and/or position.

On a more optimistic note it may be that the demands of managing change per se will act as a catalyst on managers' attitudes towards HRD and galvanise them into action with respect to their own development needs and those of their subordinates. Research conducted in 91 large UK-based companies found that expenditure on manager development was highest when it represented an integral element of corporate planning, when it was directly associated with the need to respond effectively to changing environments and when the operating market was increasingly turbulent (Parkinson, 1990). Evidence of increased manager development activity has also been linked explicitly with culture change programmes where it has been identified as an essential vehicle for engineering change (Storey and Sisson, 1993). Evidence drawn from across Europe including the UK also points to line managers increasingly accepting responsibility for their HRD role both in terms of training needs identification and the formulation of HRD policies (Mabey and Salaman, 1995). There has also been an upsurge in the use of competencies as the foundation for developing managers (Iles, 1993). It is to be hoped that, through greater involvement in their own training, managers may adopt more positive attitudes to the development of their subordinates. A key element here may be to make HRD more accessible and relevant to their needs. This certainly appears to have been an important consideration in the development of the personnel function into a 'Skills Partnership' at Xerox. In order to bridge the two worlds occupied by line managers and training specialists, Twigg and Albon (1992) suggest that HRD interventions need to switch from an emphasis on generic, off-the-job courses to work-based activities that have been designed collaboratively by the two parties to specifically address identified business needs. They particularly highlight the role organisational learning can play in drawing the two worlds together. Under this approach business needs are increasingly linked to managing change and the requirement for managers to innovate and take risks. This, they argue, is more likely to happen in a learning climate where 'experiences, whether successful or not, are rapidly assimilated by others and form the basis of learning how to cope with change' (Twigg and Albon, 1992: 86).

Self-check question

6.4 *What factors have contributed to the relatively low levels of investment in manager development?*

The learning organisation – pot of gold or chasing rainbows?

A recurrent theme running through the management literature and reflected in this book is that organisations will need to learn how to adapt to endemic change if they are to survive and flourish. There is nothing essentially new in the notion that organisations to varying degrees of success learn to interact with their environment. Indeed, learning can be identified at the very foundation of many management change initiatives such as TQM, culture change, and business re-engineering. More recently however, the status of learning has been elevated to become the modus operandi of organisations finding popular expression in the construct of 'The Learning Organisation' or 'The Learning Company' (Pedler *et al.*, 1991).

A frequently quoted definition sees the learning organisation as one 'which facilitates the learning of all its members and continually transforms itself' (Pedler *et al.*, 1991: 1). Underpinning this definition is the creation of a learning climate where everybody is encouraged to learn and the company as a whole organisation develops a capacity for learning. Drawing on the literature to unpack the concept further it is possible to distinguish a number of features of the learning organisation (Pettigrew and Whipp, 1991; Storey and Sisson, 1993; Mabey and Salaman, 1995; Lundy and Cowling, 1996):

■ learning can be derived from all experiences – successes and failures – and used to shape future behaviour;
■ learning is valuable in its own right and learning how to learn is an important part of the process;
■ learning from both the internal and external environment takes place at all levels of the organisation and there is a premium on sharing knowledge across organisational boundaries;
■ learning is a continuous process and at its most powerful when it becomes habitual and internalised;
■ unlearning and the reconstruction and adaptation of an organisation's knowledge base is a key managerial task; and
■ learning is used intentionally as an enabling mechanism for organisational transformation.

Learning, however, is difficult to evaluate. Arguably it is evident only when it results in some measurable behavioural outcome. Argyris and Schon (1978) distinguish two ways in which this interaction between learning and outcomes can occur. The first, labelled single loop learning, essentially involves detecting errors in organisational processes and correcting them in a continual cycle as organisations respond to changes in their internal and external environments. The second, labelled double loop learning, attempts to construct new conceptual pictures of organisational processes through challenging existing values, procedures and knowledge or, more simply, 'the way things are done around here'. One of our colleagues has applied these concepts to model the process of staff development. This model, depicted in Fig. 6.4, shows that, with single loop learning, if inputs (e.g. coaching) and/or outputs (e.g. competencies) do not result in goal accomplishment (e.g. customer satisfaction) attempts are made to detect and rectify errors in the process itself. With double loop learning, a failure to satisfy goals leads to the very assumptions of staff development and its goals being challenged. The increasing use of everyday experiences rather than generic training courses as the basis for management development may represent such a paradigm shift. According to Mabey and Salaman (1995) this signifies a shift from 'institutional' to 'internalised' patterns of HRD where high levels of line management commitment to HRD correspond to low levels of visible training and development activity.

At Xerox, while the organisation has not formally declared itself a learning organisation it is clear that the Manager of Human Resourcing and Development is very sympathetic to its principles. When researching the organisation Mike quickly found that the language of 'training' had been replaced by that of 'learning'. There

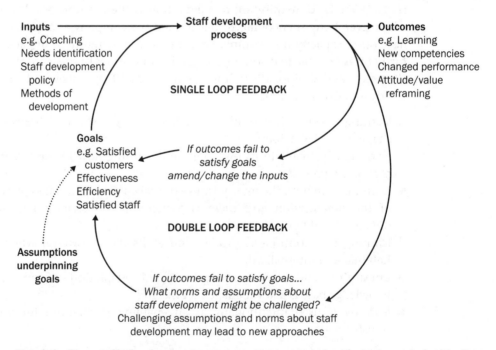

Fig. 6.4 The staff development process as an example of single and double loop learning

Source: Barry R. Baker 1997, reproduced with permission.

was a discernible shift away from prescriptive formal training provision towards continuous development built around direct work experiences. Learning appears to be an implicit feature of Xerox's HR framework.

In the context of change management the whole philosophy of the learning organisation is disarmingly seductive. The underlying hypothesis is that where learning takes place all the time throughout the organisation it will be better able to cope with change and uncertainty (Lundy and Cowling, 1996). Where the continuous development of employees is inextricably linked to the process of strategic management they 'become a major source of competitive ability, positioned to take advantage of every opportunity, while taking a positive stance when confronted with adversity' (Harrison, 1993b: 317). Others have gone further to argue that people are the only sustainable source of competitive advantage within a complex environment (West, 1994) and that organisational learning may be the only competitive advantage for firms in the future (Stata, 1989).

Viewed from these perspectives the learning organisation appears to offer the much sought after pot of gold and application of its principles has been associated with the successful management of strategic and operational change (Pettigrew and Whipp, 1991). However, against this, the concept may represent no more than an idealised construct rather than a practical working model (Storey and Sisson, 1993). One particular difficulty is that conditions thought to be conducive to learning organisations may not be readily found in practice. These conditions include: employees who are committed to and capable of managing their own continuous personal development; the presence of mechanisms that support mutual learning and which capture, disseminate and share learning; an appropriate culture that supports experimentation, risk-taking, independent thinking, discord, authority based on expert knowledge rather than status; and, dare we say, a pluralist ideology (Stewart, 1996). Organisations characterised more by bureaucracy, control and unitarism are for many of us the reality. Messengers do get shot and even where senior management espouse openness and innovation the reality may be that a blame culture operates so that employees avoid putting their heads above the parapet.

Another difficulty is that the very concept of transformation underpinning Pedler *et al.*'s definition of the learning organisation is open to criticism. How many times have organisations for which you have worked transformed themselves? Will transformation become the organisational watchword as we move into the next millennium? Mumford (1998) argues strongly that learning should be incremental rather than transformational. He questions whether employees can be equipped with the capacity for double loop learning when our HRD infrastructure has yet to deliver the widespread capacity for single loop learning. The many criticisms of HRD in the UK would seem to lend weight to his view. In this context single loop learning may represent a rational approach to problem solving and should not be jettisoned until we have validated the superiority of new learning forms (Henderson, 1997).

Perhaps, then, a construct that appears to promise so much may in fact prove to be somewhat elusive in practice. However, the journey in pursuit of the rainbow's end, like so many journeys, may be rewarding in itself. Many of the ingredients of the learning organisation appear to have merit and arguably represent common sense even if this is in reality a rare commodity! In the next and concluding section of this chapter we introduce you to an approach where organisational learning and corporate strategy come together to underpin strategic management development.

An integrating framework – possibilities, contradictions and dilemmas

Here we review how strategic human resource management (SHRM) has been used to promote organisational learning as the vehicle for developing the capabilities necessary for survival in the face of continuous change. The approach described integrates a number of themes developed earlier in this chapter, most particularly strategic linkages – both external and internal, manager development and the learning organisation. At the same time it again confirms the fragile nature of strategic interventions that are essentially top-down and insufficiently embedded in task alignment particularly amongst line managers (Beer et al., 1990). The review draws heavily on case study material reported on by Beer and Eisenstat (1996) and we would recommend that you read their full account in Storey (1996).

The approach is based on the premiss that the achievement of strategic goals is, in part, a function of SHRM which in itself is concerned to 'institutionalize an organizational learning process aimed at developing an organization capable of implementing strategy and learning' (Beer and Eisenstat, 1996: 140). The process involved with developing SHRM is depicted in Fig. 6.5. It involves four groups of players: the senior management team (SMT); an employee task force comprising a unit's best employees (ETF); process consultants ('profilers'); and teams led by general managers (GM) who report to a senior management team member.

An initial briefing meeting introduces the SMT to the process and leads to the creation of the ETF. A data collection exercise is then launched to establish what management practices, including the behaviour and attitudes of SMT members themselves, help or hinder the achievement of strategic goals. Data is collected by 'profilers' and the ETF, via interviews with SMT members and other staffing groups respectively, who then report their findings back to general managers and SMT in a 'fishbowl' discussion.

The next stage involves a series of diagnostic reviews to discern: patterns in those capabilities and behaviours identified as impediments to strategic goal attainment; the impact that these impediments have on organisational performance measured in terms of the satisfaction of stakeholders (shareholders, customers and employees); how future strategy implementation may be threatened by problems associated with the co-ordination, commitment and competence of staff; and those HR dimensions that are perceived to be the root causes of identified impediments.

Managers then develop an implementation plan starting with 'a vision of how the organization might be redesigned to implement strategy more effectively' (Beer and Eisenstat, 1996: 127) and leading to the development of HR plans to translate the agreed vision(s) into practice. This could incorporate, for example, the management style of SMT; team development; skills and competency requirements; and the

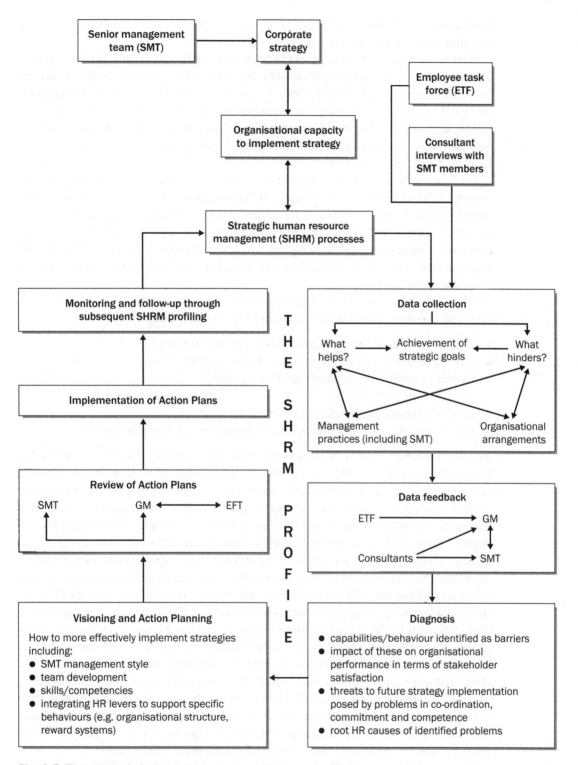

Fig. 6.5 The strategic human resource management profile

Source: Developed from Beer and Eisenstat, 1996.

integration of HR levers deemed necessary to support specified behaviours, e.g. organisation structure and reward systems.

Prior to implementation general managers discuss the outcomes of the diagnostic exercises and their action plans with the ETF, who provide feedback on the proposals, before finally conducting a review of their plans with the SMT member to whom they report. Following implementation the last stage is to monitor and follow up the extent to which planned SHRM actions enhance the organisation's capacity to implement its corporate strategy culminating, around every two years, in a further profiling exercise.

On the surface such an approach should contribute substantially to the management of change and strategy implementation. There is a continuous loop identifying and trying to resolve HR impediments with the potential for constant upward feedback underpinning the organisation's capacity to learn. However, the case study evidence, while pointing to high levels of agreement about what the HR impediments were, is pessimistic about the extent to which this knowledge can drive organisational renewal.

Beer and Eisenstat (1996: 130) reported that, on the basis of frequency of mention, the most common barriers found by the ETF were:

- difficulties in how the top team works together (100%);
- poor vertical (up and down) communication (80%);
- unclear or conflicting strategic priorities (70%);
- management style (70%);
- poor interfunctional/divisional co-ordination (70%);
- deficiencies in career development and management competence (70%).

Beer and Eisenstat (1996: 131) argue that these barriers reflect the very problems that SHRM was designed to address, i.e. co-ordination, commitment and management competence, and that organisations where they can be overcome 'will have made human resources a sustainable competitive advantage'. They found generally that managers accepted the diagnosis of their capabilities, despite the direct criticism implied; strategic human resource management gained the commitment of senior managers; and co-ordination between functions and SMT performance improved.

Against this, however, their evidence revealed that many units in the organisation failed to involve the ETF in managing the change process; some units failed to conduct a second profiling exercise; commitment to SHRM declined as you moved down the organisation; disagreements over and conflicts between strategic priorities surfaced; and there was little or no change in upward appraisal, promotion criteria (to reflect management skills) or interest in employee welfare and satisfaction. Taken together there was evidence that the case company found it difficult to confront a number of the identified barriers even though they acknowledged their presence. Indeed the very failure to confront barriers was identified as an almost universal impediment to successful strategic change and a root cause of failure among change programmes such as TQM and employee involvement.

The underlying analysis was that managerial deficiencies identified as barriers represented 'the "undiscussibles" in most organizations which managers zealously try to avoid, fearing a threat to relationships, careers and self-esteem' (Beer and Eisenstat, 1996: 130). Consistent with this management identified SHRM decisions as their responsibility where any employee involvement would run counter to managerial prerogative and the hierarchical assumptions implicit within organisation structures. Gaps between the rhetoric and reality of follow-up were attributed to SHRM being perceived as an additional burden rather than 'a business improvement process that also develops the organization and its human resources' (Beer and Eisenstat, 1996: 138). Therefore the window of opportunity for organisation and management development opened by the profiling process was closed by a management reluctant to change its core values and attitudes to embrace greater employee involvement.

The main reason for management's behaviour was attributed to 'their own discomfort and lack of skill in discussing difficult issues with subordinates' (Beer and Eisenstat, 1996: 139) which, if correct, points to an important failure in a learning process explicitly designed to impact on managerial competence and values in this very area. This scenario points to a dysfunctional consequence with which many of you will be familiar. If employees are frustrated by their lack of real involvement and perceive little improvement in commonly identified management impediments to change they are likely to approach any subsequent formal profiling exercise with great cynicism. Under such circumstances management are unlikely to generate commitment to change programmes or to discover from their subordinates the nature of any barriers impacting adversely against their success. Employees learn to stay silent!

The potential for SHRM to facilitate organisational learning directed towards successful strategic change and implementation is likely to be thwarted if it fails to engage the organisation in a deeper consideration of its managerial philosophy and values or to ensure that its managers through selection and/or development possess the requisite skills to manage change and promote a learning culture. For Beer and Eisenstat (1996: 141–2) the difficulties coalesce around the 'psychological fitness' of its managers which if absent will prevent the development of 'a high-performing learning organization'. For them fitness is largely concerned with 'managers' capacity to engage in an open, fact-based conversation' and involves the skills of 'learning how to receive feedback without loss of self-esteem, to collaborate without feeling out of control and to own up to weaknesses without feeling incompetent' (Beer and Eisenstat, 1996: 141). You will almost certainly by now have made connections with this analysis and earlier discussions about the record of HRD in the UK in general and the development of managers in particular.

SUMMARY

- Human resource development is an inevitable manifestation of organisation change and has the potential to facilitate all HR interventions. It can make a significant contribution to all three levels of strategic change, i.e. first-order corporate decisions, second-order organisation structure and operating decisions, and third-order functional decisions.

■ Unlike many of our international competitors, the national education and training infrastructure is poorly developed in the UK. Investment in post-16 full-time education runs behind many other countries and a concentration on vocational skills may obscure the importance of knowledge and theory-based learning for managing future uncertainties. A basically non-interventionist, market force ideology has pushed the prime responsibility for HRD on to employers.

■ From these perspectives it might be anticipated that HRD would occupy a central position in management thinking and practice. Accumulated evidence, however, suggests that in many organisations a lack of investment in and commitment to HRD relegates it to a relatively peripheral activity. Rather than invest in an internal labour market employers may simply resort to the external market to buy in the necessary skills ready-made.

■ The cumulative impact of under-investment in HRD at both the national and organisational levels has contributed to the emergence of critical skill shortages. Given that managing change arguably places a greater premium on HRD the portents for the future are not favourable. Against this it is possible that the endemic nature of change will force organisations to reappraise their current attitudes towards HRD.

■ The coverage given in the management literature to developments such as the learning organisation and management competencies may help to raise the profile of HRD. Increasingly approaches such as the learning organisation serve to emphasise the importance of low-visibility HRD interventions which may offer better value than more expensive, high-visibility, generic training courses.

■ There is also the possibility that greater investment in the training of managers will encourage them to acknowledge the value of HRD and internalise their role responsibilities for the development of their staff. Unless this occurs it is unlikely that managers will identify HRD as one of their key functions and give it the time necessary to make real the potential learning that can arise from every day experiences.

CASE STUDY 6.2

Human resource development at Dales Pickles and Preserves

Dales Pickles and Preserves (Dales) is a longstanding manufacturer of luxury foodstuffs. It has over 2000 employees split evenly between three food processing factories and a head office, all located in the north-east of England. This case study arises out of planned strategic change and focuses on the HRD implications of a transformation in production arrangements.

Within its market Dales enjoyed a leading but not dominant position with around 20 per cent market share. Between 1992 and 1997, however, aggressive competition based around innovative niche marketing and cost efficiency had reduced its market share to 15 per cent leading the Board of Directors to conduct a major strategic review at the end of this period.

The Board was forced to recognise that it had become complacent over the years relying too much on historical brand loyalty. The strategic review resulted in two major decisions. First, the Board determined to restore the company's market share over the period 1999–2003 and then, longer-term, to move beyond that to establish a dominant market position. Second, designation as a 'world class manufacturer' would be pursued to support these marketing imperatives. Progress up to 2003 would be evaluated internally using three performance goals: to become the lowest-cost producer in the UK; to develop a quality assurance culture that would permeate the whole organisation; and to become the market leader for new product innovation and development. These goals were to be pursued through transforming the company's Tayloristic production line systems to a high-involvement, autonomous work group operation labelled 'Workcells'.

Of the 2000 employees approximately half were engaged on direct production activities organised through 36 manufacturing departments split between the three factories. Each department produced a specific suite of products and employed 25 to 35 operatives when it was running at peak capacity of whom approximately 25 per cent would be peripheral workers on casual or short-term contracts. This reflected the need for flexible staffing arrangements to accommodate seasonal production peaks prior to Christmas and Easter. Departments were managed by a supervisor and clusters of six departments reported to a production superintendent who in turn reported to the Production Manager for each site who reported to the Manufacturing Director, based at Head Office. Parallel to this structure were a series of production service departments covering material control, purchasing, production control, quality control and plant design and maintenance. These departments were again organised on a site basis through an identical structure reporting ultimately to the Production Services Director (Fig. 6.6).

The introduction of 'Workcells' was preceded by a thorough review of current production processes against the goals of cost, quality and innovation referred to earlier. It was concluded that:

■ A rigid and expensive bureaucratic hierarchy operated against effective communication and collaborative problem solving.
■ The structure had fuelled a culture of 'management prerogative' that stifled innovation and co-operation. From an employee perspective expressions such as 'we've always done it that way', 'if it ain't broke don't fix it' and 'we know best' represented the language of management.
■ Employees adopted a minimalist approach sticking rigidly to their job description, meaning among other things, that quality issues often went unreported. Production operatives enjoyed seeing management 'dropped in it'.

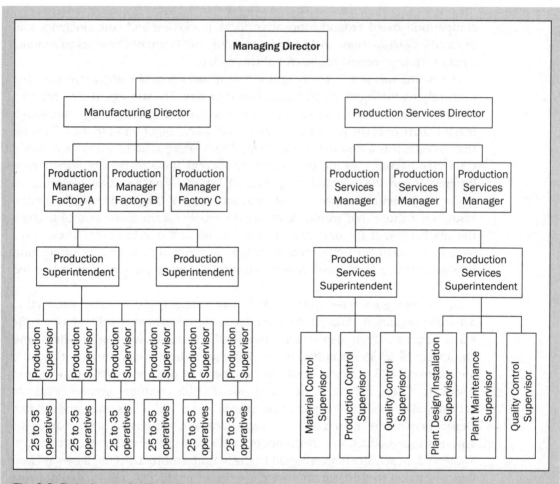

Fig. 6.6 Dales' organisation structure (production)

- Operator training reflected Tayloristic principles of job design. It was strictly geared to meeting immediate job requirements and mainly comprised 'sitting next to Nellie'. Any operating problems were reported to supervisors and after flowing through the communication hierarchy an appropriate production service specialist would arrive to rectify it. The downtime that resulted was excessive.

The manufacturing departments were to remain the basis for production but would be transformed into 'cells' using both horizontal and vertical restructuring and team building principles. This would involve employees undertaking additional roles of similar and higher levels of skill and responsibility (job enlargement and job enrichment respectively) thereby enabling each department to act as a mini-business taking initial responsibility for quality, production scheduling, inventory control, maintenance of equipment and safety.

The vital ingredient was to be the creation of self-directed teams that would be able to identify and rectify problems, communicate effectively within the team and across the organisation, operate in the spirit of continuous improvement, and adopt innovatory and risk-taking behaviours. Through employee empowerment this initiative was intended to make a significant contribution to the 'world class' strategy not least because of its potential to enrich the work experience of employees.

Consistent with work restructuring initiatives generally and the performance goals specifically the introduction of 'Workcells' would take place alongside major changes to the organisational structure. Direct production and production services functions were to be combined under a Production Operations Director and two tiers of management removed – supervisors and Production Managers/Production Services Managers – with Superintendents absorbing the responsibilities of the latter and reporting to the Director. Further downsizing would occur in the production services departments as some of their functions were absorbed into the manufacturing cells. Where possible displaced staff would be redeployed into the manufacturing cells or consultant roles which were created to underpin the transformation.

Initial and continuing staff development strategies were identified as the key to the successful implementation of the work and organisational restructuring initiatives. However, during the strategy formulation stage a number of potential human resource impediments that could frustrate management's plans were identified. A number of employees were resistant to the changes because they had doubts about their own motivation or competency. Several production services staff had intimated that they would try to sabotage the change strategies through uncooperative behaviour irrespective of whether they were to be redeployed into the manufacturing cells or consultant roles. Many managers had voiced extreme scepticism over the principles of employee involvement embedded in the work restructuring plans and throughout two of the factories there existed a strongly held view that 'all this business re-engineering stuff was just another management fad'.

Shortly before developing training and development strategies it was decided to create a 'Consultant' role which it was anticipated would help address these issues particularly through a direct contribution to HRD. Ten consultants were to be recruited, each servicing three or four manufacturing cells against the following role brief:

- Assist managers and cells to identify training needs.
- Contribute actively to the development and implementation of training strategies.
- Accelerate the development of teamworking skills.
- Improve lateral and vertical communications across the organisation.
- Support the creation of a continuous improvement environment.
- Challenge bureaucracy and inertia.
- Generally act as change agents.

▶

At this stage it was anticipated that training would need to be targeted at three different groups: production operatives, line managers and consultants.

Case study questions

1 What will be the short- to medium-term training needs resulting from the 'Workcells' initiative for the three groups identified?

2 How would you seek to address these training needs?

3 What other organisational changes are occurring at Dales besides work restructuring and how might HRD facilitate their introduction?

4 Although not explicitly stated in the case it would appear that Dales is sympathetic to the learning organisation concept. To what extent do your HRD proposals take the organisation in this direction and how do you think further progress could be made?

REFERENCES

Argyris, C. and Schon, D. (1978) *Organisational Learning*, Reading, Mass.: Addison-Wesley.

Ashton, D. and Felstead, A. (1995) 'Training and development', in Storey, J. (ed.), *Human Resource Management: A Critical Text*, London: Routledge, pp. 234–53.

Beer, M. and Eisenstat, R.A. (1996) 'American Medical Technologies Inc.', in Storey, J. (ed.), *Blackwell Cases in Human Resource and Change Management*, Oxford: Blackwell, pp. 124–43.

Beer, M., Eisenstat, R.A. and Spector, B. (1990) 'Why change programs don't produce change', *Harvard Business Review*, November/December, 158–66.

Cappelli, P. and Rogovsky, N. (1994) 'New work systems and skill requirements', *International Labour Review*, 133(2), 205–20.

Garavan, T.N. (1991) 'Strategic human resource development', *Journal of European Industrial Training*, 15(1), 17–30.

Garavan, T.N., Costine, P. and Heraty, N. (1995) 'The emergence of strategic human resource development', *Journal of European Industrial Training*, 19(10), 4–10.

Guest, D.E. (1987) 'Human resource management and industrial relations', *Journal of Management Studies*, 24(5) (September), 503–21.

Harrison, R. (1993a) 'Concepts and issues in strategic human resource management', in Harrison, R. (ed.), *Human Resource Management: Issues and Strategies*, Wokingham: Addison-Wesley, pp. 35–65.

Harrison, R. (1993b) 'Developing people – for whose bottom line?', in Harrison, R. (ed.), *Human Resource Management: Issues and Strategies*, Wokingham: Addison-Wesley, pp. 299–329.

Harrison, R. (1993c) 'Thorn Lighting Ltd, UK – A Learning Organization', in Harrison, R. (ed.), *Human Resource Management: Issues and Strategies*, Wokingham: Addison-Wesley, pp. 375–80.

Harrison, R. (1997) *Employee Development*, London: Institute of Personnel and Development.

Henderson, S. (1997) 'Black swans don't fly double loop: the limits of the learning organization', *The Learning Organization*, 4(3), 99–105.

Heyes, J. (1998) 'Training and development at an agrochemical plant', in Mabey, C., Skinner, D. and Clark, T. (eds), *Experiencing Human Resource Management*, London: Sage, pp. 97–112.

Iles, P.A. (1993) 'Achieving strategic coherence in HRD through competence-based management and organization development', *Personnel Review*, 22(6), 63–80.

Johnson, G. and Scholes, K. (1993) *Exploring Corporate Strategy*, 3rd edn, Hemel Hempstead: Prentice Hall.

Keep, E. (1992) 'Corporate training strategies: the vital component?', in Salaman, G. (ed.), *Human Resource Strategies*, London: Sage, pp. 320–36.

Kelleher, M. (1996) 'New forms of work organisation and HRD', in Stewart, J. and McGoldrick, J. (eds), *Human Resource Development: Perspectives, Strategies and Practice*, London: Pitman, pp. 138–57.

Lundy, O. and Cowling, A. (1996) *Strategic Human Resource Management*, London: Routledge.

Mabey, C. and Iles, P. (1993) 'The strategic integration of assessment and development practices: succession planning and new manager development', *Human Resource Management Journal*, 3(4), 16–34.

Mabey, C. and Salaman, G. (1995) *Strategic Human Resource Management*, Oxford: Blackwell.

Miller, P. (1989) 'Strategic HRM: what it is and what it isn't', *Personnel Management*, February, 46–51.

Mumford, A. (1998) 'Managing learning and developing management', *Human Resource Development International: Enhancing Performance, Learning and Integrity*, 1(1), 113–18.

Parker, S.K., Mullarkey, S. and Jackson, P.R. (1994) 'Dimensions of performance effectiveness in high-involvement organisations', *Human Resource Management Journal*, 4(3), 1–21.

Parkinson, S. (1990) 'Management development's strategic role', *Journal of General Management*, 16(2), 63–75.

Pedler, M., Burgoyne, J. and Boydell, T. (1991) *The Learning Company*, Maidenhead: McGraw-Hill.

Pettigrew, A. and Whipp, R. (1991) *Managing Change for Competitive Success*, Oxford: Blackwell.

Prais, S. J. and NIESR research team (1990) 'Productivity, education and training: Britain and other countries compared', *National Institute Economic Review*, London: National Institute of Economic and Social Research.

Purcell, J. (1989) 'The impact of corporate strategy on human resource management', in Storey, J. (ed.), *New Perspectives on Human Resource Management*, London: Routledge, pp. 67–91.

Schuler, R.S. and Jackson, S.E. (1987) 'Linking competitive strategies with human resource management practices', *The Academy of Management Executive*, 1(3), 207–19.

Stata, R. (1989) 'Organizational learning – the key to management innovation', *Sloan Management Review*, Spring, 63–74.

Stewart, J. (1996) *Managing Change through Training and Development*, 2nd edn, London: Kogan Page.

Storey, J. (ed.) (1996) *Blackwell Cases in Human Resource and Change Management*, Oxford: Blackwell.

Storey, J. and Sisson, K. (1993) *Managing Human Resources and Industrial Relations*, Buckingham: Open University Press.

Twigg, G. and Albon, P. (1992) 'Human resource development and business strategy', in Armstrong, M. (ed.), *Strategies for Human Resource Management: A Total Business Approach*, London: Kogan Page, pp. 80–92.

Upton, R. (1987) 'The bottom line: Bejam's ingredients for success', *Personnel Management*, March, 26–9.

West, P. (1994) 'The concept of the learning organization', *Journal of European Industrial Training*, 18(1), 15–21.

Williams, A.P.O. and Dobson, P. (1995) 'Personnel selection and corporate strategy', in Anderson, N. and Herriot, P. (eds) *Assessment and Selection in Organizations: Methods and Practice for Recruitment and Appraisal, Second Update and Supplement*, Chichester, John Wiley, pp. 1–27.

Williams, A.P.O. and Dobson, P. (1996) 'Culture change through training: the case of Sainsbury', in Towers, B. (ed.), *The Handbook of Human Resource Management*, 2nd edn, Oxford: Blackwell, pp. 416–31.

ANSWERS TO SELF-CHECK QUESTIONS

6.1 *To what extent might HRD be classified as either a vital human resource component or a poor relation in an organisation known to you?*

Clearly your answer here has to be set into the context of your selected organisation. It is, therefore, impossible for us to answer this question from your perspective but what we do here is pose a number of subsidiary questions drawn from the chapter that together will provide a framework that you can use to evaluate your organisation's approach to HRD.

■ What proportion of the organisation's total budget is spent on HRD? How does this translate to number of days training or expenditure per person?

■ What priority does your manager give to their HRD role responsibilities? How is this evidenced? How much off-the-job HRD support do they give to subordinates?

■ Is there a clear linkage between any training received and corporate strategies, perhaps through some performance management process?

■ To what extent is training activity directed at current job requirements or future development?

■ To what extent are you encouraged to accept responsibility for your own development? How does the organisation support you in this?

■ What happens when you come back to work after attending an off-the-job training event?

6.2 *On the basis of available data to what extent would you describe Xerox's approaches to HRD as strategic? Give reasons for your answer.*

To answer this question it is possible to use Harrison's (1997) construction of SHRD discussed earlier as a starting point. HRD at Xerox is clearly directed towards enabling X Teams to deliver the prime corporate objective of customer satisfaction. Further, the approach to HRD supports both top-down and bottom-up development strategies and provides all employees with the potential to shape their own development programme. HRD has a key role to play in progressing the vision of 'world class' performance and arguably promotes both organisational and individual growth.

In addition HRD at Xerox is closely aligned with other HR levers. Here the 23 'Leadership Attributes' and 9 'Cultural Dimensions' provide a very visible integrating framework around which HR processes are constructed. What is less clear, however, is the extent to which line managers have internalised their HRD role responsibilities or the extent to which evident strategic linkages are due to formalised strategic planning or have evolved over time perhaps as a consequence of bottom-up managerial initiatives.

6.3 *How might work restructuring initiatives be undermined by a failure to invest in HRD directed at behavioural skills and/or attitude change?*

Clearly as evidenced in the chapter work restructuring will almost certainly involve the acquisition of a different set of knowledge, skills and attitudes. The term skills base has been used to encapsulate the knowledge and skills (ability) requirement (Kelleher, 1996) and was seen to comprise three dimensions – technical, conceptual and behavioural.

If work redesign changes the relationships between staff and particularly where it involves a move to teamworking then a failure to address the behavioural component through HRD is likely to have dysfunctional consequences. If, for example, staff are unable to resolve interpersonal difficulties, negotiate task allocation and appraise each other's performance then the integrity of teamworking will collapse.

In our experience multi-skilling rarely embraces development of the behavioural component and a particular area of neglect is attitude change. Difficult though this area is, if employees are resistant to the job design changes being implemented they are likely to be able to find many ways of sabotaging management's efforts. Heyes (1998) provides a graphic account of how a failure to address employee attitudes militated against a work restructuring initiative. He reports how attempts to formally introduce flexible working practices foundered because they interfered with prevailing status differentials and flexible arrangements that were already operated informally by operators. The associated loss of intrinsic rewards and control led operators to resist the changes and resulted in 'the emergence of rigidities where they had previously not existed' (Heyes, 1998: 109).

6.4 *What factors have contributed to the relatively low levels of investment in manager development?*

Running through the chapter are a number of references to factors that may impact adversely on manager development. For ease of reference these might be grouped under three headings. Based on your own experiences you may of course be able to add to those factors identified here.

First, there are the direct experiences of the managers themselves. They may have got where they are with little personal investment in management education and training which may therefore be perceived as largely irrelevant. This attitude is likely to be reinforced if organisations demonstrably promote staff into management positions on the basis of their functional expertise rather then their potential management competence.

Second, their interpretation of their role may emphasise functional rather than managerial responsibilities. This may reflect a comfort zone where they find it easier to carry on much as before rather than tackle a set of difficult responsibilities for which they feel inadequately prepared. Furthermore, if the way they develop their staff is not explicitly rewarded their functionally oriented behavioural patterns are likely to be reinforced.

Third, the way they are managed within the organisation will impact on their attitudes to personal development. They may have experienced little by way of quality one-on-one development time with their manager and are therefore exposed to poor role models. Furthermore, the emphasis on short-term results may send out signals that longer-term investment in training is a low priority.

Reward management and the management of change

Having completed this chapter, you will be able to:

- See reward management as an important component of the range of HRM activities rather than a purely technical concern.

- Explain the concept of 'strategic reward management'.

- Explain the way in which reward management may assist in delivery of required employee behaviours.

- Distinguish between reward values, structures and processes.

INTRODUCTION

The purpose of this chapter is to encourage you to think about reward in a different way. We use the term 'reward' in the chapter because it includes non-pay rewards. However, the major focus of the chapter is on pay. Central to the chapter is the notion that pay is an important component of the range of HRM activities, which can play a key part in achieving organisational change.

Reward has long enjoyed something of a Cinderella status. It has been seen as inhabiting 'the turgid, unimaginative and inflexible world of wage and salary administration' (Smith, 1993: 45). But this 'world' for many organisations has changed in recent years. In this chapter we reflect this new thinking about reward. Indeed, many writers have argued that thinking about 'wage and salary administration' is in itself new. Livy (1988: 249) typifies this scepticism in describing most reward systems as 'chaotic' with 'employers having little idea about what their pay systems are supposed to achieve'. Smith (1983: 12) is equally sceptical:

> Repeated questions to managers and employees about why they pay and accept certain levels of remuneration usually result in replies which boil down to the same answer: that is the pay level is as it has always been or, in harsher terms, we don't really know. There are very few organisations where the answer is clear and positive.

Clearly, pay does not have to be so 'chaotic'. The orthodoxy which has arisen in recent years under the heading of 'new pay' (Lawler, 1990; Schuster and Zingheim, 1992) argues that the business strategy of the organisation determines the behaviours employees need to demonstrate in order that the strategy may be implemented effectively. These behaviours may, in part, be delivered by the reward strategy. Lawler (1995) notes that the reward strategy consists of three key elements: the values which underpin the reward strategy, the reward structures, and the reward processes.

In this chapter we use the 'new pay' approach. We do not do so in an unthinking, prescriptive way by suggesting that this is the way to design and implement a reward strategy. 'New pay' is a philosophy rather than a set of practices. As such it is used both as a point of departure and a device for structuring the chapter. 'New pay' is a useful way of thinking about reward management because it has the potential to complement, if not generate, organisational change (Armstrong, 1996; also Flannery *et al.*, 1996).

The two case studies in this chapter are set in quite different employment contexts, but both feature organisations which face the need for dramatic organisational change. Both have used reward as an important part of their change strategy. The first, Midland Main Line, has woven reward change into a host of other changes necessary upon its creation as a new organisation. The second, Finbank, faced the necessity to improve profitability and developed a reward strategy, which had cost reduction as its driving force.

Reward management at Midland Main Line

Midland Main Line (MML) is one of the 25 new train operating companies created upon the privatisation of the rail industry following the 1993 Railways Act. It operates the high-speed service between London, Derby, Nottingham and Sheffield. The company employs approximately 900 people including drivers, train maintenance workers, station staff, train crew and office staff. MML is owned by National Express.

The strategic challenge facing MML is similar to those facing many other organisations. Put simply, it has to achieve higher income, lower costs and a better quality service. The company faces an enormous challenge. During the period of the seven-year contract which MML has been awarded it has to increase passenger income by two-thirds. This is no easy task when set against the maximum 3 per cent annual growth rate which was achieved under British Rail. Operating costs have to be reduced by one-third during the same period. In facing this challenge, MML, in effect, has to satisfy two masters. The parent company, National Express, has its profit expectations of MML. At the same time the government, which has traditionally heavily subsidised the railways, will cease to provide subsidy by the year 2000. MML's task is made even more daunting by the government edict that regulated fares should not rise by more than inflation minus 1 per cent (Brown, 1997).

Faced with the triple challenge of achieving higher income, lower costs and a better quality service MML has radically altered its employee relations strategy in which reward management plays a significant role. However, before describing the changes which have been implemented it is necessary to examine the situation which MML inherited.

The pay structure in British Rail was, to say the least, exceedingly complex. There were over 100 different staff grades in six different groups. Added to this there were in excess of 300 components of remuneration (Greenhill, 1997). These consisted mainly of allowances which had grown up over this century. For example, drivers were paid a 15-minute allowance for reading safety notices. This allowance arose because drivers were paid only for the time they were actually on driving duty so allowances were important because they were a significant addition to drivers' wages. In another example, fitters were paid an allowance for work performed which was normally part of another craftsman's job. The complexity of this system created a 'mini-industry' in British Rail where considerable expertise was needed to interpret all the pay arrangements. It was a highly centralised national system with little autonomy given to local line managers. This was in part due to the necessity for the British Rail Board to report direct to the Department of Transport.

The creation of MML has simplified collective bargaining arrangements. There is now local company-level bargaining. Pay and other major terms and conditions of employment are negotiated by the MML company council which consists of ▶

management and representatives of the four recognised trade unions sitting around a single table. Company-level bargaining means that MML can now negotiate arrangements, which are tailored to its specific operating requirements. For example, under the new bargaining structure MML has negotiated a deal whereby drivers can complete two return London-Sheffield journeys in a day. Under the national hours agreement it was possible to achieve only 1.5 return journeys.

The root cause of this complex system of pay allowances was the low basic wage paid by British Rail which employees boosted by overtime and allowances. Examples of drivers and electricians illustrate the point. Prior to the creation of MML, drivers were earning average annual pay of £11 440 and electricians £9765. This provided an inbuilt incentive for employees to create overtime although this may not have been strictly necessary had their duties been performed expeditiously. It is not difficult to imagine how this situation may have been to the immediate detriment of customer service, since the driver, and other on-train staff, were being rewarded with overtime in the event of trains running late. The new pay structure negotiated with the trade unions has abolished overtime and introduced a far higher basic wage. Drivers at MML now have a basic wage of £20 850 for a normal working week of 37 hours although this could be increased to a maximum of 48 hours. The result of this change is that there is now an incentive for drivers, and other grades, to get the job done as quickly and safely as possible, with consequent advantageous effects on train punctuality.

The key concept underpinning the new pay arrangements at MML is employee flexibility. It is this, added to the abolition of overtime, which has enabled MML to offer a high basic salary and provide a better customer service. Flexibility at MML impacts upon the duties employees perform and when they perform these duties. Two examples illustrate the concept. The first relates to depot staff at Leeds and Derby. Here work has been arranged in multi-skilled teams consisting of various crafts that maintain trains. The teams consist of skilled and semi-skilled staff who, as far as possible, perform each other's duties. In addition, the teams operate an annualised hours system. In this system, the company may require the teams to work a potential annual maximum of 1800 hours (equivalent to 37.5 hours × 48 weeks) although the contract specifies a normal annual maximum of 1680 hours (equivalent to 35 hours × 48 weeks) spread throughout the year. In some weeks it may be necessary to work more than 35 hours, in other weeks less. The key point here is that it is not necessary to work all of the 1680 hours. Under this system there is clearly an incentive to get the job done quickly and go home. The productivity gains made have allowed an anticipated 20 per cent reduction of jobs in the depots.

The second example relates to train crew staff. MML has restructured the on-train teams. There used to be eight grades including senior conductor, chef, guard, senior steward and ticket collector. This has been reduced to three grades: train manager, senior customer host and customer host. There is a higher basic salary for each grade: £18 500 for the train manager, £15 000 for the senior customer host and £11 500 for the customer host. Once again the aim is complete flexibility between roles, which has meant a major training programme.

Clearly, reform of the reward strategy has not taken place in isolation. It is part of a wider set of initiatives which have a clear strategic intent. As can be seen there has been wide-ranging structural change. Training and development has also been very much to the fore. Almost two-thirds of the staff have been through training programmes, which are designed to change the old British Rail culture. The values which these courses are seeking to inculcate are personal ownership of problems, empathising with the customer teamworking, thinking of new ideas, recognition of the value of individual contributions and continuous improvement. Attention has also been paid to performance management. For example, performance criteria for on-train staff are competence-based and emphasise customer service delivery team development and fulfilment of on-train specification. There is an element of 360-degree appraisal in that performance feedback on customer service is elicited by consultancy which does three-monthly surveys with 1000 customers.

The future may see MML make further reward management changes. Customer Services Director Barry Brown would like as much as 20 per cent of the pay packet to consist of variable pay. This would comprise a profit-related bonus (there is already a profit-related pay scheme in which 99 per cent of employees participate, and a share purchase scheme) and team performance bonus. A significant part of this team bonus could be paid as a cash bonus not consolidated into the employee's salary until the second year provided that performance was sustained. It is thought that this will be difficult to negotiate with the relevant trade unions. They would see it as a return to a lower basic wage with supplements. But in this case the supplements would be related to organisational and employee performance. It is all a far cry from the pay arrangements which MML inherited from British Rail.

Strategic reward management

Any consideration of the relationship between employee reward and organisational change must begin with a clarification of what it is the organisation wishes to change and why. A logical starting point for this process is to clarify what it is that the organisation wishes employees to do which may be different from that which they are currently doing. Equally logical is the rationale for such changed employee behaviours: that is, they should be consistent with what the organisation is seeking to achieve through its business strategy.

The strategic reward model in Fig. 7.1 suggests that reward strategy starts with a consideration of the external and internal operating environments. Clearly this was vital in the case of MML because of the profit demands being made by both the owner and government as well as the increased expectations of customers. Armstrong (1993) notes that the internal environment consists of the organisation's culture, structure, technology, working arrangements, processes and systems. In the

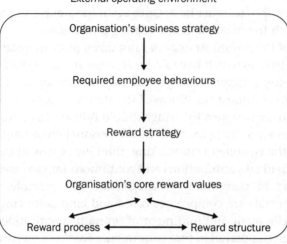

External operating environment

Organisation's business strategy

↓

Required employee behaviours

↓

Reward strategy

↓

Organisation's core reward values

Reward process ←——————→ Reward structure

Internal operating environment

Fig. 7.1 Key elements of reward system design
Source: Developed from Lawler, 1995.

MML case the business strategy is clear: to achieve higher income, lower costs and a better quality service. The employee behaviours associated with this strategy are flexibility and customer care.

As the case study illustrates, the MML human resource strategy is much wider than reward. It also encompasses contract of employment changes, training and performance management. What Lawler (1984) argues is that there should be congruence between these various aspects of the HRM strategy in that the reward system needs to fit the other features of the organisation to ensure that total human resource management congruence exists. This means that the reward system needs to fit such things as job design, supervisors' leadership styles and the types of career tracks available in the organisation.

Self-check question	7.1	_What other features of the organisation may the reward system need to fit in order that total human resource management congruence exists?_

According to Lawler (1995) the reward strategy consists of three components: the organisation's core reward values, structural issues and process features. The organisation's core reward values are what the organisation stands for; they inform the principles on which the reward strategy is founded. Structural issues include the strategy features (e.g. performance-related or profit-related pay) and the administrative policies surrounding these features. Process features include how the strategy is communicated and the extent to which employees are involved in the design and implementation of the strategy. We consider each of these in detail in the remainder of this chapter. Lawler makes the point that the stronger the alignment between the core reward values, structural features and processes, the more effective the reward strategy will be. He argues that the key consideration is the level of consistency between what organisations say and what they do. In the event of inconsistency Lawler notes that there is likely to be employee misunderstanding about how the reward strategy works with a consequence being a failure to motivate the required behaviours.

On the face of it this model of strategic reward management seems very straightforward, but it makes considerable assumptions. First, let us consider the main driving force of the reward strategy – the business strategy. Two of the complications are well rehearsed in the literature. First, there is the assumption that business strategy is a rational, top-down process rather than emergent (Mintzberg and Waters, 1989; Whittington, 1993). Even if the business strategy is clearly formulated, it is by no means certain that the HRM strategy will follow this lead. Indeed, if this is contemplated, it is often not possible to promote wholesale changes to, for example, recruitment and selection, training, appraisal and career development. What is more likely is that such changes happen incrementally over a substantial period of time.

In addition, the model is essentially unitarist in that it assumes employees will endorse the business strategy and wish to demonstrate the behaviours it implies. Moreover, it assumes that they will accept the organisation's reward strategy if the values, structure and process are consistent. This may be the case if the employees' interests are not threatened. But, as will become clearer later in this chapter, such reward changes under the heading of 'new pay' may not be received favourably by employees. Indeed, as long as one of the strategic driving forces is cost saving, such a threat is almost inevitable.

As well being unitarist, the strategic reward management model is highly deterministic. It reflects a very 'bottom line' orientation (Beaumont, 1993: 205) which assumes that an effective reward strategy will have a beneficial effect upon the performance of the organisation. This is a very considerable assumption because of the difficulty in subjecting it to empirical test. The model masks the complexities of organisational life. To think that simply designing the reward strategy in accordance with the prescription will yield 'success' ignores the host of variables which may conspire to render such an outcome unlikely. Managers often take 'short-cuts' due to the pressure to produce quick results exerted by senior managers obsessed with short-term goals (Storey and Sisson, 1993; Monks, 1998). There is often opposition to changing reward strategies from trade unions as well as from managers who feel their interests threatened. In short, the deterministic perspective is based on assumptions of rationality and unitarism which disregard the political realities of organisational life (Keenoy, 1990).

It seems that caution needs to be exercised in assuming that the implementation of strategic reward management will lead to a reward strategy which will automatically change employee behaviours in line with the organisation's business strategy. There are far too many variables which may conspire against such a straightforward cause-effect relationship. However, it would be foolish to abandon the possibility that reward strategy may play a role in contributing to organisational change. Consequently, the remainder of this chapter examines the components of

Fig. 7.1. The purpose of the analysis is to explain how integration between the HRM strategy and the reward strategy, and integration between the three components of the reward strategy itself, may contribute to changed employee behaviours.

The analysis starts with a consideration of the employee behaviours employers may wish to encourage. The relationship between HRM strategy and reward strategy is then examined briefly. The main part of the analysis is devoted to a consideration of the reward strategy's values, structures and processes.

Using rewards to change employee behaviours

The fundamental question here is: 'what sort of behaviours may the organisation wish to encourage?' The strategic HRM literature (e.g. Beer *et al.*, 1984; Guest, 1987) reflects the desire for certain key goals: employee commitment to the organisation's aims; employee competence; flexibility; and the production of quality goods and services. Among the employee behaviours which MML wish to encourage, flexibility is the most important. This entails working at a variety of tasks at variable times. This is particularly significant given the 'it's not my job' culture prevalent in the days of strict job demarcation. In addition, like most employers in competitive product markets, MML wished to encourage employees to take more responsibility for customer care by learning new skills and attitudes.

Self-check question	7.2	*What other behaviours may organisations wish to encourage among their employees?*

At this point we raise the assumption which dominates reward management thinking in general and the model in Fig. 7.1 in particular. This is that pay has the ability to motivate employees to behave in a way in which they may not otherwise behave. The theory which tends to predominate here is that of rational economic person. This has its roots in the work of F.W. Taylor (1911) who assumed that workers were lazy and needed money to motivate them to expend greater effort. The prevalence of payments-by-results schemes this century, in particular for blue-collar workers, testifies to the influence of this way of thinking about the relationship between pay and employee effort. Later, this approach was questioned by the human relations school which queried the over-reliance on money as a motivator and argued that social relationships were an important determinant of employee productivity.

Equally well-known are the theories of Maslow (1943) and Herzberg (1968). Maslow's 'hierarchy of needs' suggests that people's needs change as they ascend a hierarchy which has basic needs for food, security, etc. at the lowest level and self-actualisation at the highest. Herzberg argued that employees were more likely to be motivated by factors such as achievement and the work itself rather than simply money. While money has only limited power to motivate, it does have the ability to de-motivate employees if they are dissatisfied with the amount they receive or the way in which this amount is determined.

It is beyond the scope of this chapter to go into detail on these and the many other motivation theories. What is clear is that this is a highly complex issue. Perhaps the best we can say is that money may motivate some people to behave in particular ways some of the time, in some circumstances. What we cannot assume is a clear relationship between pay and motivation.

The point was made earlier in the chapter that reward is only part of the overall human resource strategy and that the strategic HRM literature (e.g. Beer *et al.*, 1984; Baird and Meshoulam, 1988; Miller, 1989) emphasises the importance of there being congruence between the various aspects of HRM. There is a compelling logic in this emphasis. A classic example of the existence of such congruence can be found in the case study organisation Premierco (Case Study 5.2). In this case there was a clear consistency between the effort put into the process of managing employee performance by line managers and the reward strategy which emphasised individual performance-related pay. In many organisations such consistency is less prevalent. In his study of team-based pay, Thompson (1995) reported a rarity of team pay approaches despite the fact that teamworking was widespread. Thompson reasons that this seeming contradiction may have two explanations. First, what he calls the 'lag' effect: 'organisations are seeking to develop and embed these working practices some time before they consider linking them to pay' (Thompson, 1995: x). The second explanation is more predictable. This, argues Thompson, is due to the *ad hoc* way in which UK organisations manage pay. Far from being strategic, pay, asserts Thompson, is being managed in a highly reactive fashion.

On the face of it Thompson's evidence on team pay suggests that strategic reward management in particular and strategic human resource management in general are not evident in practice in many UK organisations. However, the enormous interest which has been shown in recent years in the concept of strategic human resource management suggests that there is faith in the idea that integration of the various HR components will lead to more effective organisations.

Reward management values: their role in changing employee behaviours

Earlier in this chapter we noted the importance Lawler (1995) placed in consistency between the three components of reward strategy: values, structure and processes. In particular, Lawler claimed that an inconsistency between what the organisation says and does in its reward strategy may lead to employee discontent. It follows from this that the reward values which employers espouse are of great significance. In this section we look at five values which organisations may consider in reward management design. These are the degree to which the organisation believes in

■ paying for performance;
■ equity;
■ employees sharing in the organisation's success;
■ employee involvement in reward strategy design and implementation;
■ combining financial and non-financial rewards.

We now discuss each of these in turn.

Paying for performance

Paying for performance may take at least two forms: individual performance-related pay and team-based performance-related. As Chapter 5 indicates, individual performance-related pay has considerable potential to change the organisation's culture due to its symbolic significance (Schein, 1992) as a distinctive 'message carrier'. Indeed, research evidence (Kessler and Purcell, 1992; Cannell and Wood, 1992) suggests that moving towards a more 'performance-oriented culture' was a prevalent reason for introducing individual performance-related pay. If you would like to read more about this turn to Chapter 5 now.

Team-based performance-related pay, albeit in its infancy in the UK (Thompson, 1995), may encourage employees to work more closely in teams through giving members a clearer focus on the team's objectives and what needs to be done to achieve them. Working more effectively in teams certainly chimes with the general direction taken by many organisations in recent years as they have de-layered and flattened hierarchies, placing much more emphasis on employees co-operating with one another to get the job done with greater autonomy. This sits easily with the desire of organisations to develop a wider range of skills in their employees in order that team members interchange jobs more readily to meet demands (Armstrong, 1996).

Equity

It would be claiming too much to say that the value of equity may be a major contributor to the promotion of changed employee behaviours. But there is little doubt that if employees feel their pay to be inequitable then the change managers hope for in their new reward strategy are unlikely to materialise. This is because perceived inequity among employees will lead to a lack of employee acceptance of the reward strategy which is a key determinant of success (Lawler, 1990).

There are two ways in which employees may feel their pay is inequitable. First, there is the issue of external equity and internal equity. The former refers to the extent to which employees feel their pay is fair in relation to those doing similar jobs in other organisations. Internal equity relates to the same feeling in comparison with those doing similar jobs in their own organisation. Armstrong (1993) points out that in many organisations there is a tension between the two. The desire to be competitive in the labour market for some jobs, thus ensuring external equity, may lead to feeling of lack of internal inequity among those employees whose external labour market appeal does not afford them similar power. What is implied here is the necessity for employers to take a clear policy decision on the value it places on equity and the way in which this value is expressed.

The second way in which employees may feel their pay is inequitable is less about the amount of pay but the way in which it is determined. This raises issues concerning structure and process, which are dealt with below.

Employees sharing in the organisation's success

Organisations that wish to promote a high level of employee identification with the pursuit of success are likely to have an element of sharing in that success built into their reward strategy. The most popular form this has taken is profit-related pay. Other forms include gainsharing and schemes where employees obtain shares in their employing organisation. There is more about these schemes in the next section, on structures. However, it would be claiming a lot to suggest that these schemes play much of a role in changing employee behaviours due to the rather distant connection between effort and reward.

Employee involvement in reward strategy design and implementation

Traditionally, employers have not contemplated employee involvement in reward strategy design and implementation. Yet we take the view that the chances of a reward strategy gaining employee acceptance is that much greater if employees have a say in both design and implementation. We include some thoughts on how this may be accomplished in the section on reward management processes.

Combining financial and non-financial rewards

At the beginning of this chapter we made the point that the term 'reward' would be used in the chapter because it includes non-pay rewards. The extent to which an organisation combines financial and non-financial rewards in its reward strategy reflects a clear value position. Over-reliance on pay as a motivator is likely to be accompanied by other human resource policies which assume a scientific management perspective (e.g. no involvement in management decisions, minimum employee control over the way in which jobs are performed). Recognition by the employer that non-financial rewards may play an important part in attracting, and more particularly retaining, employees suggests a view of humanity which recognises that individuals require more for their efforts than pecuniary reward.

Armstrong (1996) notes that there are five areas where employees' needs may be met by non-financial rewards: achievement, recognition, responsibility, influence and personal growth. Of these, our view is that the first two will apply to virtually all employees. Responsibility, influence and personal growth will apply to many more than we realise. All of us like to feel that we have achieved something in our work, pride being derived from a job well done. In addition, most managers realise that a simple 'thank you' and a pat on the back for a job well done has enormous motivational power. It has to be recognised that not all employees seek greater responsibility in their jobs, or greater influence over decisions which directly or indirectly influence those jobs. This may be related to the individual's personal characteristics. But it may also be a consequence of a history of organisations not giving people the opportunity to exercise responsibility or influence. If you are dubious about the willingness of employees to accept responsibility and the extent to which this may be shaped by the way they are treated we recommend you look at Semler's (1993) account of the management style in his Brazilian company. The desire of many individuals to seek opportunities for personal growth through their work is very powerful. It may seem odd that this could be termed an employee reward rather than a vital prerequisite of organisational success. Yet many individuals rate the opportunity for personal growth higher than financial reward.

Reward management structures: their role in changing employee behaviours

Having looked at the values which employers may wish to foster through the reward strategy, we now turn to the structures which may be put in place to promote four of these values: paying for performance; equity; employees sharing in the organisation's success; and combining financial and non-financial rewards. (Employee involvement is considered in the following section on reward management processes.)

Paying for performance

Paying for individual job performance is, for many organisations, at the heart of a reward strategy. This raises what for many employees is a highly contentious issue: the putting at risk of a proportion of their salary. When most of us think about our pay we think in terms of base pay (Schuster and Zingheim, 1992): the fixed amount which traditionally has increased yearly to reflect inflation and, often, our length of service with the organisation. Base pay will also change, of course, upon promotion to a more responsible job. For many of us this has embodied our values of predictability, security and permanency – the very opposite of change. From a managerial perspective, it is not necessarily the best form of reward strategy. You will remember the desire of the Customer Services Director of MML to move to a situation where 80 per cent of pay is base pay and the remaining 20 per cent is variable pay. The very permanency which employees value is expensive. Increasingly employers are asking themselves: 'why should we build into our fixed salary costs a permanent salary bill which takes little account of changing external, organisational and individual circumstances?' Pay strategies which rely exclusively on base pay enshrined in salary scales through which employees move annually until the top of the scale is reached, or promotion achieved, are typical in the public sector. Such strategies assume that length of service equates with experience and loyalty. Neither tends to be as prized by organisations in the 1990s as in the past. Such is the pace of change that yesterday's experience may be an impediment to change. We all know that loyalty to one employer, typified by a career spent with that employer, is an increasingly outdated concept in an age where we may have a number of different careers as well as employers. In addition, pay strategies which rely on promotions for employees to increase their salaries take no account of the fact that organisations now have flatter structures with the consequence that promotion is less available. A large insurance company in which Phil did some research felt that the desire of employees to only move to jobs within the organisation which resulted in a minor promotion, and therefore re-grading, was a major obstacle to developing employees into different roles and having them learn new skills.

For some organisations base pay is of declining importance. This raises the question: 'how can the traditional reward objectives of attracting, retaining and motivating people be achieved while making the pay budget more cost effective?' The answer for many organisations has been to make base pay reflect the market rate for the job and to supplement this with a variable pay element related to individual performance, team performance, organisational performance and individual skill acquisition – or a combination of these. Central to the decisions which need to be taken is whether to pay the variable element as a lump sum bonus or to consolidate this into salary. The trend in the USA has been for variable pay to be one-off cash bonuses (Kanter, 1987). This is hardly surprising given the cost saving that the organisation enjoys. By not raising base pay, one-off cash bonuses do not affect future base pay increases or other associated payments such as overtime, and, of course, pensions.

Moving from all base pay to a combination of base and variable pay does, of course, signal, in part, a conceptual move from paying for the job to paying the person. Thus, the reliance on traditional bureaucratic forms of job evaluation is less pronounced. That is not to say that job evaluation is no longer relevant. We noted earlier that base pay still needs to be set at a level consistent with the external labour market. Therefore, some method of determining the relative importance of the job is needed. It is that definition of importance which is likely to be different in the organisation which places more significance in a combination of base and variable pay. Such a definition is likely to reflect the changed employee behaviours the organisation wishes to encourage in order to met its changed organisational circumstances. What is clear, according to Schuster and Zingheim (1992), is that internal equity will no longer be the most important consideration. The market value of jobs, and employees' skills and their impact on the organisation's strategy will take precedence over internal equity. It must be borne in mind, however, that such a strategy runs the risk of falling foul of the legislation on equal pay. This could be a major issue of which we feel you must be aware.

Before leaving the topic of paying for performance we consider structural design issues relating to two of the paying-for-performance initiatives which we mentioned above: individual performance-related pay and team-based pay.

One of the reasons individual performance-related pay has fallen from grace in personnel circles is the failure of many schemes to discriminate between differing levels of performance both in terms of measurement made and pay allocated. In one organisation where Phil conducted research nearly nine out of ten employees received a performance rating in the middle ranges of the distribution. In view of the fact that there was only sufficient money in the performance-related pay 'pot' to award an average base pay increase of 2.5 per cent, the financial reward for employees who achieved a rating just above average was negligible which resulted in a good deal of employee dissatisfaction.

The extent to which team-based pay may deliver its objectives is partly dependent on the structural features of the scheme. Principal among these features are clear definition of team membership and purpose (for example, some teams are permanent, others set up to run a specific project); members whose work is interdependent and who work well together and share accountability (Armstrong, 1996). It is inevitable that some employees will feel that they contribute more to the team than others. In view of this it may be that greater employee acceptability will be achieved if team-based pay is only one part of the payment package, together with individual performance-related pay.

Equity

The pay issue which has gained more publicity than any other in recent years is that of directors' pay. The image of directors gaining huge pay increases in a time when their organisations have been declaring redundancies and trimming general pay costs is one that has created a feeling of profound internal inequity. The facts appear to bear out this feeling. Armstrong (1996) notes that in the period between 1985 and 1990, according to a survey by the UK National Institute of Economic and Social Research, directors' pay rose in real terms by 77 per cent while the equivalent figure for all employees was 17 per cent. Reports from the Cadbury and Greenbury committees of the mid 1990s, which were designed to secure greater openness and accountability, seem to have done little to improve the public perception of unfairness. What is clear here is that employee acceptance of reward strategy change is unlikely if the general impression is that 'fat cats' are getting an unfair share of organisational rewards.

A lack of internal equity may also be evident in the case of perceived inequality between the pay of men and women. An issue which is discussed less often is the possibility of perceived inequality in the comparison between white-collar and blue-collar workers. This is a wider issue than simply pay. It relates to a range of terms and conditions of employment. It is worth noting here that many organisations which have been in the vanguard of change, in particular Japanese manufacturing companies, have featured initiatives designed to harmonise terms and conditions of employment between white-collar and blue-collar workers in an attempt to foster a greater feeling of 'community' in their workforce (Price and Price, 1994).

We cannot leave structural issues without mentioning broad banding. This is defined by Armstrong (1996: 224) as 'the compression of a hierachy of pay grades or salary ranges into a small number (typically four or five) of wide bands. Each of the bands will therefore span the pay opportunities previously covered by several separate pay ranges.' The advantages of broad banding noted by Armstrong (1996) suggest that this pay reform has, potentially, a powerful role to play in complementing, if not generating, organisational change. Among these are:

- facilitation of movement of employees across the organisation without the necessity for promotion to a higher grade to be obtained;
- development of employees' skills and competencies by removing perceived barriers to movement;
- the support of multi-skilling and teamwork by removing barriers to lateral movement;
- enabling line managers to accept greater responsibility to reward with salary increases those employees who demonstrate a greater 'contribution' (however defined) to the organisation.

<table>
<tr><td>Self-check question</td><td>7.3 What may be some of the disadvantages of broad banding?</td></tr>
</table>

We have noted the importance of broad banding under the heading of 'equity' because it has the potential to reward those 'solid citizens' who add a good deal to every organisation but who do not pursue promotion. Wider pay ranges give them the opportunity to 'grow' their salaries without hitting the barriers imposed by narrower bands which can only be surmounted by promotion. However, the role broad banding plays in organisational change is potentially very important. It complements the efforts which many organisations are currently making to achieve greater flexibility in the organisation of work.

Employees sharing in the organisation's success

A recurrent theme throughout this book is that organisational change is more likely to be achieved if employees feel themselves to be a valuable part of the organisation. Reward schemes which enable employees to share in the organisation's success (or failures) are a powerful way of reinforcing this message.

Profit-related pay has grown considerably in recent years to the point where in 1994 1.8 million private sector employees were covered by such a scheme (Income Data Services, 1994). The reasons for this are not difficult to guess since it has been possible for employees to have as much as £4000 of salary per year free of income tax. This tax advantage was introduced by government to promote a stronger awareness of the commercial performance of the employer among employees and to encourage employees to greater effort. It is doubtful if it has achieved that effect since many organisations have seen it as little more than a tax-efficient way of structuring salary. However, the last Conservative budget in 1997 announced the gradual withdrawal of the tax advantage by the year 2000. Perhaps profit performance awareness would be more effectively promoted by cash-based profit sharing schemes in which normally a bonus payment is made in the event of commercial success but not where the company has had an unsuccessful year.

Awareness of commercial performance may also be enhanced by the various employee share ownership schemes, such as the scheme which exists at MML, where employees are able to purchase shares in their employing company.

Gainsharing, which tends to be more popular in the USA than in Britain, is another way in which employees may share in the success created by their own efforts. In gainsharing the relationship between employees' efforts and their eventual reward is rather more direct than with profit-related pay. Gainsharing plans are designed so that employees share improvements in productivity, cost saving or quality with the payment being paid from costs savings generated as a result of such improvements. The employees participating in the gainsharing plan are normally part of a discernible group who have had a direct effect upon the cost savings. The resultant payment to them may be made in three ways: as a percentage of base pay; as a one-off cash bonus; or as a payment per hour worked. Schuster and Zingheim (1992) make the point that the same payment would normally go to all members of the group. They are also at pains to point out that the organisation must design safeguards to ensure that it derives financial value from the results generated from the project linked to gainsharing. This type of gainsharing differs from more traditional forms of gainsharing which have operated in manufacturing under the heading of Scanlon and Rucker plans. The principal difference is that the foundation of this new type of gainsharing is the future goals of the organisation whereas that of more traditional gainsharing plans is the historical performance standards of the participating employees. The key point here, of course, is that historical performance standards may be achieved or exceeded while the organisation's overall goals are not met.

Combination of financial and non-financial rewards

We noted earlier the importance of non-financial rewards in a reward strategy. For many employees these may be particularly important as motivational tools. This is because of their capacity to meet the employees' needs for achievement, recognition, responsibility, influence and personal growth. We note below some of the structures which may need to be in place in order that these needs may be realised. This in turn increases the possibility of organisational change consequent upon more positive employee attitudes and behaviours.

The first of these is probably the easiest and least expensive to put in place. This is a communication strategy which broadcasts the successes of individuals and teams. Many organisations do this through their in-house magazines. This combined with special 'thank you' prizes (e.g. a weekend in Paris) often will have more motivational influence than direct financial rewards. One manager Phil interviewed talked of the de-motivating influence of performance-related pay awards replacing promotions in a flatter structure because promotions were symbols of individual success highly visible to all his colleagues. He liked his colleagues to know he was successful!

Performance appraisal systems also have a significant role to play in meeting employees' needs for recognition and a feeling of achievement. Chapter 5 talks of the importance of goal-setting and giving feedback to employees about their performance in pursuit of those goals. A developmental perspective to performance appraisal rather than seeing it as a management control mechanism is likely to result in employees defining their own training and career development needs. However, this approach to performance appraisal does depend on line managers having the appropriate attitudes and skills to manage in such a way that the individual is given sufficient autonomy for personal growth to be developed. This signals a clear training need which is about encouraging managers to shed the 'technician' label they often possess and embrace new ways of managing which have leadership and facilitation as their guiding principles rather than power and control. These 'new ways of managing' are central to the concept of change given the key role line managers play in managing the change process.

Employees' needs for responsibility, influence and personal growth may also be met through imaginative job design. Among the elements of job design which Armstrong (1993) advocates to enhance the interest and challenge of work are: greater responsibility for employees in deciding how their work is done; reducing task specialisation; allowing employees greater freedom in defining their performance goals and standards of performance; and introducing new and more challenging tasks. In addition, more opportunities for employee involvement may also foster responsibility, influence and personal growth among employees. These benefits are well illustrated in the DuPont case study in Chapter 3. They may be achieved through such activities as quality circles and problem-solving groups.

All the above structural measures designed to foster the values consistent with non-financial rewards do not involve pay. However, there is one very topical form of reward which may do a good deal to promote, potentially, all the employees' needs covered above. This is skill-based pay. Skill-based pay is 'a payment system in which pay progression depends on the acquisition by employees of new skills' (Income Data Services, 1992: 1). It is at the heart of organisational change. Skill-based pay is consistent with the concept of 'new pay' in that it relates to the payment of the person not the job. Organisations normally introduce skill-based pay to increase the ability of employees to perform a wider range of tasks thus assuring greater flexibility in coping with increased demands. Although it has been introduced for manufacturing jobs in organisations such as Amersham International, Pirelli Cables and Pilkington Glass (Income Data Services, 1992) the influence of skill-based pay is spreading into white-collar jobs. You may argue that providing a financial incentive to the employee may be inconsistent with meeting the needs for achievement, recognition, responsibility, influence and personal growth. For some employees you may well be correct. Nonetheless, skill-based pay may play a part in meeting these needs through its ability to enhance the employee's intrinsic interest in the job as a consequence of being able to perform a wider range of tasks. In addition, it is likely to increase the value of the employee to the organisation. This is not only of benefit to the organisation, of course, but adds to the attractiveness of the employee to alternative employers.

Self-check question	**7.4** *What may be some of the potential pitfalls of skill-based pay?*

Reward management processes: their role in changing employee behaviours

In this section we consider key reward management processes which are associated with the reward management structures analysed above. It is our view that these processes are usually given scant attention in the reward management literature. The emphasis is invariably upon structures. However, the soundest structures based upon a clear view of the values which underpin the organisation's reward strategy are of little value if they are implemented ineffectively. If that is the case they are unlikely to lead to the reward strategy playing its part in encouraging the changed employee behaviours necessary for organisational change.

Here we do not discuss, as we did in the previous two sections, the processes associated with each of the reward management values. Instead we concentrate on two process issues: employee involvement and communication. It is these two which appear to be the most significant and which are given the most attention in the literature.

Employee involvement

We make the point in the section on values that employee involvement in the design and implementation of reward strategy is likely to lead to greater employee acceptance of the strategy. This acceptance means that the change organisations seek to generate through revised reward strategies is likely to be achieved.

Schuster and Zingheim (1992) advocate that employee involvement in the design of reward strategies may occur at five stages. In the first of these there is a feasibility study to establish precisely what is expected both from a new reward strategy and the involvement of employees in its design. In the second stage a task force is set up. This may comprise about a dozen members: managers, supervisors and employees. The group's task is to consider all the possible methods of achieving the expectations defined in the first stage and to put a proposal to senior management about the purpose and content of the new reward strategy. At the third stage the strategy is implemented. Schuster and Zingheim assert that involved employees should be held accountable for the results achieved following monitoring of the strategy. This means monitoring not only the pay strategy itself but also the process of its design. The fourth stage is particularly important. This is the communication of the strategy to affected employees and training of those supervisors and managers who have to implement it. The more radical the new strategy the more the communication effort is necessary as, for example, British Gas Trading discovered when it needed to announce details of a pay freeze for some employees and reduced rises for others in the light of a predicted downturn in the business cycle (Welch, 1998). The final stage is monitoring and evaluation where the task force meets regularly to review progress.

Schuster and Zingheim (1992) make two further valid points. The first is that organisations may consider an employee attitude survey prior to the consideration of a new reward strategy. This can be seen as an important part of the communications effort in that it sets the climate for introduction. Their second point is equally important: employee involvement will not be sufficient in itself to lead to reward strategy success. They argue that new pay plans must be technically and qualitatively sound in order that they may be effective.

The way in which employees are involved in the implementation of reward strategy is equally important. In Chapter 5 we noted how employees may be involved in the processes which are crucial to the effective implementation of performance management. Among these are the setting of performance objectives. The point here is that objectives are more likely to be accepted by employees if they have had a hand in setting them. Similarly, criteria for measuring performance which are not simply imposed by the line manager without consultation are more likely to be seen as valid by employees.

In team-based pay schemes the implementation processes which are of particular importance are similar to those in individual performance-related pay. Such decisions as the method of setting team objectives, performance measurement criteria and the method of determining the amount payable lend themselves to employee involvement. This last issue may be particularly important in team-based pay, assuming the award is given to the team based on overall team performance. The team may then make its own decision as the way in which that allocation should be distributed to team members. After all, team members are best placed to judge the contribution of individuals. We have all been in teams where some of the members haven't pulled their weight. In such cases, the hardest decision team members have to make is to allocate less to individuals whom they thought contributed least. To empower the team to give less to these individuals would be a powerful form of poor performance control – probably a good deal more powerful than that which the line managers would impose.

The potential combination of financial and non-financial rewards highlights the importance of employee involvement in reward strategy implementation. This is where employees may be involved in a choice as to how their rewards are distributed. So-called 'cafeteria' benefits systems are more popular in the USA than in the UK. They allow employees some freedom of choice over a range of benefit options within the constraint of the overall amount to which they are entitled. Although such systems are more prevalent for senior managers, most of us place different values on aspects of reward. Some, for example, would prefer to forego cash to enjoy private health benefits or a sabbatical period. Armstrong and Murlis (1994) note the difficulties inherent in managing such schemes, not the least of which are the tax complications which can arise. The point remains, however, that it may be a more imaginative use of the employee rewards which finds acceptance among some employees.

Communication

The amount of information which the organisation communicates about its reward strategy and the way in which it is implemented says a good deal about its culture. In some organisations pay is very much a secretive issue. We have worked in organisations where we have been discouraged from talking about pay to our colleagues. Such organisations are unlikely to articulate to their employees their reward values or the purposes of the particular reward structures they adopt (assuming they are clear about these purposes). In addition, the reward processes will probably be notable for their lack of openness to employees. In such cases employees will be unaware of the criteria for rewards or promotion.

It is understandable why managers may wish to veil reward issues in secrecy. Secrecy affords managers greater flexibility in their dealings with employees. This may be justifiable, for example, in certain labour market situations where it is necessary to pay some newly recruited employees at a level which existing employees may perceive as unfair. A lack of openness implies that managers have to be less accountable for their decisions than in situations where reward issues are open. This may be attractive to many managers. However, as Lawler (1984) notes, the disadvantages of secrecy surrounding the reward strategy are that inaccurate rumours may spread and a low-trust employee relations climate is generated.

Greater openness in reward matters is characteristic of the public sector. However, this is less to do with management willingness to be open than with the fact that pay levels and pay progression criteria have traditionally been determined at national level.

Our view is similar to that of Lawler (1984) in that the decision management makes over its reward communication policy is contingent upon the organisation's culture and the employee behaviours it wishes to create. Greater employee creativity and responsibility, which are among the behaviours that many employers wish to generate, may be more congruent with an open communication policy. However, this carries with it the necessity for managers to implement the policy of openness with a level of skill which may need considerable development.

SUMMARY

- 'New pay' is the philosophy which underpins this chapter. 'New pay' is a useful way of thinking about reward management because it has the potential to complement, if not generate, organisational change.

- Organisational change must begin with a clarification of what it is the organisation wishes to change and why. A starting point is to clarify what it is that the organisation wishes employees to do which may be different from what it is that they are currently doing. Such changed employee behaviours should be consistent with what the organisation is seeking to achieve through its business strategy. The aim of the reward strategy is to contribute to the generation of these changed employee behaviours.

- There are many variables which may prevent the reward strategy contributing to organisational change. Among these are the possible lack of clarity of the business strategy and the unitarist assumptions which are made about the employee relationship.

■ If the reward strategy is to make its contribution to changing employee behaviours it must contain three key components: the values which underpin the strategy; the structures which are in place to promote these values; and the processes involved in the design and implementation of the strategy.

■ The five values which underpin the reward management strategy are: the degree to which the organisation believes in paying for performance; equity; employees sharing in the organisation's success; employee involvement in reward strategy design and implementation; and combining financial and non-financial rewards.

■ Principal among the structures in place to promote the reward values are making a clear division between base pay and variable pay; individual performance-related pay; team-based pay; broad banding; profit-related pay; gainsharing; performance appraisal; job design and skill-based pay.

■ If the reward strategy is to be effective in contributing to a change in employee behaviours it must be implemented effectively. The key processes contained in the implementation of the strategy are employee involvement and communication.

CASE STUDY 7.2

Reward strategy for managers at Finbank

Finbank is one of the largest high street banks with assets of £80 000 million. It has over 40 000 employees and nearly 2000 branches. This case study is about how Finbank used its reward strategy for managers to achieve organisational change.

Finbank's business strategy was to improve profitability. This was to be achieved by driving up income and driving down costs. This had the powerful advantage of being clearly understood by all managers. Moreover, they also understood the reasons for this strategy.

The reward strategy was to make a contribution towards both the increase in income and the cutting of costs. The principal means of achieving the former was by making staff more sales-conscious. Cost-cutting was to be achieved by reducing the fixed element of the managerial salary bill and increasing the variable amount. A more detailed description of how this was to be achieved is given below.

The traditional image of the bank manager as the 'community ambassador' had changed (Cressey and Scott, 1993). The role had become that of a business manager or, less flatteringly, a 'salesman'. With this, the 'job for life' had disappeared. In addition, lending decisions about retail business had been de-skilled in that information technology made the decision for the manager by using computerised credit-scoring. All this pointed to the need for different managers. They needed to be less experienced, more commercially aware, more energetic; and they could be obtained, and retained, more cheaply than their predecessors. This suggested the need for a new reward strategy for branch managers which rewarded the procurement of sales, did not reward experience to the same extent as hitherto and, critically, trimmed the bank's managerial labour costs.

▶

The general impression was that prior to the introduction of the new reward strategy the performance of managers at Finbank needed improvement. The metaphor of the 'comfort zone' was in common use. Younger managers spoke of older managers who were 'content to take it steady and let the world pass them by'. Many of these managers had gone since the late 1980s, but still some remained. For those that remained, the new reward strategy carried the clear threat that 'under-performing' would be penalised in the pay packet.

Finbank introduced its new reward strategy in the late 1980s. It simplified the grade structure by reducing the number of management grades from eight to three; introduced a company bonus plan and improved fringe benefits; abolished premium payments for weekday overtime and introduced individual performance-related pay.

Initially, this package was well received by managers. This was not surprising given that there was a two-year settlement period where any potential 'threat effect' of performance-related pay was cushioned by a guaranteed 12 per cent salary increase which was virtually double the then 'going rate'.

The most contentious aspect of the strategy was individual performance-related pay. This was because it represented a fundamental change from the previous arrangement where employees were paid according to grade and length of service.

Finbank operated its performance-related pay scheme under the umbrella of a performance management system. The cornerstone of this system was the setting of objectives by the implementing manager for the recipient manager. These objectives were derived from the bank's objectives. The main component of these objectives was 'hard' financial targets, e.g. amount of loans, sales of mortgages, leads for the corporate managers to follow up, as well as 'softer' objectives relating to how the managers carried out the job. These objectives were assessed annually for pay. Assessment was on a five-point scale from 'outstanding' to 'unsatisfactory'.

A key feature of the Finbank performance-related pay system was the abolition of the automatic annual increase. This was a radical move by the bank and sent a powerful signal to managers that their world was changing from one which was secure and predictable to one that mirrored the intensely competitive product market in which they operated. The bank designed a pay matrix which allocated a specified amount of money to the manager based upon the performance rating received and position on the salary scale. Under the new arrangements managers receiving a salary below the median figure for the grade received a consolidated salary increment. Those managers with a salary above the median did not receive an increase but received a one-off cash bonus which was not consolidated into salary. By this means the bank was seeking to adjust base pay for all managers to a market-based level and not incur the fixed cost of paying for past years' good performance as an annuity.

The advantages to the bank were obvious, the major one being the reduction of the fixed proportion of managerial labour costs. This was vital since labour costs were by far the largest element of the bank's total costs. Since the retail bank manager labour market operated on internal labour market principles it followed that there were a high number of long-serving managers in each grade. The cost of rewarding these long-serving managers was that many junior managers were not being recompensed adequately.

Senior managers at Finbank thought the bank needed to move from a culture that emphasised bureaucracy to a 'performance culture'. Performance-related pay was a powerful symbol of culture change at Finbank.

The way that performance-related pay had been introduced served as a symbol of the declining amount of trust between Finbank and its managers. They were told that 'the sky's the limit' as far as salary was concerned, but as inflation decreased and the amount of money in the pay 'pot' reduced this promise was clearly not fulfilled. Consequently, the general impression of managers was that the bank had been disingenuous, as the real reason for the introduction of performance-related pay was cost control. Managers, in general, accepted the logic of this reason. They objected because the bank didn't admit this.

Managers were unhappy about the way in which their performance objectives were set. The official line was that objectives were negotiated with the implementing manager. Yet most managers insisted the reality was that they were imposed: by 'the bank' on area managers and by area managers on branch managers. The scope of performance objectives for Finbank managers was restricted. They seemed only to dwell on the achievement of financial business targets. This was consistent with the emphasis of the new reward strategy, but it encouraged managers to concentrate on the short term rather than build long-term developmental relationships with staff and customers. Managers were also concerned about there being too many objectives with the consequence that there was insufficient opportunity for recipient and implementing managers to focus on specific objectives. Some objectives were seen as more important than others. Some managers felt their objectives were unachievable from the outset and a significant minority had no knowledge of the targets until well into the 'measurement year'.

Finbank managers expressed concern about the subjectivity of the measurement process. Managers were worried about the lack of congruence between their views on the variables affecting achievement and those of the rating manager. The general view seemed to be 'it's OK as long as he thinks in the same way as you'.

There was little evidence that Finbank managers were receiving qualitative feedback on their job performance from their managers or learning from the experiences of others. This was blamed by one senior HR manager on implementing managers who saw performance management and performance-related pay as a bureaucratic necessity. Therefore, there was little management development taking place. Advancement was something which was seen simply in terms of salary or promotion. For the more experienced managers salary had effectively been capped, and promotion opportunities had been reduced by restructuring. Therefore, it was doubtful if there was significant motivation for managers to learn.

The most important issue for some managers was the payment of a cash bonus instead of a salary increase, depending on their position on the salary scale. This devalued the whole performance-related pay process from the perspective of those managers who received the bonuses. Another feature of recipient manager discontent was that managers knew what their ratings were likely to be, but did not know how that rating would be translated into cash. Managers would have preferred a straightforward matrix where they could 'read off' what salary increase a particular performance grading would attract. This was not the case.

A survey revealed that over three-quarters of the recipient managers interviewed at Finbank were extremely unhappy with performance-related pay. They felt that the bank no longer valued loyalty. The causes of these feelings were the abolition of the automatic annual increase and the reduced opportunity to progress through the incremental system. At a branch managers' meeting one manager spoke of managers being 'permanently on trial' as a result of a pay system which meant they would get no salary increase unless their performance warranted it.

Their major concern was how a lower basic salary would affect their pension fund. The second major practical worry was about their ability to keep up with the cost of living and therefore meet their financial obligations. Senior managers were worried about the incentive effect in the longer term. They were also concerned about the effect of the new policy on younger managers who had reached a point just above the pay median prior to the introduction of the 'no automatic increases' rule. They would suffer from the imposition of cash bonuses.

Case study questions

1 To what extent do you think Finbank's strategy amounted to 'strategic reward management'?

2 How do you think Finbank could have communicated the strategy more effectively to its employees?

3 What other measures do you think Finbank could have taken to generate the required employee behaviours?

4 Upon what factors do you think the success of the Finbank strategy will depend?

REFERENCES

Armstrong, M. (1993) *Managing Reward Systems*, Buckingham: Open University Press.

Armstrong, M. (1996) *Employee Reward*, London: Institute of Personnel and Development.

Armstrong, M. and Murlis, H. (1994) *Reward Management: A Handbook of Remuneration Strategy and Practice,* 3rd edn, London: Kogan Page.

Baird, L. and Meshoulam, I. (1988) 'Managing two fits of strategic human resource Management', *Academy of Management Review*, 13(1), 116–28.

Beaumont, P.B. (1993) *Human Resource Management: Key Concepts and Skills*, London: Sage.

Beer, M., Spector, B., Lawrence, P.R., Quinn Mills, D. and Walton, R.E. (1984) *Managing Human Assets*, New York: Free Press.

Brown, B. (1997) 'Getting there', *People Management*, 1 May.

Cannell, M. and Wood, S. (1992) *Incentive Pay: Impact and Evolution*, London: Institute of Personnel Management and National Economic Development Office.

Cressey, P. and Scott, P. (1993) 'Employment, technology and industrial relations in the UK clearing banks: is the honeymoon over?, *New Technology, Work and Employment*, 83–96.

Flannery, T., Hofrichter, D. and Platten, P. (1996) *People, Performance and Pay*, New York: Free Press.

Greenhill, R. (1997) 'All change', *People Management*, 1 May.

Guest, D. (1987) 'Human resource management and industrial relations', *Journal of Management Studies*, 24(5), 503–21.

Herzberg, F. (1968) *Work and the Nature of Man*, London, Staples Press.

Income Data Services (1992) *Skill-based Pay*, Study No. 500, February.

Income Data Services (1994) *Profit-related Pay*, Study No. 564, October.

Kanter, R.M. (1987) 'The attack on pay', *Harvard Business Review,* March–April, 60–7.

Keenoy, T. (1990) 'Human resource management: rhetoric, reality and contradiction', *International Journal of Human Resource Management*, 1(3), 363–84.

Kessler, I. and Purcell, J. (1992) 'Performance related pay: objectives and application*', Human Resource Management Journal*, 2(3), 16–33.

Lawler, E.E. (1984) 'The strategic design of reward systems', in Fombrun, C., Tichy, N.M. and Devanna, M. (eds), *Strategic Human Resource Management*, New York: John Wiley.

Lawler, E.E. (1990) *Strategic Pay: Aligning Organisational Strategies and Pay Systems*, San Francisco, Calif.: Jossey-Bass.

Lawler, E. (1995) 'The new pay: a strategic approach', *Compensation and Benefits Review*, July–August, 14–22.

Livy, B. (1988) '*Corporate Personnel Management*, London: Pitman.

Maslow, A. (1943) 'A theory of human motivation', *Psychological Review*, 50, 370–96.

Miller, P. (1989) 'Strategic HRM: what it is and what it isn't', *Personnel Management*, February, 47–51.

Mintzberg, H. and Waters, J. (1989) 'Of strategies deliberate and emergent', in Asch, D. and Bowman, C. (eds), *Readings in Strategic Management*, Basingstoke: Macmillan.

Monks, J. (1998) 'Trade unions, enterprise and the future', in Sparrow, P. and Marchington, M. (eds), *Human Resource Management: The New Agenda*, London: Financial Times Pitman Publishing.

Price, L. and Price, R. (1994) 'Change and continuity in the status divide', in Sisson, K. (ed.), *Personnel Management*, Oxford: Blackwell.

Schein, E. (1992) 'Coming to a new awareness of organisational culture', in Salaman, G. (ed.), *Human Resource Strategies*, London: Sage.

Schuster, J. and Zingheim, P. (1992) *The New Pay: Linking Employee and Organisational Performance*, New York: Lexington.

Semler, R. (1993*) Maverick! The Success Story behind the World's Most Unusual Workplace*, London: Arrow Business Books.

Smith, I. (1983) *The Management of Remuneration: Paying for Effectiveness*, London: Institute of Personnel Management.

Smith, I. (1993) 'Reward management: a retrospective assessment', *Employee Relations*, 15(3), 45–59.

Storey, J. and Sisson, K. (1993) *Managing Human Resources and Industrial Relations*, Buckingham: Open University Press.

Taylor, F.W. (1911) *Principles of Scientific Management*, New York: Harper and Row.

Thompson, M. (1995) *Team Working and Pay*, Institute of Employment Studies Report No. 281, Brighton: University of Sussex.

Welch, J. (1998) 'British Gas leaks vital information', *People Management*, 19 February.

Whittington, R. (1993) *What is Strategy and Does It Matter?*, London: Routledge.

ANSWERS TO SELF-CHECK QUESTIONS

7.1 *What other features of the organisation may the reward system need to fit in order that total human resource management congruence exists?*

Lawler (1984) refers to the way jobs are designed, the leadership style of supervisors and the types of career tracks available to employees. In addition, the type of employees recruited and selected will be important. It is of little use recruiting people with a high need for income security and predictability if the reward system is going to be marked by an absence of these factors. As with job design, it also seems sensible to arrange the training effort in order that employees are given every opportunity to acquire those skills which will be rewarded.

7.2 *What other behaviours may organisations wish to encourage among their employees?*

There are numerous examples of lists of such behaviours available. A clear example is that of Thomas Cook (Armstrong, 1996). This organisation defined the generic aptitudes necessary to perform jobs effectively. These are grouped under six headings: knowledge and skills; human relations skills (including influencing other people, leadership, selling, communicating); thinking and reasoning; numerical, logical and information technology skills; personal qualities (e.g. responsibility, flexibility); and physical skills. It is perhaps predictable that there will be a high degree of similarity in the lists of attributes produced by different organisations, particularly if they are in a similar product market. However, we are very wary of 'off-the-shelf' packages available from consultants operating in this area. It seems to us to be much more sensible for each organisation to have a go at developing its own list of required employee behaviours.

7.3 *What may be some of the disadvantages of broad banding?*

Perhaps the most important disadvantage is that employees may feel resentment at the introduction of broad banding. It overturns an established set of hierarchical principles with which we have all become familiar. Those aspiring to climb the heights of a steep, ascending pay structure are denied the opportunity of so doing and those near the top may resent that those beneath them having an 'easier' journey than that which they had to endure. (Yes, pay is an emotive topic!) In addition, it may be that the pay aspirations of lower-paid employees are unrealistic. All this points to the need for careful communication to employees in order that they understand why broad banding is being introduced and how it will operate.

Armstrong (1996) warns of the danger of broad banding escalating payroll costs. No longer do narrow pay scales inhibit the growth of individuals. Managers have the flexibility to award their more effective employees higher salaries. However, such flexibility suggests that careful control needs to be exercised.

7.4 *What may be some of the potential pitfalls of skill-based pay?*

There are two major potential pitfalls: cost, and the de-motivational effect on employees who have developed all the skills 'on offer'. Skill-based pay is obviously costly because of the considerable training effort necessary. This involves not only the direct cost of training employees but the indirect cost of, for example, attendance at college to acquire appropriate skill modules. The consideration of cost raises the issue of waste. This may occur when the organisation does not use the skills which it has gone to the trouble of developing in the employee. De-motivation in the employee who has acquired all the skills deemed necessary is understandable. This may be lessened by the introduction of an individual performance-related element to the pay package.

CHAPTER

8

Employee relations and involvement strategies and the management of change

Having completed this chapter, you will be able to:

▪ Identify a range of contemporary employee relations strategies.

▪ Discuss the role of these strategies in achieving employee relations change.

▪ Evaluate the role of employee involvement in achieving organisational and employee relations change.

▪ Analyse approaches to understanding the psychological contract and employee commitment and evaluate their links to employee involvement.

▪ Link employee relations and involvement strategies to other HR change interventions.

INTRODUCTION

In a book on contemporary HRM and change, some writers may be tempted to ignore the topic of employee relations. If we were writing this book 25 years ago it is certain that industrial relations, as it was then called, would have been the main focus because of the high level of manifest discontent that characterised industrial life. Managing the consequences of this discontent was a major concern of both personnel specialists and line managers. But since the 1970s there have been enormous changes in the way in which the employment relationship is managed. These changes are inextricably linked with the main theme of this book – wider organisational change. Changes in the operating environments of organisations in recent years mean that organisations need to be much more responsive to the demands of the product market. This in turn means greater demands on employees. An example is customer demand for longer opening hours in, for example, supermarkets and financial services call centres. This requires more flexible working arrangements and an employment contract which reflects this need.

In this chapter, we define employee relations as the relationship between the employer and the employee and the way in which this relationship is regulated. Such regulation focuses on the content of the employment relationship and the processes used to ensure that the relationship is managed in such a way that the needs of the employer and the employee are met.

In the section following the first case study, we highlight some of the main changes in the employment relationship. We then focus on one of the main process changes – employee involvement. We have chosen employee involvement because of the marked growth of interest in this area and because of its strong link to organisational change. Before explaining some of these changes in detail, we examine employee relations change at one of the UK's major private sector employers, Tesco.

CASE STUDY 8.1

Refocusing employee relations at Tesco

Tesco has the largest market share of the UK supermarket business. It has over 600 stores and 150 000 staff. Terms and conditions of those staff have been negotiated with USDAW, the only trade union with a recognition agreement at Tesco.

The supermarket business is highly competitive and Tesco realise that the future success of their business depends to a large extent on the quality of customer service. Delivering the required level of service depends on enthusiastic staff who feel they are valued. In the mid 1990s, however, there were signs that a general lack of communication with staff was inhibiting employee relations (IDS, 1998). The company's response was to agree a radically new employee relations structure with USDAW based on the principle of partnership between Tesco, its employees and the union.

The cornerstone of the existing employee relations structure at Tesco was the annual national negotiation over terms and conditions with subsequent balloting of members. Only half of the union's 85 000 members bothered to vote (IDS, 1998). It was, according to the Tesco HR director, 'a ritualistic sham' (Allen, 1998). At local level, the union represented members in grievance and disciplinary cases. There was no role in the employee relations structure for employees who were not USDAW members. Attitude surveys found that many staff felt that the company 'was not good at listening to staff'. There were few opportunities for them to air their views.

The new employee relations structure was agreed in a series of joint management and union workshops at Cranfield School of Management in 1997 (Allen, 1998). The partnership had nine 'pillars'. These are shown in Fig. 8.1. Each of these nine 'pillars' (with the exception of the second related to training) has been realised through a completely remodelled employee relations structure. USDAW representatives are trained in employee relations practices, employment legislation, Tesco's terms and conditions, business awareness and an

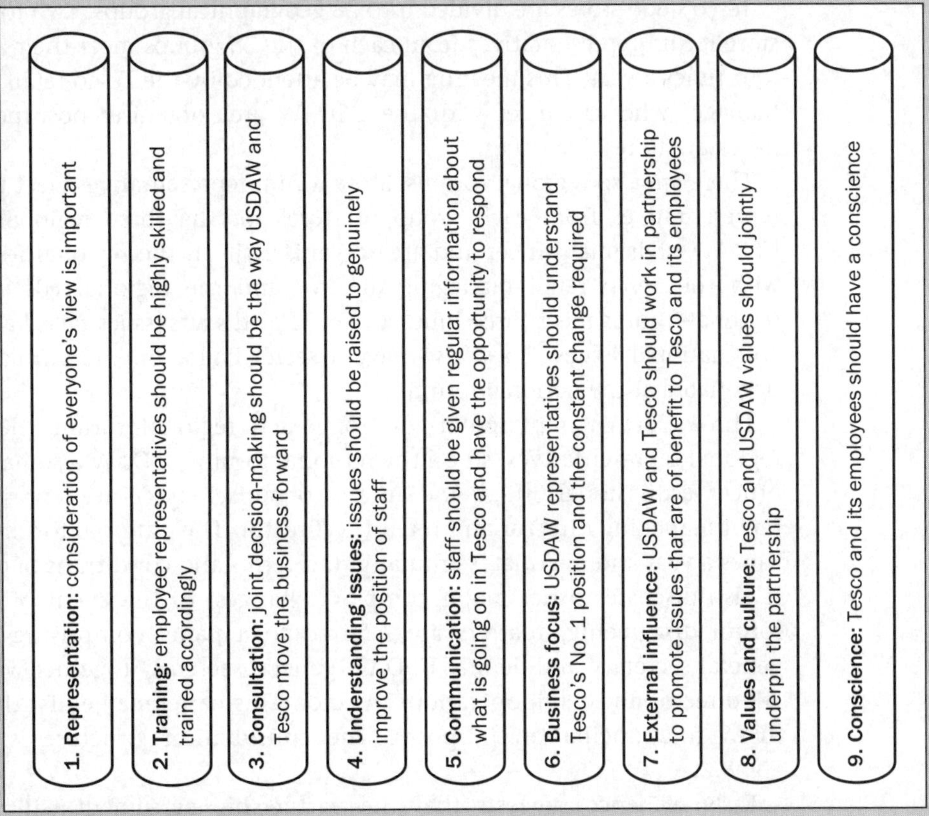

Fig. 8.1 **The nine pillars of the Tesco/USDAW partnership**

Source: Derived from IDS, 1998: 28.

1. **Representation:** consideration of everyone's view is important
2. **Training:** employee representatives should be highly skilled and trained accordingly
3. **Consultation:** joint decision-making should be the way USDAW and Tesco move the business forward
4. **Understanding issues:** issues should be raised to genuinely improve the position of staff
5. **Communication:** staff should be given regular information about what is going on in Tesco and have the opportunity to respond
6. **Business focus:** USDAW representatives should understand Tesco's No. 1 position and the constant change required
7. **External influence:** USDAW and Tesco should work in partnership to promote issues that are of benefit to Tesco and its employees
8. **Values and culture:** Tesco and USDAW values should jointly underpin the partnership
9. **Conscience:** Tesco and its employees should have a conscience

understanding of its culture and values. This is carried out by the union and funded partly by Tesco.

The basic building block of the structure is the staff forum in every store. The forums have two main aims: first, to ensure that all staff's views are represented, and second, to act as a two-way communication channel in which staff are given a greater understanding of the way the business operates and feed back their views on how the store may improve.

The store forum meets four times a year and consists of representatives who may be both USDAW and non-union members. (Participation by non-USDAW members was not popular with the union officers, but Tesco argued that non-union members made up around half of all employees and should have the chance of representation.) There is one representative per 50 staff, with a minimum of 5 representatives per store. One place is reserved for a union representative and one for a section manager. The management team with whom they meet comprises the store manager and the personnel manager. The items covered include store trading performance, change issues, points raised by staff and feedback on national issues.

Tesco's 600 stores are divided into 28 geographical groups. Two to four USDAW store forum representatives from each of the 28 groups meet their area organiser four times a year. This meeting may be attended by the Tesco retail development manager who can meet with the USDAW area organiser post-meeting if it is necessary to resolve issues.

There are also regional forums. Store forum representatives elect three USDAW representatives from each group of stores for the three regional forums. An USDAW divisional officer and area organiser sit on the regional forum together with the Tesco retail managing director and the regional HR manager. The regional forums meet three times a year. They discuss issues raised at staff forums and national issues. They also have a secret ballot on the annual pay review negotiated at the national forum.

Three USDAW representatives from each regional forum, elected by the regional representatives, sit on the national forum. USDAW also has its national officer, a divisional officer and an area organiser. Tesco are represented by the retail managing director and retail HR director. The national forum meets three times a year and negotiates annually staff terms and conditions of employment. It also discusses other major company changes. In the event of the national forum disagreeing, matters are referred to a panel comprising the USDAW general secretary and deputy USDAW general secretary together with the Tesco HR director and retail operations director. This panel may enlist the support of ACAS for conciliation purposes. The consultation structure is outlined in Fig. 8.2.

Early evidence suggests that the partnership agreement will fulfil Tesco's objectives. The 1998 pay offer was considered and accepted in a day by 96 regional representatives (the new consultation structure had not been completed at that

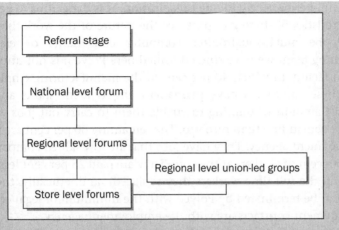

Fig. 8.2 Tesco/USDAW partnership consultation structure
Source: Derived from IDS, 1998: 30.

stage). The negotiations were characterised by a high level of information-giving by the company on the state of the business and no side-meetings (IDS, 1998).

The benefits to USDAW are equally clear. It has the opportunity for members and officials to be involved in the running of the business to a far greater extent than used to be the case. In the words of the USDAW general secretary Bill Connor, 'we have worked with the adversarial approach and it hasn't worked so let's try a new way' (interview notes).

Changing the focus in employee relations

In this section, we focus on two of the strategies used by employers to make more effective use of the workforce. The first of these is flexibility, a strategy used by most organisations in one way or another to generate greater worker productivity. The second strategy is the desire to create a workforce more in tune with the goals of the organisation – a unitary workforce. We comment on the contribution of these strategies to wider organisational change and to the way in which the changes have altered the nature of the employment relationship.

Creating a more flexible workforce

A core-periphery strategy

The concept of an organisation structure configured so that there is a core of employees surrounded by peripheral workers is one that has received much publicity since it was first highlighted in the mid 1980s by Atkinson (1984). The core consists of employees enjoying relatively secure employment status and in whom their employer invests. At the periphery are part-time workers, those on temporary contracts and the self-employed providing services to the organisation. In addition, there are those who work for employment agencies but who are attached semi-permanently to one organisation. It is dangerous to generalise about the characteristics of these groups, since the nature of the work they do is varied. They may be much-sought-after computer consultants or cleaners. But a manufacturing plant we have studied (called here Polyco) is not untypical. It has a production facility in which 40 per cent of the manufacturing employees are core workers. These employees have permanent employment status and have had a considerable amount of training to enable them to carry out jobs which are now much more demanding than hitherto. The remaining 60 per cent are the employees of an employment agency. They have jobs that are low skilled compared with those of the 40 per cent of workers at the core. They are paid 25 per cent less than the core workers (and the full-time workers they replaced), and, crucially, their working at the plant can be terminated by Polyco with the minimum of legal constraint since their employment contracts are with the employment agency.

Some indication of the extent of the peripheral workforce in Britain can be gained from a brief reference to labour market data (Office for National Statistics, 1999). Approximately 6.8 million (25 per cent) of the 27-million-strong British workforce work part-time with 80 per cent of these workers being women. Around 1.2 million of these workers have more than one job, like the redundant draughtsman who cleans our offices in the morning and then moves on to a similar job with the local authority in the afternoon. Approximately 1.8 million British workers are in temporary employment while around 3 million are self-employed (Office for National Statistics, 1999).

Polyco's rationale for moving to a core-periphery workforce was simple. The cost competition faced by the organisation from overseas competitors was such that the American parent company would certainly have closed the plant had dramatic production cost savings not been made. Hiring 60 per cent of the production workforce from an employment agency at a salary one-third lower than was previously paid to employees, with no attendant 'on' costs such as pension, NI and holidays, is an obvious cost saving. In addition, the fact that these workers are not employed by Polyco means that their services can be called on to a greater or lesser degree to suit manufacturing demands.

Flexibility of working hours

In the same way that employers may seek flexibility in their numbers of workers, they may wish to arrange the hours of workers in such a way that they are working at times when it best suits the needs of the organisation. The employment of part-time and temporary workers is clearly part of this strategy as are the traditional methods of overtime and shift working. However, we will focus here briefly on a strategy which has gained much publicity recently in the wake of the 1998 deal to keep Rover car production at Longbridge (BBC, 1998): that of annualised hours. This is the system of 'averaging working time across a year. Employees are contracted to work a given number of hours over 12 months, rather than a specified number of hours per week' (IDS, 1993: 1). The purpose of such a system is that work hours may be varied according to the needs of the business (see Case Studies 5.1 and 7.1 on Siemens Standard Drives and Midland Main Line for explanations of manufacturing, maintenance and customer service units where annualised hours have been introduced). Blyton (1994) notes that there are two types of annualised hours systems. In the first, employees work longer hours in busy periods and shorter hours when demand slackens. In the second, the number of shifts rostered (A) in the annual schedule is less than the agreed maximum number of annual hours (B). In the amount of hours equalling the difference between (A) and (B), workers are on call and can be called upon to work in unforeseen circumstances.

The advantages to the organisation of a system of annualised hours are similar to those of the utilisation of peripheral workers. Reduction of labour costs is a consequence of having to pay less overtime and not having to employ temporary workers. In addition, the employer is better able to deploy resources resulting in increased productivity.

Greater flexibility of numbers of workers and of the hours in which they work are strategies which are clearly of great benefit to employers. Managers at Polyco and those at Rover at Longbridge would argue that such strategies have done more than contribute to organisational change. They have preserved the existence of their workplaces. Both are foreign owned, Polyco by Americans and Rover by BMW of Germany. Both parent companies have the ability to switch production from the UK to plants abroad in the event of the UK plants not being sufficiently productive. It is this stark reality that has meant that in both workplaces trade unions have broadly been in favour of the changes.

But flexibility has two sides. What is good for the employer may not be good for the employee, albeit that the alternative may be redundancy. In Sisson's (1994: 15) celebrated words, flexibility means 'management can do what it wants'. On the face of it, the core-periphery model may be ideal for those at the core. But the expectations of those employees are likely to be high given their 'chosen' status. However, it is those at the periphery whose employment relationship is likely to be characterised by insecurity, unpredictability and a general surrendering of power to the employer. For every temporary employee in 1997 who did not want a permanent job there was another who could not find one (Office for National Statistics, 1999). Those workers on annual hours contracts may suffer from similar unpredictability. Not knowing when you are going to be called upon to work means possible difficulties in planning leisure time and childcare arrangements (Tailby, 1999). This, of course, is in addition to the loss of overtime pay.

The search for greater employee flexibility has extended in many organisations not only to who works and what hours are worked but also to what is done at work. It was noted above that greater demands are likely to be made of core (and possibly peripheral) employees. One of these demands is that they should take on a wider range of skills.

Multi-skilling of employees

At Polyco the 40 per cent of production employees chosen to form the core have had to make the transition from production operatives to technicians. This has meant the need to develop additional technical skills, including machine setting-up, faultfinding and general maintenance. It has also necessitated the development of people skills because the job now involves the management of peripheral workers employed by the contractor. The core workers' role is similar to that of the group leaders at Siemens Standard Drives (*see* Case Study 5.1).

Self-check question	**8.1** *What practical difficulties do you envisage in former production workers making the transition to team leaders?*

The introduction of multi-skilling can have quite a significant impact upon organisational change. Hendry and Pettigrew (1988) note the changes that this may create in the culture and structure of an organisation. So it was at Polyco. The manufacturing culture was similar to that present in Bedford Commercial Vehicles prior to the joint venture with Isuzu: 'I come here, I'm told what to do and I go home' (Open University, 1992: 18). To overcome this sense of powerlessness, the new technician group was taken to a series of one-week team building events designed to develop their initiative and confidence. Polyco's aim is to develop a team of technicians who are willing and able to make decisions about the work their teams do and the way in which it is done. The potential for organisational change is quite profound.

Apart from the obvious training implications, multi-skilling has notable implications for the employment relationship. The logical consequence of multi-skilling is the breakdown of the tradition of demarcation between tasks, possibly performed by employees who are members of different unions. At Polyco this was a factor that prompted the move to single-table bargaining (*see* later in this section) where the three unions on site join as one for negotiating purposes. You should also note the link with skill-based pay (*see* p. 205) where the move to multi-skilling may be accompanied by financial incentives.

Geary (1995) warns against assuming that multi-skilling is widespread in British industry. He notes that the research evidence suggests that employers are often reluctant to devote the necessary training costs to this initiative. It would also be wrong to think that the other flexibility strategies outlined in this section are new and revolutionary. Employers have long used temporary workers, and extended employees' hours, for example in retail organisations such as Tesco, summer ice cream production and the Christmas postal rush. But the drive for greater productivity, as a consequence of enhanced product competition, has forced many employers to think of ways of achieving those productivity gains. It would be equally dangerous to underestimate the significance of these changes in flexibility. They are set to continue, and play their part in effecting organisational and employee relations change.

Creating a unitary workforce

A constant theme throughout this book has been the HRM-inspired desire by employers to develop a more enthusiastic, committed, unitary workforce. A unitary workforce is 'an integrated group of people with a single authority/loyalty structure and a set of common values, interests and objectives shared by all members of the organisation (Salamon, 1998: 5). You may argue that such an aim is not possible, or even desirable. But the unitarist assumption underpins much of the HRM rhetoric. As such, it has been very influential in the thought and action of many managers throughout the 1980s and 1990s. Much of this book deals with techniques for dealing with employees at an individual level which have as one of their implicit, or explicit, aims the creation of a more unitary workforce. In this section, we outline some of the employer strategies that have implications for the way in which the employment relationship is regulated at a collective level. The Tesco/ USDAW agreement is just such a case.

Forging a more co-operative relationship with trade unions: partnership agreements

In the 1999 Employment Relations Bill the government captures one strand of the spirit of 1990s employee relations thinking by emphasising the necessity for employers, employees and trade unions to work together if Britain is to prosper in an increasingly competitive global market. After twenty years of steady membership decline, and consequent lack of influence both nationally and at the workplace, some unions have gladly seized an opportunity to reclaim lost ground. One of the ways this is happening is the creation of partnership agreements, similar to that between Tesco and USDAW. The content of such agreements may vary, but IDS (1998) list a number of features that are often found. These are:

- new consultation and communication arrangements;
- setting up of joint working groups;
- increased employee flexibility and teamworking;
- employee commitment to business goals;
- long-term pay deals;
- an umbrella of employment security;
- sharing of information;
- an emphasis on training and development;
- greater focus on local problem-solving activities;
- a move towards harmonisation and single status.

The creation of partnership agreements clearly has a lot to offer all parties. For the employer, like Tesco, it offers the chance of less adversarial employee relations and the chance to introduce change with the assistance of unions in what the Co-operative Bank says is a 'spirit in which we set out to reach common objectives' (IDS, 1998: 3). For employees, it at least means that they are likely to be given some form of commitment, if not a guarantee of employment security. If redundancy is necessary, partnership agreements commonly give employees, under the heading of 'employability', training to equip them for future employment that may be outside their current organisation. A good example of this is at Scottish Power where

all reasonable steps are taken to maximise the employability of staff, investment in training and development to maintain employability are (sic) driven by the needs of the individual and do not depend solely on the needs of the business .... (IDS, 1998: 6)

For unions, partnership deals hold out the hope that they may be better able to demonstrate the benefits of trade union membership to employees and employers. The consequence of this is increased membership, which the unions desperately need. The case of the USDAW partnership deal with Tesco provides a good illustration of the potential benefits to unions. According to Bill Connor, USDAW General Secretary, USDAW have in membership 97 500 of Tescos 150 000 employees and have increased the number of shop stewards from 1000 to 1500 (interview notes).

The extent to which partnership deals become a permanent feature of employee relations is debatable. It is tempting to think that they may be a rhetorical response to an adversarial employee relations climate within organisations, as in the case of the partnership agreement at Barclays (*People Management*, 1999). But the Tesco case suggests that an employee relations crisis is not a necessary precondition for such a deal. Such agreements may simply be a symbol of a new age of social partnership, with a shelf life as long as economic conditions are in their favour. In the meantime, they certainly have the potential for facilitating organisational and employee relations change.

Single-status agreements

You will note that part of the normal content of partnership agreements is a move towards single-status terms and conditions of employment. The impetus for single status has been increasing since it first appeared in the wake of the influx of Japanese companies in the UK in the 1970s and 1980s. Price and Price (1994) note that single-status is associated with a number of other change initiatives. First is the Japanese example. In the next sub-section, we note the inclusion of single-status terms and conditions of employment in the 'package' of employee relations measures introduced by Japanese companies. There is no doubting the high unitarist ring to the package, or the persuasive influence that this had on British managers. Second is the move from traditional low-skill jobs to more technologically sophisticated jobs, the creation of 'core' technicians at Polyco being a perfect example. This more technologically demanding role suggests a move from the traditional 'low-trust' employee relationship associated with manual employees to a relationship consistent with 'white-collar' employment. A third factor is the introduction of single-table bargaining. Where the workplace has more than one union representing different groups of employees this involves the collaboration of unions in negotiating with the employer as a single body. This is the case in Polyco where there are three unions on site but only one set of negotiations. Not only does this save management time by only having one set of negotiations but it reduces the prospect of 'leap-frogging' claims where union negotiators seek a better deal than the one that has been agreed with other unions at the same workplace. Single-table bargaining facilitates multi-skilling since it assists in the breakdown of demarcations between jobs. It also means that pay for different jobs is consistent with principles of internal equity (*see* Chapter 7) and equal value considerations. Equal value is the major driving force behind the 1997 single-status agreement in local government.

But the real value of single-status terms and conditions lies in the symbolic 'working together' message it sends to employees and managers about the type of organisation for which they are working. Segregated car parks, separate eating areas, different sick pay arrangements etc. are not the stuff of 'working together'. The extent to which single-status does change entrenched 'them and us' attitudes is debatable. Like partnership agreements, they may be more of a symbol of change than a real shift in direction.

Self-check question	8.2	*The introduction of single-status terms and conditions of employment may encounter some practical difficulties. What may these be?*

Single-union agreements

The signing of single-union agreements was a significant feature of employee relations in the 1980s. In a single-union agreement, one union represents all relevant employees for collective bargaining purposes. Such agreements received much publicity and analysis in the 1980s (*see* Bassett, 1987). These were particularly prevalent in Japanese companies establishing themselves in the UK. The evidence (Gall, 1993) suggests that this interest has not been maintained in the 1990s. But the employer aims behind such agreements are as relevant now as when such agreements were initially being forged. As Salamon (1999) notes, these aims are now being pursued by different means. The aim was to establish consensus in employee relations through the development of mechanisms designed to bring employees and their managers closer together. These mechanisms often included a company council for negotiation and consultation purposes, with employee rather than exclusively trade union representatives; union support for the organisation's goals; single-status terms and conditions of employment; and 'no-strike' agreements. In addition, there was considerable emphasis upon the development of multi-skilled teams through training. The extent to which single-union deals have been successful in creating a unitary workforce is unclear. But like other management initiatives detailed in this book, their real significance has been in the cultural message that has been sent to employees that union, management and workforce are essentially 'on the same side'.

We note below forthcoming legislation that will support trade unions in their pursuit of recognition by employers. In the event of new recognition deals being signed it is more likely that employers, like Tesco, will favour deals with single unions rather than have various unions representing different groups of employees.

Employers not recognising trade unions

Our assumption so far has been that the employment relationship is one that is regulated collectively, between employers and trade unions. But for many organisations and employees this is increasingly not the case. One of the most dramatic changes in employee relations in the past twenty years has been the decline in influence of trade unions. This is best illustrated by a simple comparison of the level of union membership. At its height, in 1979, this stood at 13.2 million. By 1996 the figure had declined to just 7.9 million (Office for National Statistics, 1998). There are many reasons for this decline, with perhaps the most important being changes in the labour market. Those areas of the economy which have declined, the traditional 'smokestack' industries, are those where the density of trade union membership was at its strongest. The rise of employment in the service industries has not served unions well. It is this sector which traditionally has been the most difficult for them to organise membership. The proportion of UK workplaces in which there are no union members at all has risen from 36 per cent in 1990 to 47 per cent in 1998 (Cully *et al.*, 1998). This statistic is mirrored in the proportion of workplaces recognising unions for collective bargaining purposes. In 1984, 66 per cent of workplaces recognised unions. This figure had declined to 53 per cent in 1990 and by 1998 had declined further to 45 per cent (Cully *et al.*, 1998). However, the news for trade unions is not all bad. The 1999 Employment Relations Bill promises support for those unions that can demonstrate a case for recognition through the level of membership, and member support for recognition, at the workplace.

Some employers managing employee relations without trade unions have developed alternative methods of generating the support of employees, the most prevalent of which is employee involvement (Cully *et al.*, 1998). It is to a detailed analysis of employee involvement that this chapter now turns.

Managing change through employee involvement

What is employee involvement and how may it contribute to organisational change?

Employee involvement strategies have been used by organisations in their attempts to develop a unitary workforce. In theory, these strategies are potentially an important means to bring about organisational and employee relations change. In reality, however, several other factors are likely to affect adversely any attempt to achieve this desired outcome. This section of the chapter therefore evaluates the scope for employee involvement strategies to realise this type of intended change.

As a general principle, many employing organisations want to employ people who feel involved in the work that they undertake. However, employee involvement is more specifically used as a means to promote employee relations and other organisational change. For those organisations that recognise and negotiate with trade unions but wish to move away from this approach, employee involvement may be used as a means to reduce union influence or to replace the role of unions in managing employee relations. In the previous section, reference was made to the use of employee involvement as a means to generate employee support without the need to recognise trade unions. This type of strategy has been used to avoid a change away from an organisation's non-union status and it characterises the approach adopted by many organisations that espouse soft HRM principles. However, it is important to recognise that employee involvement may also be used as a parallel set of activities to traditional employee relations processes involving unions (*see*, for example, Storey, 1992). Employee involvement is also used in the promotion of change management events that do not relate to trade unions, at least directly. For example, many advocates of quality management and continuous improvement programmes see the achievement of employee involvement as a condition for success (*see*, for example, Wilkinson *et al.*, 1992).

These examples illustrate that employee involvement is promoted by management, as a voluntary strategy specifically designed to support the change requirements that are seen as desirable by them. Recognition of the role of management as the motivating force for the use of employee involvement provides a means to differentiate this type of strategy from forms of employee participation or notions of industrial democracy. Employee participation and industrial democracy have traditionally been favoured by trades unions and principally involve the granting of representational rights and joint decision making in some areas (*see*, for example, Ackers *et al.*, 1992). The essentially managerialist and unitary nature of employee involvement is illustrated in the definitions that we now discuss.

In 1988, the CBI defined employee involvement as 'a range of processes designed to engage the support, understanding and optimum contribution of all employees in an organisation and their commitment to its objectives' (cited in Kessler and Bayliss, 1998: 125). In 1991, the CBI and the then Department of Employment launched an initiative called 'Managing for Success – Improving business performance through employee involvement'. This describes the purpose of employee involvement as follows: 'The CBI and the Government believe that employee involvement promotes business success through a combination of practices and systems designed to secure the maximum awareness and commitment of all employees in an enterprise to its objectives' (CBI/EDG, 1991). The Institute of Personnel Management (now the Institute of Personnel and Development) and the Industrial Participation Association developed an Employee Involvement Code, dating back to 1982, one of whose aims was to 'generate commitment of all employees to the success of the organisation'.

These definitions lay stress on the alleged causal linkages between employee involvement and the development of employees' commitment and contribution to their employing organisations. We evaluate these claimed linkages later in this section. At this point we develop the list of claims made about the relationship between employee involvement and various facets of organisational and individual effectiveness in Table 8.1.

Although these claims are made in relation to the achievement of effective employee involvement, they raise a number of fundamental problems. The very notion of effectiveness of employee involvement is based on the assumption that this strategy will not lead to any conflict with other organisational or personal goals. This type of underpinning assumption is at the heart of the unitary perspective. It would be difficult to see how a manager adopting a unitarist perspective could concede that an organisational strategy to promote this approach might end up generating conflict, other than to displace the cause of this! However, several conflicting aspects have been identified in the literature that evaluates the effectiveness of attempts to generate employee involvement. We discuss these areas of potential conflict later in this section. Although many of these aspects are not inevitable, they cast serious doubt on the achievement of effectiveness of many

Table 8.1 Claimed effects from the implementation of employee involvement

It has been claimed that effective employee involvement should:

■ improve employees' business awareness;

■ generate employees' commitment to the objectives of their employing organisations;

■ foster trust by employees towards those who manage them;

■ create a more customer-focused approach and improve customer service;

■ improve product quality;

■ promote greater acceptance of organisational change;

■ lead to employee flexibility;

■ encourage more effective working relationships;

■ generate employee empowerment;

■ improve employee relations;

■ improve job satisfaction and employee morale.

Source: Developed from Kessler and Bayliss, 1998; CBI/EDG, 1991; IPM/IPA Code, not dated.

employee involvement strategies. Consequently, while employee involvement is intended to promote organisational change and effectiveness, its use is likely to be problematic, and its intended outcomes somewhat less than fully achieved (*see*, for example, Marchington, 1995a).

A further fundamental problem arises from the claims made about the range of potential effects of employee involvement. The considerable range of potential outcomes shown in Table 8.1 points to employee involvement as a broad rather than a narrow concept. Employee involvement may be conceived of as little more than a range of communication techniques; or perhaps as a means to involve employees by allowing them to offer their ideas for improvement through a suggestion scheme. Both of these possibilities are restricted in their scope. However, where an organisation operated this narrow type of employee involvement it could hardly expect to achieve the broad range of outcomes suggested in Table 8.1. In this way, the potential outcomes of a particular employee involvement strategy will be limited by its scope. This will be irrespective of other difficulties surrounding its implementation or its non-acceptance related to conflicting beliefs and values.

This leads to a problem for those who claim that employee involvement is capable of achieving the range of change outcomes suggested in Table 8.1, even where an issue is not raised about the validity of the philosophical underpinnings of this type of strategy. For an employee involvement strategy to be capable of producing multifaceted outcomes such as several or all of those outlined in Table 8.1, it would need to assume a major significance in the operating processes of an organisation and become truly embedded as an underlying assumption of its culture. This raises a question about the ways in which this type of employee involvement strategy would manifest itself in such an organisation. If the adoption of certain communication techniques or a suggestion scheme indicates a narrow approach to employee involvement, with concomitant objectives, then a much more broadly based strategy would clearly require employee involvement to be infused in many different areas of organisational decision making and implementation (*see*, for example, Caldwell, 1993).

In this respect, the earlier definitions of employee involvement referred to 'a range of processes' and 'a combination of practices and systems'. Various writers have identified several employee involvement methods and some researchers such as Guest *et al.* (1993) and Marchington (1992) have grouped these various methods into related categories. Table 8.2 illustrates a number of categories of employee involvement. These categories indicate the way in which the concept of employee involvement is related to as well as affected by many aspects of organisational life. To approach this relationship from the opposite direction, there are many aspects of organisational life that are capable of producing negative employee feelings and emotions such as frustration, unfairness and alienation. Approached from this

Table 8.2 Categories of employee involvement

Main categories of employee involvement	Examples of methods used	Brief (intended) rationale
Downward communication	Team briefing; other briefing groups; corporate newspapers, journals and reports aimed at employees; videos; audiotapes; e-mail; recorded telephone briefings.	To provide information; uniform messages; to be educative or re-educative.
Problem-solving involvement and upward communication	Quality circles; quality action teams; quality improvement teams; suggestion schemes; employee surveys.	Explicit access to employees' experience and skills; gain co-operation and opinions.
Consultation	Joint consultation committees, working parties or groups; staff forums; works councils.	Providing information and testing reactions.
Involvement through structural changes at job and work organisation levels	Job redesign: job enlargement and job enrichment. Work reorganisation: team working; autonomous working groups; 'empowerment'.	To be re-educative; providing greater levels of motivation and satisfaction; empowering.
Financial involvement	Employee share ownership plans; profit-related pay; performance-related pay; bonus schemes.	To be re-educative; providing incentives and promoting effort.
Managerial style and leadership	Participative managerial style; being visible, accessible and informal; creating credibility; ensuring actions in line with key messages.	To provide support; encourage positive working relationships and trust; reduce barriers.

Source: Developed from Ackers *et al.*, 1992; CBI/EDG, 1991; Guest *et al.*, 1993; Kessler and Bayliss, 1998; Marchington, 1992; Marchington, 1995a; Storey, 1992; authors' own experience and other chapters.

Table 8.3 Organisational strategies/characteristics that may encourage or inhibit employee involvement

Broader organisational strategies/characteristics that may encourage or inhibit employee involvement	Related chapter(s) in this book
■ Organisational performance, prospects and corporate direction	1
■ Organisational culture	3
■ Organisational structures and restructuring	2 and 9
■ Training, human resource development and career management	6
■ Performance management	5
■ Other strategies such as those relating to health and safety and employee relations approaches	This chapter for ER

direction, it becomes easier to understand the nature of employee involvement as diffuse yet connected to many organisational aspects. In order for employees to feel genuinely involved in the operations of an organisation, it is therefore very likely that a number of variables capable of engendering this feeling will need to be acting in concert to produce this desired outcome (*see*, for example, Marchington *et al.*, 1994). However, in reality, this may only serve to demonstrate the difficulties and even the contradictions associated with any organisational strategy to engender genuine employee involvement. Guest *et al.* (1993) provide an example of this where employee involvement was 'crowded out' by other organisational factors, which we consider in more detail later in this section. Table 8.3 illustrates a number of broader organisational facets that will serve to enable or inhibit employee involvement.

The pursuit of employee involvement is therefore likely to be a problematic concept as well as an unrealistic one in many of the ways in which it is approached. This is because it is based on a unitarist perspective of organisational relationships. However, there are nevertheless a number of other reasons why it may be seen as a desirable outcome. Marchington *et al.* (1992) found that employee involvement 'has a mildly favourable impact on employee attitudes, or at least that the existence or promise of E I is associated with more positive attitudes' (Marchington, 1995a: 290). There is, however, less evidence that it affects behaviour or organisational commitment. A number of organisational concepts have been advanced that may help to explain the relationship between employee attitudes and the extent to which employees feel some measure of work-related involvement. One of these relates to the notion of organisational treatment (*see*, for example, Naumann *et al.*, 1995), where it is reasonable to assume that employees will prefer to be treated in a participative way by those who manage them. This relates to the concept of interactional justice that we discuss in Chapter 9. Also related to this notion of organisational treatment are employee expectations. The changing nature of the workforce in developed countries in particular is associated with altered expectations about the treatment of employees at work. 'Knowledge-based workers' in particular may have expectations about their treatment at work based on educational achievement and perceptions about levels of expertise.

Other concepts that are associated with facets of employee involvement are employee voice and managerial justification. Employee voice (*see*, for example, Folger, 1977; Daly and Geyer, 1994; Sako, 1998) allows employees to express their points of view about potential decisions which would affect them. Related to this is the notion of personal influence over the implementation of decisions that affect individual or groups of employees. The concept of justification (*see*, for example, Bies, 1987; Daly and Geyer, 1994) relates to the provision of explanations to employees for the reasons why particular decisions have been taken. This facet of employee involvement goes beyond the simple provision of information about what is to occur, where management simply 'tells' other employees, to an educative process of meaningful persuasion. The effective use of these two concepts in practice may be seen as a genuine means to promote employee involvement. However, the use of these means to promote employee involvement may require the acceptance of a pluralist, rather than a unitarist, frame of reference to be genuinely meaningful in practice. It also suggests that for employee involvement to be realised in practice it will be necessary to consider the depth of attempts to bring this about, rather than simply focus on involvement as some sort of outcome.

Problems in relation to the realisation of employee involvement

The discussion in the previous sub-section has indicated that the achievement of employee involvement is problematic for a number of reasons. We now consider these reasons in more detail, related to organisational characteristics that inhibit employee involvement, implementation problems and issues that arise from the changing nature of the psychological contract for involvement. This leads us to a final sub-section that discusses the nature of employees' commitment.

Organisational characteristics and circumstances that inhibit employee involvement

Table 8.3 indicated that employee involvement is affected by various organisational characteristics and prevailing strategies that may act to inhibit, or promote, its realisation in practice. These factors will include the effects of organisational structures on the scope for employees to influence the way in which they undertake their work and therefore the extent to which they feel some sense of involvement (*see* Chapter 2). For example, a mechanistic organisational structure may inhibit employees' involvement while a project-based structure may serve to encourage this. Other factors will include organisational performance and perceptions about job security, prospects for development and advancement in the organisation and the prevailing employee relations climate. The impact of these factors are perhaps more capable of inhibiting or promoting employee involvement than the use of many specific techniques designed to achieve this type of outcome (Marchington *et al.*, 1994). In relation to the use of employee involvement as part of a programme to realise organisational change, Legge (1995: 184) summarised the conclusion of Marchington *et al.* (1994): 'that employee involvement initiatives are as much affected by the prevailing organisational culture and environment as they are sources of cultural change'. Any attempt to use employee involvement to bring about organisational change therefore needs to recognise the impact of prevailing organisational characteristics and circumstances on the likely outcomes from this strategy.

Self-check question

8.3 *What other aspects of the way in which an organisation introduces or uses employee involvement may adversely affect its effectiveness?*

Implementation issues in the use of employee involvement as a change strategy

A simple stakeholder analysis reveals another source of conflicting factors that are capable of inhibiting the realisation of employee involvement in practice. There is a body of literature that evaluates the roles for and responses of groups of managers, employees and trade unions in relation to attempts to encourage employee involvement (e.g. Marchington 1995a, 1995b). We will briefly consider each of these from the perspective of the conflict that is likely to arise which will impair employee involvement.

Line managers are likely to play a central role in implementing employee involvement. However, line managers may feel that this type of strategy is wasteful of their time or misguided in terms of its intended outcomes. This may be because they feel that their discretion to operate as they wish is threatened or because they recognise that demands from above to use their time to promote employee involvement will not be properly resourced, or perhaps for both reasons. Given the earlier recognition of the relationship between organisational culture and employee involvement, it is likely in situations where managers feel their power will be threatened that this will also indicate a cultural state which will inhibit effective employee involvement. Storey (1992: 111) refers to the fate of an employee involvement technique in one of his case study organisations: 'quality circles had been introduced by the factory manager but they had been "killed off" by middle managers who saw in them a threat to their own role.'

Guest *et al.* (1993) undertook case study work that recognised the potential for conflict between production or financial targets and the pursuit of employee involvement. Their case study organisation, British Rail, was undergoing rapid change that involved it pursuing goals related to cost efficiencies and restructuring, on the one hand, and higher quality customer service, on the other hand. Guest *et al.* (1993: 199) found that the attempt to encourage employee involvement related to the desire to achieve better customer service was 'crowded out by the financial imperatives and the spate of reorganisations'. In less dramatic circumstances, it is possible to understand how employee involvement is 'crowded out' by the imperative of other targets, so that it becomes at best a marginal, bolt-on strategy that is 'nice to have' but only when the organisation sees some benefit from seeking to involve its employees!

Other obstacles may confront line managers in any attempt to implement a strategy of employee involvement. Their own understanding of the reasons for and intended outcomes from this type of strategy may be in need of development. They may also require skills training to be able to conduct effectively employee involvement techniques such as running a briefing group or a problem-solving session. They may also meet resistance from some of those whom they manage and lack appropriate skills to be able to overcome this. The factors discussed so far in relation to the problems confronting the implementation of employee involvement may lead to the demise of various techniques, which itself is likely to have a detrimental effect on subsequent attempts to launch new involvement approaches to bring about some facet of change.

Self-check question	8.4	*What other problems may confront line managers in their role in the implementation of employee involvement?*

Although attempts to engender employee involvement may be seen as a positive development for employees, they will not necessarily be received in this way. A number of factors will affect employee perceptions about particular attempts to introduce employee involvement strategies. One such factor may relate to employee experiences of any previous attempt to introduce an employee involvement strategy. Previous attempts that have been seen to fail, or which were perceived as attempts to increase managerial control over employees rather than to encourage their involvement, are likely to increase employee resistance and cynicism. In addition, some groups of employees may be used to an environment in which they have not been involved and will view any attempt to achieve involvement as something that they do not want (Guest *et al.*, 1993). A further factor will relate to the broader organisational circumstances and characteristics discussed earlier. Employees are likely to resist and feel cynical in relation to overtures to develop employee involvement if they perceive the existence of other threats from the organisation and inconsistencies with the way in which it treats them (Marchington *et al.*, 1994).

Attempts to introduce the notion of empowerment are a point of issue in relation to the way in which employees perceive the motives and actions of management. Marchington (1995b: 61) summarised the espoused intention underpinning empowerment and its reality as follows:

> The implication behind notions of empowerment is that employees will be allocated greater power to do things, be entrusted with authority, and achieve higher levels of control – not only over their own specific work functions but also more widely throughout the organization. In reality, of course, this does not generally happen and any increase in authority is heavily circumscribed and maintained within the confines of managerial control systems.

The study by Cunningham *et al.* (1996) into empowerment practices in thirteen organisations substantiates Marchington's conclusion. They found that non-managerial employees gained little in terms of increased control through the approach adopted. Indeed, the approach to 'empowering' employees in several of their case study organisations was narrowly conceived (e.g. introducing suggestion schemes). In others, where it involved a broader approach to empowering employees (e.g. through teamworking and job enrichment) strong managerial control was still evident through the imposition of accountability and intolerance of repeated mistakes. Sewell and Wilkinson (1992: 111) similarly posed the question 'do self-managers [so-called empowered employees] possess any real degree of empowerment?', and concluded, 'The answer is "yes", but only in a highly circumscribed form.' In relation to empowerment's role to introduce change, we conclude that this approach may be effective for the organisation (*see* Cunningham *et al.*, 1996), but that it may not involve employees in terms of promoting their organisational commitment or altering their perceptions of the way in which they are treated. This will especially be the case where empowerment is effectively little more than a means to make employees work harder (Marchington, 1995b).

In the first part of this section, we discussed different ways in which employee involvement may be used in relation to the role for trade unions. Essentially, a trade union may be offered an inclusive role in relation to the use of employee involvement. This is exemplified by the Tesco case study at the start of this chapter. Alternatively, employee involvement may be used to marginalise or exclude a trade union in relation to the management of employee relations. Trade unions will be likely to respond according to the nature of any employer's approach to the use of employee involvement, at least as they perceive it. This is particularly likely to be the case where union officials adopt a position of 'realism' in relation to the nature of the current employment climate in a situation where they are offered such a role. On the other hand, they are likely to adopt a defensive position where they perceive the use of an employee involvement strategy as a means to exclude them. This may have the effect of reducing the scope to promote involvement amongst a group of employees where they perceive its introduction as a means to impose unilateral control by management.

Recognising the nature of the psychological contract and its impact on the scope for employee involvement

We discussed the creation of a more flexible workforce earlier in this chapter. One of the ways in which this may be created is through the use of a core-periphery strategy (*see* our earlier discussion). However, while this strategy will introduce one form of organisational change, it is likely to create another, less tangible outcome related to the psychological contracts of those affected by this type of structural change. Herriot and Pemberton's (1996) contractual model of careers provides a useful framework through which to explore this transfer of employee status and any change in psychological contract. Within this model, a clear distinction is made between two types of psychological contract that emerge from this type of change.

The first contractual type is termed 'relational' (Herriot and Pemberton, 1996). It implies an ideal model of mutual commitment between the employee and the organisation involving general reciprocity. The organisation offers security of employment, training and development and promotion prospects while the employee offers loyalty, commitment and trust (Herriot and Pemberton, 1995). The second contractual type identified in the model is 'transactional' (Herriot and

Pemberton, 1996). This implies that the relationship between the employee and the organisation is an instrumental exchange implying strict reciprocity between the employee's labour and some form of compensation. While employees will be concerned about whether or not this exchange has been fair, their loyalty and commitment is unlikely to be an integral part of the contract.

These contractual types are likely to have implications for the scope to generate employee involvement, especially in relation to those who perceive their contract to be a transactional one. It may be argued that a core worker is more likely than a peripheral worker to have a relational contract with an employer and perhaps to have a higher propensity to become more 'involved' in their work. However, a peripheral worker is more likely than a core worker to have a transactional contract with an employer and to be less likely to feel involved in and committed to their employing organisation. For example, the core workers in Polyco who are now called technicians are more likely to have a relational contract with Polyco and perhaps to have a higher propensity to become involved. However, the peripheral workers are more likely to have a transactional contract with Polyco and to feel less involved due to the peripheral nature of their attachment to the organisation.

The desired link: understanding the reality of employee commitment

We recognised earlier that one of the claimed benefits of using an employee involvement strategy was the generation of employee commitment to an organisation. In turn, this is seen as a means to bring about beneficial change in an organisation. However, attempts to define, engender and measure commitment in the context of organisational behaviour have led to the recognition that this is a problematic concept (e.g. Legge, 1995). Two principal problems have been recognised. The first of these relates to the difference between attitudinal commitment and behavioural commitment (*see*, for example, Coopey and Hartley, 1991; Morris *et al.*, 1993). Attitudinal commitment refers to the strength of an employee's identification with and involvement in their employing organisation (Mowday *et al.*, 1982). Porter *et al.* (1974) operationalised this approach to organisational commitment as: a strong belief in and acceptance of an organisation's goals and values; a willingness to expend considerable effort on an organisation's behalf; and a strong desire to continue as a member of the organisation. This is the type of commitment associated with the claim referred to at the start of this paragraph.

In contrast, behavioural commitment is based on a different set of motives, at least with regard to the first two elements of the Porter *et al.* conceptualisation. Whereas attitudinal commitment is based on moral involvement and the internalisation of organisational values, behavioural commitment is founded on an individual's calculative judgement about the investments they have made in relation to their current job and the organisation for which they work – referred to as 'side bets' (Becker, 1960). In this way the time they have spent in their employing organisation will 'bind' rather than commit them to continued membership (Griffin and Bateman, 1986). This approach to organisational commitment makes clear that the desire to maintain membership of an organisation may be due to the accumulation of these side bets. Individuals may also believe that there are a lack of alternative employment opportunities. In this way, any identification with the organisation's goals may be limited to those areas that coincide with an individual's calculation about the value of past investments (e.g. pensionable service). Any effort expended may be based on an individual's calculation about what is required to maintain membership of the organisation. This approach implies an exchange relationship built on instrumentality.

The second problem relates to the number of alternative commitment foci that have been identified. Morrow (1983) identified over 25 measures of commitment, which she categorised into five forms: the intrinsic value of work as an end in itself; career focus; job focus; organisational focus; and union focus. Further work by Morrow and Goetz (1988) and Morrow and Wirth (1989) identified a professional focus. Other foci may be evident; for example, commitment to one's work group. The existence of some of these foci also indicates scope for a significant level of instrumentality, based on an individual's commitment to some external, personal, or even noble goal.

These aspects of employee commitment therefore call into question the reality of any simple relationship between the introduction and use of an employee involvement strategy and the generation of greater commitment and contribution to an organisation. Undoubtedly the use of some employee involvement strategies does have a beneficial effect for both an organisation and its employees, and may lead to some increase in employees' commitment. However, any simple and automatic relationship between these two aspects is open to question and in need of critical evaluation.

SUMMARY

- A number of employer-led employee relations changes have been outlined in this chapter. In particular, two broad strategies have been discussed. These relate to attempts to make more effective and efficient use of an organisation's workforce through implementing forms of employment flexibility and attempting to create a 'unitary workforce'.

- The principal forms of employment flexibility discussed relate to the introduction of a core-periphery labour strategy, flexibility of working hours and the development of multi-skilling.

- Attempts to create a unitary workforce range from approaches that seek to incorporate and offer a role to trade unions to other methods that marginalise or exclude them.

- One particular strategy to develop a unitary workforce, related to attempts to engender employee involvement, has been explored and evaluated in this chapter. This strategy has been associated with many claims about its alleged benefits, based on a unitary perspective of the way in which organisations should operate. These claims are difficult to realise in practice and the use of employee involvement is problematic.

■ Employee involvement may be conceived of and approached as a narrow concept, with limited objects, or as a much broader strategy. The recognition of employee involvement as a broader concept demonstrates its problematic nature. Organisational techniques to engender involvement may be negated by employee perceptions about a range of other organisational characteristics and circumstances that undermine their credibility.

■ Nevertheless, a number of other factors, considered from the perspective of employees, were discussed in relation to the pursuit of employee involvement. These relate to employees' perceptions about organisational treatment, including managerial style, employee expectations, the scope for employee voice and influence, and the provision of managerial justification in relation to decision making.

■ In spite of alleged employer benefits as well as those from the perspective of employees, a number of problems in relation to the realisation of employee involvement were discussed. These relate to organisational characteristics and circumstances that inhibit employee involvement; implementation issues around its use; the changing nature of many employees' psychological contracts; and the multifaceted nature of employee commitment.

■ The scope for this strategy to realise intended change must therefore remain open to question and evaluation wherever its use is being considered.

CASE STUDY 8.2

Employee involvement at Engco

Engco manufactures components used in a range of domestic equipment. It is a subsidiary business unit of a larger organisation, which is, in turn, a division of a multinational corporation employing 28 000 people across 17 different countries. The head office of this particular division is based in Germany. Operating policies stem from this Divisional Head Office, although these frequently cause problems for business units based in other countries, such as those based in Britain and the USA, because of different cultural and operational expectations.

Because of the threat of closure of Engco and the relocation of its work to a business unit based in another country, its management realised that they had to improve its performance. They were also concerned about the possibility of having to implement an employee involvement strategy emanating from the Divisional Head Office which they felt would threaten their freedom to manage in the way that they had in the past. Consequently, they devised an employee involvement strategy which they felt would work towards placating both of these threats. This was called 'Focus on Quality and Service'. It became known as the 'FQS programme' or 'Focus programme'.

The Focus programme was introduced across the various parts of Engco through a series of workshops. In all, about 250 people were employed in Engco. A four-day workshop was devised for senior and line managers to attend. Other grades in Engco attended a two-day, weekend workshop. The intention of the workshops was to introduce employees to the need for the Focus programme, what it was intended to achieve, and to the techniques that were to be used to involve employees in helping the organisation to achieve its goal of improving quality, service and performance. During their four-day workshops, managers received additional training intended to equip them with the skills to implement the techniques to be used. Employees attending the two-day workshops were generally reported as enjoying the experience of a weekend away at the employer's expense and a couple of these workshops quickly entered the 'folklore' of Engco for the drinking events that apparently took place into the early hours of the morning. More enthusiastic Focus programme participants were identified and offered the opportunity to become Focus Champions in their work groups.

A number of employee involvement initiatives were devised for introduction and all of these were clearly identified with the aims of the Focus programme. Improvements in communication were intended to be realised through the introduction of 'Focus briefings'. Employees were to be encouraged to become involved in the improvement of quality through the introduction of the 'FQS suggestion scheme' and 'FQS improvement teams'. Work patterns were also reorganised through the introduction of 'Focus work teams' to promote employee involvement. The announced intention of this initiative was that production processes would be remodelled to replace traditional clusters of engineering operations (e.g. machining or assembly operations being clustered together) to create 'production cells' that would be able to take more responsibility for producing particular components or sub-components. Management was also encouraged to become much more visible through 'walking the shop' and by attending Focus briefing groups and FQS improvement team meetings.

Focus briefings were arranged as a cascade with information emanating from the Managing Director. These briefings were also used to include key messages from the parent organisation and from the Divisional Head Office. However, the downward focus of the information provided was often felt to be threatening and to lead to frustration. The operating climate for the Division was reported as being highly competitive and the particular circumstance of Engco was portrayed as being 'under review'. This had the effect of creating a high level of uncertainty for employees and some reported that they felt 'very stressed' after attending a briefing session. Some managers made particular efforts to obtain supplementary information and answers to the concerns voiced by those who attended their particular briefing sessions. Senior managers had been encouraged to attend these briefing groups to raise their visibility and to show that all employees in Engco were facing the same issues and aiming at the same goal. However, their presence in a situation of evident uncertainty led to mixed reactions. Some employees turned their questions on the senior manager attending their briefing group. Other groups felt that the presence of a senior manager at the briefing group was like having a 'spy in the camp'. The result was that these groups received the information with very little discussion. Soon senior managers stopped attending these briefing groups.

The 'FQS suggestion scheme' was launched with a poster campaign around the site offering different types of prizes for individual and group suggestions that would improve performance in part of Engco. This scheme led to a significant and quick response from some parts of Engco. This took the management by surprise and led to the setting up of a panel to establish some criteria against which to evaluate the suggestions being submitted. Some of the suggestions were not felt to be viable and these were rejected with an accompanying explanation. Other suggestions were felt to be potentially viable and were entered into a further round of evaluation. A small number without cost implications were implemented within a few weeks. However, the initial stream of suggestions soon ceased with few following in the subsequent period.

The introduction of 'FQS improvement teams' followed the campaign for the FQS suggestion scheme. The Focus Champions were used to lead teams specifically set up to examine a particular process or business problem that had been identified. In some parts of Engco, these improvement teams were seen to work well and to involve employees in working out solutions to the problem identified for them to examine. The use of these teams was also felt to develop teamworking and the competencies required for this to be successful. Attendance at these teams was initially introduced as being on a voluntary basis, within a particular part of work time. After initial high levels of attendance in those areas where these teams were established, attendance in some of these areas began to fall off. This led management to require attendance at these improvement teams. However, this compulsory strategy did not help to promote the advancement of problem-solving solutions and, in some cases, it inhibited the work of these teams. Consequently, this requirement was soon withdrawn. These improvement teams continued to operate in some parts of Engco, where they were valued by both the organisation and those who participated. In other parts of Engco, they were rarely used, if at all in particular sections.

The introduction of 'Focus work teams' was associated with the implementation of various forms of job redesign and work reorganisation. The exact nature of these forms varied between the different sections within Engco. In some sections, work was reorganised to allow for the use of job rotation and some forms of job enlargement. In other sections, work was more substantially reorganised to allow for the introduction of semi-autonomous work groups that encouraged multi-skilling and job enrichment. The level of involvement was seen by those managers who took an interest in this development to be higher in those sections that adopted a more radical approach to reorganising work. The nature of the jobs that resulted in these sections allowed for greater employee influence and

▶

opportunities for development. However, those managers who took an interest in the outcome of these attempts to introduce employee involvement still felt that even in these sections, as well as elsewhere in Engco, the introduction of this strategy 'still left a lot to be desired'.

Case study questions

1 How effective was the introduction of employee involvement in Engco?

2 What factors affected the level of effectiveness of employee involvement in Engco?

3 How would you approach any attempt to encourage employee involvement in this organisation?

REFERENCES

Ackers, P., Marchington, M., Wilkinson, A. and Goodman, J. (1992) 'The use of cycles? Explaining employee involvement in the 1990s', *Industrial Relations Journal*, 23(4), 268–83.

Allen, M. (1998) 'All-inclusive', *People Management*, 11 June, 36–42.

Atkinson, J. (1984) 'Manpower strategies for flexible organisations', *Personnel Management*, August, 28–31.

Bassett, P. (1987) *Strike Free*, London: Macmillan.

BBC (1998) 'Business: The company file: Deal to save Rover plant', 27 November, available from Internet, http://news.bbc.co.uk/hi/english/business/the%5Fcompany%5Ffile/news id%5F223000/223054.stm

Becker, H.S. (1960) 'Notes on the concept of commitment', *American Journal of Sociology*, 66, 289–96.

Beer, M., Eisenstat, R.A. and Spector, B. (1990) 'Why change programs don't produce change', *Harvard Business Review*, November/December, 158–66.

Bies, R.J. (1987) 'The predicament of injustice: the management of moral outrage', in Cummings, L.L. and Staw, B.M. (eds), *Research in Organizational Behavior*, Vol. 9, Greenwich Conn.: JAI Press, pp. 289–319.

Blyton, P. (1994) 'Working hours', in Sisson, K. (ed.), *Personnel Management: A Comprehensive Guide to Theory and Practice in Britain*, Oxford: Blackwell.

Caldwell, R. (1993) 'Employee involvement and communication', *Journal of Strategic Change*, 2 (June), 135–38.

Confederation of British Industry/Employment Department Group (1991) *Managing for Success*, Launch Issue, April, London, CBI/EDG.

Coopey, J. and Hartley, J. (1991) 'Reconsidering the case for organisational commitment', *Human Resource Management Journal*, 1(3), 18–32.

Cully, M., O'Reilly, A., Millward, N., Forth, J., Woodland, S., Dix, G. and Bryson, A. (1998) *The 1998 Workplace Employee Relations Survey: First Findings*, available from Internet, www.dti.gov.uk/emar.

Cunningham, I., Hyman, J. and Baldry, C. (1996) 'Empowerment: the power to do what?', *Industrial Relations Journal*, 27(2), 143–54.

Daly, J.P. and Geyer, P.D. (1994) 'The role of fairness in implementing large-scale change: employee evaluations of process and outcome in seven facility relocations', *Journal of Organizational Behavior*, 15, 623–38.

Folger, R. (1977) 'Distributive and procedural justice: combined impact of "voice" and improvement on experienced inequality', *Journal of Personality and Social Psychology*, 35, 108–19.

Gall, G. (1993) 'What happened to single union deals? – a research note', *Industrial Relations Journal*, 24(1), 71–5.

Geary, J. (1995) 'Work practices: the structure of work', in Edwards, P. (ed.), *Industrial Relations: Theory and Practice in Britain*, Oxford: Blackwell.

Giffin, R.W. and Bateman, T.S. (1986) 'Job satisfaction and organizational commitment', in Cooper, C.L. and Robertson, I. (eds), *International Review of Industrial and Organizational Psychology*, Chichester: Wiley.

Guest, D., Peccei, R. and Thomas, A. (1993) 'The impact of employee involvement on organisational commitment and "them and us" attitudes', *Industrial Relations Journal* 24(3), 191–200.

Hendry, C. and Pettigrew, A. (1988) 'Multi-skilling in the round', *Personnel Management*, April, 36–43.

Herriot, P. and Pemberton, C. (1995) *New Deals: The Revolution in Managerial Careers*, Chichester: Wiley.

Herriot, P. and Pemberton, C. (1996) 'Contracting careers', *Human Relations*, 49(6), 757–90.

IDS (1993) 'Annual hours', IDS Study 554, December.

IDS (1998) 'Partnership agreements', IDS Study 656, October.

IPM/IPA (n.d.) *Employee Involvement and Participation Code*, London: IPM.

Kessler, S. and Bayliss, F. (1998) *Contemporary British Industrial Relations*, 3rd edn, Basingstoke: Macmillan.

Legge, K. (1995) *Human Resource Management: Rhetorics and Reality*, Basingstoke: Macmillan.

Marchington, M. (1992) *Managing the Team: A Guide to Successful Employee Involvement*, Oxford: Blackwell.

Marchingon, M. (1995a) 'Involvement and participation', in Storey, J. (ed.), *Human Resource Management: A Critical Text*, London: Routledge.

Marchington, M. (1995b) 'Fairy tales and magic wants: new employment practices in perspective', *Employee Relations*, 17(2), 51–66.

Marchington, M., Goodman, J., Wilkinson, A. and Ackers, P. (1992) *Recent Developments in Employee Involvement*, Employment Department Research Series No.1, London: HMSO.

Marchington, M., Wilkinson, A., Ackers, P. and Goodman, J. (1994) 'Understanding the meaning of participation: views from the workplace', *Human Relations*, 47(8), 867–94.

Millward, N., Stevens, M., Smart, D. and Hawes, W.R. (1992) *Workplace Industrial Relations in Transition: The ED/ESRC/PSI/ACAS Surveys*, Aldershot: Dartmouth.

Morris, T., Lydka, H. and O'Creevy, F. (1993) 'Can commitment be managed?', *Human Resource Management Journal*, 3(3), 21–42.

Morrow, P.C. (1983) 'Concept redundancy in organizational research: the case of work commitment', *Academy of Management Review*, 8, 486–500.

Morrow, P.C. and Goetz, J.F. (1988) 'Professionalism as a form of work commitment', *Journal of Vocational Behaviour*, 32, 92–111.

Morrow, P.C. and Wirth, R.E. (1989) 'Work commitment among salaried professionals', *Journal of Vocational Behaviour*, 34, 40–56.

Mowday, R.T., Porter, L.W. and Steers, R.M. (1982) *Employee-Organization Linkages: The Psychology of Commitment, Absenteeism and Turnover*, New York: Academic Press.

Naumann, S.E., Bies, R.J. and Martin, C.L. (1995) 'The roles of organizational support and justice during a layoff', *Academy of Management Best Papers Proceedings*, 55, 89–93.

Office for National Statistics (1998) 'Trade union membership and recognition, 1996–7: analysis of data from the Certification Officer and the Labour Force Survey', *Labour Market Trends*, July, 353–64, London: Office for National Statistics.

Office for National Statistics (1999) *Labour Force Survey: Quarterly Supplement No. 4*, February, London: Office for National Statistics.

Open University (1992) *'Video 2: IBC' Media Booklet for B884, Human Resource Strategies*, Milton Keynes: The Open University.

People Management (1999) 'Barclays unveils landmark pay and partnership deal', 25 February.

Porter, L., Steers, R., Mowday, R. and Boulian, P. (1974) 'Organisational commitment, job satisfaction and turnover among psychiatric technicians', *Journal of Applied Psychology*, 59, 603–9.

Price, L. and Price, R. (1994) 'Change and continuity in the status divide', in Sisson, K. (ed.), *Personnel Management: A Comprehensive Guide to Theory and Practice in Britain*, Oxford: Blackwell.

Sako, M. (1998) 'The nature and impact of employee "voice" in the European car components industry', *Human Resource Management Journal*, 8(2), 5–13.

Salamon, M. (1998) *Industrial Relations: Theory and Practice*, Hemel Hempstead: Prentice Hall.

Salamon, M. (1999) 'Collective bargaining', in Hollinshead, G., Nicholls, P. and Tailby, S. (eds), *Employee Relations*, London: Financial Times Pitman Publishing.

Sewell, G. and Wilkinson, B. (1992) 'Empowerment or emasculation? Shopfloor surveillance in a Total Quality organization', in Blyton, P. and Turnbull, P., *Reassessing Human Resource Management*, London: Sage.

Sisson, K. (ed.) (1994) *Personnel Management: A Comprehensive Guide to Theory and Practice in Britain*, Oxford: Blackwell.

Storey, J. (1992) *Developments in the Management of Human Resources*, Oxford: Blackwell.

Tailby, S. (1999) 'Flexible labour markets, firms and workers', in Hollinshead, G., Nicholls, P. and Tailby, S. (eds), *Employee Relations*, London: Financial Times Pitman Publishing.

Wilkinson, A., Marchington, M., Goodman, J. and Ackers, P. (1992) 'Total Quality Management and employee involvement', *Human Resources Management Journal*, 2(4), 1–20.

ANSWERS TO SELF-CHECK QUESTIONS

8.1 *What practical difficulties do you envisage in former production workers making the transition to team leaders?*

The greatest of the difficulties is likely to be the feelings of personal inadequacy experienced by the newly appointed team leaders. Senior managers at Polyco and Isuzu talked of the new skills and personal confidence needed to fulfil the role successfully (Open University, 1992). This is hardly surprising since the role demands that team leaders in both cases should run meetings, select, train and discipline team members. In both cases managers were delighted with the results of the training designed to create this confidence.

An additional difficulty may be the aspect of 'poacher turned gamekeeper'; that is, supervising former colleagues. In neither of these case studies was this the case. But clearly this may be a problem in other situations.

8.2 *The introduction of single-status terms and conditions of employment may encounter some practical difficulties. What may these be?*

Potentially the most important is the loss of preferential status by the former white-collar workers. 'Rounding up' terms and conditions to give former blue-collar workers the same 'privileges' as their white-collar counterparts means that these are no longer privileges. This potentially gives rise to a dispute among the white-collar workers. This may be overcome by the restructuring of the benefits package, to apply to all employees, which means the sense of 'loss' experienced by the white-collar workers may be minimised. However, this may make the whole exercise more costly than the organisation would wish.

8.3 *What other aspects of the way in which an organisation introduces or uses employee involvement may adversely affect its effectiveness?*

You may have produced an answer containing a number of different aspects. We would like to emphasis two such aspects. Employee involvement may simply be used as a 'bolt-on' strategy in an organisation. We recognise in this chapter that employee involvement is, or should be, an 'integrated' concept, affected by as much as affecting other aspects of organisational life (Marchington *et al.*, 1994). Therefore, where no attempt is made to integrate this strategy as part of the culture of the organisation, for example, it is unlikely to develop as intended. We refer to Guest *et al.* (1993), whose work indicated how employee involvement was seen as a secondary concept in their case study organisation and became 'crowded out' by other strategies seen as far more important.

A second aspect related to the way in which an organisation introduces and uses employee involvement that may have a significant bearing on its effectiveness is related to the thesis of Beer *et al.*, 1990. You may have read Chapter 2 on organisational structures and the management of change. In Chapter 2 we briefly discussed the distinction between the use of involvement as a bottom-up strategy, that is developed in the specific setting of an emergent change, and as a top-down, imposed approach. Beer *et al.* (1990) believe that the former approach is likely to be much more effective and to lead to genuine involvement. This is associated with their task alignment approach to the generation of change, that is designed to produce effective change though involving employees and building on their skills and knowledge in the context of a specific change scenario. They believe that the latter, imposed type of strategy is less likely to be effective for this reason (*see* Chapter 2).

8.4 *What other problems may confront line managers in their role in the implementation of employee involvement?*

Again, you may have generated a number of different aspects in your response to this question. The additional problems that they confront may include conflicting approaches to the implementation of employee involvement initiatives between managers. Thus, some managers may attempt to implement faithfully the initiatives that have been introduced, while others may not do so. This may result in conflict and stress. Another problem for line managers may relate to the range of initiatives that they are expected to have responsibility for and changes that emerge to the techniques that are used. This suggests that managers themselves may have a problem around the low level of process control that they exercise and the expectations placed on them in relation to top-down approaches to employee involvement.

CHAPTER 9

Downsizing and the management of change

Having completed this chapter, you will be able to:

■ Explain the purpose of downsizing and analyse the problems associated with its use.

■ Identify a range of organisational strategies to downsize and evaluate their consequences.

■ Discuss the significance of employee involvement and influence in relation to the implementation of downsizing.

■ Describe the nature of survivors' reactions to the advent of downsizing and the existence of moderating variables affecting these, and evaluate their significance for organisations using this type of change strategy.

■ Discuss the role of organisational theories and HR interventions to provide strategies to manage the process of downsizing more effectively.

■ Identify the role downsizing plays in contributing to organisational change and link it with other HR change interventions such as culture change, performance management, employee involvement and commitment, and training and development.

INTRODUCTION

Downsizing has become a major organisational change strategy used by organisations of all sizes. At a superficial level downsizing is a simple change to consider. Reducing an organisation's headcount is a more concrete idea than, say, considering implementing a culture change programme. However, although such a structural change programme may be easier to comprehend at this superficial level, in reality the process of downsizing is highly complex and can often generate a range of reactions that undermine an organisation's objectives for downsizing. In this chapter we explore these reactions and their consequences for an organisation using this type of change strategy. As a major structural change strategy, downsizing is also capable of promoting and contributing to other organisational change strategies. Indeed, our purpose will be to show how the successful use of this change strategy will require the implementation of other human resource strategies to avoid or manage the reactions which downsizing generates, as well as to gain the greatest benefit from its use. We therefore discuss the need to focus on the human aspects of change in order to have a higher chance of realising the intended objectives of this strategy.

Two case studies are used to illustrate the main points in this chapter. The first, BT (British Telecom), is set in the high-technology communications industry and illustrates the issues associated with downsizing as the organisation adapted to the private sector and increased competition. The second case explores downsizing in the power industry. This illustrates differences as well as similarities in the issues that it faced during downsizing. The second case study emphasises the role of managers in managing the people issues associated with downsizing. It also stresses the need to recognise the range of organisational stakeholders when downsizing and to develop other human resource strategies in order to achieve a more successful outcome.

CASE STUDY 9.1

Downsizing at BT

Since BT emerged as a separate company in the early 1980s it has faced a number of significant changes in its operating environment which have necessitated managing change within the organisation. In 1984 the Telecommunications Act led to the privatisation of British Telecom, with an initial 51 per cent of its shares being sold to the public. This also established the principle of competition and a regulatory body called Oftel to encourage and oversee this. Initial competition was restricted to the establishment of a second company, Mercury, so that the British telecommunications industry at that time may be seen as a duopoly. In 1991 government policy was altered to end this duopoly situation by allowing competition from a much wider range of companies, many of which had been establishing themselves through the supply of cable television (Höpfl et al., 1992; Brown, 1997). However the regulatory framework remained and for BT this meant the operation of a price cap which restricted the prices it could charge in certain markets. In practice this has led to price reductions over the course of time. As a consequence there were pressures to reduce its operating costs, including labour costs which stood at 45 per cent of operating costs in 1991 (IRS, 1993).

Technological changes in the telecommunications industry and developing liberalisation in various important national markets also increased the scope for competition. The investments required in new technology and international markets, to maintain or develop a competitive position, involve huge sums, with BT investing billions of pounds each year in the 1990s. Increasing competition between telecommunications companies is likely to lead to greater globalisation and industrial consolidation, especially as firms seek to deal with technological changes that blur the distinctions between existing industrial boundaries. In 1997, BT attempted to merge with the USA-based company MCI before that organisation announced its plan to merge with another major telecommunications firm, WorldCom. BT had already established a 'global supercarrier' called Concert Communications and is developing joint ventures in several European countries as well as investing in other markets. Increasing global competition is therefore likely to bring about future changes in the operating environment of telecommunications companies and to lead to a decreasing number of large, international firms.

The transformation of BT from a public corporation to a private sector company, operating in an increasingly changing environment, has been accompanied by significant structural and cultural changes affecting the organisation's workforce. BT's workforce stood at nearly a quarter of a million at the end of the 1980s (Doherty *et al.*, 1996; Brown, 1997). In terms of employment policy, BT's employees had worked in an environment which has been described as being characterised by 'high security, certainty and predictability' (Newell and Dopson, 1996: 12). However, a number of downsizing programmes reduced BT's UK headcount to about 130 000 people in mid 1996. The scale of this downsizing and its impact on those who had entered an organisation where job security and employment continuity had been the norm are amongst the reasons why Doherty *et al.* (1996) believe that BT is an important case to study in this context.

One of the key events towards this transformation was the introduction of Project Sovereign in 1990. This was designed to promote a more customer-focused culture at BT through the use of restructuring, de-layering and downsizing. The organisation was restructured in 1991 from 27 geographical districts, each with up to 12 management layers, to three divisions related to categories of customers, accompanied by a flatter organisational structure. This change led to the targeted reduction of 6000 managers, through the de-layering of management tiers, and the loss of other related posts (Höpfl *et al.*, 1992; Newell and Dopson, 1996). The Release Scheme related to redundancy was voluntary although 'of those targeted, few stayed' (Höpfl *et al.*, 1992: 30). The use

▶

of a voluntary strategy to achieve redundancies and organisational downsizing remained an important facet of this continuing change since it was more congruent with the organisation's industrial relations culture: as a unionised company agreement had been reached and was maintained to secure voluntary redundancies (IRS, 1994a).

By 1991, BT had downsized, including through the use of natural wastage, to about 215 000 people. The targeted nature of redundancies in BT was changed to a more general or unfocused approach in 1992. This change in strategy was introduced through a downsizing programme known as 'Release '92'. This commenced in April 1992, following its introduction through a letter to all staff in March, and followed a procedure which led to each individual being informed about the scheme, given time to consider it, and where interest was shown offered an estimate of severance terms. However, BT sought to maintain some control over the implementation of this scheme through the right to select applications that would not be allowed because the personnel concerned had competence that the organisation wished to retain. A range of redundancy terms was offered to staff whose applications were accepted, depending on their age, length of service and pension scheme membership. These terms were generous and early leavers attracted an additional payment. Leavers were also offered a range of other benefits. These included outplacement services, retraining costs up to £1000, independent financial advice, periods of temporary work over the following year, and pre-retirement counselling for those over 50 years of age. Line managers played a central role in promoting this release scheme and received training to be able to cope with this event. This training included provision of the justification for redundancies and interview skills for this situation (IRS, 1993).

The promotion of 'Release '92', driven in part by a concern that it would not attract the number of volunteers desired and combined with the terms on offer, helped to produce a situation where many more BT staff applied for voluntary severance than the 20 000 'target'. IRS (1993) reported that about 46 000 staff made serious applications, of whom just over 30 000 were accepted. This release of additional personnel to those originally envisaged was partly facilitated by allowing managers to manage workloads with smaller teams as well as by bringing forward planned closures. However, despite the fact that this release scheme, like those which followed, was based on the principle of voluntary severance, research conducted into the reactions of those who experienced and 'survived' this event at BT indicate a number of negative survivor reactions.

The implementation of the downsizing programme itself led to survivor reactions. The 'success' in attracting so many volunteers for the redundancy terms being offered led to a situation where some of those retained became 'angry and hurt' because they had not been allowed to leave (IRS, 1993: 14). Despite the fact that BT's downsizing programmes were voluntary, Doherty et al. (1996) also report that some survivors felt a sense of loss about colleagues with whom they had worked closely and were friends. This could even lead to a sense of guilt about the fact that they had retained a job while their former colleagues had lost theirs. Other findings reported in *BT Today* (December 1992, cited in IRS, 1993: 14) illustrate a different strand of survivor emotions: 'Under Release '92 there was a feeling that you were allowed to go only if you weren't that good. So some people will argue, what's the benefit of being good? It means you can't leave and get paid for it.'

Survivors' reactions also arose after the implementation of this and other downsizing programmes. Survivors found themselves in an organisation where they had to cope with increased workloads and targets. The need for continued downsizing also contributed to uncertainty and job insecurity. Related to insecurity was the loss of career opportunities which arose from the downsized nature of the organisation (Doherty *et al.*, 1996; Newell and Dopson, 1996). As a result of such changes, morale and commitment were adversely affected, according to research that has been published. IRS (1993: 14) report findings from the annual BT Communications and Attitudes Research for Employees (CARE) survey published in February 1993, that 'morale among the 125,781 respondents was low'. Doherty *et al.* (1996: 55–6) report that from their sample of BT survivors '77 per cent stated that stress had increased at work, and 69 per cent … highlighted that loyalty to BT and the amount of fun gained from work has decreased'. A survey by the Society of Telecom Executives, reported by IRS (1994b), found that 64.6 per cent of respondents believed that their workloads had increased, while 56 per cent of those responding felt that they suffered from work-related stress.

The period from 1991 to 1995 witnessed significant downsizing at BT through voluntary redundancies and other methods such as natural wastage. During this period BT's UK workforce fell from 215 000 to 137 000 – a reduction of 78 000 staff. The size of the workforce has continued to decline since this date although more slowly. BT's experience of Release '92 led it to modify its approach in subsequent programmes. Thus Release '93 did not permit volunteers from anywhere in the organisation. A number of employee categories were identified and publicised from which it was unlikely that volunteers would be accepted. In addition the leaving period for those who were accepted for redundancy was extended for up to two years. This had an important effect in terms of avoiding a particular time or short period when many thousands of people would leave. Positively, staggering the dates of those leaving would help work transitions, restructuring events and human resource planning (IRS, 1993). The scale and experience of BT's downsizing programme thus illustrates many key points about this type of change. Our own interview with one of BT's corporate personnel practitioners in the mid 1990s illustrated that the company had achieved a significant amount of organisational learning over the course of this change and that it was probably one of the most sophisticated downsizing organisations in the country. Even allowing for such learning, downsizing is clearly a significant event, affecting the jobs and security of survivors as well as leavers, and thus a complex change to manage.

Downsizing

What is downsizing?

Downsizing is an organisational strategy to reduce the size of an organisation's workforce. It is frequently used as a synonym for redundancy. Although references in the media often associate downsizing with redundancy, it may involve a range of methods, as we saw in the case of BT where significant numbers were also reduced through natural wastage. In this sense downsizing may be seen as a term that includes some of the methods that have traditionally been seen as alternatives to redundancy. These methods include the use of natural wastage, early retirement, voluntary as opposed to compulsory redundancy, freezing recruitment, redeployment and retraining. Freeman and Cameron (1993) offer two further distinguishing features of downsizing in relation to redundancy (or 'layoffs' as this is referred to in the North American literature). For them, downsizing is an organisation-level concept whereas redundancy is approached at the level of the individual. Following from this differentiation, downsizing should be approached as a strategic issue whereas redundancy is an operational one.

The purpose of and problem with downsizing

The purpose of downsizing is to provide a means to improve organisational performance (Kozlowski *et al.*, 1993). However, this statement of purpose may be criticised for being too general, since it can be associated with either a short-term goal to cut costs, or a more fundamental and longer-term aim to realise improvements related to greater effectiveness, efficiency, productivity and competitiveness. This distinction, and the fact that downsizing is frequently linked with the former goal and the use of redundancy, leads to the fundamental problem associated with its intended purpose. In practice, pursuing short-term cost cutting through redundancy to reduce headcount is likely to lead to the loss of key competence and to the creation of lowered morale and insecurity. This outcome may adversely affect, rather than improve, aspects of the performance of an organisation. Even the use of a more carefully managed and longer-term attempt to restructure and transform the organisation may still have adverse effects. Thus, downsizing is likely to be associated with the creation of negative psychological and behavioural consequences for survivors no matter how well it is managed. The management of this type of change therefore needs to alleviate the causes of such consequences as far as is possible and reduce their effects.

Organisations as well as human resource management theorists often recognise the importance of committed employees (*see*, for example, Guest, 1987). Alternatives to a strategy that encourages employee integration with, and commitment to, the goals of an organisation (*see* Chapter 8) may be to muddle along or to seek to use an approach that overtly increases the degree of managerial control over the workforce. However the use of either of these approaches may only work effectively in the short term where no attempt is made to manage the issues which arise from downsizing. In relation to BT, Doherty *et al.* (1996: 56) illustrate how commitment may have been affected, through the view of one of their participants:

> What drove us on to complete the project, even with its impossible targets, was our professionalism and our relationship with the customer to whom we were committed. It had little to do with loyalty to the company.

The need for organisational commitment and loyalty is likely to be more significant after the advent of downsizing since those who remain become more important to the functioning of the organisation. However, this is likely to be threatened if the organisation does not purposefully intervene to foster commitment, unless its employees maintain some sort of third-party relationship with its customers, perhaps related to a sense of professional commitment.

Shaw and Barrett-Power (1997) recognise that the measures typically used to assess the effectiveness of downsizing from a corporate perspective are clearly inadequate as a means to understand and manage the impact of this process on stakeholders such as work groups and individuals who survive this event. Typically, corporate measures are related to profitability, productivity, investment returns, customer satisfaction ratings, etc. While these may indicate that downsizing has had a negative impact on those who survive as employees in the organisation, they can only serve to highlight the presence of psychological and behavioural consequences for survivors. There is evidence of the existence of such consequences, and their adverse effect on expected corporate outcomes from downsizing, from the findings of a number of USA-based surveys. Mishra and Mishra (1994) cite Tomasko (1992) who reported survey research that found that just one-quarter of surveyed organisations had realised their objective of improved productivity, higher investment returns, etc. Similarly, a survey by the Wyatt Company of 1005 organisations found that less than half of those surveyed were able to agree that they had achieved a particular organisational objective related to a desire to reduce costs, improve productivity, increase investment returns, or increase profits, etc. (Cameron, 1994a).

We believe that these USA-based survey findings suggest the need for similar research in other countries to see if their results can be replicated. But in any case, our view is that the continued commercial success of many organisations that have engaged in significant downsizing programmes means that there is a need to interpret the results of such surveys with a degree of caution. Whilst a failure to achieve a key objective following downsizing may indicate the presence of psychological and behavioural reactions from survivors we believe that such consequences may be present even where corporate results do not point to this outcome. A range of contextual variables could affect, and disguise, the impact of negative reactions of downsizing survivors on the commercial performance of an organisation. These include the nature of the technology being used, the skills of the workforce, the nature of work processes, and the need for innovative behaviour. For this reason, we believe that the negative impact of survivors' reactions may be hidden from an organisation's 'balance sheet', at least in the short term.

Thus, rather than diminish the importance of the study of this area of change management where organisations continue to demonstrate commercial success, we believe that it may be claimed to increase its significance. Even where observable commercial costs are not recognised it may be the case that a significant adverse impact has occurred. This may be related to the creation of negative psychological consequences for survivors or to the altered profile of an organisation's workforce, which impairs its ability to demonstrate adaptability to altered circumstances in the future (*see* Chapter 2).

To summarise our discussion so far, it has been suggested that the intended reason for organisations to downsize is to achieve an improvement in organisational performance. However, it has also been recognised that the creation of psychological and behavioural reactions from those who survive this process may lead to the impairment, rather than the improvement, of the performance of the organisation. This suggests that downsizing needs to be examined as a 'bottom-up' process as well as a 'top-down' one. In other words, for the corporate intentions of a downsizing organisation to be realised it will be necessary to consider and manage the process from the perspective of affected individuals and work groups and the stresses which this event creates. This type of approach has led Shaw and Barrett-Power (1997: 109) to propose a definition which focuses on this perspective:

> we define downsizing more broadly as a constellation of stressor events centering around pressures toward workforce reductions which place demands upon the organisation, work groups, and individual employees, and require a process of coping and adaptation.

The nature of these psychological and behavioural reactions is summarised in Fig. 9.1 and discussed more fully, along with their implications, on pp. 259–67.

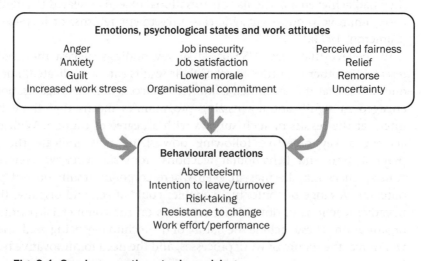

Fig. 9.1 Survivor reactions to downsizing

Source: Developed from Thornhill and Saunders, 1998.

The management of change implications of downsizing

Downsizing is a powerful means to generate organisational change. As a structural change adversely affecting the retention of people's jobs its incidence will be highly transparent and its impact pervasive. Downsizing can also contribute to and affect other forms of organisational change. For example, it may be used as a means to help to bring about a change in the culture of an organisation (*see* Chapter 3), or to introduce a system of performance management (*see* Chapter 5). Such changes may be easier to introduce in the wake of the shift which downsizing produces as organisational participants cease to believe in the notion of 'a job for life' and steady progression through the organisation. The incidence and scale of downsizing in BT appears to have introduced such a shift in the thinking of its employees (Newell and Dopson, 1996). However, the use of downsizing may also impair an attempt to introduce another type of change strategy where it produces negative reactions amongst those who survive. The process of downsizing also necessitates the introduction of other changes. For example, as events such as restructuring, de-layering, redundancy and redeployment occur, training and development needs will become apparent (*see* Chapter 6).

This suggests that downsizing can be seen as either a primary lever to introduce organisational change, or as a link in a chain of change events. Implicit in both of these interpretations is an undertaking to manage the implications of downsizing proactively, and to try and ensure that strategies to manage change are congruent. In practice, as we discuss later, this may not happen. Where this is the case, the opportunity to achieve the organisational objectives intended from the use of downsizing is likely to be impaired. This will require reactive interventions to attempt to obtain the type of change that was originally intended. The need for a reactive intervention to overcome unintended and negative change outcomes may also result from the use of inappropriate or ineffective interventions when downsizing was introduced. This is illustrated in Fig. 9.2.

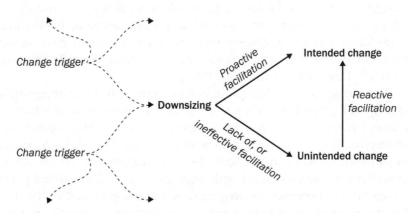

Fig. 9.2 Change implications related to downsizing

Management of change implications arising from alternative organisational strategies for downsizing

Work by Cameron and colleagues (*see*, for example, Cameron *et al.*, 1991, 1993) has identified three organisational strategies to achieve downsizing. The first of these is the workforce reduction strategy, which focuses simply on reducing an organisation's headcount. The second is the organisation redesign strategy, which involves elements of de-layering, eliminating areas of work and job redesign, so that the amount of work is reduced as well as the organisation's headcount. The third is the systemic change strategy and, as its name suggests, it is a longer-term approach intended to promote a more fundamental change that affects the culture of the organisation through promotion of employee involvement and adherence to a continuous improvement strategy. Downsizing may thus be implemented solely through reducing an organisation's headcount (the most popular strategy) or in combination with one or more other strategies which seek to reduce the amount of work undertaken and bring about structural and cultural organisational change.

Significantly, Cameron *et al.* (1993) found that the exclusive use of a workforce reduction strategy led to a diminution, rather than an improvement, in organisational performance. In a confirmatory study, Mishra and Mishra (1994) found that organisational performance was adversely affected in relation to both cost and quality where this strategy was used exclusively. Such a strategy may lead to the loss of valued organisational competence, as we discussed above, and to negative consequences for those who remain. Its benefits are seen to be short-term whereas the attendant costs remain into the longer term as the organisation attempts to overcome the loss of required competence and negative survivor reactions.

By comparison the use of an organisation redesign and/or systemic change strategy has been positively related to organisational performance in terms of both cost reduction and quality improvement (Cameron *et al.*, 1993; Mishra and Mishra, 1994). Moreover, organisations which relied exclusively on the use of a workforce reduction strategy were found to be likely to repeat the use of this approach whenever cost reduction was deemed necessary (Cameron, 1994b). Repeated use of a workforce reduction strategy has also been shown to have further damaging consequences to employee morale as subsequent downsizing programmes are revealed (Thornhill and Gibbons, 1995).

The management of change implications arising from an organisation's choice of strategy for downsizing will also be related to the extent to which the approach adopted is proactive or reactive (Kozlowski *et al.*, 1993). A proactive downsizing strategy is likely to be integrated with the organisation's business strategy, target organisational areas and competencies for downsizing selectively, and recognise the potential consequences from both organisational and individual perspectives. The recognition of potential consequences is also likely to lead to the development of interventions to alleviate or manage their incidence. Proactivity therefore implies careful planning throughout the stages of downsizing.

In contrast, a reactive approach is unlikely to consider those aspects that a proactive approach is designed to address. It is therefore more likely to be used where the aim of downsizing is limited to reducing organisational costs, and to lead to the creation of negative consequences in relation to remaining employees. The North American literature suggests that a reactive approach to downsizing may be more frequently used than a proactive one. For example, the small amount of time available to the HR managers in the study undertaken by McCune *et al.* (1988) meant that they had little opportunity to plan before downsizing. It probably also follows that managers faced with such a situation will have insufficient, if any, time to plan and develop interventions to alleviate and manage the consequences of downsizing for those who survive. The change management implications are thus more likely to be negative and, in the event, more difficult to manage, where an organisation pursues only a workforce reduction strategy, especially where this is conducted on a reactive basis.

Self-check question	9.1	*Why might the requirement to adopt a proactive downsizing strategy in order to minimise the negative consequences associated with this type of change be difficult to achieve in practice?*
	9.2	*Re-read the BT case study. How would you categorise BT's organisational strategy to achieve downsizing?*

Management of change implications arising from the methods used to implement downsizing

Our earlier discussion has highlighted the relationship between the type of organisational strategy used to downsize and the nature of the consequences which result from this process. This has suggested that a strategy which focuses only on workforce reductions, especially where this is reactive in nature, is less likely to achieve the organisational objectives established for downsizing and more likely to lead to unintended negative consequences related to survivors' reactions. We now suggest a similar relationship between the methods used to implement downsizing (for example, redundancy, early retirement, etc.) and the nature of the reactions that occur.

The nature of survivors' reactions generated by use of a particular method is likely to be linked to the level of managerial control that this method promotes over the implementation of downsizing (Greenhalgh *et al.*, 1988). For example, a high level of managerial control over the implementation of downsizing is likely to promote a lack of perceived employee influence and greater feelings of job insecurity. The use of compulsory redundancy to achieve downsizing is therefore likely to lead to low employee influence and high levels of job insecurity because it is management that exercises choice not only about method but also about selection of those to be made redundant.

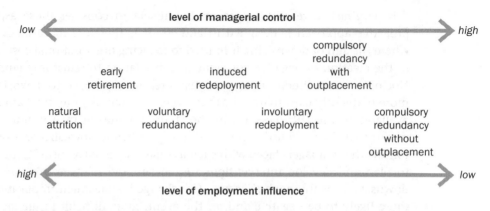

Fig. 9.3 **Downsizing methods, managerial control and employee influence**
Source: Developed from Greenhalgh *et al.*, 1988.

The use of methods such as natural wastage or early retirement should reduce the level of perceived managerial control. This is likely to reduce levels of job insecurity for those below the early retirement age as well as concerns about low employee influence since the use of such methods does not threaten these employees' continuity of employment. Greenhalgh *et al.* (1988) discuss five downsizing methods which they place on a continuum that emphasises employees' influence over their continuity of employment at one end and managerial control at the other. We have added early retirements and voluntary redundancy to this continuum (*see* Fig. 9.3).

However, even where an organisation encourages early retirements or uses a voluntary approach to redundancy, a high level of managerial control may be exercised (Wass, 1996; Turnbull and Wass, 1997). Redundancy through all categories arises as the result of a managerial decision. Although voluntary redundancy involves a decision by an employee to accept an offer of a redundancy payment, and is differentiated from compulsory redundancy which affects selected employees regardless of their wishes, managerial control over inducements to accept voluntarily have been shown to be highly persuasive (Wass, 1996). In addition, non-financial inducements to volunteer are suggested by Lewis (1993: 34): 'Increasing the target staffing reduction may add to the pressure upon employees and may further reduce morale. More volunteers may result. Intensification of work and other changes may have a similar effect ...'.

Perhaps the key point in this respect is the perception by employees of their level of influence over this change process. While careful targeting of the terms to be offered may allow organisations to exercise effective control over the implementation of downsizing, even where the process is ostensibly voluntary, employees may perceive that they still exercise choice in accepting redundancy. Alternatively there may be an exchange relationship whereby employees are willing to trade their influence over the process for a sizeable compensatory payment. There may even be a sense that employees have exercised some degree of collective control in influencing management to offer relatively generous redundancy terms to avoid particular negative reactions. However, where the method used to implement downsizing is presented as voluntary, but is perceived not to be, the outcome is likely to be the creation of negative reactions. These may be created amongst survivors as well as leavers, with consequences for the future management of the organisation (Thornhill *et al.*, 1997b). In this situation, any sense of influence by employees would be perceived to be false, with the implication that survivors' reactions may be negatively affected through this type of organisational treatment.

Self-check question	9.3	*Which other aspects related to the methods used to implement downsizing might affect managerial control and employee influence over the process?*

Management of change implications arising from the impact of downsizing on those who survive the process

The process of downsizing, through the strategy adopted and the methods to implement it, has been linked to the creation of psychological and behavioural reactions by those who survive this event. This may lead to the impairment of intended organisational objectives, either in the short term or in the longer term. We referred to the need to approach downsizing as a 'bottom-up' process in our earlier discussion. The implication is that by doing this, an organisation will be more likely to recognise the threats to the achievement of its objectives for downsizing, and therefore to understand how it might attempt to alleviate these or manage their effects.

In this section we explore the psychological and behavioural aspects of this type of change management by adopting a 'bottom-up' approach to downsizing. We start by looking more closely at the nature of survivors' reactions to downsizing and the existence of moderating variables (*see*, for example, Brockner, 1988) which affect the strength of survivors' reactions. These variables also indicate the scope for managers to intervene to manage this process. We then consider how a range of organisational theories may be used to suggest interventions to manage downsizing as a 'bottom-up' process.

The nature of survivors' reactions and the existence of moderating variables

Figure 9.4 illustrates the principal determinants and categories of survivors' reactions to the advent of downsizing. These reactions are affected not only by the actions of an organisation but also by psychological and social differences between individuals and broader environmental factors. Reactions to downsizing will vary between individuals because of psychological differences related to self-esteem, prior organisational commitment, tolerance of insecurity and individual coping resources. For example, Brockner *et al.* (1985) suggest that survivors with low self-esteem may actually improve their work performance because they experience a high level of positive inequity (i.e. guilt) about the way in which a downsizing is conducted.

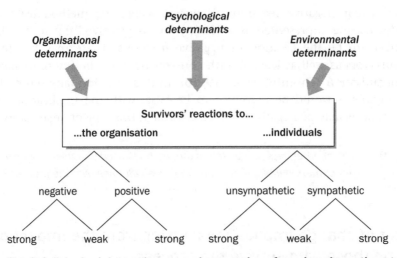

Fig. 9.4 Principal determinants and categories of survivors' reactions to the advent of downsizing

Brockner *et al.* (1992) found that the survivors who are most likely to suffer from negative reactions are those who were highly committed to the organisation before downsizing, where the management of this process is perceived to be unfair. Greenhalgh and Rosenblatt (1984) report that individuals who have a significant aversion to perceived threats such as job insecurity will experience strong reactions. Related to this last aspect, Armstrong-Stassen (1994: 612–13) found that survivors who felt more in control of their situation adopted coping strategies that reflected this feeling. This suggests that those who do not feel this will be less likely to cope effectively.

Environmental conditions may also act as a determinant of survivors' reactions (Brockner, 1988). Where their former colleagues are able to find comparable work in the labour market, survivors' reactions are likely to be less adverse. The occupational and geographical mobility of redundant employees and their economic need to work will also be likely to affect the strength of survivors' reactions (*see*, for example, Greenhalgh and Rosenblatt, 1984).

These variables suggest that survivors' reactions will vary between individuals in the same work setting. It also suggests that organisations need to be aware, in general terms, of the nature of differences between individual employees and of prevailing environmental circumstances when they design interventions to alleviate negative survivor reactions to downsizing. However, these variables should not be interpreted as suggesting that this situation is outside of the influence of a downsizing organisation and therefore that any intervention is not possible. Instead it may be seen to highlight a need to lay particular emphasis on certain interventions, such as employee communication, and to provide an appropriate focus to others such as outplacement assistance for redundant staff, so that any threats posed by insecurity or lack of coping are alleviated. We discuss these types of intervention in the following sub-section.

These individual differences and environmental factors are types of moderator variables. Such variables affect the incidence and strength of survivors' reactions to downsizing (*see*, for example, Greenhalgh and Rosenblatt, 1984; Brockner, 1988). They help to explain why the incidence and strength of psychological and behavioural reactions may be either more or less pronounced in relation to particular downsizing situations. The identification of moderator variables is therefore a very important step towards any attempt to manage a downsizing programme proactively and effectively. An understanding of possible moderator variables will permit those interested to identify possible effects and to use appropriate procedures to avoid, or at least to seek to alleviate, the potentially negative consequences of downsizing.

Many moderator variables are directly related to events in an organisation. The nature and strength of survivors' reactions may thus be partly explained by prior work interdependence with those who are to leave or who have been made redundant (*see*, for example, Brockner, 1988). The strength of sympathetic survivors' responses is likely to be much greater where survivors and leavers have previously been interdependent in terms of carrying out their work. More broadly, these reactions may be partly explained by the existence or absence of shared attitudes, values and experiences (*see*, for example, Brockner and Greenberg, 1990). Where survivors and leavers closely identify with one another there is likely to be a higher level of sympathetic survivor response.

Survivors' beliefs that they may be made redundant themselves may be another source of insecurity affecting the nature and level of their reactions. A further major determinant of survivors' reactions will be related to perceptions about the policies and procedures used by an organisation to implement downsizing. Related to this implementation variable are issues about employee expectations and avoidability, where for example unexpected or avoidable redundancies may result in strong, sympathetic reactions such as anger toward an organisation (*see*, for example, Brockner, 1988). We discuss the management of these variables later.

Our discussion so far about the nature of survivors' reactions and the existence of moderating variables points to a highly complex scenario within a downsizing organisation. Moreover these moderating variables will be likely to have a cumulative and compounding effect (Brockner, 1988). Nevertheless, managerial action focused at this level of downsizing should contribute towards the effective management of this type of change. Its intention would be to reduce the incidence or alleviate the consequences of negative survivors' reactions that can arise where downsizing is only conceived as a corporate-level (top-down) strategy. In this way the strength of negative reactions may be weakened, while any sense of legitimacy in the downsizing process combined with procedural fairness may possibly lead to the creation of some positive reactions.

Brockner and Greenberg (1990) present two opposing categories of reactions which survivors may exhibit, depending upon their perceptions of how leavers are selected and subsequently treated during their period of notice. These categories are labelled as 'sympathetic' and 'unsympathetic' and refer to survivors' reactions towards those who leave an organisation (*see* Fig. 9.4 above). In the context of a downsizing situation, they suggest that an unsympathetic reaction may include the belief that redundancies were justified, particularly in relation to those selected for redundancy, with survivors distancing themselves from the leavers and working harder. On the other hand, sympathetic reactions by survivors may include the belief that leavers have been unfairly selected and/or treated, resulting in negative emotions, attitudes and behaviours towards an organisation. These categories of survivors' reactions therefore point to the need for managerial interventions.

Self-check question

9.4 *How would you react to the redundancy of colleagues in the organisation for which you work, or in an organisation for which you have worked? (Perhaps you have actually experienced this event! If you have, how did you react and why?)*

Interventions to manage downsizing as a 'bottom-up' process to reduce the strength of survivors' reactions

Research using a number of applicable theories, such as those related to equity, organisational justice, job insecurity, job redesign and organisational stress, suggests a number of interventions for managers to consider. These would be designed to reduce the incidence and strength of negative survivor reactions and encourage more positive reactions to the downsizing organisation.

Equity theory, management decisions and work effort

Equity theory (Adams, 1965) has been used to evaluate the effects of employee perceptions about the fairness of management decisions related to the downsizing processes. For example, survivors' reactions are likely to be affected by their level of acceptance of:

■ the need to downsize or make employees redundant;
■ the lack of an alternative course of action;
■ the level of prior notification provided by management;
■ the selection criteria used and the decisions made by managers about who should be made redundant; and
■ the way in which the leavers are treated during their period of notice and offered support to find alternative employment (Brockner, 1988, 1992).

Perceptions of fairness or equity about management decisions and procedures related to these aspects may help to reduce the incidence of negative reactions. On the other hand perceptions of unfairness may either lead to positive inequity, where particular survivors feel that those made redundant had a greater claim to be retained than they did; or negative inequity where, for example, survivors identified closely with those made redundant. Positive inequity may lead to survivors experiencing guilt with the result that they work harder, whereas negative inequity may lead to affected survivors reducing their level of organisational commitment and working less hard (*see*, for example, Brockner, 1988).

Organisational justice theory: management decisions, decision making and managers' skills

Recognition of the importance of perceived fairness has been developed through the use of organisational justice theory (*see*, for example, Brockner and Greenberg, 1990; Daly and Geyer, 1994). Three types of organisational justice theory have been identified: distributive, procedural and interactional. Distributive justice is related to employees' views about the fairness of the decisions that are made – the 'outcomes' of the process. The elements of distributive justice promote an understanding of why survivors may not perceive the outcomes of redundancy decisions to be fair. Organisations are likely to make or promote redundancy selection decisions based on criteria related to business needs, efficiency and performance. However in many, if not most, cases such criteria will be unlikely to produce outcomes which match the economic need to maintain employment of those threatened by redundancy (Brockner and Greenberg, 1990). Explaining why criteria were chosen may help to reduce the consequences of redundancy decisions based on this mismatch between organisational and individual objectives. In addition, employees may perceive that the business-related criteria used for redundancy selection do not match their judgements about effective performance. The use of such criteria will lead to an outcome that is perceived to be unfair. The possibility of such an outcome has clear implications about the validity of selection criteria and the need to shape perceptions about this. Another aspect of distributive justice may relate to perceptions about whether downsizing and redundancy also affect management, or whether managers are seen to avoid this outcome (Brockner, 1992).

Procedural justice focuses on employee perceptions about the fairness of the procedures used to make decisions about downsizing and redundancies. This suggests that not only should the outcomes of downsizing decision-making be seen to be fair, but so should the procedures used to arrive at such decisions. Where negative reactions are created by outcomes which are perceived as unfair, these may be reduced by the use of procedures which are seen as fair (Brockner *et al.*, 1990). Studies related to procedural justice have focused mainly on two factors that affect perceptions about procedural fairness. These are 'voice', which is linked to employee involvement in the process (*see* Chapter 8), and 'justification', which relates to education through explanation (Daly and Geyer, 1994). The promotion of involvement in this context may include the use of consultation and communication about the process; the use of a voluntary, as opposed to a compulsory, route to redundancy; affected employees being provided with options about redeployment and relocation; the provision of outplacement facilities; and interventions aimed at allowing survivors to adjust to downsizing-related changes. Guest and Peccei (1992: 55) evaluated the effects of involvement initiatives used during the closure of a British Aerospace site and found that 'employee involvement can work as a strategy for easing the process of plant closure'. However, they also found that certain groups were less involved, with the implication that these employees may have had less favourable perceptions about the fairness of the procedures used.

Involvement or voice in this type of context allows those affected to exercise some degree of influence in relation to the process, as we discussed earlier. This type of employee influence has been linked to a number of attitudinal and behavioural survivors' reactions. Davy *et al.* (1991) found that employee influence over the downsizing process positively affects perceptions about fairness and job satisfaction, which in turn affect level of commitment to the organisation and intention to stay. Organisations may therefore genuinely seek to engender employee involvement to promote perceptions that the process used is just (Davy *et al.*, 1991). Justification may also be promoted through an educative process to explain why downsizing is necessary. A similar finding has been found for this as for employee influence in relation to the process: justification has been found to be related positively to procedural fairness and, in turn, to intention to stay (Daly and Geyer, 1994). This may be explained through the finding that employees are more likely to accept a decision, even an unfavourable one related to redundancy, when they receive an adequate and genuine reason for it (*see*, for example, Brockner *et al.*, 1990).

Interactional justice focuses on employees' perceptions about the fairness of the treatment that they and others receive during the implementation of downsizing (Bies and Moag, 1986). Line managers have a potentially significant influence over the way their subordinates react to downsizing in terms of their treatment of those who leave and the survivors. Line managers thus need to be able to demonstrate a range of skills that might be broadly described as change management skills. In addition, line managers need to be able to deal with issues that are specific to a redundancy situation. These will include communicating notification decisions, providing reasons for these, and the sensitivity with which they treat leavers during their notice period. It is therefore suggested that line managers will require preparation and training to be able to cope effectively and fairly (Thornhill *et al.*, 1997a).

Job insecurity and the role of employee communication

The central role that effective communication may play in the management of downsizing and redundancy has been highlighted above through references to equity and organisational justice theories (*see also* Chapter 8). Job insecurity theory develops our understanding of the role of communication in this context. Greenhalgh and Rosenblatt (1984) report that employees receive information through three channels: official organisational ones; organisational actions that provide them with clues; and rumours. Two points follow from this recognition. First, information from the organisation may not focus on the specific concerns of those affected, whether they are leavers or stayers. Second, in the absence of information, or of appropriate information, employees will both infer what is likely to happen from organisational and managerial actions, and rely upon rumours. Where official organisational communication does not focus on the specific concerns of those affected it will not alleviate their sense of powerlessness and perceived threat (*see*, for example, Greenhalgh, 1983; Greenhalgh and Rosenblatt, 1984).

It was recognised above that positive employee perceptions might follow from the exercise of employee involvement or voice during downsizing. In relation to job insecurity, perceptions about personal control related to the downsizing process may be positively affected through communication of the following types of information. First, most employees will benefit from knowing that they will not be affected, at least directly. This may be related to a downsizing strategy that avoids the use of redundancy, at least in its compulsory form. An organisation may also use a carefully defined and targeted approach to reduce the pool of those potentially affected. Where redundancies will occur, an organisation may provide advance notification so that insecurity about potential job loss is reduced for survivors, even though this introduces earlier issues for the management of those who are to leave (Greenhalgh, 1983). Second, where appropriate both leavers and survivors will benefit from information about how they will be affected. Leavers will need information about how they will be treated during their period of notice, what will be expected from them and what further redeployment or outplacement support they may expect to receive. Survivors will need information about how they will be affected by the changes that result from downsizing. The provision of such information will be important for survivors who will now be less concerned about loss of their jobs but who may remain concerned about the removal of those job attributes which they found attractive before change was implemented (Greenhalgh and Rosenblatt, 1984).

Job insecurity, career progression and the psychological contract

Job insecurity in this broader sense refers to uncertainty about attributes such as career progression, contractual relationships including the psychological contact, and status. Downsizing and de-layering may impair opportunities for career progression. Organisations will thus need to consider the implications of this where it is likely to lead to the creation of negative survivor reactions and resulting intentions to leave. In an attempt to avert this type of outcome, organisations will need to consider the competencies which they require, the design and implementation of career management programmes to develop these and how they communicate these aspects to the survivors (*see*, for example, Ebadan and Winstanley, 1997). More broadly, this threat to career progression and prior expectations about security may represent a breach of the psychological contract, where 'the resulting contract involved an exchange of loyalty for security' (Hendry and Jenkins, 1997: 39). This may signify a shift towards a 'transactional' contract, characterised by strict instrumentality where employee inputs are exchanged for compensation, away from a 'relational' contract involving the offer of employment security, training and promotion for employees' loyalty and trust (Herriot and Pemberton, 1996). This may occur at the very time when the need for commitment to the organisation from survivors is likely to be at a premium (*see*, for example, Hallier and Lyon, 1996). The implications of this may be particularly pronounced for middle managers, as we now consider.

Studies conducted in North America (Belasen *et al.*, 1996) and the UK (Newell and Dopson, 1996) found that work demands increased significantly for middle managers during and after downsizing. Such survivors have to engage in a broader range of roles and cope not only with their traditional management tasks but also with new aspects related to the implementation of change. This led Belasen *et al.* to report that the managers in their study needed to be 'hyper-effective' in order to cope. Newell and Dopson also reported that managers needed to work harder and longer in order to cope. However, the sustainability of this requirement, its impact on these managers' psychological contracts, and their level of organisational commitment were questioned. Both studies found that these managers felt they did not receive adequate information, leading to a sense of powerlessness, and that their psychological contracts had been unilaterally altered by the nature of the changes occurring within their organisations. Newell and Dopson reported that the experiences of the managers in their study had led several of these to reappraise the nature of their commitment, shifting their focus from work to family irrespective of career progression.

All survivors may of course experience feelings of insecurity arising from uncertainty and unilateral changes to their psychological contracts. Kozlowski *et al.* (1993) used facets of job redesign theory, related to job enrichment or enlargement, to explore the relationship between an organisational strategy used to downsize and structural determinants of survivors' reactions following downsizing. In our earlier discussion we outlined three organisational strategies for downsizing (*see also* Cameron, 1994b). The first of these simply involved the use of a workforce reduction strategy, where the intention is to reduce organisational headcount and costs. However, the amount of work which remains in the downsized organisation may not be reduced, at least on a commensurate basis. This will lead to a situation of job enlargement for survivors, where feelings of role stress and dissatisfaction may result in an altered commitment focus and intention to leave. This is likely to be associated with ineffective leadership, unclear job responsibilities, poor communication and feedback, and poorly defined performance standards, as well as role overload, following downsizing (Tombaugh and White, 1990). The use of an organisation redesign strategy, in conjunction with a workforce reduction one, will instead be aimed at reducing the quantity of work in the downsized organisation and, when effective, may lead to job enrichment where this enhances personal control in relation to job roles (Kozlowski *et al.*, 1993; Cameron, 1994b).

Recognising and managing stress through the reactions of survivors

Recent work exploring the consequences of downsizing suggests that Lazarus and Folkman's (1984) theory of stress provides a useful analytical and integrative framework to recognise and manage these issues (*see*, for example, Brockner and Wiesenfeld, 1993). Shaw and Barrett-Power's (1997: 109) definition emphasises that downsizing is a 'constellation of stressor events ... which ... require a process of coping and adaptation'. The changes that we have discussed in this chapter emanating from downsizing have indicated a significant number of potential sources of stress for survivors. Lazarus and Folkman's (1984) theory centres on two key concepts: stress appraisal and coping. Individuals will cognitively appraise whether an event will lead to stress, how this may manifest itself and what they can do about it. Coping with an event that causes significant levels of stress, such as downsizing, may involve the use of one of two divergent strategies. One of these involves an intention to confront the problem and to seek to solve it through attempts to exercise influence and control. The second involves focusing instead on its emotional consequences and perhaps seeking to avoid it. Strategies related to problem solving have been labelled as problem-focused coping (Lazarus and Folkman, 1984) or control-oriented coping (Latack, 1986). The second category of strategies have been labelled as emotion-focused (Lazarus and Folkman, 1984) or escape/avoidance coping (Latack, 1986), indicating withdrawal from the situation (Shaw and Barrett-Power, 1997).

We therefore believe that there are clear organisational and management implications from the application of stress theory to the downsizing context. In relation to stress appraisal, prior organisational treatment may be important to the way that individuals react to a potentially threatening or stressful situation (Naumann *et al.*, 1995). Thus, individuals who are employed in organisations which have proven to be supportive in the past may appraise changes as less threatening and stressful. This may be particularly significant for survivors of downsizing. Organisational support through the downsizing event itself is also likely to be important in relation to the type of coping strategy which affected individuals adopt. The aim of such support would be the encouragement of a problem-focused and control-oriented coping approach. Organisational support may be defined simply as the level of concern and care that an organisation shows in relation to the effects of its, and perhaps others', actions on its employees (*see*, for example, Naumann *et al.*, 1995). The most important source of this type of support is likely to be an employee's line manager (see our discussion earlier in relation to interactional justice). In Armstrong-Stassen's (1994) study, the survivors who performed better and were more committed and loyal to their organisation were those who also felt that they had highly supportive line managers. Survivors who demonstrated the same attributes toward commitment, performance and intention to stay were also found to be those who used control-orientated coping strategies. It therefore seems possible that some form of link exists between organisational support and survivors' coping strategies.

Self-check question	9.5	*Using the theoretical framework outlined in this section, how would you evaluate the approach adopted in BT to manage downsizing survivors?*

SUMMARY

■ Downsizing has been defined as an organisational strategy to reduce the size of an organisation's workforce. However, because its use is likely to generate a range of reactions from those who remain in an organisation, which lead to adverse consequences, an adequate definition needs to recognise the effects of downsizing as well as its aim and purpose.

■ Three organisational strategies have been identified to achieve downsizing. These are the workforce reduction strategy; organisation redesign strategy; and the systemic change strategy. An important distinction has also been drawn between the use of proactive and reactive approaches to downsizing. The use of a reactive, workforce reduction strategy has been found in some surveys to impair, rather than improve, organisational performance. Evidence exists which suggests that this approach to downsizing is widely used. Even where such evidence does not exist, there may still be a negative effect arising from the creation of negative survivors' reactions and the loss of organisational competence.

■ Some studies also suggest that where organisations use methods to implement downsizing which emphasise managerial control over the process at the expense of perceived influence by employees over their continuity of employment, this will generate further negative survivors' reactions which lead to adverse consequences for the organisation.

■ The incidence and strength of survivors' reactions are affected by the existence of moderating variables which suggest that there is scope for downsizing organisations to intervene to seek to alleviate their incidence or manage their effects.

■ A range of organisational theories, related to equity, organisational justice, job insecurity, job redesign and organisational stress, can be used to indicate appropriate human resource interventions to manage the process of downsizing more effectively, depending on the characteristics of the organisational context.

■ Downsizing has been shown to be capable of promoting significant organisational change. However, the success of downsizing will depend on the concurrent use of many of the other change strategies which are explored in this book.

CASE STUDY 9.2

Downsizing at Energyco

Energyco emerged from a large public sector provider of power in the early 1990s. This larger organisation was technologically advanced but highly staffed. As Energyco emerged into the private sector it was already known that it would be necessary to downsize the new organisation. The assets of the public sector provider had been divided between the new firms that superseded it with the result that Energyco had acquired dispersed facilities and a larger than required workforce. The company set about evaluating its requirements for both people and physical assets. It commenced this process using a benchmarking exercise that looked at the staffing requirements for power stations – the core of its business. This suggested that, in comparison to power companies in a number of countries, it had a staffing level that could be reduced by about 50 per cent or more in its power stations. In addition, a number of relatively smaller and older power stations were identified for closure. This early planning work suggested that the organisation would need to downsize by approximately 30 per cent in terms of total numbers employed in Energyco. In fact, further planning exercises resulted in downsizing which significantly exceeded this reduction, as we shall see below.

The methods used to downsize the organisation involved an ostensibly voluntary approach. As a public corporation, it had become highly unionised. As the organisation in its privatised form was now embarking on a major downsizing programme, it made sense to follow a voluntary strategy given the continued existence of strong trade union representation. In addition, the age profile, with a significant proportion of employees over 50, meant that many older workers were happy to take the severance terms being offered. The organisation was also not particularly sensitive about which employees volunteered given the highly qualified and experienced profile of the workforce, providing it with an abundance of skills in relation to the target size for the new organisation. However, the organisation did not have an effective performance management system, which made it difficult to identify effective performers. This meant that it would have been more difficult for the organisation to target those to be made redundant if it had not been fortunate in terms of its age profile and the sheer surplus of skills that it possessed amongst its workforce. The combination of these factors therefore meant that it was possible to allow most volunteers to leave even though some were identified as necessary to retain, at least for a given period.

Once initial downsizing had occurred in the operational areas the focus shifted to the support areas. It was decided to reduce the aggregate proportion of those engaged in 'overhead' activities to 20 per cent, from 30 per cent of the total workforce. The organisation again used a benchmarking approach to identify where savings could be made and an evaluation of activities undertaken. For example in relation to human resources, those who were the 'customers' of this function were asked what type of support they required with the result that this provision was restructured with the loss of over 200 jobs (over 50 per cent). Each part of the organisation was set a target as a result of this type of activity. This was accompanied by communication initiatives that supplied all members of the organisation with information about the company's plans. This direct communication to employees also provided them with details about the severance terms on offer if they volunteered.

The scale of the downsizing and its fairly open nature, combined with the age profile of the workforce, the terms on offer and the recognition that those staying would have to adapt to a new organisational culture, meant that the strategy adopted was successful in attracting volunteers. However, there was a conscious effort on the part of those managing the downsizing process to control the acceptance of the terms on offer in those parts of the organisation where there was no future demand for employees. A number of tactics were used to achieve this acceptance in practice. The terms on offer included an additional payment for early leavers. Additional benefits were also offered to those in areas where they

▶

were not considered to be core to the future of the organisation. Line managers were given discretion to discuss each employee's future status and to offer certain inducements such as additional training or outplacement interventions to encourage those who were reluctant to volunteer in areas where there was no future demand. Consequently, the use of this approach ultimately proved to be highly successful in achieving its aim to facilitate the downsizing of the organisation and without the need to consider a compulsory strategy in such a highly unionised environment. In fact so successful was this strategy that the organisation had downsized itself by approximately 60 per cent after about four years of privatisation, related to the identification of further efficiencies and its response to market changes. Further workforce reductions have since occurred.

The role of line managers was recognised as being of importance in the management of this change process. All of the organisation's line managers, numbering several hundred in total, and including its directors, attended a two-day training programme which focused on communication and counselling skills to prepare them for their role in managing the downsizing process. It was recognised that this change had damaged morale, even though employees remained committed to the purpose of the business. It was thus part of the line managers' role to demonstrate appropriate change management skills to provide a sense of direction and a face-to-face means of communication to address concerns about the future of the business. Communication, involving the line managers as well as other means, was seen to be an important link between the establishment, or re-establishment, of the link between morale and efficiency.

In this way, the use of communication and the skills of the line managers were two of the ways in which the culture was changed around the incidence of the downsizing and restructuring programmes which occurred in the organisation. The use of communication and the skills of the line managers were also intended to be focused on creating a positive impression amongst a number of key stakeholders involved in, or around, the advent of downsizing. The organisation was consciously attempting to retain the goodwill of those who left the organisation – the creation of 'happy leavers'. It also wished to avoid negative publicity or any industrial action which might have adverse effects on its share price or its industrial relations. It was also concerned about the perceptions of those who stayed in the downsized organisation – the survivors of these changes.

The treatment of those who left the organisation, the use of direct communication to employees and the emphasis placed on the role of line managers were not the only initiatives aimed at those who remained in the organisation, with a view to involving these employees in the fulfilment of its mission. Energyco introduced a performance management system, which was linked to a career development plan for each employee. This was a powerful means to indicate the concurrent attempt to bring about a change in the culture of the organisation. The previous public sector ethos of a job for life was intended to be replaced by an attempt to make tangible the concept of 'employability', linked to a performance culture associated with performance related pay. To quote the Personnel Director of Energyco at that time:

> the intention is to create a situation where we will treat employees well, pay them well, develop them but recognise that we cannot guarantee them a job for life. If it becomes necessary to release any employees, they will leave as high quality and well developed individuals.

Case study questions

1 How would you categorise the nature of the approach to achieving downsizing in Energyco?

2 What are the threats and opportunities of a downsizing programme for other forms of HR-related change? Use Energyco as an example.

3 How might you explain the assertion that although 'it was recognised that this change had damaged morale, employees remained committed to the purpose of the business'?

4 What concerns may employees have experienced as a result of the change initiatives at Energyco?

5 How would you seek to manage these concerns?

REFERENCES

Adams, J.S. (1965) 'Inequity in social exchange', in Berkowitz, L. (ed.), *Advances in Experimental Social Psychology*, Academic Press: New York, 2, pp. 267–99.

Armstrong-Stassen, M. (1994) 'Coping with transition: a study of layoff survivors', *Journal of Organizational Behaviour*, 15, 597–621.

Belasen, A.T., Benke, M., DiPadova, L.N. and Fortunato, M.V. (1996) 'Downsizing and the hyper-effective manager: the shifting importance of managerial roles during organizational transformation', *Human Resource Management*, 35(1), 87–117.

Bies, R.J. and Moag, J. (1986)'Interactional justice: communication criteria of fairness', in Lewicki, R., Sheppard, B. and Bazerman, M. (eds), *Research on Negotiation in Organizations*, Greenwich, Conn.: JAI Press, 1, pp. 43–55.

Brockner, J., (1988) 'The effects of work layoffs on survivors: research, theory and practice', in Staw, B.M. and Cummings, L.L. (eds), *Research in Organizational Behavior*, Greenwich, Conn.: JAI Press, 10, pp. 213–55.

Brockner, J., (1992) 'Managing the effects of layoffs on survivors', *California Management Review*, Winter, 9–28.

Brockner, J. and Greenberg, J. (1990) 'The impact of layoffs on survivors: an organizational justice perspective', in Carroll, J.S. (ed.), *Applied Social Psychology and Organizational Settings*, Hillsdale, N.J.: Erlbaum, pp. 45–75.

Brockner, J. and Wiesenfeld, B. (1993) 'Living on the edge (of social and organizational psychology): the effects of job layoffs on those who remain, in Murnighan, J.K. (ed.), *Social Psychology in Organizations*, Englewood Cliffs, N.J.: Prentice Hall, pp. 119–40.

Brockner, J., Davy, J. and Carter, C. (1985) 'Layoffs, self-esteem, and survivor guilt: Motivational, affective, and attitudinal consequences', *Organizational Behavior and Human Decision Processes*, 36, 229–44.

Brockner, J., DeWitt, R.L., Grover, S. and Reed, T. (1990) 'When it is especially important to explain why: factors affecting the relationship between managers' explanations of a layoff and survivors' reactions to the layoff', *Journal of Experimental Social Psychology,* 26, 389–407.

Brockner, J., Tyler, T.R. and Cooper-Schneider, R. (1992) 'The influence of prior commitment to an institution on reactions to perceived unfairness: the higher they are, the harder they fall', *Administrative Science Quarterly,* 37, 241–61.

Brown, M. (1997) 'Dial C for change', *Management Today,* July, 65–71.

Cameron, K.S. (1994a) 'Investigating organizational downsizing – fundamental issues', *Human Resource Management,* 33(2), 183–8.

Cameron, K.S. (1994b) 'Strategies for successful organizational downsizing', *Human Resource Management,* 33(2), 189–211.

Cameron, K.S., Freeman, S.J. and Mishra, A.K. (1991) 'Best practices in white-collar downsizing: managing contradictions', *Academy of Management Executive,* 5(3), 57–73.

Cameron, K.S., Freeman, S.J. and Mishra, A.K. (1993) 'Organizational downsizing', in Huber, G.P. and Glick, W.H. (eds), *Organizational Change and Redesign,* New York: Oxford University Press.

Daly, J.P. and Geyer, P.D. (1994) 'The role of fairness in implementing large-scale change: employee evaluations of process and outcome in seven facility relocations', *Journal of Organizational Behaviour,* 15, 623–38.

Davy, J.A., Kinicki, A.J. and Scheck, C.L. (1991) 'Developing and testing a model of survivor responses to layoffs', *Journal of Vocational Behaviour,* 38, 302–17.

Doherty, N., Bank, J. and Vinnicombe, S. (1996) 'Managing survivors: the experience of survivors in British Telecom and the British financial services sector', *Journal of Managerial Psychology,* 11(7), 51–60.

Ebadan, G. and Winstanley, D. (1997) 'Downsizing, delayering and careers – the survivor's perspective', *Human Resource Management Journal,* 7(1), 79–91.

Freeman, S.J. and Cameron, K.S. (1993) 'Organizational downsizing: a convergence and reorientation framework', *Organization Science,* 4(1), 10–29.

Greenhalgh, L. (1983) 'Managing the job insecurity crisis', *Human Resource Management,* 22(4), 431–44.

Greenhalgh, L. and Rosenblatt, Z. (1984) 'Job insecurity: toward conceptual clarity', *Academy of Management Review,* 9(3), 438–48.

Greenhalgh, L., Lawrence, A.T. and Sutton, R.I. (1988) 'Determinants of work force reduction strategies in declining organizations', *Academy of Management Review,* 13(2), 241–54.

Guest, D.E. (1987) 'Human resource management and industrial relations', *Journal of Management Studies,* 24(5), 503–21.

Guest, D.E. and Peccei, R. (1992) 'Employee involvement: redundancy as a critical case', *Human Resource Management Journal,* 2(3), 34–59.

Hallier, J. and Lyon, P. (1996) 'Job insecurity and employee commitment: managers' reactions to the threat and outcomes of redundancy selection', *British Journal of Management,* 7, 107–23.

Hendry, C. and Jenkins, R. (1997) 'Psychological contracts and new deals', *Human Resource Management Journal,* 7(1), 38–44.

Herriot, P. and Pemberton, C. (1996) 'Contracting careers', *Human Relations,* 49(6), 757–90.

Höpfl, H., Smith, S. and Spencer, S. (1992) 'Values and valuations: the conflicts between culture change and job cuts', *Personnel Review,* 21(1), 24–38.

IRS (1993) 'Natural selection: BT's programme of voluntary redundancy', *IRS Employment Trends 533,* April, 11–15.

IRS (1994a) 'BT unions lobby shareholders on compulsory job losses', *IRS Employment Trends 566,* August, 4.

IRS (1994b) 'Stress levels surveyed in wake of BT's redundancy programme', *IRS Employment Trends 569*, October, 3.

Kozlowski, S.W., Chao, G.T., Smith, E.M. and Hedlund, J. (1993) 'Organizational downsizing: strategies, interventions, and research implications', in Cooper, C.L. and Robertson, I.T. (eds), *International Review of Industrial and Organizational Psychology*, New York: John Wiley and Sons, 263–332.

Latack, J.C. (1986) 'Coping with job stress: measures and future directions for scale development', *Journal of Applied Psychology*, 71, 377–85.

Lazarus, R.S. and Folkman, S. (1984) *Stress, Appraisal, and Coping*, New York: Springer.

Lewis, P. (1993) *The Successful Management of Redundancy*, Oxford: Blackwell.

McCune, J.T., Beatty, R.W. and Montagno, R.V. (1988) 'Downsizing: practices in manufacturing firms', *Human Resource Management*, 27(2), 145–61.

Mishra, A.K. and Mishra, K.E. (1994) 'The role of mutual trust in effective downsizing strategies', *Human Resource Management*, 33(2), 261–79.

Naumann, S.E., Bies, R.J. and Martin, C.L. (1995) 'The roles of organizational support and justice during a layoff', *Academy of Management Best Papers Proceedings*, 55, 89–93.

Newell, H. and Dopson, S. (1996) 'Muddle in the middle: organizational restructuring and middle management careers', *Personnel Review*, 25(4), 4–20.

Shaw, J.B. and Barrett–Power, E. (1997) 'A conceptual framework for assessing organization, work groups and individual effectiveness during and after downsizing', *Human Relations*, 50(2), 109–27.

Thornhill, A. and Gibbons, A. (1995) 'The positive management of redundancy survivors: issues and lessons', *Employee Counselling Today*, 7(3), 5–12.

Thornhill, A, Saunders, M.N.K. and Stead, J. (1997a) 'Downsizing delayering – but where's the commitment?', *Personnel Review*, 26(1/2), 81–98.

Thornhill, A, Saunders, M.N.K. (1998) 'The meanings, consequences and implications of the management of downsizing and redundancy: a review', *Personnel Review*, 27(4), 271–95.

Thornhill, A., Stead, J. and Gibbons, A. (1997b) *Managing Downsizing and Redundancy*, London: Financial Times Pitman Publishing.

Tomasko, R.M. (1992) 'Restructuring: getting it right', *Management Review*, 81(4), 10–15.

Tombaugh, J. R. and White, L.P. (1990) 'Downsizing: an empirical assessment of survivors' perceptions in a post layoff environment', *Organisation Development Journal*, 8(2), Summer, 32–43.

Turnbull, P. and Wass, V. (1997) 'Job insecurity and labour market lemons: the (mis) management of redundancy in steel making, coal mining and port transport', *Journal of Management Studies*, 34(1), 27–51.

Wass, V. (1996) 'Who controls selection under "voluntary" redundancy? The case of the redundant mineworkers payments scheme', *British Journal of Industrial Relations*, 34(2), 249–65.

ANSWERS TO SELF-CHECK QUESTIONS

9.1 *Why might the requirement to adopt a proactive downsizing strategy in order to minimise the negative consequences associated with this type of change be difficult to achieve in practice?*

The literature on which this sub-section is based certainly points to the need for a proactive approach to downsizing as part of the means to minimise and manage negative survivors' reactions that may adversely affect organisational objectives. However, the factors referred to in the literature (e.g. a strategic planning and environmental scanning capacity) that underpin a proactive approach may not be present in many organisations (Kozlowski *et al.*, 1993). In addition, the existence of an integrated, human resource management approach is more likely to exist in larger organisations or those that are part of a larger group of companies. Such managerial capability and competence may not be present in other organisations. These other types of organisations may have a tendency to muddle along and be more likely to adopt reactive approaches where environmental factors create pressures that cannot be ignored. This reactive approach may also be more symptomatic of organisations in decline.

9.2 *How would you categorise BT's organisational strategy to achieve downsizing?*

The evidence presented in the case study and the research which this draws on points to the presence of all three of the Cameron *et al.* (1991, 1993) strategies being used. The organisation certainly engaged in workforce reductions, decreasing its workforce by over 100 000. There is also evidence of the use of an organisation redesign strategy, through restructuring and de-layering for example. The organisation also sought to introduce other longer-term changes to the way work was conducted through the use of new technology, culture change programmes, etc. There is also evidence that this downsizing was proactively planned, especially given the fact that the organisation staged its downsizing over several years. This allowed for a process of incremental learning, and policy and practice modification. Stakeholders such as the trade unions were also involved in strategy formulation. However, there is evidence to show that even with this level of proaction on the part of the organisation, problems may still arise. For example, Release '92 led to a degree of reactive behaviour given the unexpectedly large number of volunteers. 'According to the unions, the management of Release '92 was rather chaotic, particularly as BT was constantly "reshuffling the pack" for who was, or was not, surplus to requirements and where vacancies would arise' (IRS, 1993: 14).

9.3 *Which other aspects related to the methods used to implement downsizing might affect managerial control and employee influence over the process?*

Targeting those to be made redundant, or who will be offered some inducement to accept voluntary severance, is a further way of increasing managerial control over the implementation of downsizing. Targeting relates to the ability of an organisation's management to focus workforce reductions in areas (i.e. a particular function or layer) requiring action to overcome the effects of technological obsolescence, reduced product demand, or for some other reason. The alternative to a targeted approach to workforce reductions is to engage in either unfocused or across-the-board reductions, perhaps related to a general cost reduction strategy. Such an alternative approach has been associated with cost reduction strategies, short-termism and a low level of managerial control. This approach is likely to lead to the types of post-downsizing organisational problems discussed in the main body of the chapter.

The use of selection criteria offers a further means to exercise managerial control in relation to the downsizing process. Selection criteria may be used in relation to an ostensibly voluntary approach. Whereas targeting (see above) may be used to identify work areas or groups for downsizing, the use of selection criteria, in relation to targeted areas, provides a check in relation to particular individuals whom the organisation wishes to retain. Selection criteria may also be used as the only filter where volunteers are sought from across the organisation. The alternative to any form of selection in relation to a voluntary approach to redundancy is made clear by Lewis (1993: 28): 'the volunteer population may become an irresistible force and the pattern of volunteers may largely determine the distribution of actual redundancies'. The outcome of this lack of managerial control could be a mismatch between actual and required human resource profiles of the downsized organisation.

9.4 *How would you react to the redundancy of colleagues in the organisation for which you work, or in an organisation for which you have worked? (Perhaps you have actually experienced this event! If you have, how did you react and why?)*

Your response to this question will clearly be personal to a certain extent. However, if you are persuaded by the theory being advanced in this chapter you will have made connections to the approach of the organisation in terms of its downsizing strategy. You will have also reflected on the methods used to implement downsizing, or, more precisely given the question, the method of redundancy. Where the organisation simply used a workforce reduction strategy, without much thought about those who survived, or who would survive, this event, you may be expected to experience fairly negative reactions. Where the organisation did not consider those made redundant you may be expected to experience fairly strong or strong sympathetic reactions to those so affected. This may not be the case where you feel that those selected for redundancy were appropriately selected. This may be even more the case where they are fairly treated. However, there may be a number of reasons related to your psychological characteristics, the prevailing employment circumstances and the need for your redundant colleagues to find work, as well as the closeness of your working relationships, beliefs and values etc., why you would have, or did have, sympathetic reactions towards your colleagues. You can see what a potentially complex picture can emerge from this type of event. We hope that you do not have to experience this! Where you have to manage this situation we hope that the ideas in this chapter provide at least some help!

9.5 *Using the theoretical framework outlined in this section, how would you evaluate the approach adopted in BT to manage downsizing survivors?*

The voluntary nature of BT's downsizing programme undoubtedly helped to alleviate many potential issues which theories related to equity and organisational justice suggest may occur. In general terms, however, the information in the case study indicates that even using this voluntary strategy could not wholly alleviate the incidence of feelings of inequity. In particular, the exercise of selection criteria in relation to Release '92 created feelings of negative inequity with some survivors feeling angry that they were not being released. Negative inequity would also be related to the reported perception that good performance prevented some from being selected to leave. Paradoxically perhaps the organisation may have learnt that the exercise of more control through targeting leavers should help to reduce the possibility of this incidence of inequity since expectations would not be raised about the possibility of leaving.

The perception that good performers might be prevented from leaving also relates to distributive justice, since the outcome of the decisions made about who would be allowed to leave was judged unfair. In a similar way this would also link to perceptions of procedural injustice or unfairness. However, the scope for redeployment, the provision of various forms of outplacement support and generous redundancy terms would all help to promote feelings of procedural justice or fair treatment. Whether the survivors felt that they were being treated fairly themselves in relation to Release '92 is perhaps open to question. IRS (1993: 14) reported the view of one of the unions that 'great care was taken to smooth the passage to redundancy for those leaving, but scant attention was paid to those left behind with higher workloads or reallocated duties'. This may be related to job redesign theory. Positively in this respect BT redesigned work as well as downsizing the organisation.

In terms of interactional justice, BT recognised the important role which line managers would play and trained them to be able to explain why change was occurring and to manage the change process. Supportive line managers are also one of the key means of facilitating the management of workplace-related stress. However, while the use of the voluntary strategy helped to reduce feelings of job insecurity surrounding those to be made redundant, the changes associated with downsizing appear to have promoted insecurity as job attributes associated with the past were removed. In this way, the opportunity for career progression, for example, was seen to be adversely affected, which in turn affected the nature of some survivors' psychological contracts and commitment (*see* Newell and Dopson, 1996).

Evaluating and promoting change

Learning objectives

Having completed this chapter, you will be able to:

- Understand the need to evaluate and promote change.

- Assess the appropriateness of evaluation research and action research approaches for different change initiatives.

- Outline a range of strategies and techniques which may be used to gather data about changes in different situations.

- Identify the complexity of issues associated with feeding back findings about changes.

INTRODUCTION

Effective evaluation and promotion of change requires the systematic collection of data that are subsequently analysed and the findings presented in some form. These data may have been collected through monitoring what is happening within an organisation over time or specifically to evaluate a particular change intervention. However, without the ensuing evaluation the effectiveness of one or a series of change interventions is likely to be less certain. The knowledge gathered through this process of research, we would argue, helps organisations to have a clearer understanding of what is happening and, of equal importance, the impact of particular interventions. In addition, the actual process of research can help promote the change. Yet, despite this, evaluation is rarely carried out (Toracco, 1997).

Toracco (1997) argues that this lack of evaluation of change is due to difficulties associated with the long time frames required for organisational change. In particular it is often difficult to be certain of the precise impact of particular interventions. In addition, where external consultants have been involved in the change process they have long since separated from an organisation by the time indications of success or failure emerge. These observations are supported by others (for example Randell, 1994; Lewis and Thornhill, 1994), who also emphasise the difficulty of designing studies and obtaining data of sufficient quality to disentangle the effect upon an HR intervention from other stimuli. They also stress the negative impact of organisational politics, especially where poor evaluation findings suggest that the change was a function of an incorrect decision higher in the organisation's hierarchy (Lewis and Thornhill, 1994). Despite these difficulties, Toracco (1997) argues that it is important to undertake research to evaluate changes against key organisational goals, even where improvements cannot be wholly attributed to a particular change intervention.

The need for data and its subsequent use in evaluation is emphasised by models of the change process. These usually incorporate 'information gathering' and analysis phases (Hendry, 1996) which emphasise the importance of knowing and understanding the current situation and strategic direction of an organisation prior to initiating change. The phases are likely to include data on the external environment as well as internal objectives, organisational capabilities and the need to communicate information within the organisation (Burnes, 1996). For example, the Beer *et al.* (1990) emergent ('bottom-up') approach to task alignment outlined in Fig. 3.6 initiates the change process through a joint diagnosis of business problems involving data gathering, sharing, surfacing norms and answering questions such as 'where are we now?'.

Traditional 'scientific' approaches to research often seek to minimise the amount of involvement between those collecting and analysing the data (the researchers) and those from whom data are collected on the grounds of maintaining objectivity (Robson, 1993). Within such processes researchers are seen as separate from, rather than working alongside, an organisation. Findings are disseminated only to the sponsor of the research rather than to all those affected. This conflicts with much that we have discussed in this book in terms of managing the change process and, in particular, our focus upon managing change through people. Such conflict is, perhaps, not too surprising where the purpose attributed to the research is to understand and explain. We would argue that research can also provide useful insights about managerial problems and business issues associated with specific organisational changes. However, in using research to evaluate and promote change we believe it is often necessary for the researcher to be within or to become part of the organisation. Analysis of data collected should not take place in a vacuum and judgements need to be made within the context of the organisation.

In this chapter we therefore tend towards the perspective that the use of research to evaluate and promote change needs to involve those affected within the organisation as fully as possible. This is not to say that research can only be undertaken by people within the organisation. Rather it implies that where people external to the organisation are used, their role should be to help those within to perceive, understand and act to improve the situation; an approach akin to Schein's (1988) 'process consultation'. As part of this we recognise that, depending upon purpose, one or a number of research strategies might be more appropriate. Research may take place over a range of time scales. These can range from one-off case studies perhaps answering the question 'Where are we now?', through cross-sectional studies which benchmark HR practices, to longitudinal evaluations perhaps using a series of employee attitude surveys. Similarly, we recognise that to address particular objectives some research techniques are likely to collect more appropriate data than others are. For example, a questionnaire survey of employees is less likely to discover their true feelings about a recent downsizing than face-to-face interviews in which the interviewer takes time to gain the employees' confidence.

The main points in this chapter are illustrated by two case studies both taken from the service sector. The first, Barclays Edotech, is an electronic print and mail organisation. This case study illustrates how a range of data collection techniques have been used to evaluate the impact of changes, and help generate suggestions for further interventions by the organisation. It also describes ways in which findings were fed back to all employees. The second case study outlines research undertaken within Telesales Incorporated, a large telesales company. This focuses upon the approach used by the organisation to evaluate the suitability of new approaches to employee training relative to an existing method.

CASE STUDY 10.1

Evaluating change and the development of Barclays Edotech

Barclays Edotech is part of Barclays Technology Services, the division that is responsible for service delivery, production and marketing of information technology services principally to the Barclays Group. As part of the Service Provision Cluster (*see* Fig. 10.1) Edotech provides high-volume electronic laser printing, mailing, consulting, data presentation and data archive/retrieval services for both the Barclays Group and external customers. This includes the production

▶

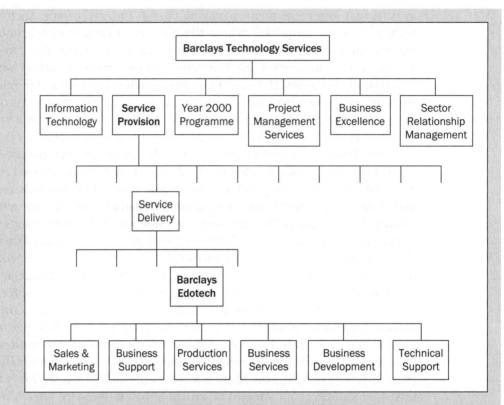

Fig. 10.1 Barclays Technology Services Organisation Chart

and mailing of all Barclays UK bank statements and reports as well as printing Barclaycard statements; more than 10 million items are mailed each month. Edotech's Computer Centre is one of the largest single-site print and mail operations in Europe. In 1998, Edotech employed approximately 330 people at their Computer Centre as well as a small number of people at a separate information technology development unit.

Although the computer centre has been in existence since the late 1970s Edotech has only been in existence since October 1993. Prior to this date the site had concentrated upon the processing (formatting and printing) of data for the Barclays Group. Research undertaken within the division suggested that this approach to service delivery was unlikely to be sustainable in the longer term and that change was needed. The creation of Edotech represented the start of changes towards a market-driven service, which focused on clients' needs. Rather than waiting for their customers to ask for print and processing innovations, Edotech was to become proactive in developing and selling new ideas to its clients within the Barclays Group as well as offering outsourcing of print and mail services to external clients. Print production facilities, although separate from Edotech at this time, were amalgamated on one site and there was considerable investment in new technology. This included:

- sophisticated document composition software to enable forms and data (such as the Medici Bank Statement) to be printed at the same time;
- facilities for data output onto CD-ROM as well as archive and retrieval services;
- leading edge print and mail equipment to support both bulk mailing to customers and the more bespoke services required by Barclays Insurance and Unit Trust pensions etc.

A simpler grading structure for print production staff was introduced as part of these changes. This reflected the shift to a production orientation and the refocusing of the required skills (*see* Fig. 10.2). The rotational shift work pattern was also revised to take account of increasing work volumes and short-term contracts were used increasingly to match staff numbers to work volumes. Consequently, the skills required of employees on the same grade now varied considerably. Skill variation was greatest within the new grade 'Operator B' some of whom were nearly working at Senior Operator (Operator 4) level. Local management believed the new grading structure required revision to take account of these skill variations. However, they felt there was a need to evaluate the true level of staff feelings and, in particular, job satisfaction rather than just relying on their own hunches.

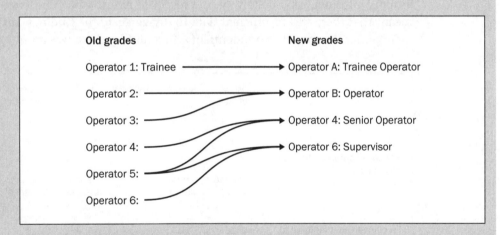

Fig. 10.2 Grading structure changes for production staff

Since 1996, employees at the Computer Centre had taken part in the annual staff attitude survey for the division. This used a generalised questionnaire and was administered through the internal mail across those areas within Barclays Technology Services that were responsible for the delivery, production and marketing of IT services. The aims of this survey were outlined clearly in the letter that accompanied the questionnaire with a strong focus upon identifying strengths and areas that require improvement:

- To compare your views ... today with what you had to tell us at this time last year. ...
- To feed back your comments [on the recent changes] to us so that we can act on them to make each of the areas even more effective in the way we meet the needs of both staff and customers.

The content of the questionnaire had remained substantially the same between years to enable comparisons. Approximately 80 questions were used to ascertain employees' views on areas of leadership, policy and strategy, people management, resources and processes, customer satisfaction, people satisfaction, the impact of the organisation upon society and business results. Virtually all questions employed five- or six-point Likert-type scales to record answers (examples are shown in Fig. 10.3). In addition, there were spaces for comments and a few open questions to provide an opportunity for respondents to 'highlight some of the key issues, and to add detail on how these might be resolved'. Locational information such as job role, broad salaries band and site were collected to allow comparisons.

Summary results of the annual staff attitude survey had been fed back to all staff through a four-page *Headline Results* document. Unpublished site-specific tables had enabled managers to compare the response of site staff with others in the group. Unfortunately a relatively low response rate (24 per cent) from the site meant that there was insufficient data to disaggregate the findings further while maintaining respondent confidentiality. In addition, there was an informal view

	MUCH BETTER	BETTER	THE SAME	WORSE	MUCH WORSE	I AM TOO NEW TO KNOW
How would you rate working in Barclays compared to one year ago? Is it ...	1	2	3	4	5	6
	STRONGLY AGREE	TEND TO AGREE	?	TEND TO DISAGREE	STRONGLY DISAGREE	
I feel involved in helping to achieve objectives	1	2	3	4	5	

Comments ...

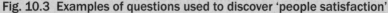

Fig. 10.3 Examples of questions used to discover 'people satisfaction'

among managers that site-specific issues such as the re-grading of production staff might have impacted upon response rates, perhaps making the results less reliable.

It was decided, therefore, to conduct a 'one-off' local staff survey. Again, the aims of the survey were outlined clearly in the accompanying letter from the management team: 'we want to focus on issues that are relevant to us all locally and to improve how we work'. Assurances of anonymity were provided and line managers were asked to ensure that employees were given time away from their work area to complete the survey. Designed by internal consultants in conjunction with site managers the survey consisted of approximately 30 Likert-type questions along with locational information such as gender, salary band and work group.

The main issues from the local survey were fed back to staff through question and answer sessions at existing three-monthly team briefings. Summaries of findings were also placed on notice boards. A key part of the feedback was informing staff about the resulting 'actions'. These included broadening the Operator B salary grade to enable staff to be rewarded according to their skills and responsibilities.

Findings from the annual staff attitude survey combined with the low response rate for the site provided further impetus to other research initiatives. As before the focus was upon identifying strengths and areas for improvement. One major initiative used the Business Excellence Model (BEM) self-assessment process (British Quality Foundation and European Foundation for Quality Management, 1996). The 1996 assessments were based upon semi-structured interviews with a random sample of 60 site staff stratified by work function and grade. Internal consultants undertook interviews with pairs of staff of similar status. These lasted approximately one hour and covered the same areas as the annual staff attitude survey.

After the interviews, the consultants analysed the data. Their findings supported those from the 1996 annual staff attitude survey and suggested that the site:

- was strong in the areas of processes and business results;
- needed to improve in areas of people management, leadership and policy and strategy.

Responses also helped illuminate issues raised in the earlier questionnaire surveys. As a result, a site-based improvement team was established to develop an action plan to address these issues. This involved staff from different grades and work functions at the site. Changes introduced as part of their action plan included:

- walkabouts by management team members;
- a poster campaign to highlight the values of Barclays Technology Services as a whole;
- the introduction of regular question and answer sessions at which staff raise local issues with a senior site manager.

Research by internal consultants had also highlighted the need to integrate print and production with the business development and support services provided by Edotech. Consequently, printing production services were amalgamated with the existing Edotech and the organisational structure outlined in Fig. 10.1 came into being.

Site personnel who had been trained by the internal consultants undertook the 1997 BEM assessment. The findings indicated improvements of at least 25 per cent in the areas of people management, leadership and policy strategy and suggested that the interventions introduced were having a positive impact. An improved response rate and responses to the 1997 annual staff attitude survey supported the finding from the BEM survey that there had been improvements in these areas.

Approaches to evaluating change

As we outlined in the introduction to this chapter, the process of evaluating organisational change is often termed research. Like all research it should be undertaken in a systematic way and used to find things out. The term 'systematic' suggests this evaluation will be based upon logical relationships and not just beliefs or hunches. The term 'finding out' emphasises the use of data as a background for decision making rather than relying upon assumptions and guesswork for diagnosing problems. However, within this broad definition of research the purpose and context need to be considered in more depth and alternative approaches explored.

The purpose and context of evaluation

Research textbooks, including our own (Saunders *et al.*, 1997), often place research projects on a continuum according to their purpose and context (*see* Fig. 10.4). At one end of this continuum is evaluation undertaken to advance knowledge and theoretical understanding of processes and their outcomes. This is often termed basic or academic research. At the other end is evaluation that is of direct and immediate relevance to organisations, addresses issues which they consider are important and presents findings in ways which can be understood easily and acted upon. This is usually termed applied research. The evaluation and promotion of change is, not surprisingly, placed towards the applied end of this continuum. Such research is oriented clearly towards examining practical problems associated with change interventions or making decisions about particular courses of action for change within organisations. It therefore helps organisations to establish what is happening and assess effectiveness of particular interventions. This orientation is clearly visible in the twin purposes of research at Barclays Edotech, that is to identify aspects within the organisation that require improvement (i.e. where there may be problems) and areas of existing strength. Evaluation can take place at any time during change. Evaluation during the early stages of a change programme to

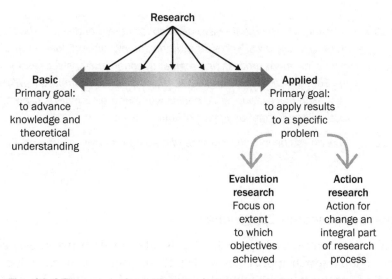

Fig. 10.4 The research continuum and approaches to evaluating and promoting change

improve or fine-tune the process is often referred to as formative evaluation. That which occurs towards the later stages, perhaps to assess impact, determine the extent to which goals have been met or establish whether to continue with the process is termed summative evaluation.

Applied research can take place at a number of levels. Widely cited work by Hamblin (1974) identifies five levels at which this might occur (*see* Fig. 10.5). Although Hamblin relates these specifically to training evaluation, general principles about the levels at which applied research may take place and impact of the research can be deduced. In particular Hamblin's work highlights that research can be undertaken to evaluate operational changes (levels 1 and perhaps 2), to enable medium-term or tactical changes to be evaluated (level 3 and occasionally levels 2 and 4) or it can focus upon more strategic change (levels 4 and 5). In Hamblin's discussion of training these include trainee learning (operational), job performance (tactical) and the wider contribution made by the organisation (strategic).

Level	Evaluation	Impact
Low	1 Training as in the post-course questionnaire.	*Operational*
	2 Learning in terms of how the trainee behaves.	
	3 Changes in job performance.	*Tactical*
	4 Changes in organisational performance.	
High	5 Changes in the wider contribution the organisation now makes.	*Strategic*

Fig. 10.5 Hamblin's five levels of training evaluation

Source: Developed from Hamblin, 1974.

Self-check questions

10.1 *Four ways in which data have been collected are outlined in the Edotech case study, namely: divisional staff attitude survey, 'one-off' local staff survey, BEM self-assessment process and regular question-and-answer sessions. Re-read the Edotech case study and establish at which of Hamblin's (1974) levels each has taken place. You should decide whether their impact is likely to be strategic, tactical or operational as part of your answer.*

10.2 *How do you believe the purpose of research is likely to differ between these levels?*

Evaluation and action research approaches

Within applied research, a distinction is often made between evaluation research and action research approaches (*see* Fig. 10.4). Evaluation research is concerned with finding out the extent to which the objectives of any given action or activity, such as the introduction of a new training intervention, have been achieved (Zikmund, 1997), in other words it is concerned with testing the effectiveness of the action or activity. As part of this evaluation, it is necessary to gather data about what is happening or has happened (monitor) and analyse them. This can be undertaken using a range of strategies including experiment, survey and longitudinal studies as well as through a variety of techniques such as interview, questionnaire and observation (these are discussed later in the chapter). Findings based upon the analysis of these data are subsequently disseminated back to the sponsor.

The term 'action research' was first used by Lewin in 1946. Action research makes use of the same strategies and data collection techniques as evaluation research. Although it has been interpreted subsequently by management researchers in a variety of ways, there are three common themes within the literature. The first focuses upon and emphasises the purpose of the research, for example the management of a change (Cunningham, 1995) such as organisational downsizing. The second relates to the involvement of practitioners in the research and in particular a close collaboration between practitioners and researchers, be they academics, other practitioners or internal or external consultants. Eden and Huxham (1996: 75) argue that the findings of action research result from 'involvement with members of an organization over a matter which is of genuine concern to them'. Therefore the researcher is part of the organisation within which the research and change process are taking place (Zuber-Skerritt, 1996).

The final theme suggests that action research should have implications beyond the immediate project; in other words it must be clear that the results could inform other contexts. For academics undertaking action research Eden and Huxham (1996) link this to an explicit concern for the development of theory. However, they emphasise that for both internal and external consultants this is more likely to focus upon the subsequent transfer of knowledge gained from one specific context to another. Such use of knowledge to inform other contexts we believe also applies to others undertaking action research such as practitioners.

Thus action research differs from other forms of applied research such as evaluation research due to an explicit focus upon action, in particular promoting change within the organisation (Marsick and Watkins, 1997). In addition the person undertaking the research is involved in this action for change and subsequently application of the knowledge gained elsewhere. It is to the implications of these differences for evaluating and promoting change that we now turn.

From evaluating to promoting change

Evaluation research

Evaluation research commences with a clear understanding by the person undertaking the evaluation of the action or activity that is to be evaluated (*see* Fig. 10.6). Recently Adrian and Mark were employed as external consultants by an organisation's senior management team to discover employees' opinions of the way a recent management buyout had been managed (Thornhill and Saunders, 1998). This 'change initiative' had involved the organisation in downsizing and the creation of a new private sector organisation. The precise objectives of the evaluation were defined clearly with the organisation's senior managers in relation to the change. They included ascertaining employees' opinions about their line managers' styles and skills, the senior management's commitment to the changes, communication processes, the future direction of the organisation and employees' commitment to the organisation. While there was no agreement that the senior management team would act upon the findings of the evaluation, the fact that they were interested in evaluating what had happened suggested that they would be willing to take action to remedy any problems that arose.

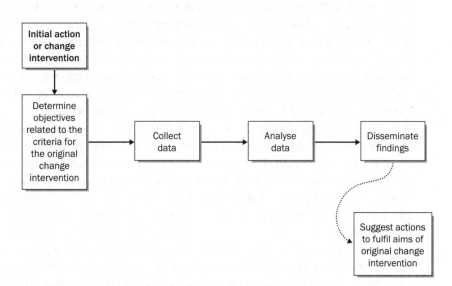

Fig. 10.6 Evaluation research

Adrian and Mark collected data using a variety of techniques including a questionnaire administered to all employees and interviews with a sample of employees. This process raised employees' awareness of both the issues outlined in the previous paragraph and the concern of senior managers. Data collection also introduced the expectation that something would be done to address issues raised by employees. In other words, it promoted the expectation that there would be further change. The data were analysed and the findings disseminated to the sponsors, in this case the organisation's senior management team in the form of a report. Senior management took the findings seriously. They informed employees of the key findings and developed an action plan based upon these. After this, further change interventions were made by senior management to address issues raised by the evaluation. Adrian and Mark were not involved in this aspect.

Thus, although evaluation research does not contain an explicit requirement for action, the work undertaken by Adrian and Mark illustrates the potential for the findings to promote change. Initially the research process highlighted the importance of what was being evaluated to employees, as their senior managers were willing to invest both time and financial resources. In being part of the data collection, in this case through completing questionnaires and for some also being interviewed, employees were reminded of the principles, purposes and practices of the change that was being evaluated. Randell's (1994) research suggests that such investments are likely to be interpreted by employees as implying the change was effective.

Action research

By contrast, the promotion of change is explicit within the action research process. This is emphasised by Winter (1996: 23) who also highlights the link between practitioners, researchers and change arguing that those who engage in an action research approach are not consultants in the traditional sense of the term: '[We] are not consultants, advising others how to change, nor unchanging catalysts of others' development. We are part of the situation undergoing change.' As such their goal is to work out what change is needed, implement the change, monitor and evaluate the outcomes and subsequently revise the change intervention as necessary.

The action research process commences with an initial idea for a change intervention (Fig. 10.7, cycle 1). This is likely to be expressed as an objective (Robson, 1993). Reconnaissance (fact finding and analysis) about the change intervention is undertaken in order to generate an overall plan and a decision about the first steps to be taken. The remainder of the first cycle is concerned with carrying out this plan, monitoring and evaluating. Subsequent cycles involve revising the change intervention to ensure it meets the needs of the organisation using information gathered through the monitoring and evaluation process. Planned action steps are amended and implemented to take account of unforeseen changes. Their effects are monitored and evaluated and further amendments made (Fig. 10.7, cycles 2 and 3). In the Barclays Edotech case study the initial idea for change was the move towards a market-driven service focusing on client's needs. After fact finding and analysis, action steps were planned. These resulted in the creation of Edotech

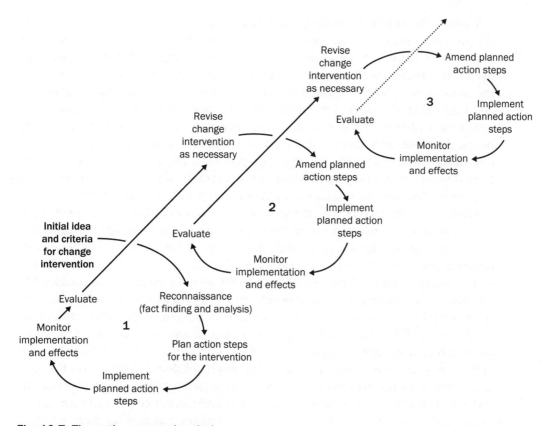

Fig. 10.7 The action research spiral
Source: Developed from Oja and Smulyan, 1989; Robson, 1993.

and print and mail production facilities being amalgamated at one site along with considerable investment in new technology (Fig. 10.7, cycle 1).

Evaluation of the changes through the Group Planning Operations and Technology (GPOT) annual staff attitude survey and the local staff survey indicated the change interventions required revision. Planned action steps were therefore amended in a variety of ways. These included the review of salary grade bandings so that staff could be rewarded according to their skills and responsibilities outlined in the case. Changes were monitored and evaluated using a range of techniques including the annual staff attitude survey and the Business Excellence Model (BEM) self-assessment process (Fig. 10.7, cycle 2). A further cycle of revising change interventions, amending plans, implementing, monitoring and evaluating followed. This resulted in the amalgamation of Edotech and print and mail production facilities (Fig. 10.7, cycle 3).

The additional strengths of action research are therefore:

■ a focus upon change;
■ the recognition that time needs to be devoted to reconnaissance, monitoring and evaluation;
■ the involvement of employees (practitioners) throughout the process.

Schein (1995) emphasises the importance of employee involvement throughout the process, as employees are more likely to implement change they have helped to create. Once employees have identified a need for change and widely shared this need it becomes difficult to ignore and the pressure for change comes from within the organisation. Action research therefore combines both information gathering and facilitation of change. The reconnaissance stage is often seen by employees as recognition of the need for change (Cunningham, 1995). Planning encourages people to meet and discuss the most appropriate action steps and can help encourage group ownership by involving people in the changes. These plans are then implemented. Once monitoring and evaluation have taken place there is a responsibility to use the findings to revise the intervention as necessary.

Action research can have two distinct foci (Schein, 1995). The first of these, while involving those being researched in the research process, aims to fulfil the agenda of those undertaking the research rather than that of the sponsor. This does not, however, preclude the sponsor from also benefiting from the changes brought about by the research process. The second focus starts with the needs of the sponsor and involves those undertaking the research in the sponsor's issues, rather than the sponsor in their issues. These consultant activities are termed 'process consultation' by Schein (1988). The consultant, he argues, assists the client to perceive, understand and act upon the process events that occur within their environment in order to improve the situation as the client sees it. Within this definition the term 'client' refers to the persons or person, often senior managers, who sponsor the research. Using Schein's analogy of a clinician and clinical enquiry the consultant (researcher) is involved by the sponsor in the diagnosis (action research) which is driven by the sponsor's needs. It therefore follows that subsequent interventions are jointly owned by the consultant and the sponsor, who is involved at all stages. The process consultant therefore helps the sponsor to gain the skills of diagnosis and fixing organisational problems so that she or he can continue to improve the organisation on their own.

Schein (1995) argues that the process consultation approach to action research is more appropriate because it better fits the realities of organisational life and is more likely to reveal important organisational dynamics. However, it is still dependent upon obtaining data which meet the purpose of the change evaluation and are of sufficient quality to allow causal conclusions to be drawn. Many authors (for example Randell, 1994) have emphasised the difficulties associated with obtaining such data. For example the data collected may well be suspect, as in the 1996 annual staff attitude survey responses for Edotech, due to low response rates. We now turn to the need to establish the precise purpose of research and strategies for obtaining data.

| Self-check questions | 10.3 | Contrast the key differences between an action research approach and an evaluation research approach. |
| | 10.4 | Why do you think organisations might choose to adopt each of these approaches? |

Clarity of purpose and strategies

The need for clarity of purpose

Probably the most difficult aspect of any evaluation is coming to a clear understanding of what is being evaluated and why; in other words the precise purpose and objectives (Saunders *et al.*, 1997). However, this issue is often bypassed within the evaluation process. For example traditional corporate measures of the success of a redundancy programme are often related to profit, production levels, return on investment and perhaps customer satisfaction (*see* Chapter 9). A numerical fall in such measures may suggest that the redundancies have not been successful and may have had a negative impact on employee commitment. However, they do not actually measure employees' commitment to the organisation or the link between redundancies and commitment. Similarly training courses are often evaluated in terms of the trainees' enjoyment and thoughts on the perceived usefulness of the intervention rather than the impact upon their observed behaviour in the work environment (*see* Chapter 6). Simply enjoying a training intervention does not prove that it is effective, unless producing enjoyment is one of the aims! (Rushmer, 1997).

One way of helping ensure clarity of purpose and objectives is to spend time establishing and agreeing these with the sponsor. This is unlikely to be as easy as it might seem and will be time consuming. As part of the process, we believe it is essential to ensure that both the person undertaking the evaluation and the sponsor have the same understanding. Another, and equally important, aspect of ensuring clarity of purpose relates to the understanding and insight the person undertaking the evaluation brings to the change situation. While her previous experience is likely to be important, her understanding is also likely to be drawn from reading about others' experiences in similar situations, a process more often referred to as reviewing the literature. Indeed, your reading of this book is based upon the assumption that you will be able to apply some of the theories, conceptual frameworks and ideas we have written about to change situations you are managing or will have to manage.

Strategies

Once a clear purpose has been established, a range of strategies may be adopted. We divide these into five categories (Saunders *et al.*, 1997), namely:

- survey
- case study
- experimental
- longitudinal
- cross-sectional.

These strategies should not be thought of as mutually exclusive, for example a case study of an organisation may well involve collecting data using a survey (*see* Fig. 10.8). Similarly an experimental strategy such as testing the relative impact of a

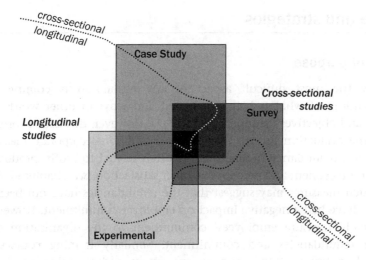

Fig. 10.8 Overlap between categories of strategy

number of different interventions will often be undertaken at a number of different time points, that is longitudinally. However, despite this overlap these categories provide a useful way of representing the main strategies.

Using a survey to evaluate change

Surveys are perhaps the most popular strategy for obtaining data to evaluate change. Using this strategy, a large amount of data can be collected from a sizeable population in an economic way (Saunders *et al.*, 1997). As illustrated by Midland Main Line's quarterly customer survey (*see* Case Study 7.1), the strategy is often based around a questionnaire. Questionnaires enable standardised data to be collected, thereby allowing easy comparison. They are also relatively easily understood and perceived as authoritative by most people. However, the questionnaire is not the only data collection technique that can be used within a survey strategy. Structured observations such as those frequently associated with organisation and methods (O&M) research and structured interviews involving standardised questions can also be used.

Survey questions can be asked to both individuals and groups of individuals. Where groups are interviewed, their selection will need to be thought about carefully. We would advocate taking a horizontal slice through the organisation to select each group. By doing this each member of an interview group is likely to have similar status. In contrast using a vertical slice would introduce perceptions about status differences within each group (Saunders *et al.*, 1997).

Self-check question	10.5	*How have findings based upon a survey strategy influenced the development of Barclays Edotech since 1993?*

Using a case study to evaluate change

Robson (1993: 40) defines case study as the 'development of detailed, intensive knowledge about a single "case" or a small number of "related cases"'. This strategy is used widely when researching change within an organisation or, as in the Barclays Edotech case study, part of an organisation. The data collection techniques used can be various including interviews, observation, analysis of existing documents and, like the survey strategy, questionnaires. However, this is not to negate the importance of comparative work, benchmarking or setting a case study in a wider organisational, industrial or national context. This might be achieved by using available secondary data, that is data that have already been collected for some other purpose.

Using an experiment to evaluate change

An experimental strategy owes much to research in the natural sciences, although it also features strongly in the natural sciences, in particular psychology (Saunders *et al.*, 1997). Typically it will involve

- definition of a clear hypothesis;
- selection of samples from known populations;
- allocation of these samples to different groups of experimental conditions;
- introduction of a planned change to one or more of the sample groups;
- control of as many other factors as possible;
- comparison between the groups.

This approach is illustrated clearly in the evaluation of computer-based training in Case Study 10.2.

Longitudinal and cross-sectional perspectives

The final two strategies, longitudinal and cross-sectional, offer two mutually exclusive time perspectives for the other strategies. The main strength of a longitudinal perspective is the ability it offers to evaluate change over time. For example, a major purpose of Group Planning Operations and Technology's (GPOT) annual staff attitude survey was to enable comparison of current employee views with those held by employees a year previously. By gathering data about people or events over time, some indication of the impact of interventions upon those variables that are likely to affect the change can be obtained (Adams and Schvaneveldt, 1991). In contrast a cross-sectional perspective seeks to describe the incidence of a particular phenomenon, such as the information technology skills possessed by managers in one organisation, at one particular time.

Gathering data for analysis

The data-gathering techniques used need to be related closely to the purpose of the evaluation. For all change evaluations, it is important that data appear credible and actually represent the situation. This issue is summarised by Raimond (1993: 55) as the 'How do I know?' test and can be addressed by paying careful attention to data-gathering techniques. This is especially important for longitudunal evaluation (Golembiewski *et al.*, 1976) as techniques used and the questions asked at the start of a change process may be inappropriate if transformational change has occurred. For incremental change the likelihood of techniques and questions no longer being appropriate is far lower. For example, the impact of a management development programme might be evaluated using data gathered by one or a number of different techniques dependent upon the focus of the analysis. These might be cross-sectional, for example in-course and post-course questionnaires and observations by trainers and others, and/or longitudinal attitude surveys and psychological tests before and after the event. Data already gathered by existing appraisal systems might also be used. Such data that have already been collected for other purposes are known as secondary data (Hakim, 1982).

Secondary data

When considering data for evaluating change most people automatically think in terms of collecting new (primary) data specifically for that purpose. Yet, despite this, secondary data can provide a useful source from which to begin to evaluate a change intervention. Secondary data include both raw data and published summaries and can have been collected within the organisation or externally (*see* Fig. 10.9). Most organisations collect and store a variety of data to support their operations such as payroll details, copies of letters, minutes of meetings and accounts of sales of goods or services. Increasingly these data are stored in electronic form, in the case of human resource data often as part of a computerised personnel information system. Although data have been collected for a specific purpose, they can also be used for other purposes. Data collected as part of performance and development appraisal might be combined with data on competencies for career management or

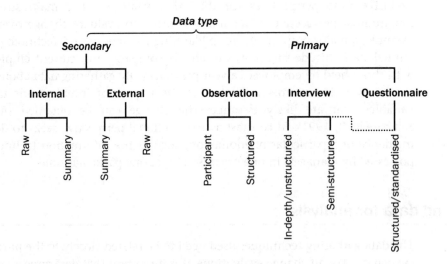

Fig. 10.9 Main techniques of obtaining data

succession planning. For example reports can be produced that match employees' profiles with the requirements of future vacancies due to retirements within the organisation, thereby highlighting specific training needs (Kingsbury, 1997).

External sources of secondary data tend to provide summaries rather than raw data. Sources include quality daily newspapers, government departments' surveys and published official statistics covering social, demographic and economic topics. Publications from research and trade organisations such as the Institute for Employment Studies at Sussex University and Income Data Services Ltd. cover a wide range of human resource topics such as performance-related pay and relocation packages.

For certain change research projects, possible improvements will be sought by comparing particular HR processes with those other organisations. Such process benchmarking is concerned not only with the measure of performance, but also with the exploration of why there are differences, how comparable the data are between different contexts and how potential improvements may be transferred (Bendell *et al.*, 1993). However, where limited appropriate secondary data are available, primary data will need to be collected specifically for the purpose.

Primary data

Using observation to obtain data

Where change is concerned with what people do, such as how they respond after a particular training intervention, an obvious way to collect the data is to watch them do it. This is essentially what observation involves: the systematic observation, recording description, analysis and interpretation of people's behaviour (Saunders *et al.*, 1997). There are two main types of observation (*see* Fig. 10.9). Participant observation is qualitative and derives from the work of social anthropologists earlier this century. It has been used widely to study changing social phenomena. As part of this, the researcher attempts to become fully involved in the lives and activities of those being researched and shares their experiences not only by observing, but by feeling those experiences (Gill and Johnson, 1997).

By contrast, structured observation is quantitative and, as its name suggests, has a high level of predetermined structure. It is concerned with the frequency of actions such as in time and motion studies and tends to be concerned with fact finding. This may seem a long way from the discussion of evaluating and promoting change with which we started this chapter. However, re-examining the evaluation and action research processes (*see* Figs 10.6 and 10.7) emphasises that this is not the case. Both these research approaches require facts (data to be collected or reconnaissance/monitoring to take place) before evaluation can occur and, in the case of action research, change be promoted.

We would discourage you from thinking of one observational technique, or indeed any single technique, as your sole method of collecting data to evaluate change. In the Edotech case study, the site management's hunch that the new grading structure was causing dissatisfaction was based at least partially upon observation in which they had adopted the role of complete participant. However, on its own, participant observation provided insufficient evidence for the management team. Often, as in this case study, it is necessary to supplement observation with other methods of data collection such as interviews and questionnaires to triangulate (check) the findings. We will now consider the first of these.

Using interviews to obtain data

Interviews have been described as 'a conversation between interviewer and respondent with the purpose of eliciting certain information' (Moser and Kalton, 1986: 271). They may be unstructured and informal conversations or they may be highly structured using standard questions for each respondent. In between these extremes are intermediate positions, often referred to as semi-structured interviews. Unstructured and semi-structured interviews are non-standardised. Unstructured interviews are used to explore the change situation in depth and are often referred to as 'in-depth' interviews. There is no predetermined list of questions although the person undertaking the interview needs to have a clear idea of those aspects of the change she or he wishes to explore. These are often noted down prior to the interview as a checklist. Interviewees are encouraged to talk freely about events, behaviours and beliefs in relation to the changes and it is their perceptions which guide the interview (Easterby-Smith *et al.*, 1991).

In semi-structured interviews such as those used in the Edotech case study as part of the BEM assessment, the interviewer will have a list of themes and questions to be covered. As in these interviews, questions may vary from interview to interview to reflect those areas most appropriate to respondents' knowledge and understanding. This means that some questions may be inappropriate in particular interviews. Additional questions may also be required in some semi-structured interviews to enable the objectives to be explored more fully. The nature of the questions and the ensuing discussion means that data from semi-structured interviews are usually recorded by note taking. However, as with in-depth interviews, tape recording may be used providing this does not have a negative effect on interaction within the interview (Easterby-Smith *et al.*, 1991).

Using questionnaires to obtain data

We would argue that structured interviews are in reality a form of questionnaire. This is because, as with other ways of administering questionnaires, the respondent is asked to respond to the same set of questions in a predetermined order (de Vaus, 1991). For this reason, we have shown structured interviews as a type of questionnaire in Fig. 10.9. Questionnaires are one of the most widely used data collection techniques. Because each respondent is asked to respond to the same set of questions a questionnaire provides an efficient method of gathering data from a large sample prior to analysis.

Responses to questionnaires are easier to record as they are based on a predetermined and standardised set of questions. In structured interviews, there is face-to-face contact as the interviewer reads out each question from an interview schedule and records the response, usually on the same schedule. Answers are often pre-coded in the same way as those for questionnaires (*see* Fig. 10.3). There is limited social interaction between the interviewer and the respondent, such as when explanations are provided, and the questions need to be read out in the same tone of voice so as not to indicate any bias.

Questionnaire data may also be collected over the telephone, by delivering and collecting the questionnaire or, as in the case of the Group Planning Operations and Technology annual staff attitude survey, by a postal questionnaire. However, we would like to include a note of caution concerning decisions to use questionnaires. Many authors (for example Oppenheim, 1992; Bell, 1993) argue that it is far harder to produce a questionnaire that collects the data you need than you might think. Each question will need to be clearly worded and for closed questions, such as the two in Fig. 10.3, possible responses identified. Like other data collection techniques, the questionnaire will need to be pilot tested and amended as necessary. The piloting process is of paramount importance as there is unlikely to be a second chance to collect data. Even if finance for another questionnaire were available people are unlikely to be willing to provide further responses.

Self-check question	10.6	Outline the advantages that are likely to accrue to an organisation using a range of techniques, rather than just one, to obtain data to evaluate change.

Analysing and feeding back

Analysis and feedback are important in both evaluation research and action research. Evaluation research ends usually with the presentation to the sponsor of findings from the analysis. In contrast a researcher involved in an action research project, perhaps as a process consultant, is likely to be involved also in developing actions and revising the change intervention as necessary.

Analysis

Analysis of data is obviously a precursor to feedback. While a full discussion of the techniques available is outside the scope of this chapter some key observations can be made. The most important of these is to ensure that analysis evaluates the change against the agreed objectives. Both the questionnaires and the BEM quality assessment in the Edotech case study were designed to collect data so the objectives could be met. Subsequent analyses addressed these objectives looking both for areas where the organisation was doing well and where the business could be made more effective. The introduction to the *Headline Results* document for the 1996 annual staff attitude survey (Garrard, 1997: 1) emphasises this:

> The purpose of this briefing is to present the results. They are presented in two parts. The first shows those aspects ... where in general terms your experience seems to be particularly positive. The second shows those where your experience has not been so good, and where therefore you consider there are distinct areas for improvement.

Analysis of large amounts of data, whether quantitative or qualitative, will involve inevitably the use of a computer. It almost goes without saying that those undertaking this analysis should be familiar with the statistical or qualitative processes required. However, we believe it is important that those who are going to analyse the data are also involved in the design stages of the evaluation. People who are inexperienced often believe it is a simple linear process in which they first collect the data and then a person familiar with the computer software shows them the analysis to carry out. This is not the case and, as some of our students could tell you, it is extremely easy to end up with data that can only be analysed partially. If objectives, strategy, data collection techniques and analysis had been better integrated then their data could have been analysed more easily. Another pitfall is that readily available software for data analysis means it is much easier to generate what Robson (1993: 310) describes concisely as 'elegantly presented rubbish'!

Feeding back

Findings based upon data analysis are fed back to the sponsor, usually in the form of a report and perhaps a presentation. Where the report contains findings which may be considered critical of the organisation in some way this may create problems. However, we would argue that to maximise benefit it is important that these findings are fed back rather than being filtered so as not to offend. Typically, especially where large groups are involved, a summary of the feedback is cascaded from the top down the organisation. This may make use of existing communication structures such as newsletters, notice boards and team briefings. Alternatively, if rapid feedback is required then additional newsletters and team briefings might be used. The research sponsor sees the full report of the findings first. Subsequently a summary may be provided for circulation to all employees. As part of the team briefing process each managerial level within the hierarchy is likely to see its own data and is obliged to feed the findings down to subordinates. Managers at each level are expected subsequently to report about what they are doing about any problems identified, in other words the actions they intend to take.

Schein (1990, 1995) argues that such a top-down approach may be problematic in managing change as it reinforces dependency on the organisation's hierarchy to address issues identified. If some issues raised by the evaluation are ignored then employee morale may go down. It also places managers in a difficult position as they are in effect telling their subordinates about issues that the subordinates thought were important. Then they tell them what they (the managers) are going to do about it. Instead, Schein advocates an alternative of bottom-up feedback that he argues also helps to promote change from within.

In bottom-up feedback, data are shared initially with each work group who generated them. This process concentrates upon understanding the data and clarifying any concerns. Consequently the focus is on the area where change is needed rather than the whole organisation (Zuber-Skerritt, 1996). Issues arising from the data are divided into those that can be dealt with by the group and those that need to be fed back to the organisation. The work group is therefore empowered by more senior managers to deal with problems, rather than being dependent upon the organisation's hierarchy. Feedback continues with each group in an upward cascading process. Each organisational level therefore only receives data that pertain to their own and higher levels. Each level must think about issues and take responsibility for what they will work on and what they will feed back up the line. Schein (1990) argues that this helps build ownership, involvement and commitment and signals management's wish to address the issues. In addition, it emphasises that higher levels of the organisation only need to know about those things that are uniquely theirs to deal with. While it may take longer to get data to the top level Schein believes that this approach is quicker for implementing actions based upon the research.

Thus, a top-down approach to disseminating findings can enable relatively rapid communication. It also allows management to maintain control of the process and decide the nature of the message, who receives it and any actions that will be taken. By contrast a bottom-up approach involves employees thinking about issues, deciding and taking responsibility for the actions they will take, and selecting those issues they need to feed back to their line managers. The latter is inevitably more time consuming, but will only work where an organisation's culture allows employees to be empowered by managers to take ownership of the changes. However, it would be wrong to think of these two approaches as mutually exclusive. Rather, the approach to feedback, like the rest of the evaluation process, needs to be tailored to the precise requirements of the organisation and that particular change intervention or stage within a change process.

SUMMARY

- Evaluation and promotion of change involves the systematic collection of data that are subsequently analysed and the findings presented in some form. Despite the importance of such evaluation for assessing the effectiveness of change interventions, it is rarely undertaken.

- The evaluation of change is classified as applied research. Within this a distinction is often made between evaluation research and action research.

  - Evaluation research is concerned with finding out the extent to which the objectives of any action or activity such as a change intervention have been achieved.

  - Action research uses the same strategies and data collection techniques as evaluation research. In addition, it has an explicit focus upon action to promote change.

- Prior to evaluating change it is important that a clear understanding of the precise purpose and objectives of the evaluation is reached. This needs to be the same for either the person or persons undertaking the evaluation and the sponsor.

- The main strategies are survey, case study and experiment. These should not be thought of as discrete entities and may be combined in the same research evaluation. In addition, strategies can be either longitudinal or cross-sectional.

- Evaluation of change can make use of both secondary and primary data. Secondary data have already been collected for some other purpose. Primary data may be collected through a range of techniques involving observation, interviews or questionnaires.

- Feedback typically involves cascading a summary of the findings from the top down the organisation. Another approach is to share data first with those who generated it. This is more likely to generate change. Subsequently issues that cannot be dealt with may be fed up from the bottom to higher levels of the organisation.

CASE STUDY 10.2

Evaluating a possible change to training methods at Telesales Incorporated

Telesales Incorporated is a large company operating in the UK insurance sector. Amongst its workforce are telesales operators selling a range of motor vehicle and life assurance policies. Telesales was considering the introduction of computer-based training (CBT) for courses such as 'introductory telesales'. However, prior to deciding to make this change they needed to establish whether CBT was as least as effective a medium as their existing 'traditional' training approach. Discussion between the internal consultant assigned to the project and personnel department employees combined with a review of published literature enabled 'effective' to be defined in terms of training outcomes such as observable changes in employees' use of the telephone and associated knowledge. It also helped the formulation of three interrelated questions the research needed to answer:

- How effective is CBT for self-study relative to the existing approach?
- How effective is CBT for group study relative to the existing approach?
- Is CBT study in groups more effective than CBT self-study?

In order to describe and explore the effect of CBT on training outcomes the internal consultant, in conjunction with the training manager, designed a study which examined the effectiveness of this type of training over six months. The review of the literature suggested that four distinct groups would be needed:

1 *Self-study CBT*: using the CBT software individually without a trainer to facilitate and provide input.
2 *Group study CBT*: using the same CBT medium but studying as a group of trainees without a trainer to facilitate and provide input.

3 *Existing training course*: using the message and content of the CBT but applying it to a facilitated group in which computer-based training was not used and the input was provided by a trainer;

4 *Control group*: where no training took place during the study period to provide a benchmark.

A representative sample of 120 of Telesales' employees who required telesales training were selected and 30 allocated to each group at random. Data were collected over the six-month period using the combination of questionnaires, observations and interviews outlined in Table 10.1.

A confidential questionnaire to measure quantitatively any changes in individuals' knowledge and a structured observation of individuals' telephone manner were designed and pilot tested. These collected data on knowledge and skills that should have been developed by the training interventions. The control group was also tested, despite receiving no training, to record any changes in manner due to other factors. In addition, questions were included in the questionnaire to measure trainees' reactions to various aspects of the training as well as assess the representativeness of the sample.

Earlier reading of the academic and practitioner literature had suggested that the social context in which training took place would also influence its

Table 10.1 The approach to evaluation research

Group	Data collected			
	Immediately before training by:	During training by:	Immediately after training by:	Six months after training by:
Self-study CBT	Questionnaire and observation of telephone manner	Descriptive observation	Questionnaire, observation of telephone manner and separate interview	Questionnaire and observation of telephone manner
Group study CBT	Questionnaire and observation of telephone manner	Descriptive observation	Questionnaire, observation of telephone manner and separate interview	Questionnaire and observation of telephone manner
Existing training course	Questionnaire and observation of telephone manner	Descriptive observation	Questionnaire, observation of telephone manner and separate interview	Questionnaire and observation of telephone manner
Control group	Questionnaire and observation of telephone manner			Questionnaire and observation of telephone manner

▶

effectiveness. Descriptive observation was used to collect data on the behaviour of each of the three groups of trainees, paying particular attention to events and associated actions and behaviours.

Statistical analyses of data collected through the questionnaire and through the structured observation of telephone manner both indicated that immediately after training knowledge and telephone manner had improved significantly for both employees who had undergone group CBT and those who had followed the existing training course. This suggested that both approaches were 'effective'. Improvements for those employees who had undertaken self-study CBT, although still statistically significant, were less marked, suggesting that self-study CBT was less effective. Interviews and descriptive observation data collected during the training offered a range of possible reasons for this such as the lack of group discussion.

Analysis of data collected six months after training revealed a more complex picture. While significant improvements in telephone manner and knowledge were still evident for those employees who had received either group or self-study CBT, statistical analysis showed their effectiveness to have declined significantly from that recorded immediately after training. By contrast, there had been no significant decline in telephone manner or knowledge for employees who followed the existing training course. The control group's effectiveness, measured by the questionnaire and structured observation of telephone manner, remained the same over the study period. This suggested that changes were unlikely to have been caused by other factors. The training manager therefore concluded that the existing training course was more effective in the long term than either of the CBT interventions considered.

Case study questions

1 At which of Hamblin's (1974) levels was evaluation taking place in this study? Give reasons for your answer.

2 Which strategies were adopted in this study?

3 What were the benefits of adding a longitudinal dimension to this evaluation?

4 What benefits do you think were gained from using multiple methods of data collection?

5 Why do you believe an evaluation research rather than an action research approach was adopted?

REFERENCES

Adams, G. and Schvaneveldt, J. (1991) *Understanding Research Methods*, 2nd edn, New York: Longman.

Beer, M., Eisenstat, R. and Spector, B. (1990) 'Why change programs don't produce change', *Harvard Business Review*, November/December, 158-66.

Bell, J. (1993) *Doing Your Research Project*, 2nd edn, Buckingham: Open University Press.

Bendell, T., Boulter, L. and Kelly, J. (1993) *Benchmarking for Competitive Advantage*, London: Pitman.

British Quality Foundation and European Foundation for Quality Management (1996) *Guide to Self-Assessment 97*, London: British Quality Foundation.

Burnes, B. (1996) 'No such thing as … a "one best way" to manage organizational change', *Management Decision*, 34(10), 11–18.

Cunningham, J.B. (1995) 'Strategic considerations in using action research for improving personnel practices', *Public Personnel Management*, 24(2), 515–29.

De Vaus, D.A. (1991) *Surveys in Social Research*, 3rd edn, London: University College and Allen & Unwin.

Easterby-Smith, M., Thorpe, R., and Lowe, A. (1991) *Management Research: An Introduction*, London: Sage.

Eden, C. and Huxham, C. (1996) 'Action research for management research', *British Journal of Management*, 7(1), 75–86.

Garrard, K.J. (1997) *GOT Staff Survey November 1996: Headline Results*, Internal Communication, Barclays Technology Services.

Gill, J. and Johnson, P. (1997) *Research Methods for Managers*, 2nd edn, London: Paul Chapman.

Golembiewski, R.T., Billingsley, K. and Yeager, S. (1976) 'Measuring change and persistence in human affairs: types of change generated by OD designs', *Journal of Applied Behavioural Science*, 12, 133–57.

Hakim, C. (1982) *Secondary Analysis in Social Research*, London: Allen & Unwin.

Hamblin, A.C. (1974) *Evaluation and Control of Training*, London: McGraw-Hill.

Heifetz, R.A. and Laurie, D.L. (1997) 'The work of leadership', *Harvard Business Review*, 75, Jan./Feb., 124–34.

Hendry, C. (1996) 'Understanding and creating whole organizational change through learning theory', *Human Relations*, 49(5), 621–41.

Kingsbury, P. (1997) *IT Answers to HR Questions*, London: Institute of Personnel and Development.

Lewin, K. (1946) 'Action research and minority problems', *Journal of Social Issues*, 2, 34–6.

Lewis, P. and Thornhill, A. (1994) 'The evaluation of training: an organizational culture approach', *Journal of European Industrial Training*, 18(8), 25–32.

Marsick, V.J. and Watkins, K.E. (1997) 'Case study research methods', in Swanson, R.A. and Holton, E.F. (eds), *Human Resource Development Research Handbook*, San Francisco: Berrett-Koehler, pp. 138–57.

Moser, C.A. and Kalton, G. (1986) *Survey Methods in Social Investigation*, Aldershot: Gower.

Oja, S.N. and Smulyan, L. (1989) *Collaborative Action Research: A Developmental Approach*, London: Falmer Press.

Oppenheim, A.N. (1992) *Questionnaire Design, Interviewing and Attitude Measurement*, London: Pinter.

Raimond, P. (1993) *Management Research Projects*, London: Chapman & Hall.

Randell, G. (1994) 'Employee appraisal', in Sisson, K. (ed.), *Personnel Management: A Comprehensive Guide to Theory and Practice in Britain*, Oxford: Blackwell, pp. 221–52.

Robson, C. (1993) *Real World Research: A Resource for Social Scientists and Practitioner Researchers*, Oxford: Blackwell.

Rushmer, R.K. (1997) 'How do we measure the effectiveness of team building? Is it good enough? team management systems – a case study', *Journal of Management Development*, 16(2), 93–110.

Saunders, M.N.K., Lewis, P. and Thornhill, A. (1997) *Research Methods for Business Students*, London: Financial Times Pitman Publishing.

Schein, E.H. (1988) *Process Consultation Volume I: Its Role in Organizational Development*, 2nd edn, Reading, Mass.: Addison-Wesley.

Schein, E.H. (1990) 'A general philosophy of helping: process consultation', *Sloan Management Review*, 31(3), 57–64.

Schein, E.H. (1995) 'Process consultation, action research and clinical enquiry: are they the same?', *Journal of Managerial Psychology*, 10(6), 14–19.

Thornhill, A. and Saunders, M.N.K. (1998) 'What if line managers don't realise they are responsible for HR?: lessons from an organisation experiencing rapid change', *Personnel Review*, 27(6), 460–76.

Toracco, R.J. (1997) 'Theory-building and research methods', in Swanson, R.A. and Holton, E.F. (eds), *Human Resource Development Research Handbook*, San Francisco: Berrett-Koehler, pp. 114–37.

Winter, R. (1996) 'Some principles and procedures for the conduct of action research', in Zuber-Skerritt, O. (ed.), *New Directions in Action Research*, London: Falmer Press, pp. 13–27.

Zikmund, W.K. (1997) *Business Research Methods*, 5th edn, Chicago: Dryden Press.

Zuber-Skerritt, O. (1996) 'Emancipatory action research for organisational change and management development', in Zuber-Skerritt, O. (ed.), *New Directions in Action Research*, London: Falmer Press, pp. 83–105.

ANSWERS TO SELF-CHECK QUESTIONS

10.1 *Four ways in which data have been collected are outlined in the Edotech case study, namely: divisional staff attitude survey, 'one-off' local staff survey, BEM self-assessment process and regular question-and-answer sessions. Re-read the Edotech case study and establish at which of Hamblin's (1974) levels each have taken place. You should decide whether their impact is likely to be strategic, tactical or operational as part of your answer.*

Research has taken place at a number of different levels during the development of Edotech. These are outlined in Table 10.2 (*see* Fig. 10.5 for the meaning of the levels).

Table 10.2 Levels and impact of research at Edotech

Research undertaken	Level	Impact
Divisional annual staff attitude survey	5	strategic
'One-off' local staff survey	3	tactical
Business Excellence Model (BEM) self-assessment process	4	strategic
Regular question-and-answer sessions	1	operational

10.2 *How do you believe the purpose of research is likely to differ between these levels?*

Your answer to question 10.1 should help you in answering this question. The divisional annual staff survey was a regular questionnaire survey administered to all staff in the division. Its strategic purpose was to identify strengths and areas that require change (improvement) throughout the division rather than just the site. By keeping the majority of the questions the same from year to year, changes in employees' perceptions could be monitored. Comparison of these perceptions between clusters and sites was also possible.

In contrast the 'one-off' local staff survey was concerned with exploring specific issues that had risen at one site at one particular time. Here the focus was on a need to better understand local (site) issues at one moment in time in order to make changes and improve. Because of the shorter time horizon, this research can be considered tactical.

The BEM self-assessment process also collected data about the site. The strategic purpose was to identify strengths and areas for improvement and monitor changes from year to year. However, these data were also intended to check (triangulate) findings from the other surveys. Detailed responses to open questions also helped managers to understand and interpret questionnaire findings.

The purpose of the regular question-and-answer sessions was to allow site employees to raise local issues with senior managers. Recent issues have included the provision of lights in the bicycle sheds and overnight food in the canteen.

10.3 *Contrast the key differences between an action research approach and an evaluation research approach.*

The three key differences, which should be highlighted in your answer, are outlined below:

1 The most important difference is the promotion of change as an integral part of the action research process. However, this does not preclude evaluation research from promoting change implicitly. We have argued that the process of evaluation research is likely to raise an awareness of change amongst employees and that the findings have the potential to promote change.

2 Another difference is the involvement of employees/practitioners throughout the action research process and, in particular, the close collaboration between practitioners and those undertaking the research. In contrast practitioners' involvement in evaluation research is often limited to sponsoring the research and being subjects from whom data are collected.

3 The final key difference relates to the wider implications of research findings. We have argued that action research should have implications beyond the immediate project, in other words, the results should be used to inform other change situations. This is not to say that evaluation research can not be used to inform other change situations, rather that the intention to inform other change situations is only explicit in the action research process.

10.4 *Why do you think organisations might choose to adopt each of these approaches?*

Your answer to this question is unlikely to be in the same format as ours. For both evaluation and action research we would hope your answer includes the desire to gather and analyse data in a rational and systematic manner in order to find out the extent to which any change intervention has achieved its objectives. However we would also expect you to have discussed at least some of the following reasons, although we recognise our list is not exhaustive!

Organisations might adopt an evaluation research approach to evaluate a change intervention when:

- the evaluation is not considered to be a necessary part of a change process;
- they are uncertain whether they will wish to act upon the findings of the evaluation;
- they require the research to be undertaken by people who are obviously separate from the organisation so that the findings are more likely to be seen as objective rather than biased by the sponsor's beliefs;
- there is a desire to maintain close control of the evaluation process;
- there is a desire to maintain close control of the findings and the extent to which these are fed back to their employees.

In contrast organisations might adopt an action research approach to evaluating change when:

- the evaluation process is seen as an integral part of facilitating change;
- they wish employees to work alongside those undertaking the evaluation throughout the process;
- they wish to engender employees' ownership of the changes;
- they wish to develop evaluation expertise within the organisation;
- they intend to transfer the knowledge gained from evaluating the change to other projects;
- they intend to adopt a process consultation approach.

10.5 *How have findings based upon a survey strategy influenced the development of Barclays Edotech since 1993?*

The survey strategy has been used widely in the development of Barclays Edotech since 1993. Three surveys are outlined in the case:

- the Group Planning Operations and Technology (GPOT) annual staff attitude survey of all employees in the Barclays Technology Services division;
- the 'one-off' local staff survey;
- the BEM self-assessment process undertaken at the site with a sample of employees.

A low response to the 1996 annual staff attitude survey implied that there were issues related to the changes at the site. These were explored in more depth using the local staff survey, which highlighted problems such as the new grading structure for production staff. It also suggested that the site was strong in the areas of processes and business results, but needed to improve in the areas of people management, leadership and policy strategy. These findings were subsequently supported and a better understanding gained of the associated issues through the BEM self-assessment process.

Findings from these surveys led to the creation of the site's Improvement Team and a range of changes such as walkabouts by management team members, a poster campaign to highlight the values of the division and the introduction of regular question-and-answer sessions. The findings also probably influenced the amalgamation of printing production services with the existing Edotech. However there is no direct evidence of this within the case.

10.6 *Outline the advantages that are likely to accrue to an organisation using a range of techniques, rather than just one, to obtain data to evaluate change.*

One technique on its own is unlikely to provide sufficient data to evaluate fully a change intervention. While secondary data can be used to benchmark the evaluation against an industry or perhaps national context there is often still a need to collect a range of data.

By selecting appropriate techniques, the data collected can be matched to the objectives of the research more closely. Different techniques are better at collecting different types of data. For example, to gather information from a large number of people and answer 'what?' questions, questionnaires are an efficient method. However, to explore the same situation in more depth and gather information to answer 'why?' or 'how?' questions, techniques such as unstructured interviews are likely to be more appropriate as the interviewee can talk freely about events.

Using different data sources also enables finding to be triangulated. If, as in the Edotech case study, the findings all suggest the same outcome, you can be more certain that the data have captured the reality of the situation rather than your findings being spurious.

Index